WAKE UP AMERICA!

Water and Energy (WE)

Charlie Pedersen

Author's Tranquility Press
MARIETTA, GEORGIA

Copyright © 2023 by Charlie Pedersen.

All rights reserved. No part of this publication may be reproduced, distributed or transmitted in any form or by any means, including photocopying, recording, or other electronic or mechanical methods, without the prior written permission of the publisher, except in the case of brief quotations embodied in critical reviews and certain other noncommercial uses permitted by copyright law. For permission requests, write to the publisher, addressed "Attention: Permissions Coordinator," at the address below.

Charlie Pedersen/Author's Tranquility Press
3800 CAMP CREEK PKWY SW BLDG 1400-116 #1255
Atlanta, GA 30331
www.authorstranquilitypress.com

Ordering Information:
Quantity sales. Special discounts are available on quantity purchases by corporations, associations, and others. For details, contact the "Special Sales Department" at the address above.

Wake Up America! /Charlie Pedersen
Hardback: 978-1-959453-81-9
Paperback: 978-1-959453-82-6
eBook: 978-1-959453-83-3

Acknowledgement

Special thanks to the people who have shared their precious time for the completion of this book; Samuel Prince(Editor), Lynn Pedersen (Tran), Eddie Pedersen(Contributor), Hector Galindo(Contributor), Fareed Zakaria(CNN), Bill Maher (HBO), and Cortnie Schmidt(24-Hour Fitness). Thank you very much!

CONTENTS

PREFACE 1

What's Underneath the Bubble? 17

The President presents his ideas to the
Vice President and Secretary of the State 45

Washington DC Selling the First Lady 73

The Morning Briefing - The Cabinet 97

Calgary Canada 117

The First World Tour 203

The President and Congress 267

The President Speaks to the American People 277

The President and the Lobbyists 341

The White House and Camp David 365

The United States and Australia Speak 369

One More Trek around the Globe: Beijing;
Moscow; Europe; and Vienna (Home of OPEC) 377

Back to America 431

The President Speaks to the People and Congress 441

Postlude 451

Conclusion 467

ABOUT THE AUTHOR 481

Key Issues: Xenophobia, Oil, the Chaotic State of World Affairs... Almost a Frenzy of conflicts...

Xenophobia is basically fear, hatred, or mistrust of any group which is foreign, especially strangers or people from different countries or cultures.

In the Middle East, Oil is the one key to their economics, and self-belief and they want to perpetuate the status quo, at higher prices.

Frenzy: the world is in an irritated state: Middle East, Europe, the USA, China, and Russia, and the world, and existing in a climate of uncertainty over energy resources (source, price, availability, direction) in an unstable state (civil war, terrorism, immigration, etc.) from key supplier nations, (Iraq, Syria, Iran, Libya, Nigeria, Egypt, Saudi Arabia, Qatar, Yemen, and others.) This creates fear and aggression, and easily flips into war.

PREFACE

Wake Up America!
- World trade;
- Energy (low cost and clean);
- Honesty

We seem to be trending towards perilous ends. Our position and initiatives in **World Trade** have followed creating a world market with the rise of standards of living around the world, along with other mega exporters like Germany, Canada, England, China, Japan, South Korea, and more. Meanwhile, retail dominance and profits seem to be ignored when assessing the trade balance. Companies like Walmart are world leaders, yet their product line (clothing) is dominated by products from China and Vietnam. Where are the studies that show the effects of profits from low-cost sources? What about the consumer benefits from a lower cost of living? World trade is much more complex than a pure trade imbalance. **In a world where buyer markets are 95% outside the U.S.A., we need to treat the world outside the USA as customers who benefit from economic improvement. World trade is an ally to our success, not an evil temptress. Honesty** is the USA's mantra, but apparently, the modus operandi of our political dialogue is to tell citizens anything and deny or change it the next day. Honest dialogue is well thought out and morally grounded governance, and peace is the expectation. The USA's economy is stagnating because of tight markets; *look to anti-trust as the solution.* General Motors now sells more vehicles in China than in the United States. Apple sells more smartphones in China than in the US. China has 1.3 billion people. India will soon be larger than China.

The 21st century is the Pacific Century. Economic activity will be strongest around the Pacific Rim. (Population) When you consider food and agriculture, you see the inter-relationships between world markets and the cost of living in a society with rising populations. We need aggressive suppliers of low-cost food, medicine, technology, and lifestyle products with open competition. It's not a game, it's what we do. The success of PC's, telecom, internet, smart phones, etc. has given rise to companies like Intel, Microsoft, Google, Apple, Amazon, Cisco, and **more who sell up to 85%** of their products overseas. Don't dampen the shining light. Embrace the world and embrace our positive leadership and participation. Freedom, democracy, worldwide sales, and service are driven by innovation, not monopolies trying to hold on to market share and suppress change. The world sees America as a (historical) force of change. What drives our innovation and immigration is a society open to change, backed by an extremely resilient yet stable legal and education system that encourages improvement. This is our mantra, our key to the future, not bullshit.

Honesty

"Honesty or truthfulness is a facet of moral character that connotes positive and virtuous attributes such as integrity, truthfulness, straightforwardness, including straightforwardness of conduct, along with the absences of lying, cheating, theft, etc. Honesty also involves being trustworthy, loyal, fair and sincere."

Apparently, the modus operandi of our political dialogue is to tell citizens anything and then deny or change it the next day. Our resolve must be reset to honesty, straightforward dialogue, well thought out and deeply discussed, with morally tested governance as the required approach. We may be slow, but in the long run, we're not stupid. We have discovered the power of food and international relationships. Consider that Egypt's domestic revolutions were ignited by rising food prices. In 10–12 years, the world's population will increase by another billion. Expansion of oil is not the goal, its **Water and Energy (WE).** Our technology, with intelligent applications and worldwide distribution, has shrunk the world. Ninety-five percent of the world's population is outside of the USA.

Most people did not realize that behind the USA, there are large Organizations.

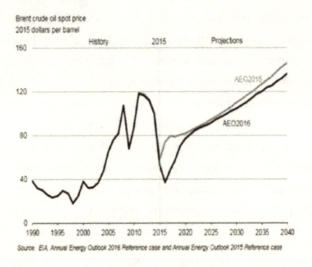

The Energy Information Administration (EIA), tracking everything about Energy; and the Central Intelligence Agency (CIA), tracking all the nations in the world. The EIA has forecasted that oil will be up to $100 per barrel by 2025. How can we plan without an understanding of the dynamics? **If we want to expand our economy, we must embrace the world, not retract from it.** We need to be the best world partners. Or are we an island of isolationists, only out for short-term gain? Failure to shift direction in world trade, honesty, and energy will rattle our future. Five (4.6) percent of the world's population (the USA) can gain market share. China projects an additional 1 billion cars on the planet in the next 10–30 years. With only a ten percent share, that's 100 million cars. Last year, Americans bought 17,000,000+ new cars from all sources—USA, South Korea, Japan, Italy, Germany, India, and China, etc. We want nonpolluting vehicles, backed by citizens that empower world trade, not protect bad, old ideas. How can the USA in a 4.6 over 95.6 world prosper? Honestly and openly, Wake Up America!

When you look at the state of our world affairs and the proliferating isolationist values and actions we seem to be trending towards, we are diverting and distracting towards perilous ends. Our position and initiatives in **World Trade** have followed creating a world market with the rise of standards of living around the world along with other mega exporters like Germany, Canada, England, China, India, Japan, South Korea, and more. Meanwhile, retail dominance and profits seem to be ignored when assessing the trade balance. Companies like Walmart are world leaders, yet their product lines are dominated by clothing products from China and Vietnam. Where are the studies that show the effects of profits from low-cost sources? What about the consumer benefits of a lower cost of living? World trade is much more complex than a pure trade imbalance.

In a world where 95+ percent of the world's buyers markets are outside the USA, we need to treat the world outside the USA as customers who benefit from economic improvement. World trade is an ally to our success, not an evil temptress. Honesty is the USA's mantra, but apparently, the modus operandi of our political dialogue is to tell citizens anything and deny or change it the next day. Honest dialogue well thought out and morally grounded governance and peace are the expectations. Our economy has stagnated because of tight markets; look to anti-trust as the solution. General Motors now sells more vehicles in China than it does in the United States. Apple sells more smartphones in China than in the United States. China has 1.3 billion people.

India will soon be larger than China. The 21st century is the Pacific Century. Economic activity will be strongest around the Pacific Rim (population). When you consider food, agriculture, and commerce, you see the inter-relationships between world markets and the cost of living in societies with rising populations. We need aggressive suppliers of low-cost food, medicine, technology, and lifestyle products with open competition. It's not a game, it's what we do. The success of PC's, telecom, internet, smart phones, etc. has given rise to companies like Intel, Cisco, and more who sell up to 85% of their products overseas. Don't dampen the shining light. Embrace the world and embrace our positive leadership. Freedom, democracy, worldwide sales, and service are driven by innovation, not monopolies trying to hold on to market share and suppress change. The world sees America as a (historical) force of change. What drives our innovation and immigration is a society open to change backed by an extremely resilient yet stable legal and education system that encourages improvement. This is our mantra, our key to the future, not bullshit.

In 1900s, if we said, "Forget gasoline, and we're sticking to wood and coal," we would look like fools today. In the late 1800s, a man in Germany named Benz invented the Internal Combustion Engine (ICE). In the late 1900s, many US private and public initiatives invented the Fuel Cell Electric Vehicle (FCEV), which is a hydrogen-based electric car, and the electric vehicle (EV), in the last decade, has taken off. Simultaneously, the hybrid vehicle, gasoline and electric, has unfolded.

Now, we have a way to create fuel without drilling, fracking, or mining, even artificial fuels. This book is about our numerous options. We could form the equivalent of a "Manhattan project group," let's call it the WE project (Water and Energy), and mobilize our people to act against high-priced, dirty energy and in favor of generating fresh water, ushering citizens of the United States, Germany, Japan, South Korea, and, yes, India, China, and Russia (and others) into an era of *energy productivity* and low pollution, as well as producing an unlimited supply of fresh water, the target of the 21st century. It sounds too easy. That's because it is finally ready to roll.

When you realize that the world will bring another billion people to the planet in 10-12 years (timeframes vary) and forecasts are that Africa will experience famine to the tune of 20-30 million people, it's time to stop horsing around and act. You will quickly see why, because almost every three months more innovations and commitments about other choices are announced from countries like India, China, Norway, Canada, Germany, and the USA, yet politicians are flying blind because of the constant expansion of war and the dominance of industry and national international oligarchies, and cartels are holding onto the status quo. The USA is dragging, and the world is taking off. These dynamics are explored in this book.

Some congressional conservative supporters said, "The problem is everyone is paid. Everyone. "Dems, Republicans, Independents, Media, etc." This common theme needs explanation. The media is part of the problem. If you watched CNN, for example, during both the 2016 conventions, the closer you got to the nominee acceptance, oil and gas dominated the advertising, literally almost every couple of ads. The hidden agenda of O&G is visible; "the status quo." (Medium is paid for via advertising).

Have you read a recent in-depth review about lobbying? Yet it's well documented on OpenSecrets.org. In fact, over the last decade, **lobbying spending has jumped from $1 billion+ to close to $3.5 billion per year**. Lobbies have bought our constitutional rights! The Supreme Court hasn't realized the consequences of its action (the Citizens United decision): They would say, "You want to change the results, change the law." Change a law that gives Congress unlimited campaign contributions (media funding)? Is that going to happen? The almighty dollar triumphs over the constitution and the power of the people. If you have money, you can buy Congress, the Presidency, and apparently be ignored by the Supreme Court. They, of course, would violently disagree, because they agree that monopolism in a 70 trillion-dollar world economy is Congress's and the executives' job. The Supreme Court's attitude is that they don't create laws; it's up to Congress and the President to change laws they don't like. The Supreme Court's job is to interpret the law, not create economic policy?!

This book explores the following conundrum. We must: drive energy costs to $1.00 per gallon of fuel; defund ISIS (oil profits);

stop propping up Kingdoms and Dictatorships; stop depressing world economies (control supply); and, most importantly, free up the stifled US economy (cost and supply). IT'S TIME TO STOP LOOKING FOR MORE WHEN WE NEED DIFFERENT. The US has had solutions paid for by the US taxpayers for years, but politicians, paid by powerful economic interests, apparently would rather draw us toward war in the Middle East than transform the world peacefully. Clean energy would put US-China relations in a positive direction i.e. *solving China's and the world's pollution problems*, delivering true peace in the Middle East (while vastly fueling the risk of the US dollar being rejected in world markets, ultimately causing double to triple inflation at home), and turning our deficit around by generating sorely needed profits in our economy, We must be world partners, and yes, make sure everyone insists on good and fair (tariffs, controls) business deals.

In this **fictional** journey, reality leaves us exposed to nations who could refuse to buy our debt (funding, T-bills), which gives us almost no alternative but to raise our T-bill interest rates (which directly impacts commercial and consumer debt, and threatens inflation estimated at 2x and 3x inflation's stability). Today, much of the world's trade is exchanged in dollars, a privilege we took over from England since WWII. We take over the Presidency and travel throughout the world to review policy while seeing national and regional issues in each country. (All the facts are consistent, regardless of the quoted date, not materially different). What should we do?

The problem with US policy and actions is that we have been brainwashed for over 75 years into believing that O&G were in diminishing supply and alternatives were years away. Meanwhile, universities and government run power research, under the watchful eye of universities, the US Energy Department, the Air Force, and others, have funded solutions (Sun gas, Syngas) to increase clean supply, as well as the worldwide discovery of alternative sources, mostly inspired by US inventions such as horizontal drilling and fracking. Yes, with the US second-guessing fracking, the rest of the world is moving forward. Oh yes, and the USA has already moved forward with fracking, putting us in a world leadership production status for O&G (nat-gas or oil), and reducing costs by over $1 per gallon. How did we reclaim energy production leadership? Against what's happening around the world with US assistance? This is not dismissing concern; it's reinforcing the conflict of actions and reactions. Obama let it happen (fracking), because he couldn't deny reality. When you see what's happening in Australia, you will (historically) find major US companies and major Chinese oil conglomerates all over it. **(Note: Australia's efforts are stalled due to loss of funding in a $45-$50.00 per barrel market (Coober Pedy, Aus. with estimates equal to Iran).** Anywhere in the world, where there is energy to be found, there are American companies present, providing technology, execution, and knowledge. WE seem to excel at striving for more when we need something different.

Look at what's also happening in the world:

Most people don't know that Germany created fuel artificially, representing 40 percent of their supply, *in 1940*. In 2015, a South African company (SASOL) is creating gasoline directly from natural gas and has tried to establish it in Louisiana, but they're stymied about getting funding.

This company is totally in control this situation. The issue is under their control.

THE US ENERGY DEPARTMENT AND THE AIR FORCE funded alternative energy projects which have produced **usa1007** usa1007@fedex.com **SUN GAS** (hydrogen from water and sunlight) and **SYNGAS** (hydrogen through chemistry), which has been pursued in Germany, Canada, and the US. This is proven technology, and the same process could be modified to provide an unlimited fresh water supply.

Australia has been developing vast facilities to mine natural gas and create enormous Liquid Natural Gas (LNG) facilities to ship worldwide. Qatar is the current leader. Australia plans to be the largest, but then they'll be surpassed by the USA and Canada. The USA is soon to be a fuel exporting nation. This is to provide large facilities to support nat-gas power plants and convert NG to liquid NG for compressed shipping (LNG) Imagine what's undiscovered in Australia, Russia, and more. The point is, we are close to oversupply. We just have to utilize it more, preferably in transportation. (NG and converting NG to Hydrogen).

Methane Hydrate, a natural gas **equal in mass to** *all other fossil fuels in the world combined*, has been successfully extracted in Alaska and Japan. This, as a reserve, changes everything, whether we use it (now) or later. Supply and demand economics means increased supply and lower costs as it becomes more productive.

The US, Australia, and others are building distribution centers for Liquefied Natural Gas (LNG) for worldwide distribution. The US pipeline to Louisiana will enhance our export of LNG if the pipeline is used for that purpose, even partially (currently not).

Cyprus has discovered Natural Gas in the Mediterranean equal to all the Natural Gas supplied by Russia to Europe. Israel and Cyprus have discovered Natural Gas off their shores in the Mediterranean. Natural Gas is being discovered all over China. The largest users of natural gas cars in the world are China, followed by India, then Iran and Pakistan. Over 7,000,000 cars? Why? Natural gas cars are cheaper than building large-scale oil refineries, even an issue for Iran. If the world market is more profitable and natural gas is more effective for their people, why not provide the market with high-priced O&G.

Tesla (USA) and Panasonic (Japan) have built a major battery manufacturing plant in Nevada—Gigafactory—to lower cost and increase capacity. Simultaneously, Tesla is deploying "home energy storage" so Solar energy is available 24/7, rain or shine, which is the secret behind Solar's long-term viability.

Canada, Scotland, Denmark, and Germany are planning an alternate energy strategy, leveraging wind and sea power. Norway sees it as a clear and continuous supply of non-carbon energy.

In 2016, GM built more cars in China than in the United States; Apple sold more—*iPhones in China than in the United States; 40% of USA S&P 500 profits in the United States came from overseas; and the USA-inspired global village is working. With India and China approaching three (3) billion people, our opportunities are boundless if we understand it and act that way in global trade. This should be the number one topic in international and national strategy... trade.*

Solar "panels" can now be painted on windows in a translucent (see through) form, which is the long-term answer for cities, along with battery backup.

Silicon solar cells will soon be replaced by super crystals, increasing solar cell density by, at the start, by 50%. This rollout will dwarf all other events when fully absorbed. (Time-frame unknown).

An efficient method to convert coal to hydrogen has been developed. Currently, coal to hydrogen is an industry well in place worldwide, but enhancements proceed in the USA.

Chevrolet has a 200-mile "BOLT" in 2017. Tesla is expected to announce the price of its midsize car. Toyota delivered the "Prios-Prime" for 2017. Its advantage is that, with a gasoline backup, it has a 600-mile range, meaning you can't get stuck (with the current distribution shortfall). (Real progress must include convenient refueling.)

Saudi Arabia has announced a strategy to evolve their economy beyond oil and gas by 2030 (not completely, obviously, but they see the handwriting on the wall, so they must diversify).

Norway has announced they will eliminate new gasoline-powered cars in 10 years. This is a country that became rich because of oil and gas in the North Sea.

China owned "VOLVO" announced that in a few years all their autos will have electric engines, as well as, in many cases, an internal combustion, or other, engine. (Partially owned Warren Buffet)

China is also losing 4,000 people a day to *pollution*-related terminal illnesses.

India has announced an electric vehicle strategy that will be implemented within the next ten years. WHAT IS OUR CONTRIBUTION AND SHARE FOR THE NEXT BILLION CARS? What is our trading relationship with China and India over the next few years since they estimate the growth? Only a ten percent market share would be 100 mm cars! China today builds more electric cars than all other manufacturers in the world combined.

Meanwhile, *all* major auto manufacturers in the world have announced "hydrogen cars" in 2015/2016. Again, the lack of refueling depots status is the challenge, *the secret behind O& G's staying power*. Alternative-fuel cars have been introduced in the USA, but there are almost no refueling stations. This is the challenge of all alternative-fuel cars.

By the way, the world population is expected to grow by over 1 billion in ten to twelve years. Where? Western Asia, the Middle East, North Africa, Africa, and South America. Is this their problem, or should we be robust partners?

Nigeria is expected to be pressing towards the USA's population in 30 years. African growth is expected to result in half the world's population by the end of the century.

Where was the issue of population growth during the last election cycle, given its impact on energy, water, food, **business**, and potential WAR? The US makes up about five percent of the world's population. That means that the world population is 95% opportunity. The 21st century has been declared "The Pacific Century," because of the population and economic dominance of the "Pacific Rim," which includes the Americas and West Africa.

These are the challenges and the opportunities. Let's check out the world!

Prepare yourself by withholding judgment if you can. Yes, energy and water are a problem with policies, societies, and warfare endlessly and corporate cartels that policies must endure and often complicate and often shift towards compromised solutions. So, to address this, I must take over the Presidency (in character) and take you throughout the world to move you from ignorance to knowledge and then propose solutions that include the "Clean Movement" rapidly towards active solutions. Numbers are always updated, so although I will use them extensively, fundamentally they are always true. For example, when oil prices fell due to US shale, it was because the industry had to hide in plain sight, and while OPEC argued about how to limit production, supply and demand appeared to be working. US energy innovation has made supply exceed demand. (Volume, not quality)

"Wake Up America" is fictional because to fix the problem, I have to take over the Presidency and travel the world, visiting heads of state, to get a world view on changes that have to happen in order that we, the world, survive. The facts are as current as necessary. WE (Water and Energy) is a strategy of change.

If you check out the graph below, you'll see that energy prices are projected to be climbing to over $100 per barrel by 2025 by the Energy Information Administration (EIA) (2016, 2017), the center point of all USA government energy information. The point is, if you want to change the outcome, including the cost and capacity and quality of water and energy, you must change the productivity of energy at massive levels. My recurring theme: if we want to grow the United States in an 8.5-9.5 population world, we must lead internationally and excel in water and energy (WE) execution, particularly around the Pacific Rim, but globally.

EIA Forecasts

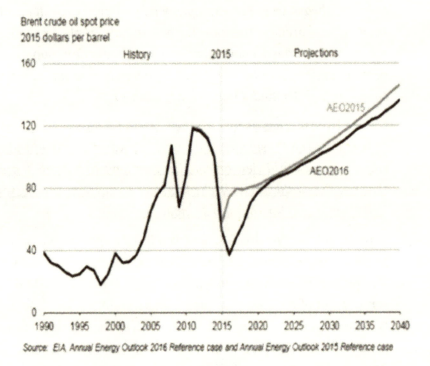

Source: EIA, Annual Energy Outlook 2016 Reference case and Annual Energy Outlook 2015 Reference case

CHAPTER I

What's Underneath the Bubble?

You hear a lot about energy independence and the desire for the United States to get out of the Middle East and <u>stop relying on its oil. That is fine, but it takes courage—a courage that</u> apparently Republicans, Democrats, Tea Partiers, and other progressives and conservatives simply do not want to display. And it's so easy. We are trapped and swimming around like too many goldfish in a small aquarium. The pressure for action just builds.

Wake Up America (WUA) presents the challenge and assembles a worldview and action plan. Here are three reasons for fixing the problem:

    1. There is an opportunity to change the world and shake off the economic chains of oil dependency. Unveiling all the twisted history that has secured us to this status quo must be done before our energy crises crashes into the forthcoming water crisis (to be discussed later in this book).

    2. The key is doing this while we work on our debt reduction. IN WUA, we explore how we can change.

3. The current US world strategy seems to be to make oil dependency so painful that we simply will do and pay anything just to be sure we can get more oil. It's like classic addiction, and we keep trying to avoid rehabilitation, a chain we must break. Short term, aggressive actions will make us feel like winners, but if we don't step up to change, we will become a third-rate country.

After September 11, 2001, we created an energy bubble, spent more than four trillion dollars on Iraq and Afghanistan (globally), and unleashed war on multiple countries, but the pain of the attack escalated further. Bin Laden's scheme is working, because the price of a barrel of oil grew from $21 a barrel in 2000, to $35 in 2004, $50 in 2005, $57 in 2006, $75 in 2010, $102 in 2011, and $91 in 2012, $101 in 2013, and $110 in 2014. But innovation is trying to break through.

We absorb the costs and complain, but we wander deeper into the quagmire and are frustrated that the economy hasn't really rebounded. This is branded "okay" and "natural" because of the presumption of increasing demand and diminishing supply. Have you noticed there are *no* recommendations on how to break the chains, the invisible handcuffs? Well, *in WUA, we* rebuff all of that. We look at current energy innovation and alternatives and recognize that we can exploit benefits and invest in delivery and solutions for the *Water* and *Energy (WE)* crises. Yes, they need to be addressed together. And yes, it's fixable, soon and without unacceptable pain.

To accomplish this, I fictitiously take over the President's persona as I travel on a world quest for the transformation of the 21st century. I will show you the way out and offer a true direction for us very quickly.

You are quite frequently told these ideas are decades away, but you should realize that many of the wealth holders of the world really want to delay it as long as they can in order to squeeze every dime out of you. In your gut, I know you know it, don't you?

That is all well and good, except the population, agriculture, food, and energy dynamics are such that to continue this charade is killing the economies of the world and stagnating the inspiration of our youth. We are limiting nations from expanding the progress that is needed to prevent economic catastrophe and, importantly, the capacity to achieve what we call the American dream: education and reeducation; a job becoming a career; a family; a home; automobiles; food; and peace.

Instead, we focus on downsizing medical support, where shrinking Medicaid will, in my opinion, destroy the Republican Party. Why have they pushed, in the Senate redo of healthcare, to destroy Medicaid in 2021? They are trying to jump over the next election cycle because destroying senior citizen healthcare is beyond mean; it's un-American. We can't save our way to prosperity; we need to ignite innovation and leadership. If we do it, shame on us. As the world population soon crosses the (8) billion mark, the dynamics change because the need for massive amounts of water can only be generated by **low-cost energy**, not to mention worldwide agriculture, and livestock. If 15 years ago, I told you that public phones would virtually disappear by 2015, you'd ask me, "What are you smoking?" I forecast that the average new car will produce 100-150 mpge (including the cost of battery recharging) by 2040.

As with AT&T in 1982, we need to open the market. Besides breaking up the communications giant, the breakup of AT&T separated the equipment business from the communications business. Opening the handset business is behind the entire cell phone and smartphone phenomenon, a virtual revolution. Likewise, when energy density is truly realized, the applications of wireless applications will be staggering.

As we speak, the population of the world increases by one billion every ten to eleven years. There is a bubble that must burst and there's a need for a freshwater revolution, including food production. The harsh reality:

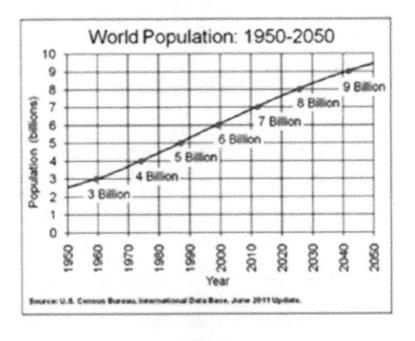

Source: US Census Bureau, June 2011. World population growth over the last hundred years has approached 1 billion every 10-12 years. I used 2011

data because it never changes. Based on history, there are only two directional choices: war or change.

The current leadership is too condescending to the one (1) percent of people who govern ninety-three (93) percent of the add-on wealth (that is, of the *increased* profits, one (1) percent of the population has experienced ninety-three (93) percent of the financial benefit). In WUA, we invent a leader who is willing to embrace the ninety-nine (99) percent of what must be done to create a renewed economy and world peace. The problem is, our journey makes us realize that this lack of leadership over the last fifty-seven years (1962–2019) has put us in a precarious position. There have been no new ideas or action plans, just prewar rumblings from the old school and war itself.

In WUA, you will see one dramatic position: take over the Presidency and inject what necessary to get us out of the quagmire is called oil and put us on the road to the real 21st century. There is a necessary realignment that is a solution for someone with the guts to take it on. Of course, avoiding war would be a great start. For the first decade of the 21st century, we were just wallowing in the aftermath of the 20th. We must change, but the only things that persist are the quest for oil and ethnic rivalries more than a thousand years old.

Have you noticed that since and including Korea, we (the United States) have never truly succeeded in war since WWII? Yes, South Korea is great (look at their TV's and cars) if you ignore the collective atomic bomb chaos called North Korea. Yes, we're negotiating, but the North Koreans feel that nuclear weapons are their power. Vietnam, Kuwait, Bosnia, Iraq, Afghanistan, Syria, and North Africa? Soldiers and civilians die every week, every year. The breakup of the USSR was a great peace dividend, but the independence of those around the Black and Caspian Seas and the "istans" is threatened, all squabbling over oil rights.

Oil, oil, and oil: a one-dimensional quagmire.

It is all about oil and energy but should also be about needing effective water strategies and agriculture. In our society, agriculture feeds not only us but our livestock as well: beef, chicken, pork, lambs, and yes, fish farms. As countries gain wealth, they demand more meat.

North Korea's headaches are about atomic energy and weapons, and Vietnam, Korea, and China's are about oil rights in the South China Sea. Everyone wants more. All the troubles revolving around Bosnia were about Muslim/Christian/Jewish religious trust issues. World War I issues have reemerged since the breakup of the USSR. Multiple generations (Bosnia, et al.) had passed, yet when Yugoslavia was broken apart, all the old religious sects were back in place, and after fifty years of "peace", all parties were ready to fight once more. That's because what's needed is a breakup of the status quo. No money reconciliation for the 99.9%, we're marching to war.

You can draw a wide circle around these cradles of civilization, including Eastern Mediterranean and Somalia, Ethiopia, Sudan, Egypt, Libya, Tunisia, etc. to the south and west Africa, you have defined the desert and energy zones that want to stir up trouble in the world (or should I say with each other?). When the Iron Curtain was lifted, those religious differences rose as if they had been dormant, even though generations had passed. Many of the Middle Eastern Islam nations had never accepted the Western powers, plus Russia, carving out Israel and restoring it back to the Jewish people (post World War II).

Meanwhile, the conflict of the ages is still with Abraham's children. Ishmael is linked through Mohammed as a sign of legitimacy (Sunni). Where Isaac's links are, are the passion of the Shiites. Both these links ascend through Abraham, who some Muslim's claim wasn't a Jew, in the historical genealogical sense. It doesn't matter because that's how the two groups evolved. Now, 85-90% of the 1.6 billion (worldwide) are Sunni s, and 10-15% are Shiites, although in the Middles East, it is more dramatic:

Distribution of Middle Eastern Muslims

Country	% Shiite	% Sunni
*Syria	35	65
*Turkey	7.5	85
*Lebanon	38	23
Jordon	10	90
*Iraq	68	37
*Iran	89	9
*Azerbaijan	70	29
*Afghanistan	19	80
*Pakistan	20	77
Kuwait	30	70
Saudi Arabia	9.3	90
UAE	15	8
Yemen	30	70
Bahrain	30	70

Iran is the most dominantly Shiite, Saudi Arabia the most dominantly Sunni This situation is the underlying problem in the Middle East.

The second problem is a historical seeming monopoly on oil, which is starting in full retreat.

When you look at the Sudan (northeast Africa), you see the classic problem. Put the Middle East Muslims in the north, by the seaports and close to the Middle East. The black Africans are in the south, where their oil is. Darfur is in the west, black Muslims, and they have nothing, not even adequate water. Now call it a country, and voila, the entrapment of our times whose primary resource is oil.

The Brewing Storms

This first layer (number one) is what you could call "prima Armageddon," or "the world according to the major Bibles and religions, through let's say AD 800, and what could explode into "Armageddon." This is the core of the Middle East, including Israel, but historically North Africa, and even China as the Eastern trader, but never a warrior.

These bubbles from all the dominant religions were claims of pre-eminence, including the Christians, Crusaders, and traders. Then came the oil demands of the industrial age—electricity, cars, airplanes, and war. What must be understood is that any demand to dominate the human spirit will be usurped like a small hiccup. To believe that locaition dominance is permanent is to not understand the march of history, which includes the British Empire, the French, the Belgians, and the Germans. The world's population grew from over two billion people to over seven billion in the 20th century. It has become time to redefine new solutions. Throughout history, discovery has often resulted in opportunity for people. Unfortunately, this often leads to claims of God's will or other acts of manifest destiny (OIL). The real issue is how you best exploited your luck, or in contrast, how you blew opportunities to enhance mankind.

The next layer is two: China, India, Russia, Bosnia/Serbia, and Spain, the western push of the Byzantines, with strong historical links to layer one through war and commerce.

Then you have layer three, the WW1/WW2 Euros, the Americas, China, Australia, and Indochina, Korea, and Japan. This layer is kind of the *modern world*, most dominantly from the two world wars, progressively interacting with numbers one and two.

Note that I have China in all three layers. They haven't invaded anyone but are effective traders and, lately, manufacturers, have evolved into the catalyst position in war or peace. It's finally their time, so you may think. The fact is their demands for anti-pollution and higher productivity energy will provide no choice but ask the USA to get out of the way.

WUA has a task. Take all three layers and promote harmony; prevent war; and move energy and water to a new paradigm. We can put a new spin on the conflict zones without causing World War III or Armageddon (or as I call it, the collapse of the cradle of civilization, in old world terms.)

But what if a whole other direction emerges? Energy creation by a whole other approach? And the creation of hydrogen from air and water? What I refer to as "Water & Energy" (WE) rather than the seemingly Middle East paradigm (ME), or as I define it, Monopolistic Energy (ME), creates a desire to change the world and establishes the stage for our real challenge. Is water the pie in the sky or is it the real goal that can only be achieved with clean, inexpensive energy or energy dominance in Saudi Arabia? This is the advent of technology in the 20th and 21st century where now advanced chemistry, scientific drilling, and meteorology where atmospheric (Wind, Sea) Chemistry are in play.

The real issue is population growth, which demands a change in attitude. WE versus ME. At the end of the day, a nine trillion population world requires a WE mentality, or USA, get ready to be a second-tier nation!

Without significant change, the ME drives us in one direction: higher costs with reactionary actions. You will discover. Alternately, real change is possible and practical.

For a moment, let's look at the top oil producers. This is actual production, including imports and reserves:

World Oil imports, production, and reserves 2015-2016

BBL Billions of Barrels per day		billions of Barrels	
Country / Region	Production	Imports	Reserves
USA	10.55 BBL	BBL	256mm
Saudi Arabia	10.05		212mm
Rusia	9.415	9.08	264mm
IRAQ	4.59		121.35
China	7.6	11.8	234
Canada	3.677		155
Iran	3.3		148
UAE	2.82		97.8

Country / Region	Production	Imports	Reserves
Kuwait	2.56		104
Brazil	2.53		110
Venezuela	2.53		95-298
Nigeria	2.317		37.2
Libya	3.64		48.01
South Korea	2.815	2.95	
Netherlands	1.884	1	
Philippines	1.503	1.45	
Italy	1.395	1.34	
Spain	1.349	1.24	
France	1.174		
UK	1.047		

Many countries have 90+ percent of their oil production coming from a single company within and usually owned by the government of the countries on this list, only the United States, Canada, and selected EU's, China, and Japan have multiple private companies (that also work with the other countries). Note that Venezuela, which sells more than 40 percent of their oil to the United States, is actually number one in oil reserves in the world, making them appear unproductive, but really, they have "heavy oil". With the robust oil discoveries in the United States and Australia, and the dominance of Russia, China, and more, we are clearly in a direction that will minimize the Middle East dominance in oil dependency. The real question is when Australia will step up to the plate in terms of oil production. Natural gas production is well underway.

This is the first major revelation: the power of the Middle East over oil will soon diminish to about 35 percent, and the major industrial users (United States, Europe, China, and Japan) both know it, and must orchestrate the evolution or change, not fight over it.

The approach of this book is to "take over" the oval office in the White House and figure out how to move the world to the point of excess clean energy and clean water while transitioning the United States and the world into a "clean" planet that is free of pollution and toxic air and water. The goal is to enable the system to support the current seven and then grow to nine to ten billion people while eliminating famine, genocide, and deep poverty. Yes, I know, control growth, but it will never happen. Growth slows only when people feel economically and medically secure. For example, Africa has been projected to house half of the planet's population by the end of this century! This may sound impossible, but you must recognize the power of technical progress that is at hand now and Africa's struggle with lifespan.

This is bold, but by taking over, you can see a worldview and the aspects of different countries. For example, Australia, which is not even in the top ten, is investing heavily in liquid natural gas (LNG), building conversion facilities to make it the world's number one (1) exporter of natural gas. This is the cumulative effect of a seven-billion-inhabitant planet where centuries of scientific knowledge and amazing low-cost computerization are fully in play. Australia is well positioned to support the Pacific Century (21st). Qatar, in the Middle East, currently leads LNG exports by substantial margin.

Australia is also producing hydrogen from coal. The march toward renewable hydrogen is progressing along several different fronts, aided by solar power as well as biomass, wind power, and tidal power. That technology is already beginning to ease into the marketplace in northern Europe. This is strangely part of what will define the 21st century as the "Pacific Century," where the Pacific Rim countries dominate the world's economies and science:

Look at India, China, Indonesia, and yes, Japan. Computerized bridges and the world Internet bring the EU, Russia, and East Coast America's science right at hand, but overwhelming population growth in Asia and Africa demands that political courage see that the Global Village is in play and regression or retraction is so last century, that it's a follower's path to yesterday, not tomorrow, and the time to act is today.

Given all the Noise about Russia, China, and soon India:

> 1. We need to work with India and China as equal partners in executing change to reflect the forthcoming water, energy, and population challenges over the next decade. We're interested in sales and share, while they need to survive a soon to be combined three billion people, not survive, and grow a strong middle class. If we aren't a leader and solution partner, we will be declared a follower and treated that way.
>
> 2. Our principal issue is being a trading partner, with obviously fair arrangements in a growing market. **We need to leverage our five percent of the population, particularly in delivering clean, low-cost energy and expanding fresh water at scale,** *which can't be done without low-cost energy, self-perpetuating the status quo.*
>
> 3. The move towards isolationist nationalism will end America's role as a leader in the free market, an unfortunately declining player in an eight-plus-billion

population world economy. The Americas need to be vibrant leaders in the global village and can demand fair trade as well as water and energy leaders, not isolationists.

This is happening around the world. Countries see the dilemma of potential interruptions in energy, water, and food supplies and are aggressively looking for solutions. Then, the United States finds a way to harvest oil and gas through shale and invents fracking and horizontal drilling (drilling laterally-literally down and then across a shale rock formation), adding other sources of energy to our list: shale oil and gas, methane hydrate (below permafrost and the bottom of the ocean), Perhaps the last of the old ways...drill baby drill. So now shale, oil sands, and aggressive exploration are providing a plethora of new fossil fuel sources (locations) around the world and outside the Middle East.

During all this, the USA's team of the Energy Dept., the Air Force, and university partners, with US government funding, determine how to create hydrogen through science and convert it to a virtually unlimited energy source (Sun-Gas). It sounds like too many questionable sources, but the answer is who can do it at a lower cost with energy productivity. Don't worry about it; over time it will be resolved. Like many things, the rigors of science will prevail. What used to be physics is now chemistry, i.e. science has succeeded in isolating elements and rearranging them to produce fresh water, hydrogen, etc. efficiently. This changes everything.

We need to step beyond the "old way" to a new frontier. Meanwhile, people project a mid-western dust bowl where the heart of our wheat belt is. Especially since the "Arab Spring revolts" were largely due to rising food costs. International trade is more than just buying and selling. When it's a large volume, people become dependent on it, including the cost. So now they have to consider that increased sales in energy, food, water, and minerals are creating more world dependence. The larger the population, the deeper the dependency. Somehow, balance must be established. Get it? Less dependent on the Middle East for energy, but more dependent on the Middle East (and North Africa) for food and water. When we build markets, we build dependencies. When we supplement farms to keep prices down, we create and extend global dependencies. Real competition.

What's really occurred lately is that we have found more energy than we "need", although population growth and technology dependency quickly erase that (electricity). We just must find an alternative to how to use this "gift" from the Earth. And then the real need is for more fresh water. So, if we have a water and energy (WE) strategy that can work, we can reengineer the world's resources to survive population increases and energy capacity...a water and energy strategy.

I call this the change from a ME (Monopolistic Energy) mentality to a WE (Water & Energy) mindset and action plan. "ME to WE".

What will work to raise worldwide economics?

Since 1970, the allies (including Asia, Africa, and Central and South America) have created a global village. We haven't been self-sufficient with oil since then. We formed deep dependencies that have evolved into military support, which we give to these countries, and it has become like a bad dream. Before we dive into the president's agenda, let's take a brief look at Egypt. Egypt has been quiet under its military dictatorship since the seventies. Its agenda has been modified by struggles having to do with discourse with Ethiopia over access to water supply. The Nile supplies 100 percent of freshwater to Egypt, and the source of the Nile is in Ethiopia. When the Muslim Brotherhood, comprising about one-third of the core population, won the election, they didn't accept the strong western influences the military would recognize, affecting religious tolerance, tourism and more. This includes their well-maintained army, with a $1.3 billion US subsidy. When the army felt this was damaging their stability and welfare due to the Islamic influence on the culture, they took over the country. This also has the dominant influence of Sinai and Israel-Egypt peace. I bring this up for reasons you'll clearly see later. It's important to understand why the Middle Eastern countries have been swept into the "Arab Spring" phenomenon. When the Ottoman Empire was crushed after World War I, the European leadership broke the region into countries to meet their needs. Typically, nations were set up with minority leaders (e.g. Shia) so they wouldn't have a largely political population base. So, the revolutions occurred to gradually reconstitute the normal or natural national leadership. Also, after World War I, came the rise in oil demand. Additionally, water came to the fore, with issues like the source of the Euphrates in Turkey feeding into Iran and Syria, and then, after World War II, Israel was recreated. In the 1970s, the United States' energy demand exceeded its domestic supply. In the last 25 years, populations have grown, and climate change has aggravated the water supply issue. . Syria is squeezed next to Iraq and then Iran, and once constituted the heart of Persia. The US military was brought into Saudi Arabia (500,000 Desert Storm) to "protect" Saudi oil fields (and stop Hussein), and now China is building refineries in Saudi Arabia to support their needs as their volume exceeds the United States Saudi demand. (Aided by the innovation of "shale" in the USA). Meanwhile, aggressive oil and gas exploration worldwide has now resulted in a large percent of oil now being found *outside* the Middle East (China, the United States, Canada, Brazil, Venezuela, Australia, Russia, and North Africa).

Europe is heavily dependent on Russia for natural gas, but new discoveries of natural gas have been made in the Mediterranean, i.e. Cyprus, Israel, etc. This is trouble for Russia. But it is representative of a world in change, energy-changing events all over the world, and we are locked in the troublesome Middle East.

Methane Hydrate

Meanwhile, methane hydrate, representing gaseous energy (NG) larger than all fossil fuels in the world combined, is being successfully extracted in Alaska (test cases) (under the sea) and actively mined in sea locations like Japan (tests already occurring), raising the specter of energy independence for Japan. Everyone is cautious, but how can they resist? All this means we must look at our energy sources and "change" how we use energy (transportation, heating, electricity, etc.) But isn't this a new version of "drill baby drill?" Yes, vaster, but perhaps riskier? (Methane from the ocean, fracking, etc.)

Remember, the Arab Spring emanated from three sources: inflation in food costs; pressure from surrounding nations over water; and marginal participation of citizens in energy profits. Trade embargos are caused by alarm felt by nations in the UN due to civil war, chemical weapons, and related issues. Meanwhile, over five million people are dispersed throughout

Syria, Lebanon, Turkey, and Iraq. To an extent, pressure on water sourcing is normally not a problem in Syria, except that growth of the population, increased industrialization, and expanding agriculture without improving irrigation techniques and war have created a crisis. In other words, civil war doesn't allow them to progress while the demands caused by societal growth continue. The problems between Iran and the United States, plus their inability to find a norm in post-Ottoman Empire, their society has been frustrated by American and British intervention (i.e. Shah and their Iraq war, which should fall under post–World War II Western colonialism), and the resulting rise of Iran's Muslim nation since 1980. America's problems post World War II in Iran somewhat relate to Venezuela, what I'll call CIA-based nation-building, or interference. All the Middle East Muslim nations never accepted the European imposition of Israel, except for temporary peace with Egypt and an alliance with Saudi Arabia over oil sourcing with the United States in exchange for military protection of their oil fields. Of course, this occurred under the umbrella of the Cold War. Asia's oil demand, the emerging energy boom in Australia, and post-1990, Russia have rearranged the supply/demand chain for oil and NG (natural gas) with their vast energy resources. Of course, the USA announced it is now the leader in oil and gas production. Yes, the leader in the one resource that guarantees our decline. The world is pressing towards alternatives, with China as the number one producer of electric cars. While this is rearranging the energy potential of the world, we need to drag world history along for the ride. Iran has to carry the legacy of post-World War II into the future; the images of past glories; reconciliation with Israel; and reconciliation with the United States (with its own cold war legacy of manipulation of global governments in the Middle East and South America), which has to find a path through energy transformation to a new era where human initiative and independence of capitalism reconcile with a "more even" distribution of life's necessities (water, food, individual freedom, health, etc.), made painfully obvious by the visibility of disparity through the communications revolution, including the internet and continued miniaturization of electronics marching toward the "quantum age" (I'll explain later). It is becoming painfully obvious that we must change through energy and transportation. The reason is that the convergence of science and discovery will not be denied.

The point is that once again, the first quarter of this century must be parallel to the twentieth century in discovery and transformation, and to some extent, fix or update the innovations of the twentieth (e.g., cars, airplanes, electricity, energy, computers, etc.) to accommodate eight to ten billion citizens. Remember, the first quarter of the 20th century was WW I. What was the first quarter of the 21st century?

The only way this can change is through improved productivity mandates in the form of water and energy. (WE)

*We must recognize that **our true challenge is not only to prevent global warming but to prevent global warfare.** In the next ten years, what's likely to happen first, the melting of the polar cap or war?*

*It's warfare that has almost bankrupted America and put us in the largest recession since the 1929 depression. (Yes, stupid financial deregulation and the desire to provide everyone the opportunity to qualify for a home exasperated that. We have tried to bury our war costs since Vietnam and provide the **appearance of progress** to poor people. How did that work out?*

Through the anti-warring initiative, we will cause the desired effect on climate change and probably (assuredly) faster than the current path of *progress (if that's the word that you could even use to define our current state of affairs in energy).*

The world can share blame as well as admiration for its advancements made. We've made so many mistakes since World War II through the super consumption and exploitation of resources that we need to just apologize and move forward. So, we jump into the oval office, and our quest begins.

We know the world is trapped in its own history and actions, so we will carefully sweep that away and break open the invisible *handcuffs* (our derived rules of international politics and corporate influences on innovation that are strangling the *"invisible hand"* *of capitalism) and find a way to adapt a water and energy strategy.

From here on, this is what should happen. You may ask: Why can't it?

*definition of the invisible hand: a term coined by economist Adam Smith in his 1776 book "An Inquiry into the Nature and Causes of the Wealth of Nations". In his book, he states:

"Every individual necessarily labors to render the annual revenue of society as great as he can. He generally neither intends to promote the public interest nor knows how much he is promoting it. He intends only his own gain, and he is in this, as in many other cases, led by an invisible hand to promote an end which was no part of his intention. Nor is it always worse for society that it was not part of his intention. By pursuing his own interests, he frequently promotes that of society more effectively than when he really intends to promote it. I have never known much good done by those who are affected to trade for the public good."

You see, the key to freedom and innovation, yes, in modern terms with appropriate measures and controls, is to open doors to unimagined consequences. The key is "open" and not suppressed by dominant market leaders. The Adam Smith version of capitalism is the opposite of suppressing socialism. This is what defines America, and most Americans don't get it.

So, back to today... Is there no end except for drilling and war? The simple, unadulterated answer is, "Yes, there is an answer whose time has come. But to appreciate it, i.e. you must understand it across the globe, what about the Middle East (of course, Israel's support is essential and unequivocal, *so don't go there*). How many people have to die... for what? Meanwhile, the US put an Exxon executive as Secretary of State and a Texan in charge of energy. Think about it for a while.

The need for M.E. oil is conjured up... much like Vietnam and Iraq.

Of course, for the price of oil we kill thousands of our young soldiers, and the Middle East has disrupted Europe's economy and social status (immigration, death by terrorism, etc.), while we listen to OPEC arguing with each other on how much to increase our oil prices by (or disrupt supply, and more). Europe is overrun by a few million Syrian refugees. Iraq and Syria are under siege by ISIS, while no one has an answer to Russian influence and the Russian supply of natural gas in Europe, although Cyprus is coming.

What we must overcome is the brainwashing we've had for over 75 years that petroleum, etc. is a diminishing resource. That's 20th century thinking, and it's over. The 21st century mindset is based on plentiful clean energy and fresh water. Any other direction is reactionary. Even Saudi Arabia has developed a 2030 vision and plan to augment O&G as its primary GDP engine. They are the world leaders in desalination, providing over 75% of their fresh water supply.

How do we create an open market? Can we move forward without major investment? This is part of our story.

By 2050, Muslims are expected to have a population equal to Christians. This alone, is a reason to reduce the business to: clean supply > demand. We can't (and shouldn't) replace a thousand years of history with Sharia law.

Immediate action must be taken. No special "carbon tax exchange" is necessary. In fact Fossil Fuels obviously can be in the final answers, as would hydrogen, electric, and natural gas. Geographically, you may extend choices to nat gas, electric, hydrogen, and gasoline, or design it to plug in up to three additional choices, **the right answer-choice**. A design of at what will that due to costs? Energy choice could also be rolled out in regional segments e.g. California Nevada, Oregon, Washington or NY, NJ, Conn, Pennsylvania, Delaware, Maryland, Wash D.C.!

Meanwhile, China is choking on pollution, the world's population is expected to grow by one billion in a decade, and 20-30 million people are endangered by famine. Our trade policies, with our $20+ trillion budget deficit, are threatening the dollar's stability, and our taxpayers are expected to choose between fiscal soundness and senior citizens' healthcare? Essentially, the millennial generation is pitted against baby boomers with their parents' and grandparents' welfare at stake.

(Dems and Indies-wake up). If you don't think China and India will solve pollution, low-cost clean energy, and water, you are living in complete denial, and quite frankly, you are championing the demise of the USA as a world leader and denying the one thing that can spark our and the world's economies. **The Middle East represents a bygone era of oil shortages, so we are planning to fight for nothing.**

If he cleared the O&G swamp and used this investment for massive debt payback, he would get world leadership, jobs, and payback for all players, except maybe Russia, who must transform their economy, as Saudi Arabia has announced they will do. It is a tough one, which can be fixed with a robust economy, worldwide, and can be used to get clean air and fresh water. **When OPEC meets, all they discuss is how to reduce oil output. This is classic monopolistic behavior...Their only goal is to manipulate supply to raise the price. All illegal actions in the USA are due to the Sherman (1890) and Clayton (1915) antitrust acts,** *which we ignore...*

OPEC, the largest swamp alligator in history, is disrupting our foreign policy. I find it difficult to even call it a policy... It's really piracy, totally supported by the good old USA and its energy conglomerates.

Let me summarize two points:

> 1. We are overpaying for O&G by over $1 per gallon because of illegal cartels. What will our appetite for participation in war be when we recognize we've been lied to and kept away from solutions because of oil greed and the lack of courage of the status quo? Think of it. Why are we bound in a struggling and constant quagmire? We need to open our markets, not retreat into "safe" nationalism.

2. **This is the 21ˢᵗ century. I repeat:** *Global warming isn't our only problem, its global warring.*

USA strategy? Increase military spending, create discourse with Iran, and lead in oil and gas, and decrease energy diversification, and pollution standards, limp on fresh Water, and decrease R&D on energy and diversity in general?

Choice: USA, Asia, Middle East, Europe, Russia...Monopolistic Energy (ME) vs Water & Energy (WE).

This is the paradigm; the Dems should engage (are you listening), "Okay Donald, Drain the Swamp! Let's start with oil and gas! (Sorry for rerepeating the obvious)Let's be aggressive traders & support the Global prosperity."

How are we going to raise the prospects of our people by isolating our own growth while the other 95% of our world keeps expanding? Are we just competitors, or do we want to be participants in the future of the world? What does our history say? Why did Nixon and Kissinger raise the prospects of China? Why did we spend a good percent of the twentieth century supporting India? Why did we invest our technology and resources to support their growth in outsourcing? Because it raised our profitability. Don't we want our partners to be our competitors? When they are seven (7) times our population with a growing middle class, these are markets where they want what we have! And we should grow market share, not deny our potential future.

If the Independent Media is not paid off, when was the last expose or study done on the lobby industry purchasing our democracy? In exchange for the 1% or 99% profit sharing insult to capitalism and free enterprise. Show me the reports and TV exposes. Go ahead; show me a comprehensive study on lobbying in the last 10 years, 20 years, and 30 years? Where is the media? Media is chasing high ratings and advertising revenue, not an intentional restraint, just a matter of fact! The two teams that should be addressing this at CBS 60 minutes and HBO VICE. Why is this not exposed? American wealth is fungible, American character and open persona, isn't.

Remind yourself that the Vietnam War and Iraq wars were started with Government Lie's. Gulf of Tonkin? WMD's? They are dwarfed by the Middle East...the heart of the swamp.

I don't choose to pick on the media... but the point is that short-term competition has ignored the real issues...that we have sold our democracy to the highest bidder that is the lobbies and financial giants who want to keep things as they are. And the Supreme Court has underwritten unlimited unaccountable political spending. Medicine and Pharma has transformed us into pill popping... I could go on and on, but that's later. The first choice is Water and Energy (WE) leadership because besides sparking our economy and world leadership, we will stop sacrificing our children and grandchildren to a twentieth century formula for success.

The fact that Vermont is sieged with heroin addiction should make us demand an "Elliot Ness" solution, except the Mafia is now the Americanized Mexican Cartels. President Trump is on the move in this area, and we need to erase the scourge on our society?

Since only HBO (VICE) does real investigative reporting. Syria, China, ISIS and more, will someone open the lid on lobbies... and give Drain the Swamp to have real direction? Or do we want to institutionalize killing off our children and grandchildren every 15-20 years.

So, where are the Dems in all this? Apparently, they are too weak (or not innovative enough) to stand up to the lobbies, except for Bernie Sanders, (the problem is how to break the lobbies, that is. Quantitative easing has run its course and the Dems don't seem to have real economic expansion ideas, except for Bernie Sanders, i.e. address the lobby and power-broker issue (No not socialism, America, prudent government diversification, like we always have done, not wasteful spending). I won't even get **into "Citizens United", where the Supreme Court institutionalized the power of money over the power of individualized voters...** If we shake up the world markets with trade tariffs, just pray that the world doesn't rebel by discontinuing using the dollar as a standard for monetary trade settlement... estimated that an unstable dollar will cause double or triple inflation. (Rising T-bill rates). Organizations like BRIC (Brazil, Russia, China, India) are already planning new currency standards for O&G and international commerce... bypassing the dollar. Why? With 20+ trillion-dollar deficits, our currency seems to be dangerously unstable. The dollar is the standard bearer, because of its extreme strength and stability. What if no one wanted to buy our T-Bills? We need the equivalent of a "Manhattan project", I call it a Water and Energy (WE) project which could be used to sort out the detail of electricity/NG/hydrogen with a target of phased rollout in less than a year. The world is ready for Energy (hydrogen/ Electric, NG, gasoline) choice and independence. Start it by incentivizing expanded fuel choice at the pump, with innovative home, office, and retail options. **But without a refueling distribution system, we're stuck. The fossil fuel lords (dictators?) have won.**

It's simple, put out a tax credit strategy for refueling choice, and the marketplace will decide. At its core, the world should know the USA is going to expand choice through the addition of

Natural Gas, Hydrogen, and Electric battery, and gasoline refueling at the pump. The markets will respond after the naysayers try to kill it, and they will. Notice to Green movement, don't worry about fossil fuels, **worry about clean fuel distribution. Without it, you have nothing. Get it, nothing**. So, marshal your finances to open refueling outlets.

Drain the Swamp... Let's start with the best payback! The world won't change energy unless the USA leads... we are so dominant in transportation and energy (5% of world population, 25% of energy use.) A clear and speedy message is required. Drain the swamp. Bring in Germany, Japan, South Korea, Canada, China and a few others into the equation they'd sign up yesterday, but our consumption...*Drain the Swamp. Yes Donald, we're ready to keep your promise. The Democrats should embrace this, unless they are just paid off by the lobbies, which means they are part of the problem. Remember Trump and Sanders drew people in with the hope of real change, which will only occur by taking money, to a large extent, out of the political equation. The only thing equally available is the Internet and the streets. (In a good way).*

Prepare yourself by withholding judgment if you can. Yes, Energy and Water is a problem with policies, societies, and warfare endlessly and Corporate Cartels, whose policies must endure and often complicate and often shift towards compromised solutions. O&G compromise...never!

So, to address this I must take over the Presidency (in character) and take you throughout the world to move you from ignorance to knowledge and then propose a solution that includes the "Clean Movement" rapidly towards active solutions. Numbers are always updating so although I will use them extensively, that fundamentally they are always true. For example, when oil prices rocketed downward, because of USA shale, it was because the industry had to hide in plain sight and while OPEC argued on how to limit production, it appeared that supply and demand was working. US energy innovation made supply exceed demand. (Volume, not quality). Now science can transform that with clean energy- Natural Gas hybrids, Hydrogen hybrids, electricity stand alone with hybrids.

Trust me, all will be forthcoming essential understanding... the wide world of choice.

Eighty-five percent fossil fuels still underlie the majority of energy consumption fossils in GDP and exports: Achieving diversification is key **Kuwait, Saudi Arabia and Oman are the three countries with highest earnings from fossil production,** predominantly oil in these cases. Fifteen of the sample of 67 countries are net exporters of hydrocarbons, in economic terms. Nigeria, Kuwait and Qatar have heavy dependence on exports although these shares have declined in the last ten years.

CHAPTER II

The President presents his ideas to the Vice President and Secretary of the State

As his second term has commenced, the President pauses and considers what he sees as too many missed opportunities, too many legislative bills held up, and to be frank, too many mistakes. He doesn't like the direction of the world or the United States, and he's starting to doubt himself and doesn't like it one bit. He calls his Vice President (VP) and Secretary of State (SOS) in for a free discussion and sets aside half a day. They join him in the oval office and then move to the situation room. We have put ourselves in the President's shoes (so his point of view is the author's).

(I'm taking you through this so you'll see what will become obvious, and that **the time for change is now.**)

I want to set a direction that will restore some resilience in the world's conditions. When we look at what should be opportunities, we are frustrated by a Congress that only has this two-year vision. Some seem to think the purpose of governing is to get reelected. Our opposition thinks their role is to not pass any positive legislation so they can blame the economy on this administration in two years. It's the reason we seemingly can't accomplish anything, and they think the voters are too dumb to see it. (A clear cry for term limits and maybe a 3-year house term and campaign spending limits).

It seems we've begun to believe the only thing that matters is maintaining the status quo and getting reelected. The government's agenda is about continuity of the party, while the people's agenda is pure need: water, food, energy, jobs, education, reeducation, and support or help when extraordinary weather or events take place.

Politicians rant about too much regulation. **The problems we have had, fiscally, were because of lax regulations and too much abuse of power in all branches of government**. Yet somehow, it's the regulations we diluted or eliminated that led to the financial crisis, not mishandling expanded regulations. It's probably because, without true leadership, we can't help writing mountains of rules. Details always bend to the "influencers".

The Vice President (VP) intervenes: Well, *step* back and consider. We pushed an agenda of more liberal credit and stimulus; the opposition turned that to "less overhead," and we agreed to both. So, we helped ease credit and they helped free the financial sector to abuse financial discipline in a quest for short-term profit and less regulation. But regulation didn't cause the problem; ignoring the wisdom behind regulation did! We passed laws to take out controls that were needed. Better said, we allowed the system to succumb to greed. Remember, at least 97 percent of the banks didn't adapt to foolish lending practices. Three percent achieved this by repealing Glass-Steagall and corrupting regulators by allowing investments while manipulating their banking components. You see, the top ten financial institutions own more than 77 percent of all customers' assets and liabilities in the USA. They thought it was just numbers and math models, not real life. In real life, you don't make a loan and then bet against it, especially when you loosened the standards of credit. Any real banker knows that.

Secretary of State (SOS): Yes, we often do that, and it produces failed policies and blind acts such as "throwing money at it" or "taking money from it" in the executive and legislative branches, and yes, sometimes in the Supreme Court. The court case, Citizens United, and its unlimited electoral advertising budgets Our Supreme Court can't see (or care) that the way to vote can be manipulated with money? Really? We had lots of progress and problems in the 1980s and '90s, and then came September 11. Remember, we felt "moderately unencumbered" and successful before 9/11. Although nations were sizzling with technological growth, we outsourced labor to different countries, so efficiencies developed, the Internet spread, etc. We loosened our purse strings, and our credit standards were lowered to stimulate consumption. Then we became traumatized by Bin Laden on 9/11. (The guy we armed in Afghanistan). We were in shock, needed resources to "get even," and used finance instead of hard work to move ahead. We also increased our militarism, probably as Bin Laden expected. After all, we did it in Vietnam; why not challenge inflation again? Vietnam resulted in interest rates of 20%; Iraq has a debt of more than 21 trillion dollars. Look at some of the pricing data. (He hands out a chart.)

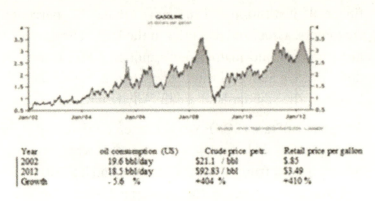

50 years of price inflation

Well you can't blame all the 21 trillion on Iraq...No, it just got us into financing our future, just like "guns and butter" in Vietnam, and that, pushing out our payback, added up to 20+ trillion in debt.

We fed Asian growth, real estate expansion, and the legitimate prescription drug conglomerates kept innovating. We then agreed to finance ourselves into substantial war debt to chase Bin Laden and anyone we thought was an evil contributor (such as Hussein). The President Johnson "guns and butter" economic policies (the notion that we could fight a war and keep everything rosy at home) failed in the 1960s, but we didn't want to make our citizens feel the pain of war, so we financed everything. We set ourselves up in the 1980s and '90s with the power of money, and then, after being punched in our gut, we felt we needed to "get even" with Bin Laden. Yes, we had to legitimately respond to evil, but not on a credit card. Meanwhile, we stimulated Asia by using their cheap labor to create efficiencies in the United States, enriched the Middle East with high oil prices, and quite frankly, ignored the poor (except letting them "qualify" for home loans), and poisoned the environment. So, we figured out how to expand the money supply by selling T-bills in exchange for trade policies in other words, more imports.

China had its own brand of unfettered growth, including building cities with no plan to occupy. They even duplicated Paris (Eiffel Tower and all) with almost no occupation plan. Most people didn't see that. Everyone was crazy and bypassed any real water and energy agenda, even though droughts persisted and storms leveled towns and cities, and food costs grew enough to create the "Arab Spring" revolts.

Overlying this, the US allegiance of greed was conveniently believing economic cycles were things of the past because profit growth and real estate values seemed unchained (when they never are); and not seeing that energy productivity has given way to energy growth outside of the Middle East.

From 2001–2013, oil went from $21 per barrel to $100 and US energy consumption declined under extremely high oil prices. We used cheap real estate financing to promote the appearance of wealth, pushed the envelope on debt with things like credit card eligibility, and created a credit bubble. We ignored the realities by driving cheap money into the market and allowing debt expansion to grow by financing war and easing consumer access to debt. Well, that didn't work in Vietnam, and now it's not working in the Middle East, and soon people couldn't pay their debts. All it took was slightly raising interest rates. No wonder they're gun shy to raise rates, now. Probably, it's the knowledge that our economy is a house of cards.

Now, it has come home to roost, and we're 20+ trillion dollars in the hole of government debt. Mortgages, and credit card debt are defaulting, with pauses due to real growth, and we've been paying upwards of four dollars per gallon at the pump, until we unleashed "shale oil and gas".

Real growth is stymied without access to expanded low-cost money, and depressing efficiency, or should I say minimal real productivity in energy, and stagnant economic growth in business and jobs.

We should have prices like 20 dollars per barrel of oil and less than one dollar per gallon of gasoline (effectively due to oil productivity—i.e. 100 mpge)(e for the added cost of electricity in plug in hybrids), under five percent interest rates, a balanced budget, and a four and one half percent unemployment rate. Meanwhile, Bin Laden is dead, and the Middle East and North Africa are increasing in chaos. The Internet, PC, telecommunications, and super intelligence like Google were real progress in the 1990s and since the turn of the century, and throughout the 2000s, but the jobs have been taken, and there was low incremental labor wage growth. The next big thing was smartphones, but the labor growth was mostly in Asia because of expanding world growth and outsourcing of manufacturing jobs and customer service via telephone. The model is Apple Corporation, with seventy thousand US employees and one million Taiwan contract employees.

In the real world of cars, airlines, water, and food, we are driven by progress, real sources of new wealth. They are driven down by our declining resource progress: water, food, oil, and transportation, caused by war, not economic expansion. The emerging economies want what we defined as progress: cars; air transportation; electronic everything; and food; yet they're tied to restraint by energy caused stagnation (cost too high) and shrinking water (shrinking reservoirs and expanded population!

Why is the Ogallala Aquifer, Located underneath the US Midwestern Breadbasket (eight states along the Great Plains), which is among the larger wheat providers in the world, etc.

The constant NOISE inside and outside the US will unfold and provide clarity throughout this story:

There is a Middle East Oil & Gas share is rapidly diminishing and will become irrelevant.

The Energy resonance led by Germany, Canada, and the USA and the effort is well underway. Don't forget that Germany invented the Internal Combustion Engine (ICE) and is not going to sit around and be blackmailed into high Natural Gas (NG) prices (by Russia or anyone else.) It's already a fact that the Fuel Cell Electronic Vehicle (FCEV) provides more productivity with hydrogen (the universe's most plentiful element) and no exhaust pollutants. (H20 is the exhaust). These aren't ideas, they are ready to begin implementation, and the car manufacturers all the world are stepping up. But something is missing.

The Middle East is a 20th Century experience and it's time to move on to the 21st Century. The M.E. is at a cross roads where W&E strategies must be put in place to accommodate the billion people that will add to the challenges in 11-12 years (yes that's right). Ignorance that the global village is upon us and can't be ignored has recently been highlighted by the EBOLA events. Saudi Arabia has used their wealth to provide desalination for 75% of their fresh water. The Jebel Ali desalination plant in Dubai, a dual-purpose facility, uses multistage flash distillation and is capable of producing 300 million cubic meters of water per year. They all ring out one answer...manufacturing cost (energy to create steam) is too expensive. Where was the rest of the Middle East and North Africa? At war. What is needed is a fresh look at water creation and desalination, perhaps focusing all sun, wind, etc. energies as well as derivatives of artificial gas (shuffling the element deck) on fresh water. **You can't directly follow Saudi Arabia, because they are energy rich. They can afford fresh water, the elixir of life.**

The 21st Century is the Pacific Century and the Energy leader in Europe is Germany and of course the USA, who, temporarily owns 25% of worldwide demand, with Canada and Germany are fully participating, is right in the middle of the Energy reinvention. What is the worldwide Headlines? War and Revolution in the Middle East and North Africa tells us that now is the time to become informed and insist on rapid progress.

Is there something wrong with this picture? Well, absorb this and let's go back to the USA story and then the world. It's necessary that you see the big picture and then we'll take you back to what a bold President and a responsive Congress must do.

Why is the Ogallala Aquifer, located in the US Midwestern Breadbasket (eight states long the Great Plains), which is among the larger wheat providers in the world, is expected to go dry in 20-30 years, with no action plan? We are so engrossed in war prevention and then expansion, that the people have been left out of what must be done, and more importantly, what can be done.

Inclement or lack of weather impacts Canada, Russian, and US wheat production and drives the cost of food up all over the

Middle East. The same forces affect pork, chicken, and beef costs. The Middle East is primarily importers of these core necessities. A large amount of US food exports are to the Middle East.

Instead, Congress ties up the executive branch under critiques of managing embassy security, debt ceilings, and gun crises. Congress is fiddling while Rome (in this case, North Africa) burns. This is because of a new idea. If we don't pass any laws, the President gets blamed, and Congress will use that to win future elections: a real people's agenda. The Dems picked up just where the Republicans left off, except without congressional control. However, the Republicans are trying to save their way to prosperity, clearly not President Trump's agenda. You can't save your way, you need economic expansion, and that means diversity and choice.

That's an example of voters sorting through the banter and still reaching for the truth. Reaching, but still not finding it. But it's an indication of what the invisible hand is. You can't see all the dynamics, but clearly the people wanted the President to persist. The voters know a different approach is necessary, but no one is providing it, **yet**. Hands continue to be tied, by factions of the status quo, the one percent.

It has become an underlying technique to avoid the real issues until the next election cycle in two years. So, we curtail any real strategies while progress in water, food, energy, and technological innovation are subordinated. Stagnation curtails real change because green strategies are face to face with new fossil fuel growth, yet we don't know what to do? Energy is the one subject every citizen should be cognizant of. After all, we are fighting wars over it. And yes, you face the gas pump every week. *You know something is not right, don't you?*

We need to confront the citizens with real water and energy strategies and priorities and take on the oligarchies (a network of companies that control a particular business and cause it to stagnate, i.e. antitrust), and quite frankly, show our citizens that the "capitalistic invisible hand" is enchained by invisible and visible handcuffs of illegal national and "international cartels and multinational monopolies".

We are so enchained; we can't even imagine real solutions. The innovative ideas that have been baked into Americans' brains are entrapped by invisible handcuffs. For example, you are brainwashed into believing there's an energy shortage when our reserves are highest in history, yet no one is willing to show you how we can unlock the handcuffs and have excess supply and true energy productivity, *which has and will mean lower prices. Note: US military bases are continuously changing, but the point is we are poised for offensive action.*

How many people know that more than two-thirds of world oil reserves are under the control of Saudi Arabia, Russia, the USA, Venezuela, and China? Or why oil and gas are Socialist (government owned and controlled) or oligarchy/cartels (international business conglomerates), all illegal under the Sherman and Clayton antitrust acts of 1890 and 1914? How can free enterprise and innovation break those chains? There must be a way.

We caused a good part of the 2008 financial debacle by the Clinton administration and Republican Congress canceling the Glass-Stiegel Act in the 1999 which was written in 1933 to force the separation of investment houses from banks. We forgot all we learned in 1890–1914 and in 1933. No one ever talks about the fact that more than ninety percent of the banks didn't allow sub-prime mortgages (mortgages to low creditworthy borrowers) because they are stupid business ideas that ignore perpetual positive and negative business cycles. But small banks aren't dominated by an investment side of the company. So, we pass laws and stifle small Banks with regulation.

Bankers know loans must survive downturns. We acted as though real estate values would perpetually increase and consumer debt could be unlimited. Ignorance bubbles always blow up: Always. Yet government is paralyzed by the power of the dollar. We keep putting T-bills into bonds and in effect refinance our debt, kicking the loan down the street. Yes, T-Bills are loans to the federal government. What economics will free up the economy so we can get more taxable income? The energy business needs to be open for growth and change.

The handful of conglomerate multinational banks and investment groups in and outside the banks did everything against what the Glass-Stiegel Act was created for, and in effect, recreated a modern version of 1929. It is all one thing: too much bank or investment company-integrated strategies and operations, accumulation of bad debt, and too little competition and supervision causes abuse from the ultimate flaw of mankind—greed. No Gordon, excess greed is bad.

Investment management didn't buy into bankers' stupid interfering ideas calling business economic cycles (i.e. reality) when business bubbles burst; real estate, the Internet, and bad real estate investments hiccup, people pull in their money and put it on the sidelines. Always.

Globalization and seven billion people on earth have made the system so large it isn't manageable because we put up with government submission to money interests paying lobby payments for campaign funding. All sorts of "graft" propelled products that we rationalized as legal but were poorly conceived of in a down turning market. Trust me, China was no better. They came from a lower individual economic level and their leadership-built cities no one came to, cities without job opportunities. Now they have their own bubbles to contend with. And they're serious.

So, when the real estate market collapsed, all those sound-minded banks that didn't make stupid loans got pulled in to the bad market by the foreclosing loans from the big Banks. Neighborhoods funded with mostly large bank loans, induced government control holds a barrier between the people (i.e., voters) and the work the government is supposedly to do for its constituency. Nothing gets done in Congress because "our" representatives have been "bought out", afraid to act against their benefactors, and energy productivity is dismal, *caused by an energy production, costs exceed other expenses and that's bad. The impact of invisible handcuffs on price mismatches keeps unit cost way above what the invisible hand would. Prices were so extreme, that when shale energy increased productivity, we saw the dollar reduction as a benefit, not a signal of what should be.*

From 1962 to 2017, the dollar grew in value to about 7.40–7.60, but energy costs (gasoline, oil, etc.) grow to $15–17 compared to the 1962 dollar. That is, the 1962 dollars. Now, in 2017, with costs at $40-50 per barrel, we must understand that prices should be driven to below $20 per barrel when cartels are colluding on how to reduce supply in order to drive prices upward. The market needs to dismiss OPEC and create the necessity to free the market.

Meanwhile, energy company profits were (and are) at record highs. Yes reduced, but nowhere near market driven reality. Capitalism has been replaced by "oligarchies, multinational monopolies" (illegal by Sherman/Clayton antitrust acts), controlled price, and product availability, and zero new ideas about Energy, except Horizontal drilling and fracking. And quite frankly, to an oligarchy, customers are not people, just numbers on a spreadsheet.

The Secretary of State (SOS) catches his breath and resumes his dialogue: Congress got our citizens to argue about capitalism versus communism yet run world oil enterprises as Socialism/Oligarchy combination out-stepping true competition and regulation, which is the problem. Any supply interruption causes price increases, while well run companies are supposed to have reserves for that. Sometimes a supply interruption or even a threat causes a retail price increase even though the impact is way down the road. That's the result of oil monopolies *and we all know it. Remember, reserves are greater than ever.*

I think we've outplayed our cards, and someone must straighten out the deck or face another round of "let's go to war and let the victors sort out the economic nightmare". But after one failed one after another, we are hesitant, yes?

The President pours a club soda and gulps it down.

President (to the VP and SOS):

I appreciate your realism. You're trying to make me understand reality. Think you can scare me back into the oval office to write speeches? Guess what? Speeches don't create jobs when innovation is suppressed. We must change.

No, we weren't punished enough by the Affordable Care Act. Yes, I know oil and gas and the military industrial complex make insurance and medical lobbies look like child's play. Yes, it's true, we haven't even figured out how to combat the NRA's hold on Congress. The NRA feeds the public on a supposed pro–second amendment advocacy, but they really support **gun sellers**. Sell more guns! Americans know this but don't know how to fix it.

What a great plan: suppress the economy and convince the citizens they need more guns. No, I'm not shutting down the second amendment, just trying to control sales to drug dealers.

Then un-employ our youth, and you can see the next tragedies in the press almost weekly. No wonder we're killing each other in our cities: youth unemployment, although declining. I see it coming, driving us to war over oil fields, and then cycle up for more debt. Meanwhile, the soul of American spirit is held hostage by invisible handcuffs. Let's give everyone guns and every corner can be the O.K. Coral.

The teachers' unions must compromise job security (tenure) for innovation and performance-based pay increases through student performance, but nothing happens, because tenure is a sacred cow. So sacred we're willing to let education falter. Yet our great teachers suffer. It's crazy. Where are the spirits of ingenuity and innovation? The point is the problem of lack of productivity is not only oil. And then let's discuss healthcare, no that's the next book about monopolistic control.

Subject after subject, we argue and then postpone action. We are just creating more bubbles and setting ourselves up for inaction. And then an election cycle comes and we have a media spending war, endorsed by the Supreme Court through "Citizens United." This is not what made America great: people made it great, not money. People created money, now money is more important than people? Our Supreme Court doesn't know that? They respond, we just interpret the law, if you don't like it, change the law.

Well, *we are going to take it on*, and we will bring the world with us. Because otherwise we are headed toward World War III and I refuse to contribute to this downward cycle towards war.

SOS: What about the oil pricing downturn?

President: The adjustment to resupply, or should I say increase in supply, is a short-term pricing phenomenon waiting for the sources to adjust production rates that will cycle down until pricing can recover. Under the current market structure, until OPEC is eliminated, and it will be, and true competition can stand up to the existing oligarchy or the government control mechanism (which is fundamentally illegal). You must cause the mix of energy use to change, and the providers be subject to an open market, or we will quickly be back to the $3-4+ pricing range, when in contrast, a truly open market will deliver $1.00 per gallon and less (much less). This is wide open because the combination of energy storage innovation and the ability to create energy will transform our efficiency. What's the biggest factors? Battery evolution and productivity of the hydrogen fuel and gasoline "creation processes", which will only improve transportation productivity: 100 mpg, 150 mpg, 200 mpg, 300mpg... etc. Are you skeptical? If you were Big Oil, what would you do? Acquire the competition! Check your pulse after you absorb the factual and logical input throughout this book. It requires only recognition that the paradigm has changed... curtailed deep drilling and mining. Just rewards for those that will create clean energy and fresh water. Remember places like Libya and Nigeria already extract oil at about $1.00 per barrel. (42 gallons or barrel) Change or find new uses for your sources of energy. Don't forget fresh water and the population increases. It will become clear. It's time to change and we have the science and resources to do it. Do we have the discipline and persistence?

Absorb all this and get ready for the next generation of America, because it's been about time to change for at least two decades.

Here is where I want to go: Energy productivity is the one problem that leads to the prospect of war. Water and energy shortages assure it. Decreased water means less food. We need higher capacity, while we reduce the cost by one-half, so we can afford to invest in water desalination and other sources of water generation. Water is the key: food must expand; we need water for famine elimination. And the world is adding a billion people to the mix. This must be the 21st century challenge. We must prepare America and the world for a new paradigm. You may be thinking, *how can you cut energy costs in half?*

The Arab Spring was caused by water and climate problems in the United States, Russia, Canada, and elsewhere. It was unleashed by citizens because of skyrocketing food costs and low participation of citizens in oil and gas profits by dictators whose profits have skyrocketed over the last ten to twelve years, have grown steadily over fifty years. **You must understand what years of excess profits produce. When you look at it, profits are 4x or 5x what they should be. This creates feelings of superiority and produces unrealistic and uncompromised delusions of grandeur.**

The United States is going to embrace the real problems as if we entered a new world war. Let's call it Citizens United for World Peace by increasing competition and innovation for water and energy change that is dynamic and comprehensive. Not more, just different.

Every person and company must be on one side of the water and energy line or the other. Pro–water and energy for America versus anti-America or anti-world. If we are to battle, it won't be with the Middle East or China or Russia. It will be within our borders. **We are going to "change the mix" of energy supply by increasing it beyond demand and generating an excess of fresh water while normalizing trade in the Americas through higher volume, low pollution, and lower prices, and increased profits, through diversification and expanded markets.**

When you recognize that all the world turmoil persists around a rich status quo minority, minority in population, not dollars, I'm afraid you simply have to look for Kings, dictators, and Power monopolies and then edit for a dominance of "oil GDP" and you'll see the problem. The only way to solve it is to internally fix the USA, Germany, and China, soon to be followed by Japan, the EU, and others that will cause a crush to efficiency and the funding of a fresh Water revolution. The rest of the world will "self-adjust" under changes that will become obvious.

When you see we can change the mix of how we use energy, we will unleash a new generation of innovation. The challenge is to get the green movement and the fossil movement to synergize around energy efficiency, for example energy productivity. *That's the road to the real green: money.* Money to pay for freshwater generation, pay down our debt, and still reduce energy costs for a renewed economy.

We will increase energy competition and innovate with efficient resources. *We will increase the use of natural gas and hydrogen in vehicles; employ wind and solar power for desalination* *and agriculture and invest $50 to $100 billion to increase battery density by three- and five-times current battery storage capacity. The problem is we need guaranteed solutions, not just ideas. If it was easy to massively increase battery density, wouldn't Elon Musk (Tesla) have done that already. He's creating scale through his Giga-factory with Panasonic (Japan) in Nevada. That's a double but we need a home run.*

We will increase energy efficiency in order to get 100 to 150 mpg across the board, produce an abundance of freshwater, including joint projects with Mexico, Canada, and the Americas. America will produce a major increase in world oil and gas production and will be leaders in assuring "non-leakage" of methane and near zero defects in mining, production, and distribution. But don't worry, we have plenty of capacity and will also share our engineering breakthroughs with the world like we always have (as a participant). We don't fear competition because our commitment will be unparalleled and supported by our technology and our people. What you need to understand is that diversity stimulates innovation. Too bad the 1000 mile battery wasn't easy -probably the reason it's not.

Look at Venezuela: They have more than twice our oil reserves, yet we triple their production. The quality of their O&G makes using of their reserves troublesome. And its Venezuela's resources and we must prove that we have turned a new leaf in international non-interventional (CIA, etc.) relationships. But Venezuela's socialism is a mess, right now, probably ending on social violence. It can't ignore the universal invisible hand. Think of it: Our Monopolistic Energy (ME) society suppresses the invisible hand, while twentieth century socialists ignore it... definition of the "problem". Open market mentality and personal freedom will restore their direction.

We have more because we're good at it, planning, mining, excavating, drilling, extraction, and distribution. Now we'll add energy productivity and near zero-defects drilling. That is, we will engineer near zero defects methane distribution. We will use our expertise to assure that we engineer effective drilling that does not release methane to the atmosphere. Yes naturalists, we'll close all the loopholes and mandate quality control. I know even people in my position voted for loopholes, but that was the old me. Not the WE-ME. But that doesn't quite do it, does it?

Our Water and energy actions will make it clear that we will assure clean energy by emphasizing both the fuel cell electric vehicle (FCEV) and EV engines with electric, natural gas, hydrogen, and fossil fuel-mix (gasoline) hybrid autos with dual and single fuel alternatives. Pakistan and Iran have cars that run on natural gas and petroleum. The third and fourth largest in the world. Of course, we expect petroleum competition and conversion, but we expect the FCEV to dominate because of superior efficiency over the internal combustion engine (ICE), until the battery innovation exceeds expectations. It's been proven that the FCEV beats the ICE by three times, without hybridization. We can leverage NG and at the endpoint convert NG to hydrogen (in your garage). And if ICE autos match the efficiency and cost, so be it. We'd also expect many EV successes, as soon as battery density exceeds three to five times today's standards

I repeat, EV's and FCEV's are the same, EV pure electric, FCEV electric engine, hydrogen fuel. The only questions are, which will achieve density (driving range) sooner, and which can provide convenient refueling faster and cheaper.

Understand this: we got to the moon for two reasons. One, we committed to it. Two, our engineering was spectacular, even before the silicon chip, and as the movie said, our Germans were better than "their" Germans. Well our Germans are now the 21st century alternative fuel leaders in Europe. And they're good.

All this includes government subsidies for fuel distribution across America and the planet and we could spend $50 to $100 billion or more on battery development and implementation is much better than spending four trillion dollars or more on war (Iraq, Afghanistan, etc.), but we don't have to.

The math is simple. **Energy productivity is so much cheaper than war!** And yes, even more profitable than war. And we don't accomplish anything in war but support the status quo. We don't want more soldiers and military equipment; we want longer lasting batteries and inexpensive and clean fuel, and fresh water for drinking and farming. The key to progress is refueling at the gas pump. No change, no progress. This is well understood by the status quo. It's the answer.

Our delivery target is production and distribution of natural gas, hydrogen, electric and gasoline hybrid cars, with over 100 mpge available within 3-5 years with energy market price assimilation and staged rollout underway within three-five years. We expect engine conversion from three-five years (after deployment) to sixty five percent and more depending on the speed of refueling station rollout, especially with the EV and FCEV. We will realign taxes as we convert to FCEVs and EVs equal to 50 percent of energy productivity improvement, and low-cost energy will enable funding of desalination and other water-creation-purification initiatives, as provided by the low cost energy for operations. (Which clearly could be a job for Solar and wind power.) After we exceed 50 percent market penetration, the demise of the internal combustion engine (ICE) may be at hand, but with lower gasoline prices, it could hang in there if **ICE reaches for our 100–150 mpg equivalent standard, which is easy with universal hybrid proliferation. That's okay because that improvement in ICEs to that level reduces pollution by over two-thirds.** But when a market is freed by accessibility to alternative fuels, watch innovation kick in. The expanded uses of this productivity will exceed lower fuel prices (free markets), but with spectacular worldwide results, watch attitudes change.

Although we always have worldwide ambitions, we will succeed by using tax incentives to reduce emissions, but internationally, that's nation by nation. We are open to any good ideas in the Far East, Middle East, Europe, Australia, and Africa. Once the world sees it has the resources and the will to compete, they will join us. The world is ahead of us. The reason we know we're behind is that Pakistan and Iran have more than seven million natural gas powered cars. Think about that: Pakistan and Iran. Isn't that ironic? Why? It's cheaper than building refineries. It's pure economics. Sell the world oil at high prices and leverage low-cost natural gas for them. Nat gas doesn't need expensive oil refineries, so natural gas deployment is cheaper.

This is a "war" for the success of free enterprise, and we will engage our citizens as if they are creating the legacy for the next several hundred years. And we're always being usurped by new ideas, especially from fusion, fission, and even petroleum, given our efficiency and clean Water and Energy (**WE**) objectives. And we will be sure to let our military leverage our enterprise, although as this system rolls, military demand should decline. Water and Energy need a Manhattan Project or Moon landing project with a JFK type vision to raise battery density by (eventually) three to five times for automobiles. It will change the world. And the core research has been done by government funded universities. (A strategy we already have in American R&D, and in the Military, is, The Air Force.) Politicians hold back about the USA's Energy Department role in funding energy research since WW II, people would rather say, Government is stupid, in spite of the facts and science that has been slowed by the resistance of the status quo. Mistaken beliefs that market pacifism will prevent war. Twenty first century pre-WWII attitudes about Germany.

So, we will tell Cabinet members, we want you to prepare for multiple world development tours that will solicit both feedback and participation over the next month. We will engage our constituencies, lobbies, and international governments over the next few months and then present a plan to our citizens and Congress.

We are also going to fund this from investment credits and taxes, with the expectation that water investments will leverage energy productivity gains, making a five-to–ten year goal of a "tax-neutral" solution, with a target price of the equivalence of below one dollar per gallon for petroleum at 100–150 mpge (e includes electrical cost to support hybrid FCEV's and EV's..) We expect oil and gas to be ardent supporters of this effort, with the expectation that this enterprise will be pro-America, pro-net productivity, and anti-oligarchy, cartel, and monopoly. We also believe our market management will be free-market and American driven, but once the bar is set, watch Germany, Japan, Italy, and South Korea to come aboard to name a few. (I repeat the Germans are already in front). As China and India rise to the level of the largest world consumers, we expect American companies to remember who they owe their innovation to. Remember, General Motors already sells more cars in China, then the USA, and now Ford is accelerating Pacific Rim investment. This is all good with the USA S&P 500 already yielding 40% of its profits overseas. Growth is the second layer of tax contribution, the one element that will wipe out our 20+ trillion-dollar debt. In fact, it's already started with mediocre economic improvements in tax income from new profits. The answer is market expansion, not isolationist-withdrawal. America is the bastion of free enterprise and will remain so for at least the next five hundred years, if we recognize and expand our role in the Global Village. This is, it must be pointed out up front, an economic-social-ecological transformation supported by the American people and Industry will extend, not retreat from, our economic and leadership momentum, our shining light on the world.

While gas dramatically over road oil, the oil market rapidly was consumed by events, all driven by Middle East events, except 2014- The introduction of shale oil- USA US history Crude Oil Prices @ price per barrel.

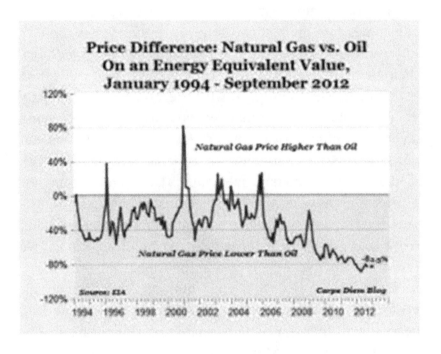

	Year 0	1	2	3	4	5	6	7	8	9
1960's	2.88	2.89	2.90	2.89	2.88	2.86	2.88	2.92	2.94	3.09
1970's	3.18	3.39	3.39	3.89	6.87	7.67	8.19	8.57	9.00	12.64
1980's	21.59	31.77	28.52	26.19	25.88	24.09	12.51	15.40	12.58	15.86
1990's	20.03	16.54	15.99	14.25	13.19	14.62	18.46	17.23	10.87	15.56
2000's	26.72	21.84	22.51	27.56	36.77	50.28	59.69	66.52	94.04	56.35
2010's	74.71	95.73	94.52	95.99	87.39	44.39	38.29	46.17		

Price jumps - 1979 US importing, 2001, 9/11, 2014 shale oil & gas.

The Secretary of State responds: Okay, we get it. America is to restore its technology and energy leadership. Energy leadership is not more, it's clean diversity available at the pump, and home. To continue the old way is to assure the decline of market share and profits. Somehow, we are going to make energy costs one-half of today's and the oil and gas companies will embrace it. Right? When China realizes it can't compete with progress, they will jump onboard the Water and Energy (WE) express and lead the world in non-ICE autos, **and diverse consumers will benefit from dramatically lower pollution, (a key point with China.)**

VP (the expression on his face is droll, and his forehead is sweating):

You only live once and *Americans* will embrace change from Canada to Argentina, and especially Venezuela. I get it, you crazy, inspired leader. But the obvious question is how to extract Hydrogen from water and make a viable source of fuel, and perhaps from seawater and create a viable source of fresh water. We forget that the seas are 70% of the world's space, but over 98% given its depth.

President: Thanks to our past leadership, we already funded and executed on that science and engineering. Now we must go back and say, we agree, let's translate prototypes into an international movement. Because look at the...

EIA Forecasts

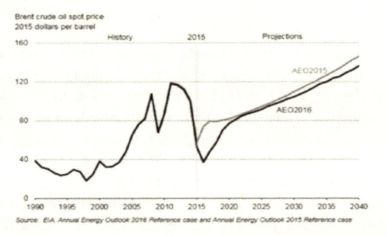

According the EIA, after production settles by 2025, we resume the march to $100+ per barrel. Frankly, you and me, and the rest of a powerless constituency. This must be reversed, soon.

VP: I want to be there just to see the expressions on their faces.

President: Look at the current oil stats: World Oil Production and Imports 2015-2016

Country / Region	Production	Imports	Reserves
USA	10.55 BBL		256mm
Saudi Arabia	10.05		212mm
Russia	9.415	9.08	264mm
IRAQ	4.59		121.35
China	7.6	11.8	234
Canada	3.677		155
Iran	3.3		148
UAE	2.82		97.8
Kuwait	2.56		104
Brazil	2.53		110
Venezuela	2.53		95-298
Nigeria	2.317		37.2
Libya	3.64		48.01
S. Korea	2.815	2.95	
Netherlands	1.884	1.2	
Germany	1.884	1.25	
Philippines	1.503	1.45	
Italy	1.395	1.34	
Spain	1.349	1.24	
France	1.174		
UK	1.047		

CHAPTER III

Washington DC Selling the First Lady

(Inside the White House, post-election second term.) The President decides to have dinner with his wife in their bedroom.

The President usually has dinner with his family, but occasionally he wants a one-on-one session with his wife. The First Lady (FL) knows he is thinking about pushing the envelope, and she grits her teeth. Not only does he take on an agenda, but depending how far he wants to go, she worries he'll set himself as a hate-group target, and then she worries about the children. Of course, the secret service is risk cognizant, but she knows the drill. *She must temper him and support his ambitions.*

President: Honey, thanks for giving me some one-on–one time. It was a dreadful campaign, but I need to bounce some ideas off you. You know I've been disturbed and am going to make some game-changing moves, so you need to be onboard because it is going to be rough. I think the "caldron" is boiling, and if I am being drawn into a fight that could be fraught with upheaval, you need to be ready.

First Lady (FL): Sweetheart, you know I am here for you, whatever the outcome. Just don't forget American resilience under pressure. Don't be afraid to ask for the people's support. With the way congress is behaving, it's not a question of whether there will be trouble, but what kind of and who should back you up.

President: I'm going to call a secret meeting with our North and South American allies and then hold a series of one on ones around the world. I am going to include Israel in this first meeting, so they do not get their information secondhand. I know this is way out of line, but I feel it will tell our American partners what our Middle East and border policies are in a straightforward manner.

I will follow this with direct meetings with our European family, as well as Japan, South Korea, Australia, Russia, India, and China, and yes, the Middle East. I am posting this as "this is what we'll do", without question, and I need our American allies to recognize this for what it is and join us. I feel if I do not do this, the next world war is a short-term inevitability, so no matter what, millions will die. I am compelled to act. How close? I don't know, but this is about the consequences of years of US inaction, a cleansing, a change Americans will need to step up to see as they evolve to a majority and then a movement. Yes, American resilience must be tested, and stagnation is no longer acceptable. It's about Water and Energy (**WE**), and it will raise the bar for everyone, so I need to enlist my voters. The problem is, I feel there is no acceptable scenario where the oil and gas industry would not take me on. So I will get pushback from both parties and industry. I also expect the green movement to weigh in, struggle, and then get it. Our sell must very clear. If they don't, we haven't made them see the position. It's ugly, but I feel world engagement is assured. I've highlighted this with VP and SOS, and although they are concerned on many levels, they'll fight the fight. You see, our energy capacity, our economy, and our opportunity are culminating right now, and I see it burgeoning all over the world. Our reliance on the Middle East is declining, we will support Israel through whatever, and it's time to transition to a Water and Energy (**WE**) strategy, and the American people must embrace this as they have in a world war.

First Lady: Okay, I'm listening.

President: Basically, I'm fed up. I feel the system is breaking. No, it's not the end of America, but we are entering the Pacific Century, where momentum surrounds what is going on in China, India, Japan, Korea, Indonesia, Australia, and the Pacific region, even Mexico. Fortunately, the United States and the Americas are as much in the region as we are in the Atlantic. It's like positioning that only God could have engineered. No, the Atlantic is not dying; it is being repositioned with the world population. All our allies know this. It still has the momentum of its history but now must adjust to a world shrunk by the computer, GPS, satellites, Google, Facebook, and so forth. But to China and India (soon to be almost three billion people) it's not an idea, it's an accelerating reality.

Ultimately, the next adjustment, after a period, is the emergence of Africa, which will take time but must and will happen. The Americas will have to fundamentally change, driven by energy, technology, and our role of assuring the emergence of everything south and north of us. But make no mistake, we must fundamentally change, and for that to occur, something must be done to prevent what seems inevitable in the Middle East and the Mediterranean.

No, Europe is not dying, but it needs to join the revolution, the revolution that crosses borders and the traditions brought about from the two world wars and its predecessors: Europe versus Russia, the Bosnian and South Eastern Europe connection with the Middle East and North Africa; essentially the reestablishment or rebirth of the relationship of the cradle of civilization to the history of the world. The balance will be brought back into a truly global village with the reemergence of Africa, but that will include innovations we cannot see yet. South America is emerging, and now Venezuela has more oil reserves than Saudi Arabia. We must realign with Venezuela, but you know that's a problem because of socialism, Cuba, etc. Yet it's inevitable because of the times. There is the ultimate result of the telecommunications revolution, the impact of population growth with global markets, and the conflict of the environment with the current course of change and with world population. But it can happen in a good way because of focused innovation. I want Venezuela to participate. When they see world momentum, they will choose to participate, I guarantee it.

The 21st Century has been noted as the Pacific Century. Population increases and the rise of India and China, targeting three (3) billion people. USA, targeting 450 million people is 1/7 their number. This doesn't downplay the Atlantic regions, EU, etc., It's a wakeup call to the Global Village. For example, China estimates car use to increase by one (1) billion. In 2016, new cars in the USA from all sources was approximately seventeen (17) million. If that's 100 million cars, if the USA could get 10% of the expanded market, that's a striking example of the Pacific Century. **Wake up America!**

The world evolved from Africa, the Tigress/Euphrates, the Empires, and has been pulled back into the cradle from some force that only God knows, to the Middle East *due to oil*. Before 1900 and the emergence of the automobile and the airplane, the Middle East did not even know they had the real volume and power of oil. America and England helped them find it. World War I set the Middle East back, sort of, through the destruction of the Ottoman Empire. It is like *inevitability*, a force that refuses to quit. But so is America and its wealth of resources, as is Russia, as well as Australia, Canada, Mexico, Brazil, and more. Maybe the population explosion and human intelligence is confronting the history of the physical earth, a finite resource, and its growing population? We do not know, but its time has come. And that time is now because failure to leverage change in a good way means change will pass you by. And we can't forget Venezuela and that means we must rationalize their history and open the door!

Our historic missteps in Central and South America need refreshing. The era of CIA based attempts to support influencing governments is over, yet to many, we must prove it (not as a sign of weakness, but a sign of learning. Why? We have to plan for 8-9 billion person planet, forward planning, not isolationist withdrawal into an enclave.)

What is true is that the earth's limits are not really being tested. What is tested is mankind's greed considering an obvious dysfunction between the 1 percent who control world incremental wealth and the 99 percent who permit the disparity to persist! I am perplexed by how many citizens vote against their own well-being. Maybe a better way of saying it is: How many just do not trust government? After all, government gave us the housing and economic crisis in 2008: Iraq and Afghanistan, and maybe 9/11 based on our response, and we (the world) can't seem to make the proper decisions to assure peaceful evolution. The power holders are fixated by wealth and feel our military exists for them. No surprise, but populations grow and grow in poverty, and wealth flows to the top. But the needed midlevel reactions have been timid against "power money".

First Lady: You've succeeded in scaring me. My God, just pressing on health care raised the roof. Now you're taking on oil and gas, the military industrial complex, and the most powerful lobbies. What can you accomplish besides destroying the Presidency? I'm saying more than I should, but I am expressing my fear for you and our children. You must tell me more.

President: America will announce it has made great discoveries in energy and is prepared to make major changes that will lower our cost to provide funding for a great freshwater initiative. We will continue to do energy business around the world but largely away from OPEC, not the countries behind them. Water and Energy (**WE**) break the bond between the Middle East and the private and state-owned energy companies. Not by obtrusive action but real-world changes in supply and demand. Let the markets persist and innovation will take hold. Remember, we are not pro or anti anything or anyone. We are just responding to the ardent facts of *resource discovery and technological innovation*. We can no longer ignore it! We are going to leverage our energy gains and expand our momentum to Water and Energy (**WE**) in order to provide irrigation to support the vast consumers of our vegetables and meat around the world. We are going to point out the changes and show that we and the world must prepare for the next level of population, energy growth, and water shortage by reconciling the implications of the dichotomy between Water and Energy (WE) and solve the problem through transformation. And we will do it in a free market!

We will announce, with congressional agreement, that America, in order to preserve its free enterprise system, will adopt "wartime" actions until we have transitioned our energy supplier/provider relationships and our energy mix to a new paradigm. Not our usual war, but the acceptance of the American people that it must go through an adjustment period, we must "change the mix" of water and energy consumption. We will, as a government priority, complete the pipeline from Canada to Texas and add internal links. We do this to support the availability of petroleum while we transition to a new mix of resources. We are no longer scared of the threat of needing more petroleum, but we will deal with dirty oil sands as a matter of business.

We will announce a priority toward Natural Gas, Hydrogen, Electricity, and Fossil Fuel/Gasoline toward the market target equivalent of below $20.00 per barrel and through the cost effectiveness of 100-150 mpg energy productivity, but we know we have to take some steps to rectify the supply/demand imbalance to a petroleum price equivalence of no more than one (1) dollar(s) per gallon, probably less. This is not an arbitrary number but one in line with inflation over the last fifty years an acceptance that demand will finally be met by technological efficiency and clean supply.

All the excuses for lack of capacity and a diminishing supply will go away because we have the capacity and the will to change. I call it "energy productivity" but it really means our use of gaseous, electric, and liquid energy will change. We will "change the mix" or how we will use the assortment of fuels that are available. Knowing that the Americas have the capacity for one hundred plus years, we will step forward and count on fusion, electric. And hydrogen to take us through the next thousand years. Hydrogen, and improved electric will emerge much sooner, so we will change to clean supply through lowering the cost of obtaining fresh water by low-cost transformation of seawater and other recycling of "used" water.

If we sleep, we will rush to be a follower, followed by being considered irrelevant, no longer the shining light of freedom and progress. Increased battery efficiency as already been demonstrated in science on many levels. This is the beginning but will evolve to a mobile storage capability that will change the world. Once the breakthrough occurs, we will exceed these efficiency levels. We always do. For example, we must overcome the energy expense it takes to boil saltwater and make hydrogen and fresh water. This technological innovation is already in progress, but US governance and science and industrial understanding must open a new era of innovation and certainty. This is like knowing what we can do and announcing it, like the moon voyage, or cyberspace, before we have proven it could be done. This is because science, in the space shot, proved it could be done. And we stepped up. Now science knows we can rekindle Water and Energy (**WE**). This is something we're good at. This is our "WE (Water and Energy) project for the 21st century.

US-funded research and development (R&D) is well positioned in batteries at numerous locations. We will provide tax credits for the energy distribution companies (gas stations, homeowners, and apartment complexes, and more) to provide an effective energy distribution system across America. This commitment, along with the commitment to extended-capacity batteries, will change the world. We will leverage gaseous and liquid power points, efficiently, and convert natural gas to hydrogen in our garages, and provide pure hydrogen delivery systems, as well as electric delivery. Remember two existing networks are in place: Natural gas and electricity.

The success of super dense and quickly charged batteries, along with wireless systems, will be a spark for numerous wireless inventions, maybe wireless buildings with inline battery backup. But you watch innovation stir, excite, and deliver. This is America, and this is the World.

We will not interfere with competitive choice but will promote trucking and airline industries to aggressively move forward with "warlike" determination and transform their energy choice, with appropriate tax incentives. This, in the short automotive term, has to do with Natural Gas, Hydrogen, direct electric, and battery capacity, we will work with the consumers and producers to focus on them because I know it can be done quickly. Science and engineering will guide us as to how fast hydrogen will take over, but there are natural gas-to-hydrogen converters that could serve the Hydrogen Fuel Cell Electric Vehicles (FCEVs). We will show our citizens that the road to clean is through hybrids gasoline, electrical, natural gas, and hydrogen as a matter of efficiency and as a bridge to zero emissions. Remember. They will soon discover that Sun-Gas is the path to fresh water.

We must enable the distribution system to give them competitive refueling locations and capability including home and business places, airports, and fuel depots. We must enable diversity and convenient access. Remember, we know natural gas powers more than seven million cars in Pakistan and Iran. Our automakers already support natural gas cars, and Germany and Japan have large hydrogen and FCEV engine initiatives. And Europe will aggressively support biodiesel. America is behind and must step up, or lose market share, dimming our shining light.

When asked what's our strategy and focal point, our answer is simple...**distribution, distribution, and distribution.**

Just like the automobile could not have changed the world without government financed roads and freeways, government must take a directional role in enabling diversity. The point is, it's a free country, but the importance of this is the equivalent of World War II technology in warfare. Not dictating the answer as many will accuse us of, we must free up **choice.** We will expand and refocus our energy exchange with Canada, Mexico, South America, Africa and Middle Eastern suppliers, and recognize that our cost and efficiency targets will begin transforming in three to five years. Simultaneously, we will increase American production internally with "warlike" fervor. Not "nation yielding" war, but rather "Water & Energy (**WE**) yielding" war, the victory of clean supply over demand. When water creation takes hold, the Middle East will be there as eager participants. Yes, it's hard, but only returning them to the status of where they would have been in a truly openly competitive market, in the first place.

Once the momentum demonstrates that change is assured, private enterprise will run to transformation in a free market. And then all those sidelined trillions will fuel innovation with confidence. Like our economy, we are hindered by a mitigated belief. We will allow all nations to participate. Cost efficiency goals are established to assure worldwide demand for low-cost clean energy achieved by increased natural gas, petroleum, hydrogen, electric vehicles, and technological vehicle efficiency. Everything I'm talking about is in play. And the American public can choose the rate of change. We are going to change the approach, and now is the time to take it to production.

No one really believes that costs of energy can go down, the secret behind all bubbles—real estate, Internet, technology, and yes, energy. This blind thinking always leads to bubble bursts—including the energy bubble.

This allows a huge opportunity for traditional and enhanced petroleum and diesel. We will encourage consumers and business to make a choice for efficiency and air quality. It is no longer acceptable for the system to drag its feet over maximizing price and quarterly returns in return for laggard industrial economics and stifling business and consumer costs. It is expected that cost efficiencies will be returned in fewer than five years and full transformation will be rolling in full motion in fewer than ten. Profits will soar from increased utilization. However, these improvements will not occur without the cost of change. And we welcome Middle East and other providers to support the new value train and lower cost paradigms. We will welcome lower prices, but it will not deter our resolve toward: clean energy freedom; lower cost; and a clean environment.

If traditional oil and gas drags their feet, they will be the horses and railroads of yesterday. We will meet with Mexico and establish a new paradigm regarding our borders, addressing the drug trafficking problem, gun control, and agri-business across the border including new initiatives to produce clean water on both sides of the border. The clean water initiative will be combined with energy producing initiatives that generate steam for power (turbines) and convert the steam to fresh water.

This crosses all energy fields, including well-defined, safe, and clean atomic power; natural gas; hydrogen; and coal to natural gas and hydrogen conversions. Power for nationwide electrical generation will continue toward natural gas, synthetically generated gas, including coal synthesis to natural gas and hydrogen, water, thermal, and atomic power. The transformation is already taking place because of the price of natural gas. Government is not inventing anything; it is supporting the obvious, and really acting to support gaseous and electric engine power. We just cannot allow this **monopoly of stagnation** to create the obvious outcome of high prices and war. Natural gas prices are currently low because it suits the acquisition priority of oil and gas over coal. But they can't wipe out coal and then raise prices like a monopoly (or oligarchy). They must see the energized future and the rebirth of American initiative. They must see the world market with its growing population of over a billion people, understand this, in 10-12 plus years.

This is our moment to catch the energy productivity, establish goals, and hold industry to transformation. And you will see, transformation is many-fold. The energy companies must see the future and let low-cost natural gas create new markets. Not price controls by government, but failure to respond will lead to their breakup or competitive demise. They must see the economic rise of methane hydrate to complement shale gas extraction.

We will also introduce a military/FBI Mexican and antidrug border patrol and drug agency of at least fifty thousand troops and antidrug agents and announce an agreement with gun manufacturers to provide electronic tracking of all weapons from manufacturing to the final point of distribution, including an electronic imbedded id's with industry oversight of privacy assurance for all Americans that do not commit crimes. We will address the second amendment issues with a fervor and priority that reduces the hard drug culture and no longer sacrifices our youth due to misplaced notions of our will to change. This is not a desire but a mandate, and we will insist on comprehensive change that wipes out crystal meth, cocaine, heroin, and opioids. This is not easy, because people self-suppress their anxiety. Competition will help, but on a nine-billion-person planet, it's a challenge. Allowing our youth to be drugged is the most heinous pacifism in our history.

We will stop the distribution of illegal drugs inside America and promote legalization of marijuana. There will be no war on illegal drugs, just their elimination. We will develop free-trade agreements and international oversight of pharmaceuticals. (Yes, drug lobbyists, you heard it.) The elimination of illegal drugs will be trumpeted as a requirement for educational and other innovations, not the least of which is we oppose the destruction of our children. We will not let Big Pharma to just replace cocaine, opioids, and crystal meth, and the heroin supply will be destroyed, including originations from Afghanistan, embarrassing itself as the world leader in heroin (poppy) distribution. And Mexico, and South America.

We want our youth educated, not medicated, certainly not drugged.

We will also find out what's behind ADHD and autistic disease and attack them as soon as possible (ASAP). Complacency is not tolerable when we see the signs of war or the signs of peril. These two epidemics will be countered until they're cured. My

God, we have some elementary public schools with students' populations, 50 percent doped up to "treat" ADHD. It's sick.

We will introduce a constitutional amendment to control the per person contributions to political candidates and, the elimination of unhealthy lobby money with a sterner definition of graft; the reduction of cross-state candidate contributions,; assurance of state sovereignty regarding candidates; and national election of the President and Vice President by popular vote based on the percentage distribution of representatives in Congress (winner take all by state). This will eliminate the Electoral College, providing the rebalance of pure voter majority with the current distribution of representatives in Congress. This provides the balance of small state and large state strength in our republic, preserving our republic. Our strength in automation will eliminate abruptly, cybercrime yet provide a unified system.

We will redefine the role of corporations in the voting and campaign contribution aspects of election and policy making. This provides the value of assuring the absolute imbalance of smaller states to the most heavily populated states and the value of regional consideration, farm states versus city states, etc. This is completely in line with national governance since 1789 and reflects population change but postpones a referendum on the role of a republic in a borderless Internet state of being. We clearly plan to permit lobbying and significant intellectual contribution but will eliminate graft. And graft will be called graft.

The current dominance of both liberal and progressive and conservative special interest lobbies in all processes of government is the underlying reason our republic and our democracy have allowed strong "special" financial interests to have dominance over common sense. It is the underlying reason for financial insolvency as we preside over energy lobbies, medical lobbies, insurance lobbies, the military industrial complex, farm subsidies, and much more.

In the world of Internet and global communications (properly over sought), the power of choice must return to the people. States need to elect their officials, the nation should elect its President and Vice President, and the balancing of the two should be consistent with our Republic structure. (Power not dictatorship).

The United States and the world are underperforming because of the dominance of nations and entities (corporations, international agreements, etc.) over the independence of free enterprise. The status quo is a strong supporter of human rights, free enterprise, health, and other core institutions and values. They just prioritize money. We emphasize energy productivity, water creation, efficiency, and economic growth and prioritize voter participation over money-based campaigning. But the dynamics of global commerce, the age of the multinational conglomerate, and the dynamics of the shrinking planet, both resource and communications-wise, require that the United States establishes a new paradigm, one that benefits us and our global family of nations. We need to free entrepreneurial spirit before it succumbs to multinational population and money dynamics. We have to reset the paradigm with the dominant direction of eliminating graft, becoming energy independent, providing a clean low-cost source of water and energy, and providing momentum that will allow a seven to ten billion person world to survive in peace, with available resources that allows the health, welfare, and productivity of its citizens to be in balance, at least from the opportunity perspective, and freedom, as defined by regional distinctions.

Understand I didn't say we are eliminating lobbies. I said we will assure the democracy is enhanced and the energy paradigm will be recast along with water and natural resources, and people will have a clear vision of peace and opportunity. The individual vote will stand up against money interests, and all states will have their identities strengthened. So, what I'm saying to major lobbyists, don't say I don't know what good lobbies do. You know exactly what I'm talking about.

We recognize that natural gas is only a transitional action with its own air quality deficits, but it's a necessary bridge to hydrogen, fusion, and other clean power. But once the bridge is crossed, we not only achieve energy independence and lower cost and produce cleaner energy; we have changed the delivery system. We are not the innovators, Iran, Pakistan, Brazil, and others have been well ahead of us. We are just "catching up" in a productive way. We will employ our technologies to achieve better results. What we will reassure, just like during the late 1800 and early 1900s, that the United States must do this without the reigning incumbencies and government manipulation inhibiting competition.

We must leverage our natural gas discoveries and change the supply/demand side of the equation. That will be the factor that reasserts America's leadership in the world's technology, energy evolution, and truly free enterprise. Yes, free, but fostered and protected by government within the framework of our constitution, and very anti-monopoly.

Now don't cower under the fear of antitrust. The breakup of AT&T gave the electric handset revolution what it needed to produce worldwide revolutions on many levels. America will produce twice the energy with twice the reserves of the Middle East. It will just be deployed differently. Based on cleanliness standards and consumer choice. I should point out that a solar energy recharger has been developed to recharge batteries for free if placed strategically in many transportation hubs and interstate commerce freeways around the United States. This will augment battery evolution. It's probably more efficient, however, to have swappable battery boards (for example, to pop out the low power batteries and pop in fully charged ones). This is an enterprise and is wide open to free-market alternatives.

First Lady: Well, you must let me absorb this. My primary concern is how you can manifest support of this initiative without being killed—figuratively and literally. You saw what happened with the insurance and health industries under attack, and you clearly see the impact energy is having on the instability of the world. But to take a full shot at lobbies and lobbyists makes most of the powers in Washington and the states, regardless of the political leaning, your enemy. You will be called a Socialist, a Communist, and an obstructionist with what will be claimed by the status quo. People just do not need the compounding effect of "oligarchy ism" in the name of preserving free enterprise. Oligarchies and cartels mmm... "Oligarctels." (I think I created a new term).

President: Not the people's enemy, the people's enabler. Someone must change the paradigm and take the heat. Someone must free the forces of peaceful innovation. We will ask the American people to enable a peace-economy, a sacrifice, no, an investment, led by those businesses that love America but understand our need to be on the other side of the revolution chain with solutions that will not only transform America but provide a paradigm that will raise the GDP of the world along with energy volumes and fresh water. No one is our enemy, except the forces that inhibit free enterprise and peaceful change. Remind yourself that like it or not, our planet will absorb another two (2) billion people.

Quite frankly, all the talk of free enterprise, with all the follow through that inhibits the same, makes me sick. I know that deep inside our citizens feel this, but we need to recognize when we have gone too far. The problem is the people do not trust the monopolies and do not trust government, including government pervasiveness and oligarchy closeness to government (business manipulating government), and our challenge is to promote the temperance of governance with the insistence of necessary change. And this challenge must be led by energy. In fact, oil and gas is mostly socialist, with the US/EU participating as oligarchies and multi nationalist corporations that almost behave like governments. We just supply the armies (and so do our allies).

Energy can take the lead because we have already discovered the resources and the engineering to make it happen. This general acceptance will lead to innovation and further discovery. Most importantly, the impact of cleaner, more productive energy and a commitment to freshwater volume will ripple through the economies of the USA and the world.

Our people need to learn the difference between government interference and bureaucracy and standing up for its people. By God, they understood it in 1890, and they can understand it today. And they will see it with water and energy change. They will understand what I have learned about choice, capacity, and capability.

First Lady: But the money that will be spent proving you are the enemy could crush the real memory of the truth. How will we prevent the trillion-dollar forces of the status quo from stopping needed change?

President: We will make Americans see the realities of needed change while enabling benefits almost immediately. In fact we will use peoples' investment incentives just like in WW II.

What we take you and our people through is how the evolving world imbalance of money interests will result in an international conflict that will shake the foundations of human society, when the alternative is to recognize the real imperatives are all within the context of our constitution and our founding fathers. We will free the will and capacity to expand and change.

I, by the way, will ask you to promote a massive Internet vehicle that will open the path of government to and from citizens. We'll decide where to put it, but it will be the next thing in government citizen open communications and transparency. We need to open exploration with Microsoft, IBM, Google, Yahoo, Facebook, and others. I truly believe that we need to focus on Cyber security with worldwide standards and the USA, Russia, China, EU, and Asian oversight. Remember, our Cyber executives are true American heroes. And we don't need to twitter, we need our high schools to be reviewing and understanding bills in progress and the scope of regulatory reach. It will be a premise in participating in the world market.

Trust me, this is historic. By the way, look at Venezuela. Their voting system is better than ours, yet their democracy is in chaos. So it's not technology, but our constitutional commitment to freedom and free enterprise and a division of power and responsibility.

Government adjusted in the late 1800s, the 1930s, during the wars and the introduction of weapons of mass destruction and computer technology. It is just that the multiplier effect of population, military, and commerce power, the tightening of our physical borders, technology, and the concentration of financial might is heading toward incidents of destruction beyond human imagination. I will embrace the Congress and I know we can produce the results to let this evolve into something better.

You will find that the great industrial and financial minds of our time, like T. Boone Pickens and Warren Buffet; may not agree with all these tactics but will align with the direction and more. Silicon Valley is behind this. Properly positioned, the trillions in cash that have been on the sidelines will unleash when everyone sees we are committed, and it is becoming a success. Not immediately, but it will happen quite soon.

I cannot agree to preside over the real act of self-destruction through "more of the same". We must believe that our foundations, so well considered in 1789, with a few notable exceptions (like slavery and women's rights), were established to support significant change. I am willing to test our resolve and commitment of our citizens to a future. Citizens will feel it and appreciate the results.

If we do not do something, the power to resolve the forces of stagnation will make the United States a follower, when our destiny is to, once again, lead the world to the next level. If we do not, the necessity of innovation will come from the population centers and those not entrapped by existing infrastructure. If we don't do it, the emerging societies will, and we will be cast aside. Our opportunity comes from a better infrastructure to allow new generations of ideas and action to come from our heritage, amended constitution, and individuals that can lead through teamwork and resolve. Our system promotes innovation when it is not locked down by the status quo and money interests. We need to free the invisible chains and handcuffs that are tying up the invisible hands of capitalism. We will clean up the balance between, say, capitalism and regulation. The founders of our constitution will be trumpeted, and our technologies will enable clean energy change and bountiful fresh water.

First Lady: Why couldn't you present this to the Saudis and see if they can see the forest for the trees? Won't Israel feel we are abandoning them?

President: For quite some time, the Israelis have been preparing for war. Islam sees the world from an ancient perspective. Hopefully, their new generations can see that the status quo needs to be changed from within. The historical Arabic view needs to be tempered by not being able to dominate events with their power over energy. Science and engineering have moved energy and lack of fresh water to a 20th century point of time. Don't worry about the Saudis, they have seen this coming for a long time.

That is the bridge to cross to save the world for tomorrow. If the Sunnis and Shiites feel they need to ally because they are the center of energy, they would be making the wrong choices. The Middle East is no longer the center of energy. Remember, the inevitability of Armageddon was formed in a flat world they knew from the Roman Empire to China, not a circular sphere of influence shrinking through mass communications and fearing about mass destruction in a world of nine plus billions with mass technology. Although that old world is highly at risk, the Middle

East must believe that the new paradigm is at hand. And they can participate and benefit.

If they don't want to be part of inevitable change, they will be marginalized by history. And the Saudis look at one thing. If Iran takes over Iraq to reconstitute Persia, Saudi oil fields will be at extreme risk.

Remember, the wealth of those nations is held at the top, by heads of kingdoms and other autocracies and the new paradigm, the flow of change, is clean, something they can be part of, but it demands highly efficient delivery of all three, together, and soon. What must be recognized is that through technology and exploration, new capacities and capabilities have emerged. The world has changed. It must be enabled. We need more energy efficiency to create the economic capacity to produce massive fresh water. We buy water through energy efficiency.

First Lady: But why should we move now? Why now?

President: It's simple; we must because we can at a time when the United States will grow to four hundred-fifty million and world to eight or nine billion people. We need funding to safely restore freshwater to our aquifers, and the Middle East, Africa, and Asia all need massive sources of freshwater. It's time to Wake Up and for America to reestablish its leadership on many levels, especially regarding food, water, and energy.

WE need lower cost and low pollution. The world needs it more. We are the leading user of energy Population and societies, need more fresh water. You can't get more fresh water without low-cost energy. It's that simple.

The great populations of the world have given the Middle East a greater shot than most over the application of wealth over world economics and wellness. They can open worldwide efforts to improve efficiency and price. An efficient internal combustion or other engine that achieves 100-150 mpg is perfectly acceptable. It may be perceived as not solving the problem, but will accelerate competitive change, and all will drive us to productivity and clean energy. Remember, 100-150 mpg on an ICE engine reduces automotive energy pollution by two thirds. I say this with the understanding of the advantages of the FCEV and the EV. When the public understands it and sees the performance, the FCEV and EV will be a tough competitor, in yet a free market.

> In fact, we want that, with entrepreneurs openly competing for new paradigms, including fossil fuel sources. The only real difference is that the call for change is with warlike determination, and our people will get it, and they'll understand why and how. We have the capacity and volume to enable change.
>
> Remember, we are a four-trillion-dollar government that can't harness hard drug trafficking...it's pathetic. We will free ourselves of the chains of the past.

First Lady:

> Just promise that you will listen before you act or travel. My idea is that I want you around, please. You are tampering with trillions of dollars. Those who have it will use it against you.

President:

> Let me flush it out...find its legs. They kiss and go to bed. The president looks out the window and sighs. WE' the people: water and energy growth, efficiency with clean water and energy. If I don't do it, who will? The only excuse is fear of the money interests versus the opportunity of needed change for billions of people.

CHAPTER IV

The Morning Briefing - The Cabinet

Oil production and consumption 2017 Source CIA Fact book: I'm jotting down some statistics so you can understand the players in the energy or game those most impacted by change. This is a point of reference for all discussions regarding oil. I repeat it over and over because its government's forecast.

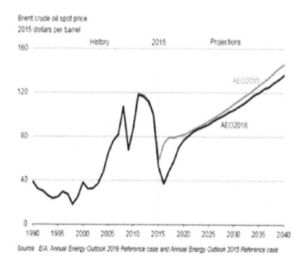

His cabinet meets at 9:00 a.m. in the situation room. The President hands out a book to his cabinet members: including the Vice president (VP), secretary of state (SOS), secretary of defense (SOD), secretary of Treasury (SOT), agriculture (SOA), Secretary of Energy (SOE), it will be unnecessarily strife-ridden, so under no circumstances should this leak. Covet this document as if your life depends on it. The meeting will have a mixed attendance from the highest officials in Canada, Mexico, Venezuela, and a few senior auto and airline execs from the US and Canada. Yes, I previously and privately set it up. I will meet with you individually over the next two days, so you should prepare accordingly. No lobby representatives should be aware of this. None! I've confidentially included Israel. Several weeks from now, it will not matter because I'll present to Congress and the American people, so hang in there.

I will meet with congressional heads tomorrow and lay out my plan. You have influence, which is why I asked you to join the movement. But you must learn the administration policy and back us. If you cannot, I will accept your resignation by tomorrow. I should point out that this is historical, requiring your utmost attention, but you have to be prepared to be part of history or be left behind. I need a team that can guide me across the river and around the pitfalls. Water and Energy will be crossing all government and corporate boundaries in the next two weeks, and I will present to congress and the American people directly after. This is not a political gamble. It is a certainty that I want you to be part of. It culminated yesterday. People are afraid of lobbies and pressure groups, and quite frankly, that is so pathetic it should make all Americans sick and tired, except for the graft merchants that don't care about the next billion people on earth, they just worry about their sponsors' quarterly profits. Many of them feel that's the role of war: population reduction and leadership clarification. Really?

So, here's the agenda: We will announce certain actions that, when fulfilled, will indicate a line in the sand, a move up to new ground, and an effective momentum starter of needed change. The document I gave you is an outline but represents more line items than I am presenting right now. I need you to consider who the players are that we need to spend time with; the goal of having a clear airing of their opinion. Those opinions will be abruptly influenced as I weave a world political alliance.

We will partner with the Americas first towards a new Water and Energy (WE) policy. We will cut across the Middle East and North Africa and perhaps the "istans" from the old Soviet Union and we wish to establish a new extension for our energy policy (Water & Energy) and to an equal extent, foreign policy. I call it the WE project as opposed to Monopolistic Energy (ME). We want innovation and peace, a new platform for dramatic, peaceful change. We will target a per barrel equivalent of a market price of $20.00 per barrel of oil and an automotive efficiency of 100 mpg on the way to 150 plus mpg equivalent, meaning the full effect of fuel, engine, motor, energy storage, or "well to wheel efficiency". We will consider investing at least 50 to 100 billion dollars in battery/energy storage media with a minimum target of three to five-time density improvement. We will remilitarize by redeploying tactically around the world and provide at least a 50,000 personnel, troop, and agent level for the US or Mexican border, *as well as city-focused, intra-US operations.* Troops will come from other countries and redeployment to Homeland Security, FBI, etc. until hard drugs are wiped out. I need to equally explain our tactics to the

Americas, the Middle East, the EU, Asia, and Russia. Call it what you may, I call it **"Elliot Ness",** as a recognized strategy.

We will stop illegal immigration and provide the necessary tools to eliminate gun running from American weapons manufacturers. We will stop the flow of cocaine, opioids, heroin, and crystal meth into the United State and be sure we do not create pseudo-equivalent Pharma drugs as a replacement. We will expel heroin from the states. We will legalize marijuana but have strong penalties for sale to minors. We will work with the Mexican government to offer freshwater sources on both sides of the border and offer worker passes to farms on both sides of the border. We will integrate the tariffs on produce with the goal of lowering price and volume to support wider vegetable volumes and support for biofuels, although probably mostly from algae. As you will see, biofuel will not be the primary focus, but will endure.

Most importantly, we will develop a plan to provide freshwater to both sides of the US-Mexican borders. Our view to agriculture is greater efficiency, and the functionality that the Americas will lead world food sourcing by expanding capacity and lower unit cost and improved quality of food.

We will complete the Canada-to-Texas Pipeline for oil and natural gas with additional distribution for the large points of fracturing across the nation. Fracturing will be regulated to a near zero defects leakage target. Not that it will be perfect, but it will be macro containable. I know you're skeptical, but when we get rid of the loopholes, you would be surprised what America can do. The flow of energy has a place in the world. Not a dominant place, yet important.

We will encourage the trucking industry to switch to natural gas and other gaseous paradigms like hydrogen, and Hybrid/Electrical paradigms as well as encourage biodiesel and other biofuels to support the trucking and airline industries at the target efficiency levels. Of course, electrical and gaseous paradigms could reduce biofuel choices to algae and specialized volatile plant life. We will fly under the banner of Water and Energy, and rapid evolution to zero pollution tolerance to stand for American's commitment to a clean excess of water and energy, including any opportunities opened by coal to gas/hydrogen (the universes most plentiful element) conversions; and high efficiency fossil hybrid form in fuels, including methane hydrate. *(I'll explain later)*.

Keep in mind that as the water problem is solved, the expansion of biofuels is available because food manufacturing will expand all over the world. This doesn't mean food and agriculture lower costs will kill that market, it just means food and biofuel will take its place in the new order of natural resources. Remember, the earth needs to absorb a billion more people in 10-12+ years. We need to behave like it's our problem to overcome. It's good business in a world where we are already a major supplier of the Middle East with vegetables and meat Africa will own half of the world's population by the end of the century. And what does the modern world see in Africa: natural resources and pandemic disease (AIDs, TB, Ebola, etc.). Don't kid yourself, we need to be as close to Africa as possible. They are the source of history and life. They are an incubator and must be participants in global change.

We will establish tax credits for the expansion of an all-access distribution system for Nat-Gas, Hydrogen, biofuel, electric charging, and swapping, and fossil fuel delivery as well as encourage/incentivizing home, office, and retail electric charging and Nat-Gas refueling. We expect results to start manifesting themselves within three years with a five-year all-out distribution enhancement and a ten-year overall completion cycle (in full motion, not complete). We will also support the next step research in hydrogen, fusion, batteries, and fissionable alternatives, and allow accelerated chances to move the technology forward.

Don't gasp for air, you'll see how it will come together.

We will also establish, as a side project, a constitutional amendment that intends to eliminate lobby money graft, change the voting process to ensure states' rights, and eliminate the electoral college by a direct voting method that will align each state's congressional voting blocs equal to the number of representatives in each state winner take all by state, (Pres and VP) to assure that the elector's vote balances pure population with the intended balance of small state power to assure the contribution of the broad community of states that represent farming and other small state benefits—the balance that is America. This is only related to the President and VP.

But none of that matters, if you just promote the doctrine of choice, invest in choice and the people will decide on the rate of change. Open the door, open the market. Understand that the status quo will not change unless the people can see the partially open door. We spend over 700 billion dollars on our military, so 10-15 billion (2.5-3.75% of budget) on transportation fuel choice is 2.5% that could transform the world. This is just an incentive for those who want to invest in the near term. The money is to allow choice at the fuel pump: gasoline; natural gas; hydrogen; and direct electric recharge.

Together, these efforts will invigorate innovation, clean low-cost energy, and political responsiveness. We will ride the new generation of employment with low-cost clean energy as well as begin building unlimited access to fresh water through combined fresh water and energy initiatives. We will recapture our world leadership by leading the direction to regional energy self-sufficiency and importantly, diversity of power and clean water. Water is attached as a direct result of driving the cost of fuel down to $1.00 and automotive productivity to 100-150 mpge (including the cost of electric recharging). Driven by the market, then attach a Water tax for desalination and other water purification initiatives.

(The president pauses, looking at the pale expressions on his cabinet members' faces.)

We will open our relationships within the Americas to assure free trade, but also expanded self-sufficiency. This will all happen because we will, step by step, bring the American voter into the mindset that will make the personal ownership for change crystal clear. We will challenge the power of money versus the power of the vote. We will restore the credibility of the United States to Argentina, Brazil, Venezuela, and most assuredly Central America, Canada, and Mexico. We will lead through smart enterprise, not a clandestine CIA. Venezuela will have to know that. We will be sure that our trade relationships are tight, but fair.

We will engage China, India, Russia, the Middle East, and others to work together toward clean, low-cost Water and Energy. (WE). All will be self-regulated...if China, or North Dakota don't want to change, they can fall behind, but they won't, will they?

The cabinet members all pause, figuring out how to act. They heard it all and then thought about health care and the gun lobby, as a point of reference, not a feeling of assuredness, believe me.

Vice President: Well, you will need a one on one with the oil and gas companies, Israel (this is real danger), and the Mexican border. How will Saudi Arabia react? What will you say and do to assure your price targets are met? The auto companies, even the Japanese and South Korea? What about Europe and Russia; a very serious one on one with China? The trucking companies and airlines? How will the general public understand a "warlike" position? I don't get it.

How do we overcome gas hikes or worse in the beginning? If Canada and Mexico pull together, who will stop getting their business or even just get less? How much can we get from Brazil? Argentina? Venezuela, I shudder at the thought. What if OPEC gets its South American partners to not play: Below $20 per barrel for oil, how much revenue is impacted for the US companies, for OPEC? How much more or less revenue for the Americas? How long will it take for the trucking companies and airlines to adjust? Won't the airlines require a huge capital investment? How long will it take for distribution to be accessible for trucks? Are there startup issues for biofuels? I do not know how we can transition this water for food and energy.

Won't China get closer to the Middle East? What about foreign aid and military positions? What will Europe and Russia be like? Have you considered all this? If we blow this, the party is dead; what gives you the right? Will you be impeached? Sorry for the stream of consciousness.

President: It's okay. I, of course, thought these things through and before rising to a near stroke, emotionally, I tempered my focus to the new paradigm, a return to honesty and a clear state of mind. So, try for me to restore tranquility through common sense. Honesty, it's a renewed idea whose time has come. It's hard, but I know you have it in you to show all the reasons that now is the time for change. We must have effective, clean, low-cost energy in order to restore the equation of more clean supply than demand and the elimination of pollution in our atmosphere. We are trading gasoline for clean air as well as providing water so that famine and drought can be eliminated once and for all. And don't shake at $20 per barrel. That's market driven, not dictated. Once the direction is clear and progress seen, the market will adjust to where they should be. Don't worry about China. They already make more electric cars than the whole world combined. Volvo (a Chinese company) just announced that in a few years, all Volvos will have an electric motor, including gasoline powered cars.

Secretary of State: Wow! It is all about persistence. None of it will work without Canada and Mexico and south; and bringing in the Africans. Why won't they all hold you up on price? Venezuela: we are 40% of their oil exports and 42% of all their imports is with the United States. That's amazing when you hear the rhetoric about socialism and anti US dialogue. This love-hate relationship could rock to the negative. It always has been about price and adherence to OPEC. But the Middle East is in dire straits right now, with a growing percent of oil coming from outside the Middle East and I assure you, this number will grow to at least 65%, and the Arab Spring, dynamics of Europe, the United States, Australia, Syria, Iran, and China leave the cards on the table.

But who will upset the game? That means you need some guarantees, some protection. The situation with China is precarious, given their take on the potential with the Middle East under these conditions.

President: Except the US, Canada, and England, none of the top oil companies are bastions of capitalism. In fact, the top twelve oil owners outside the United States Canada, and England are state-owned and state capitalists, which really means the oil and gas business is dominantly socialistic, and the democratic countries are forms of a monopoly or oligarchy aligned with OPEC when it comes to energy supply. That is so last century it makes me ill.

Secretary of Health (SOH): I will pass for now...I am still recovering from the Affordable Care Act and the American Health care initiative. But I'm intently listening and taking Rolaids.

Secretary of Defense (SOD): Clearly, we can pull our armed forces from several places...Germany, Japan, and others to establish a zone on the Mexican border. Yes, having a clear vision of Canada, Mexico, and South America is the priority. But when you invest in a way of business over a 20 or 30-year period, they will resent you when you pull out and see it as an act of withdrawal of support. Therefore, you are wise to bring Israel along from the beginning. We need to show some evidence that our military support of Israel is stronger than ever, stronger than words.

It is too bad the Arab Spring is not bringing forward clear democracies as opposed to theocracies. Although, clear democracies in Arabic terms could be Sharia law because there is no clear belief in a secular government or freedom of religion.

The liberals tolerate other religions. So be careful what you wish for. You may get multiple Iran's, or worse. Isn't democracy what George W. Bush said we were fighting for? Countries that want to, can choose to follow, but they will see the outcome of the WE nations.

American democracy, to a Muslim, is like trying to understand English without a teacher. To Muslims, democracy is theocracy, a very conservative theocracy. Sharia law would set back western democracy 1000 years, so it's a choice to self-discrimination. Remember, USA, China, and India and the EU will lead, amongst others, so we're in good company.

Now, how to get a clear vision for the rebirth of Mexico in an environment where the United States must be prioritized even greater than today. You simply must get cooperation when you need it, especially up front.

President: I agree but remember I didn't say pull all troops from anywhere, just enough to solve the drug or crime problem. Mexico is back to the old party and the Mexican people want to see change. They have a stagnant economy, although improving, but the people want to see the cartels go away and law and order restored. That is our opportunity, along with the border economics stalemate lifted. We'll give Mexico whatever they need, and I assure you knock the Cartels out of the USA. I feel we can do it, and one of our challenges is the NRA, or making the NRA feel we are not destroying the second amendment. This is a good excuse for the gun lobbies to say we are attacking them when in fact this is an international issue that must be addressed. I'm not sure what the new business model will be. Maybe we'll write our own laws instead of the lobbies writing them, the lamest idea I've ever heard of. A new experience. Maybe the lobbyists will have to come back to the Congress. At least half of them were at one time part of the executive or legislative branches of government.

Gas price targets will take care of themselves, by the victory of clean energy diversity over controlled supply. They are fixated over an idea that no longer holds water: Clean supply will soon exceed demand and is no longer is controlled by OPEC. Most oil is produced outside of OPEC. America will develop the distribution system it needs and extended storage of batteries that will break the weak supply and demand cycle of dirty energy and water by changing one fundamental thing. I'll show you, and as soon as we show that clean energy productivity is real, the markets will adjust, as soon as they reconcile that our supply chain is so deep. Of course, we need to re-educate America what's been drilled into our brains for 75 years, Clean Energy is plentiful and it's an unlimited future resource. We also will counter the idea that fresh water is a limited resource.

DOE: All the lobbies want to know what they did wrong. Interfering with the symbiotic relationship between the Congress and lobbies is a road to impeachment. Shake that cage, and you will hear rationalization and embitterment at a new level. If you think freedom of the press is under assault, wait until the financial key to everyone's election is perceived as threatened by empty coffers. How will we overcome that one? We need to think it through.

President: What did the lobbies do wrong? Let's see...Lobby money spending has risen from $1.56 billion in 2000 to $2.61 **billion in 2006 to $3.28 billion in 2012. Double in the last 14 years. And its start to fund clean Water & Energy. The world needs low cost energy and cheaply created clean water.**

*US opensecrets.org 3/2014

Yes, it's time for the elected government to realize that the honeymoon with money is over. It's easy...just do it! At the right time we'll redefine what's right and wrong about unlimited funding of elections.

OE: Now wait a minute, you can't dismiss lobbyists with declaratives. It's complex and fully part of an understood and function is part of "the system" that's well embedded.

President: Simply said that's Bullshit and you know it.

Of course, it's all part of the status quo. My intention is to circle the globe and involve our key partners i.e. the EU, Canada, China, Japan, Australia, India, and yes Russia and the Middle East in our progress and objectives. A key part of this is Germany, whom I've had multiple consultations with, and they are fully supportive and ready to partnership with us, quite frankly, Russia's actions using NG to influence European behavior is going to result in a backlash, led by Germany, Cyprus, and more. **Energy and Water are the Berlin wall of the 21st century.** And the wall will be dismantled, Lobbies and more, or they can choose to participate, or self-eradicate.

We must preempt everyone and deliver a solution. As we succeed, including many smaller efforts in this area, like letting small entrepreneurial efforts around Water and Energy (WE) takes place, we will choose solutions that will replicate themselves around the world. If a state or country goes "all electric" that's fine, but I think they'll want to reciprocate with their neighbors.

Once that path is clear for all to see, the economics and results will raise the world GDP many folds. But if we let all the efforts consolidate into a few large conglomerates, we will see prices escalate to bring percentage of profitability back to these abysmal levels (i.e. the old order). I do not mean large corporations or entrepreneurial efforts to increase share are wrong, but they must adjust to the fact that the potential around the world is so great that the return will be greater than squeezing the population through a suppressed productivity level. These acts are expansion. This is not a rollback, it's an expansion due to population and a rise in worldwide living standards.

Our own populations are living below expected levels, because their degree of participation in the productivity effect is diminished by the suppression of free enterprise. The smart companies will get it or fall the way of the nineteenth century railroads. Many will say they see a lot of small business and free enterprise. Remember, in the late 19th century, antitrust was about railroads and oil. Now it's automotive and oil, as well as heating and air conditioning.

I need you to see Water and Energy as **(WE)** a matter of scale, and they will need to participate in a peaceful but ardent way, away from the current paradigm, or more easily, toward a new paradigm. One that all, except for those who insist on not recognizing the world population of seven to ten billion requires a new level of productivity and volume, initially in Water and Energy (WE) but ultimately in the vast product of the world. Other parts of the world have many problems that we do not have, including a caste system; dictatorship by committee; and monarch or military power. We need to embrace our diversity and our freedoms that we're so carefully spelled out in our constitution. We must take our democracy and republic to the next level. Once the world sees our success and commitment, and our commitment of shared success, our path will be clear. Remember, we are not just moving deck chairs around, we're leveraging American innovation, exploration, and engineering to a new paradigm, a *new mix*. And the world will benefit.

Or we could take the military route and linger for another hundred years. Remember, real war is way beyond what we've been doing since and including Korea. This is exercising an adjustment to a new paradigm. And the opportunity is surprisingly easy to accomplish, if we have the character and foresight to see it and follow it through.

SOA: I see it and would love to participate in such a grand stance, but as you know, when the hierarchy of the status quo feels threatened, you will face forces that will make the insurance and medical lobbies look like little league. You, Mr. President, will have to enlist our true financial leaders like T. Boone Pickens, Bill Gates, Warren Buffet, Larry Page, Sergey Brin, Michael Bloomberg, and a few others who can see the forest for the trees. I say this because you have a marketing challenge that is unprecedented. But why not? We only live once, and so do our children.

Armageddon is a choice for those who are afraid of humanity, or God, as if he has lost patience with this. Evolving the world is hard, and we can't hide behind theocracy. But yes, we do need moral support. The United States has underlying moral fiber. And they'll change, given the chance. But everything is twisted because of dollars. I know no one wants to admit that real problem. But pause. We are in the Pacific Century and we either change or are runners up. By the time I'm through, you'll get it. The world of 8.5-9 billion people, it can't tolerate famines and war. I know I sound crazy, but you'll understand how critical now is. They say by 2100, Africa will own ½ of the world's population.

I concur with the cabinet, but make sure Mexico, Canada, China, Saudi Arabia, and Russia are well understood. And fix our relationship with Venezuela. And the EU is seemingly unstable. The dynamic of oil not traded in dollars is beyond my own comprehension. What are our alternatives? EU is Easy, just participate with Germany.

But someone needs to buy our T-Bills to finance expanded debt; that is for sure.

President: That is a key issue. The problem is that the issue of OPEC abandoning the dollar, as a threat, has not been publicized enough. People do not see the relationship to near hyperinflation. We will work on this. But confidentially, between us, unless we do something outside the box, the actions by OPEC, BRIC, and others are already in play. I think they are using our debt to back us into a corner. Or is the extending of debt needs to be over. Our actions will reduce our balance of payments and our debt will reduce dramatically, by virtue of our rising economy. Debt isn't our enemy; the state of our economy is. So, we will offer up a rock-solid economy. This will mitigate inflation. We already are experiencing a slight economic improvement with our balance of payments down to $890 million, although recent government deficit spending, in attempt to prop up the economy, so, a real upturn will rock our profits (and taxable income, with a strong business tax rate.). They must see our power and commitment. Is the world run by those who fill the tank, or those who invent, manufacture, drive the automobiles, and fly in the airplanes? We are turning over the reins to the drivers of the cars and the passengers on the planes.

But the steadfastness of the dollar as a reserve currency is about to fold. The Chinese have cornered the world market for gold. They are approaching the way the dollar used to be when dollars were backed by gold- dollar for dollar. The Yuan has gold behind it and the dollar has 20–22 trillion in debt, *outside the USA*. So, we must be bold and create massive energy productivity. Bring its normalized state below $20.00 per barrel of oil and under $1.00 per gallon of gasoline (equivalence) and the world will respond with economic growth resulting in finally restoring our fiscal soundness and really cutting our debt. **Equivalence means that if you pay $2.00 per gallon, but a gallon takes you three times further, that's only $.66 per gallon equivalence. Efficiency is not an enemy, but must be balanced, in a nine trillion people earth. Our culture must be shared.**

DOD (Department of Defense) Saddam Hussein broke away from the dollar, and within two years we invaded Iraq, hung him, and restored oil trade back to the dollar. Maybe Iran and Saudi Arabia need to be reminded of that.

President: You need to understand this. The BRICs have announced that they will start using their own currencies to purchase oil and all other import and export related transactions. They represent half the world population. Additionally, with the embargo on Iranian oil, Iran is trading with India with gold and rupees, and with China in Chinese Yuan. We have it in good understanding that within several months, all OPEC trades will settle in Chinese Yuan. So, this trip and the presentation to the public are set to preempt that event. We want to be paid back for the last fifteen years or so. We need to change the discussion.

The Fed and Treasury are exploring other ways to sell T-Bills at par, which is currently at 1.5 (varies) percent at base level. We are handling this, but ever *since China started to exceed the United States in Saudi oil purchases,* the activity around Saudi Arabia has changed. The Chinese are even building a refinery in Saudi Arabia. We will endure because of a robust economy, no other way.

Our only real choice is to solidify our markets for T-Bills through reinvigorating the economy:

>1. Define a strategy for keeping the dollar as a strong reserve currency through clean profitable growth.
>
>2. Build an effective alliance for change with China; and then Russia.
>
>3. Show everyone that we will invent the next generation, just like Silicon Valley did. Technology will dominate Water and Energy **(WE)** engineering as well as the next round of electronics, commercial, and military power. Do you want to stay in the 20th century or join the 21st?

Recognize that the challenge to the dollar as the trade standard is already out of the box, or I should say out of the house. United States must take actions that show our resilience including dramatically reducing debt through increased GDP and increased profits resulting in revenue that will restore our budget this is a very big deal, but the consequences of our debt and the growth of China and India. India spends half its energy finding and pumping water. They will see us as world trading partners, not unreasonable competitors.

It is hard to believe. We will drive energy productivity and water resilience so hard; we will find out who our friends are, and who will lead commerce, antipollution, and economic growth. The Chinese must see that Yuan stability will not fix their massive pollution problem and they can't build a middle class with ICE based automobiles and high energy costs? We must show our strength, even, as some say, without gold in Fort Knox. Just expect to receive travel itineraries to Calgary, Canada, in two weeks. If you do not want to participate, tell me by tomorrow, along with handing in your resignation.

The cabinet realizes they don't have much of an option. After all, the choice to resign is an easy decision. No? Courage may be a resilient asset for leadership. We have to show that a strong Water and Energy (WE) program will show the world markets that we are leading the world in strengthening the backbone of the Americas, the Middle East, north Africa, Asia, and our allies by adjusting the realities for the next billion people and the next 100–200 million Americans, Canadians, and Mexicans through dynamic Water and Energy **(WE)** initiatives.

We must understand that the solution to our debt ceiling is an obvious thrust of massive profitability and the understanding that our initiative will sweep the world in a way that will pull China, Russia, and more into a wave of inevitability-free of pollution, with fresh water, and free of debt.

Believe me we are bringing you in at first so you can prepare yourselves for the inevitable and without any CIA or clandestine agency-based shenanigans, just our hopes for the success of the Americas.

Veep:

We just took all the issues and spun ourselves into a void.

We've got a whole lot to do and our liberal spin produced a bunch of B.S. ish ourselves, into a whole new spin. We need to find real answers. Ambition is natural, but so is peaceful coexistence, we just must accept multiculturalism as a way of the 22nd century.

CHAPTER V

Calgary Canada

Calgary, Canada: United States, Canada, Mexico, Brazil, Israel, Venezuela, GM, Ford, Cummings (Canadian natural gas cars), American Airlines, United Airlines, Delta Airlines all meet.

The president arranges a one-on-one session with the above parties. He positioned the meeting as important for all. They know it is about oil and the Middle East, but the president made them understand that it is about much more than that. He left them with a curious sense of something big is forthcoming.

Mexico

It is unusual for the Mexican chief of state to be meeting in Calgary, Canada. The US president chose this because US oil efforts are in this area and it is a key hub of Canadian oil, including the pipeline that will reach all the way to Texas. Particularly, the president wanted to be on "neutral" ground with Mexico. The president brings the SOS, SOE, SOD, and their Mexican counterparts with their heads of state.

US President: I appreciate your meeting with me on such short notice, but you and I have many political issues to discuss. With your new political victory, perhaps it is a good time to establish this dialogue. I am going to highlight our short-term actions and raise some opportunities with you. I want you to hear this first from me, so we can start a dialogue, and although I plan on starting action soon, because I must, we have time to consider alternatives, and, of course, anything you would suggest. You will see that I'm sincere and am opening a very large door. You know how unsettling things are in the Middle East and in the world economy, and quite frankly, the United States must change things as delicately as possible, but in this, there is not much room for delicacy. Quite frankly, this is hard, but I must take challenges as opportunity. And the changes I want are the hardest to succeed with in my own country.

We will succeed; let me assure you of that. You know Mexico and the United States have four major issues: our existing oil relationship; illegal immigration; drug trafficking; and sales of weapons to the drug cartels. But beyond that, we have generic issues like how to resolve the farming issues on both sides of the border, water, and potential for new expanded opportunities. And yes, balance of trade.

Besides drugs, I think dynamic issues in water can revolutionize our mutual relationships. I have to say I will take several short-term actions, but the real meat is in finding a path around the four issues and changing both countries to the positive by jointly acting on the underlying generic issues. You know, for example, the United States and Mexico have a common problem in water scarcity. This is more critical than any political or military situation. Although we have common ground in illegal drugs, and both of us have huge internal issues, I assure you that the cartels will be expelled from the United States, along with crystal meth, cocaine, heroin, and opioids. Let me assure you, that era is over!

Mexican President: Yes, I need to find a path away from the horrible drug issues and related crime syndicates and find out how I will restore law and order from the cartels. My true agenda, likes yours, is national and finding solutions to the food and water issues, and our economies. I am open to ideas, especially those around immigration. Remember, the drug problem is largely my supply and your demand, although the drug source is still largely Central America and Afghanistan. So, the challenge is multinational. Mexico is just the current conduit. Central America is sending drugs to Europe through Africa because they, the Africans, don't control their airspace.

US President: Please, let me lay out my plans and ideas, and we can then explore your suggestions and prioritize the agenda. We call the project Water & Energy (**WE**) which will happen very quickly. Now of course we are in discussions with the Saudis and others, and the degree may change, but not the result. I have congressional support and I know I must have the major plan enacted in the next two years. Not completed, but clear steps down a long path, this is a reality of the American election process. This is also a major issue for many US corporations, and that is being addressed at this time. The two things that should be on both our minds are:

Our people are tired of this economic situation and the constant threat of war, and it is time for a change.

We must find a way out for Americans and the world. The population bubble will drag us into world war, and quite frankly, not on my watch. I'd rather go down trying to change. But I won't go down, so we'll change. Why? Because we must. The 21st century can't wait any longer. Yes, we're moving from an oil bubble to a population bubble, and a water un-bubble.

We have Israel at this meeting, clandestinely, because we want no confusion to get to them secondhand. I am trusting, up front that you'll keep this quiet for the moment. Short, but full of potential overreach. The presence of Israel means our commitment is unbreakable.

Mexican President: A comment: your relationship with the Saudis over the last forty to fifty years has been awesome and potentially dangerous. Also, you must be aware of China's role and they've stopped trading oil in dollars, which they've done already, given your debt. I see the quicksand of difficulties for many reasons.

US President: Yes, we will get to that. That is why the actions we take with Mexico and Canada are at the very front of our Agenda. We already get more than 2 million barrels of oil *per day* from Canada, more than 1 million from Mexico, and about 1.5 million (at peak) barrels from the Saudis. The other important source is Venezuela at 800,000 barrels, and 600,000 barrels from Russia. That of about 10 million barrels imported overall, so we must address this declining demand. You generally know that we have been discovering shale oil and natural gas in large quantities, and changes are likely. Forgetting the politics for the moment, we are going to change over our trucking to largely natural gas, biofuel, and electric and a tactical direction to hydrogen.

This is based of course on supply over demand, so you must understand it and lead your own transition. However, you know there is still profit in that and volume will increase dramatically as the supply chain kicks into the increased transportation energy use.

Balanced world issues are that governments and large corporations acquire all this income, but large quantities never work its way to the people. So, lower prices cut into 1% or 99% equation, while lower energy costs cut through all segments of society, across the board. Notice that the world governments, regardless of type, hold their wealth at the top. For want of a better term, greed reigns supreme, even with socialists. This will help drive the income increases more evenly.

Simultaneously, we will be taking advantage of the new oil and gas technologies as well as the benefits from fracturing (fracking) under environmentally sound conditions. We will administer zero-defects quality controls. Although you can see timidity and turmoil in the existing situation, you will see us come together. When we exploit all our opportunities, Canada and Mexico will be beneficiaries. In a new paradigm, China will go for price. Like the Nixon presidency, our path to world peace and a green world is through China, or should I say, the Americas, Russia, and China. This may sound scary to you but hear me out. The Americas will be the largest energy producer with the United States, the world's largest producer, Canada, Mexico, Venezuela, and below, soon larger than the Middle East. Americas' leadership will result in clean lower-cost energy and robust supplies of clean fresh water. And then Asia, Russia, and Australia will be bigger that the Middle East. We need lower cost clean fuels to pay for the agenda. The Americas need it, Asia, Russia, and Australia need it, the Middle East needs it, and the Euros need it.

Further, our efforts in fusion, battery storage, and hydrogen will be preparing for the next one thousand years. Mexico needs to be part of that. It will happen and I can prove it. I know this is like a punch in the face, when it comes to what we expect from the status quo and the current price of energy, but the United States is spending too much foreign aid, in fact, defending the status quo, instead of supporting the changes that the world needs including Water and Energy (**WE**). Mexico needs to be an integral part of Water and Energy (WE) and a leader of the southern American nations. You can help with Venezuela. Remember, we have issues with them, yet we buy 42% of their oil and much more in other goods. Venezuela has the largest oil reserve in the world, larger than Saudi Arabia, but are cautious about leveraging it, and it's the type of oil that's very expensive to refine.

Our geologists have studied North America and know that the potential for Canada and Mexico exceeds that of the US, including the offshore Gulf, Pacific, and Atlantic.

I know your politics include not being overly reliant on the United States, the same for Canada. What you need to understand is that the technologies for the next ten years will continue the acceleration of change, and the key is to be part of it. Like other countries like Brazil and Australia, the position as a key resource supplier to the Pacific Rim will make you a player in the Pacific Century, the 21st century. For many reasons, the Americas will be a friendly place to do business with free markets dominating as opposed to the Middle East and other dictatorships in Africa and elsewhere.

This is the true genesis of the Arab Spring, food and water, once the marketplace is reconsidered. China may be considered the beneficiary of western decline of business from the Middle East, but *when they see what they really need is not cheap oil, but clean energy productivity and fresh water, they will quickly join the revolution, or I should say the rapid evolution.* But the Americas must have consensus. China's and the United States' needs remarkably coalesce. China just needs more than four times the United States' volume, and more as their economy progresses. They won't get it without cheap oil or equivalence. And their pollution problem is pandemic.

As they and India enter the automotive market in a major way, they must follow the trends of antipollution. Nat-gas; electricity; more efficient engines, including Fuel Cell Electric Vehicle (FCEV), Electric Vehicle (EV), and an improved internal combustion (ICE), biofuel, and more. Imagine if those two nations adapted high-efficiency, low polluting strategies. Technology will reign supreme, and even the Middle East will have to lower their prices and participate in the market, not controlled by the suppliers, but the users of Water and Energy (WE). Remember, the people inherently own the land, and they fight the wars. We will introduce artificial Hydrogen and augment our fueling depots, nationwide. Note that India and China are making dramatic moves with the Electric car. China has made several cities have all electric public transportation, even all cabs.

Now, let me continue into the more difficult part of the discussion.

Mexican President: Yes, immigration and drugs.

US President: Yes, we are pulling our troops from various places around the world and are placing at least fifty thousand law-enforcement personnel around the US-Mexican problem, or should I say, the Americas problem. On the US side, we are stopping illegal immigration and drug trafficking. We will implore, including congressional action, our gun manufactures to provide a privately-owned database that will track the distribution of arms to its end-user, or last holder. These are warlike conditions, as we eliminate all sources of crystal meth, cocaine, heroin, opioids, etc.

Citizen's rights will be supreme, but the penalties for guns reaching criminals will be severe for the sellers. Additionally, we will decriminalize marijuana, but stop hard drug trafficking including the "Pharma" equivalents. This is not another war against drugs; it is a commitment to free the minds and prisons of our youth. Now this has major implications for Mexico, but you should treat drugs as a dying market and reestablish law enforcement considering it. We will have time to work this out, of course, but I need to position you as understanding the United States is tired of its failures and will reestablish our law enforcement to have fewer prisons and an old fashion agenda. Now, the NRA will tell everyone that the public would be seeding too much to the government, and we will respond to that. We are solving the major crime problem of our time and the people want us to eliminate drugs and related crime, so we are doing it. So, if they want guns, don't let drugs persist. But we will use trained agents, not gun toting militia.

But for an analogy with Pakistan and Bin Laden, we can't have Cartel heads sitting on a mountain planning drug trafficking in the US. To us it seems like a good drone application. We can talk about this in a while.

Mexican President: And I fear a discussion of drones.

US President: Drones are easy. What if we supply you with a squadron, train your people, and let you have at it? Only kidding, I think.

Now, here is the important part. We want to establish the Water agenda including the expansion of freshwater and Energy (solar, nat-gas, thermal, etc.) along the borders and create the farming opportunities across borders that will produces both food and biomass but leveraging both sun and technologies to create energy centers with both agriculture and water as a byproduct. Where practical, we will use seawater as an Energy source and use the steam by-product as a source for freshwater. We will decide how to manage ownership between us, but you should understand that the intellectual capital achieved here has worldwide application. This will take up to three to five years to start but will be part of a history that will be part of the rise of Mexico. I say this, with all candor because we know the potential within Mexico's terra-domain, your potential energy and special metals resources. As energy costs decline, we will partially reinvest in massive saltwater desalination, etc. You have already invited US oil and Gas in, so I believe you know you must increase production. The enrichment of South America will be parallel, but as neighbors, we feel our opportunity is unprecedented. This, by the way, is also true for Canada because of the richness of its northern slopes. Between us, the true terra-opportunity in the world is Russia due to its northern vastness. China has it too, but its issues regarding people management is their true challenge of the 21st century (percent males versus females), and an aging society (worse than the United States' baby boom). China needs to address that but become part of the energy solution challenge. We will be so successful that for China to ignore it will be an internal political and health disaster.

http://www.theatlantic.com/matthew-schiavenza/

There soon will be more old people in China and fewer young people able to help them.

Mexican President:

Of course, this is daunting, and I really need to study oil pricing elasticity and water potential. Where do you think the Middle East is in this equation?

US President:

Obviously, this is the question of the century. Like everyone on the planet, they have to decide, in a secular way, what the national roles in an energy-neutral world, are: neutral meaning that supply exceeds demand through market forces. Taking it out on Israel will not work because of Israel's firepower but promoting peace must be part of a Middle East solution. And Israel is not an energy player, yet.

Demand will still give the Middle East product strength. Somehow a more efficient delivery of energy must create a way to share the financial benefits with the people of the energy provider's nation-states. They will benefit by elongation of their reserves, due to productivity and choice as well as they're being a robust source of natural gas and maybe hydrogen. You will notice that Israel is creating an economy based on their education and power of delivering medical and electronic technology to the world. The Sunni and Shiite nations have been too reliant on oil as a percentage of their GDP, but since it has not trickled down as much as it should have, they can still evolve the economies of their nations. Remember, the world will change its delivery paradigm due to resource and delivery mix but the gaseous prices, including hydrogen, must stay below coal, in terms of well-to-wheel efficiency, to give it a baseline with electrical energy, if it can increase its production. Note that the generic fuel price isn't the effective price; you must include the cleanup factors that make coal more expensive and a "more acceptable" fuel source, as China is currently doing. But sooner or later coal will evolve to a gaseous fuel supplier. As cars evolve to FCEV and EV engines, vehicle exhaust will be primarily water or nothing.

This will drive coal to the gaseous paradigm.

Do not get me wrong; natural gas prices can still almost double and still be below the "effective" cost of coal, and many providers, particularly Saudi Arabia and Russia, will benefit. Of course, Russia would not like us to deliver natural gas to Europe. We'll see. Quite frankly, they should be more concerned with natural gas from Cypress than anything we have. It's oil that is out of step with energy productivity. What Mexico needs to do is aggressively join the quest for natural gas and join the supply of the changeover to mobile energy for trucking. Cars will be right behind them. It is just a matter of the distribution system to ratchet up and America is going to make that happen in the states. The war is against price, and that means lost revenue, unless your revenues increase by increased production. Once the price is realistic, with historic depletion adjustments; and that means almost half of the current price; then demand will rise with increased air transportation, and a renewal of world GDP growth. The goal is increased population wealth and that means electricity growth and automotive growth.

And America will help Mexico by increasing United States' demand for energy from the Americas. We also need you to help us with Argentina and Venezuela in recognizing the benefits with an Americas strategy. Not for us, but for them. **Remember, if the United States electorate knows the importance of a shift, they will support it with "warlike" fervor.** All they need is to believe, but like your country, with all people, they must recognize the honesty of the change. Once they see that, there is no stopping proactive evolution.

US citizens are tired of war, tired of the 1 over 99% equation of wealth distribution, tired of a declining middle class. They will see and believe the technology and the product and that energy sources are available and know the economy will turn. The key is piercing the $50 to $100 per barrel oil paradigm for good, and that time is now. Current EIA estimates show oil growing to $120 per barrel, assuming no dramatic change in use. And they'll understand we can't do it without "changing the mix" of fuels and have access to a flexible distribution pipelined network for fuel delivery. When we can economically provide access at homes and retail establishments, it's over.

Recognize that with transportation change, the demand for oil will drop prices to at most $20.00 per barrel of oil, no matter what. Supply will exceed demand, no matter what. Prices will restore to not lead inflation but curtail it. We believe in energy productivity as the cornerstone of a Water and Energy (**WE**) strategy.

As the dominance of natural gas changes to hydrogen and denser hybrid batteries raise energy productivity, and new sources of methane are brought online, the era of the internal combustion petrol motor is over. This is not a hypothetical. It is available and necessary. The real question is whether the EV or FCEV will dominate; it's kind of like technology and science versus Mother Nature. Once fusion is delivered, it seems like the EV will be supreme, but you never know where we will find inexpensive hydrogen. (Boil or chemically rearrange seawater, of course.)

But remember, don't mistake the United States' will to resist change as a weakness. We will defend all our partners to whatever level we're pushed. **Some countries need to discover that oil is not the center of political power, energy**

productivity is. When that's reconciled, along with freshwater generation, then the century will have fulfilled its destiny.

Mexican President: All this could be good, but we need your support on geological analysis, and drilling. It will be my job to sell the plan. Now the more difficult job is our problem with the drug cartels. Between us, we all know our corruption is deep seated and widespread, and they must realize the game is over. You know the resistance to change by gun suppliers in the United States and elsewhere is a formidable challenge, especially with Russia promoting its weapons production capabilities. China is also a weapons manufacturer. But you have drones. Note that China has formed a B$ company to manufacture drones, who knows what's next? We must draw the line somewhere.

But understand, our underlying problem is to simultaneously improve our economy and extract the cartels, and improved trade and investment in Mexico while improving our fresh water capacity. In other words, we're like the rest of the world, including America. There is always a bad element, championing something bad, along with the "usual problems".

US President: Yes, but that is why the United States needs to show an unstoppable resistance at the border and will demand the support of the gun lobby. I just must make sure the violence does not shift to your side of the border. This is where you must exercise your military muscle. But the cartels must see the United States' determination and that their world has changed. It's time for them to go legit or die. As I said, drones are another matter, which you may consider for Mexico.

Mexican President: Yes, that is obvious. I am pondering, however, how to present our side of the story.

US President: Remember, we are going to share all the work of our travels. You will have time to join the global view. We must make a joint presentation or a parallel presentation that includes our high-level action plan, whatever is politically correct. I think that your new regime is the perfect opportunity. The message is simple.

We are both sick of this lingering and painful border situation and economic doldrums, and drugs and its criminal element. And the right way to stop it is to raise the economies of both countries and just stop the bleeding on the borders. And eliminate the crime and hard drugs. You must be part of the solution of world growth and demand, and this is the time to begin the rebuilding. The transitions that you will be part of will be steps to create a new economy for Mexico, the Americas, and the World: The Water and Energy era, symbolically, WE.

Remember that underneath it all, the time of supply and demand imbalance in energy is over, and we've committed to fresh water enrichment and expansion. Make that clear to your electorate. Price is not an inhibitor; energy productivity is an enabler at every level. And its productivity will give rise to the new era of fresh water and low pollution. It's an integrated strategy: we are not for or against oil, we are for energy productivity and freshwater expansion.

Mexican President: This is expected by my people, but we have never succeeded at fixing our economy with the core of our citizens. You have your own challenges. You are subject to your own free markets, after all. Mexico must be price sensitive also. If oil could go to $100+ per barrel, how do we sell our people on

$20? Our case must be strong. It will be part of a worldwide energy deflation, I understand that. Once the distribution system is diverse and available, it's over. Make it happen in the USA, China, and Japan. Make it a clear trend, otherwise, $20 per barrel must be a trading norm, or we'll have a big problem.

President: It will be with our increased purchases and our pursuit of agriculture and water. The price will gravitate by itself when the supply side sees that vehicle efficiency, battery capacity, and mix of product toward the gaseous engines and fuel cell electric vehicles (FCEV) simply lower demand. It will not be about retaining high prices but remaining competitive. Once the synergy of innovation takes hold, it's downhill, pricewise, from there. When you see the ripple effect it has on technology and transportation, it's a positive evolution to a balanced economy and the end of a debt anchor that's been holding the economy back.

The opportunity and money available to drive this idea into the status quo is there because when you have the best, most efficient product, people will come to you. Yes, the keepers of the "flame" will cry socialism, communism, and more, and then their flame will die out. That is why a clear understanding with Canada and Mexico is essential. It is a new wave of Americana, one that benefits both continents. Our challenge is making everyone see that this is not just a new round of imperialism, or other terms for corporate bullying.

It is just leading a new paradigm that will benefit everyone. *Remember, price has made the energy consumer underserved.* This is a growth market, and *Water* will open up the agriculture markets around the world and fix the "border problem." It is very important to establish the strategy as Water and Energy.

The second and biggest problem is eliminating the hard drug culture and all its bad influence on our youth and more.

We need to come to terms with Venezuela and others that could see it as capitalism versus socialism. Well, between us, even China must see that without entrepreneurial spirit, and wealth building in their middle class, their brand of economics and politics just will not work. Russia just made a different implementation than the USSR. Autocracy capitalism has one flaw. It doesn't allow the people to engage in entrepreneurial original innovations (as much). China's challenge is still bringing their 99% into the fold, as is ours, and as is your economy and corporate cultures. China's early success was largely driven by infrastructure spending, and consumerism has a way to go. But China must face choices in antipollution and automotive engineering.

The good news is that China realizes that without widespread low-cost clean energy and water, no system works, especially for them. They should build their infrastructure with courage and conviction. Coal and oil are not the way. When energy productivity moves forward, where will they be, with us or trailing? And we will move forward, now! Their place in the 21st century will be determined based on how soon they "get it". The pressure will be based on population boom and the impact of India becoming the leading world population.

These, at the end of the day, are the forces trying to rebalance Energy supply and demand. With that in some sense of balance, growth will serve everyone. One hundred years from now, in a nuclear fusion and hydrogen world, this will be seen as so obvious. Ah, but the transition.

Can it be done without World War III? The answer is, it must be done, because oil economic suppression will drive us to war anyway. I'd rather invest our precious dollars in battery density, fresh water, clean energy, and agriculture.

That's the point. And we have emphasized clean Energy, and now we are talking Energy productivity, which will result in clean energy and fresh Water, but through a lower cost strong clean paradigm, Energy productivity.

US President: Yes, we are all trying to rely on current technologies to create wealth when, as you say, the need for a new paradigm is painfully obvious. On its surface, we just want more oil at high prices. Just like OPEC. That is a big change in attitude that must occur: *Energy productivity and clean Water.*

What's clear is that America is evolving to self-sufficiency, like in the 1960s, and China needs lower-cost clean energy and a way to produce fresh water at low cost. And they can't successfully pursue fracking, without a water strategy. They have more shale deposits than the United States, but no water strategy to get it. It is clear because most energy generators use steam as a turbine force. Steam is the path to desalination as well as reconditioning dirty water aftermath of industrialization. Integration of water and energy is the point, an integrated approach.

Mexican President: The paradigm of water and energy is a solution and stimulus for all of us on the planet. Most gas turbines are driven by steam. And America is rapidly driving energy generation to natural gas with steam turbines.

US President: We must do it. More than slow, incremental, change is required. I will provide you a video cam of this meeting so that no one can accuse anyone of wrongdoing, which they will do anyway, and snippet this up into erroneous sound bites. God bless the free press and the lobbyists. Please limit its distribution until after our joint announcements. And remember, Mexico is on the Pacific Rim and India and China are approaching three (3) billion people with a rising middle class... this is opportunity that will transform the Americas.

Mexican president: I will get back to you soon. So much of this is subject to misinterpretation and second-guessing. The Cartels and the oil executives will raise the roof. Whatever you do, don't start drone-attacking cartel hideaways like those in Pakistan. I implore you. We'll participate, but worldwide commitments are between Asia, Russia, the USA, and the Middle East' we're followers.

The Mexican president leaves the room.

Canada

An hour passes while the DVD is created. It's astonishing how a DVD can be created and duplicated almost immediately. Of course, telecom and the internet is usurping all that. (The cloud). Next time it will be all online.

The Canadian nation PM enter the conference room.)

Canadian PM:

Thank you so much for sharing the discussion with Mexico by DVD. It makes my somewhat-astonished reaction, somewhat tempered, I think. Maybe I should be in apoplexy? Or maybe this is a point to exercise leadership, as with Cummings with natural gas or hydrogen cars.

US President:

It is important that you hear the complete Mexican discussion. This is completely unedited, I promise you. It is important to keep it confidential, but you can see how it will make our discussion easier to have. What is clear to me is that the northern tiers of the world, Canada, Alaska, Russia, the Scandinavian countries, Finland, and a few others have differing points of advantage...but all with bountiful resources. Although it is even beyond oil and gas—for example rare earth, and probably precious metals and probably graphite to graphene futures—it is in deep supply in the northern world. Graphene is a source of deep porous capacity which will lead to much greater densities for batteries. We all have our geologists working in the area, but we do not really know how much there is. We only know that it is way more than we expected, given the new technologies. We must get at it and it's a global market. And the advent of graphene revolutionizing electronics in so many ways will change everything. Imagine ultrathin, malleable yet powerful steel. This will mean you can roll up video screens. This is the step until dense holograms take over. That's part of the quantum revolution, the next phase of dramatic innovation. You know my pitch, but America is on a quest for self-sufficiency, which we will all happen someday, but needs a deep commitment across the continents while the world realigns the chess pieces. And our notion of self-sufficiency includes the Americas. We must strengthen our Canadian ties and share invention in the name of huge market capacity.

Canadian PM:

You know our short-term commitment is to the Canada-Texas pipeline. The questions are simply how much and when? And starting when, regarding a pipeline commitment guarantee? We are still assessing our natural gas potential, but I know it is vast. I know I agreed to have you invite Cummings Auto to this meeting, so I presume you see a deep penetration into automotive natural gas and hydrogen. But how fast can it play out? We all have a huge investment into distribution infrastructure, but what do you think? We also have commitments into biofuel and cellulosic ethanol as bio-efficient endeavors.

US President:

> Just relate the economics to the cost and folly of war. The easiest payback you could hope for. This plus the sixteen hundred mph airplane is the present and the future.

Canadian PM:

> I am sure you are aware that China is prepared to establish a long-term relationship with Canada for at least a decade. Europeans are also scrambling for position. I am not sure what you are considering, but the timing of lower fuel cost is critical for us, as a user instead of a producer. But remember, with our population and location, we are a producer nation.

Look at Chinese investment, overseas:

Chinese Investment 2005-2015 @

High level: ($B) USA 72, Australia 61, Canada 39, Brazil 31, Indonesia 31, UK 24, Russia 21, Nigeria 21, Saudi Arabia 20,Nigeria 21,Venezuela 18, Pakistan 18

Chinese Investment (sectors) 2005-2015@

$ B: Energy 396, Transport 135, Metals 125, Property 86,

Chinese Investment Company's 2005-2015 @

IBM, Barclays, Bp, Ford, GM, Volvo, Peugeot, Lenovo

@ Heritage Foundation /American Enterprise Institute

Clearly, China has the resources to diversify, and the US and Canada are in play.

US President:

> That's why I'm moving. We just need Canada to team with us to a future. We need your current level of about 1.5 million barrels per day to be ready to ramp up to at least 3 million, and that is with the guarantee of the pipeline in place. We don't see the pipeline as an issue if it is done right, because we want significant "mix change," to the point where oil must compete for clean efficiency or be crushed. That increase is the equivalent of Saudi Arabia. I know you have a deal with Libya, so we only want assurances that we can get it in the pipeline in short order, if necessary. I need to know any other price enriched deals. I think the world market will transform very rapidly, so there will not be much price lags. Once the supply or demand shift is visible, it's a self-regulating reality.

Once the world sees we have a strategy that is executable, we will see market reaction. The futures market will become bear on oil very rapidly. I think that by us having a longer-term guarantee, your added benefit will be stability. The one thing you must recognize is that an extended natural gas or hydrogen strategy will drive the inflated price down. Remember, for decades oil averaged $23 per barrel. People will have to wake up to the fact that supply will no longer be the "red herring".

Frankly, you and the rest of our energy-consuming world must reconcile a single fact. We have been benefiting and suffering from oil costs that are about double what they should be since about 1997 and have been on an unconscionable path since September 11, 2001, resulting on a net drag on the world economy. The United States is leading the blame, but that is not the point. Canada is in interesting position because their available product exceeds the demand of their population.

After all, your population is more than 33 million, while ours is more than 330 million, almost ten times larger than Canada's You must see the big picture more than we do to buy into the scenario. However, you have several reasons to buy in, even though you may have certain potentially negative near-term impacts, if prices decline rapidly. Understand the economic model and then rethink your marketplace, Think of north and sub-Sahara Africa with a robust water supply. It's the Water and Energy revolution fulfilled. We both need to be active players, not adversaries, which we aren't in any form.

But think of 33 million versus 330 million, but the India and China's soon to be almost three (3) billion. When the economy is reinvigorated, you will harvest many benefits, mostly increased consumption worldwide. And you will have the Canada to Texas pipeline. But you could be deeper into the auto market with Hydrogen, NG, and Electric cars and hybrids. But the thrust of these changes will require more production, more discovery, and new sources of wealth, including cleaning up oil sands petroleum. With Asia and elsewhere adding a billion cars, you could be a major provider, even with India and China dominating. Look at how well GM is doing in China and soon Ford, who is already a major international player.

So even though unit per barrel equivalent revenue may decrease, overall revenue will increase due to the rising tide of the world economy. And you are close to production of rare earths, and I'll bet you've got plenty of graphite. By you being in from the beginning, you will be vesting, with quite frankly, the benefits of your earth and mineral holdings and expertise, in the new chapter of world history. Which side of history do you want? High prices and pollution, or clean energy productivity and growth? I'm impressed with your collaboration with northern Europe.

You can imagine the perceived impact on the Middle East; perhaps more perceived change than everyone else. Under the umbrella of raising world GDP; and Middle East and Africa GDP, especially, the positive act of addressing change can be the best for people of those regions, but I doubt the Monarchs and dictators will see it that way. I used the term "perceived change" because with the rise of the world economy, and reduced likelihood of war, they may be the ultimate beneficiary.

They have powerful gaseous assets. The other reality is our and China's actions will lower the cost of oil per barrel anyway. It's a guarantee, because many regions such as European regions, Australia, and Japan will grow.

Never forget that at current rates, the world grows by one billion in population every ten to 11+ years. In a broadened economy, that is a lot of cars, electricity, and agriculture. India and China will have to be smarter or they'll miss the hook on the train of progress.

The only point: we've been here before, with Japan in the seventies. They bought and they sold. By us concentrating as partners and co-competitors, we rode the wave. Yes, we gave up share in automobiles, but the new world is plus one billion in cars, and our additions in China in auto factories is merely our position in the Pacific Century. It's not just winners and losers, its players that are so intertwined, conflict is no option.

Canadian PM: I can see this, but we are tampering with billionaire leaders across the globe, not the least of which is the United States, the Middle East and "istan" empires, and many small yet concentrated wealth spots run by generals and other pseudo empires. Be very careful. We have military alliance reasons not to have you and our European brethren pull us into war by treaty. And you know we have backed you up through storm, including World War II and everything since. We want to support progress and avoid war.

JPM

So, what if half your country was hydrogen and ½ electric?

President: Diversity and competition all clean and green…my dream. Even 1/3, 1/3, and 1/3 gasoline. All at $1/00 per gallon (at 100 mpge). The economy would sing.

Keep in mind, Canada is moving upward because it is emphasizing free markets and has a low corporate tax rate 15 percent, all secured by a booming energy business. So if we can replace price with volume and capacity, then go for it. But if you think you are helping Unions by resisting free markets, you are sadly mistaken. Price effective volume still reigns. And the world market is what it is. If you did not want it, then Europe and the United States should not have created it. Although you must admit, it really started with Germany and Japan, under the American protective shield in the 70s.

Accept this! The world market had to unfold, but it took American technology to light it up. After all, US technology did crush the USSR without a nuclear exchange. Reagan's strategy of "spend till they bend" worked. You were just blinded by 1973 and OPEC and then 9/11/2001. Almost thirty years in the middle, and countless lives and refugees sustaining the unsustainable.

US President: Therefore, we will communicate. Understand that we believe that failure to act with courage and conviction will draw us into a conflict of grand scale; we just can no longer wait until there is another 9/11 with even greater consequence or Iran/Israel atrocity. Internally, if we must, we will go back to Sherman/Clayton if necessary; it certainly worked with AT&T when we released the telephone equipment business from the phone companies. The energy business must be completely reassessed. We need to unleash that competitive spirit. I know it is there. As usual, the standard bearers will not release it. So, government, once again, must act. The USA can open simply by passing a tax credit to diversify distribution (refueling) at the pump, retail outlets, and even to homes, apartments, and elsewhere.

Canadian PM: Just remember, the world is used to killing itself over oil. I believe the Middle East sees their control over energy as God's will, God's gift to them. If you think about it, it must change, a neutralization of competitive advantage brought to you by mother earth and American know-how. God's will is that Middle East oil dominance is over! Maybe they had their chance and squandered it. You and I must know that to play our hands, without change, just won't work in an 8.5 billion people planet. If we move swiftly our people can benefit, but to stagnate is to want to fall behind. Once in a lifetime. There is the opportunity to strike one for the open market.

Who are you see next?

President: Israel

Remember, we are keeping Israel involved and well informed. They have seen we won't lead from weakness. God's will, or nature's, there is obviously geographically, broad diversification, with no "willed" dominant geographic regime. If internationally we don't take a stand, just turn the century to the Pacific Rim, including Canada, Mexico, South America, and the USA. This reality will draw in Europe, Russia, and yes, the Middle East.

Israel: The President prepares the Mexico and Canada DVDs for Israel's perusal. After a few hours, the leaders meet.

Israeli PM: Thank you for preparing the Mexico and Canada materials. I understand why you invited us, although it should be clear that providing as much secrecy as possible about our participation is certainly desirable. You know that Israel prepares for Iran, Syria, and more as if we can assume, we must defend our own interests, although you know we are grateful for your and other NATO member's aid and support. Our position in the Middle East is always precarious, but defensive acts are well thought out, internally, and with our allies. Remember, you have millions of lives and billions of treasures to deal with, but we always must consider *survival* as well as prosperity. I understand your disdain for the situation. You are feeling closer to our state of mind as you see elements of Armageddon, at least in the Middle East. We, perhaps more than you, have more instincts about Iran, the Saudis, and Syria, and I know the sacrifices in men and treasure that you have laid out, to some extent as a by-product on our behalf at least as a residual result. It just turns out that as your financial and political interests align with ours, the more tensions are raised.

I am not sure war is inevitable. I feel your own questioning of motives and 2019-20 reality, leaves them no alternative except change. Get China and Russia to agree, and then they are faced with inevitability. I, like you, do not want to measure our success or failure in body count and deficit spending. I also know Russia is far more precarious as an energy provider with weak diversification. I know the pressure of the world economy and getting out of this recessionary funk is critical for the real economic and political path to a restored economy. If there were any way to get the Middle East leadership and the oil and gas oligarchies to affect peaceful evolution, I would be the first to suggest it. Maybe if we could force Palestine to close as an issue, maybe a period of Pax-Middle East could prevail. But Iran and Saudi Arabia don't really care about Palestine (strategically). Unfortunately, we know that a false peace will be perceived as a capitulation, a selling out to both your, European, and Middle East oil interests, so the result is "business as usual". You may invariably "change the mix" but the pressure for you to slow down is inevitable.

You know we have felt for some time that the result in Iran is "almost" inevitable, and we will bomb their nuclear sites. We see the Arab Spring and see the faltering Syrian dictatorship, but with bad choices, a new government would probably be worse. Then the pressure to live by Sharia law is inevitable in an Islam theocracy. I know Egypt is another matter because of their history with the Western powers. We believe the people simply deserve a bigger share of the oil economy and a chance to build institutions, education, and industry. But the dominance of the people holding the purse strings never seems to reconcile with those wanting more share of the economics and hope. And other countries, upstream, keep building dams on the Nile Now that's a water crisis. Of course, we all have that problem, don't we?

Even as you negotiate to the extreme, you always include in interim solutions, more military aid…even with us. So, this lack of trust and what we would call situational greed or financial compromise, seems to settle the situation with "more of the same". I can assure you this, our tiny world population of about 15 million Jews (worldwide) versus 1.6 billion under the banner of Islam, will stand up and be counted. And as you know, we are well armed and will not allow our nation to be intimidated under the threat of nuclear annihilation.

We are a small nation; and cannot allow even one nuclear missile to enter our boundaries. So, what you do and how you do it is very important to us. Just know if we think a weapon is close to completion, we will destroy it, no matter what. It is an unstoppable force and we have an unshakeable will. What I need to see and know is how Saudi Arabia can stop providing America and its NATO allies with the oil they need at a fair price. It seems impossible, and I would have thought, improbable. They think the power of embargo is still within the power of OPEC, and that OPEC is the center of the oil world. But I see the changes and don't know what to think. Why, Venezuela has almost more oil reserves than Saudi Arabia. That's a place where you can fix your relationships, but their need is far more than they would even let you give. The Americas are a new Middle East? Russia and Asia and Australia are a new Middle East? Better said, the Middle East doesn't have the dominance to control price, but they are a powder keg.

China and India are to become the world's largest consumer, and their commitment to succeed is unstoppable. Look at Apple and GM!

What you are seeing are the effects of world population and the incentives of energy motivating demands like China, Russia, the Istans, and India. You're also seeing the emerging of the 21st century as the Pacific Century. Energy will be repositioned as a resource, not anything to fight over. It must be available. Blockades are like blockading Japan before WWII. It leads to war. We're not going there. But nature and science is screaming: change, so carefully, we will. In many respects, tariffs are like block aids they only impede progress.

President: You're not telling the USA anything we don't know or that my military and economic advisors have not discussed. But we know we can produce what we need if we "change the mix" of energy use between home, industry, and vehicle energy. The invention of longer-term batteries is at hand, the discovery of vast quantities of oil and gas is real, so should we let our economics falter, our nation drag, and our debt consume us? Should we just continue the clearly unacceptable state in our own country, not to mention, Africa, the population of the monarchy-led Middle Eastern states, and let the drive to elevate Asia just linger? Quite frankly, no one can stop Asia's need for change.

We believe the actual mix of energy use will change and the result is not against anyone, it is just the fact that we do not need as much Middle Eastern oil and OPEC's high prices and market control. It is becoming less relevant, especially when we introduce vastly denser batteries and gaseous automobiles driven by natural gas and hydrogen. Germany is already feverishly developing the next generation of vehicles, they must. Iran and Pakistan have more than seven million cars that can use natural gas or petroleum. The United States is falling behind.

We recognize this is the first time since, say, 1960, that the supply and demand equation can actually balance to the supply side, with clean Energy. And the water demand, especially in Africa, can be solved with low-cost energy, the economic balance of power is at hand...low cost energy financing desalination costs.

Understand that we will support Israel, no matter what, but supply side oil economics is ending, and the world needs to translate new levels of energy productivity and lower costs stimulating booming economies all over the world, including creating the wealth to invest in desalination or other forms of freshwater creation. Oil costs must come down, if we want reasonably costed fresh water. Key reservoirs in the United States are experiencing rapid water table declines, even in the breadbasket states which supply the Middle East, North Africa, and others with wheat, meat, and other vegetation and that will provide the true potential for a thriving 9 billion people, at the least. Simultaneously, China, India, and other super-populated regions will begin to thrive with newfound resources that can change the life for billions of people and create markets that will benefit the Middle Eastern people as well as the globe. Once the water problem is addressed in Asia, the Americas, and Africa, anything is possible. This is the agenda that we need Israel behind and fully conversant with.

Just understand that in the last fifty years, doubled populations have lived in a world based on certain assumptions. The fact that technology can alter the mix of solutions at lower cost will demand that this evolves in some rapid acceptable manner. It must. When you confront what others take for granted, this always spells trouble. But we must accommodate billions more people without catastrophic famine, plague, genocide, or war! So at some level, you can't be denied. And you know as well as I, we can't control their population, we can improve they're water & Energy opportunities, but they have cultural issues to overcome. Look at what happened when China tried to artificially control family size. A near disaster that hasn't fully played out.

And the first stage of that will be the Americas becoming self-sufficient in transportation, home, and industry energy and we will engage in a very visible water initiative. America must exercise its leadership or become a second-rate nation. It is our destiny, our role in the 21st century! We need Israel to leverage the new paradigm for the benefit of yourselves and your neighbors.

We are open to any ideas you have and will include you in all tactics going forward. We understand this will be subject to many unknown repercussions, but, quite frankly, society cannot allow the continuation of paying double the real profitable rate for energy and we need more clean, fresh, water. Supply and demand have to come back into balance. We see lower per unit costs and about 100 to 150 plus mpg equivalence (mpge). And that is just after the first three to five years or so.

Once the paradigm shifts and refocuses on expandability, we expect many, many enhancements. Sooner or later, this moment had to come. If the Middle East cannot adjust, then what will be, will be. But they'll see reality and change, if they're smart. It is our assessment that it will be rough, politically, but once the evidence is clear, our people, industry, and the world will embrace the opportunity. Science and Engineering has raised its head. On one level, China and India will benefit the most, so that makes them stronger competitors. We just cannot ignore what is under our feet, so to speak. And the green movement, which will balk at a compromise, will see that breaking the chain, as well as insisting that free enterprise versus consolidation of all natural gas providers under the oil companies, will open the gates for entrepreneurial action. Creating a strong energy storage capability with quick recharging will change the world.

All the car energy initiatives coupled with storage capacity and fast recharging will give it the range that will open the industry. And they will have to do better three to five times storage density and mileage will transform all transportation.

The stepping-stones: natural gas, hydrogen, and gasoline hybrids and electrical fuel outlets, across a sea of water and energy innovations. Ll cars will be hybrids. This will open the door and *ride the FCEV and EV engines into the horizon of a pollution free automotive future. But we won't dictate it, we'll incentivize choice, let the marketplace decide. Status quo or change.*

Meanwhile, air and truck transport will rely on multiple iterations of natural gas, hydrogen, as well as biofuel, and electrical generation and storage will be the baseline of real change. Further, the economic benefit can be partially leveraged into a bountiful fresh, clean, water phenomenon that will among other things, refill aquifers around the world, as well as solve the US-Mexico border issues as well as restore American leadership in agricultural product and more. Embrace this change like the inevitability it represents. The Middle East can embrace the new phenomenon by using aggressive pricing and investing with other nations to find new freshwater development. Although uncertainty may make the next year a challenge, erasing uncertainty, with our support, will transform your nation and the world. And the door to artificially created oil and petroleum is wide open. If you do nothing, you lose.

Israeli President: We certainly wish it so, that peaceful change can overcome an extreme status quo.

President: If the EU, the Middle East, and America's are stagnant, Asia will move forward, and leave us behind. Absorb this...With India and China approaching three (3) billion people, they have to move forward. Stalling is killing them with pollution, water, and energy problems (shortfall), so we need to step up.

The President confers with some industry execs to explore how the whole system can leverage the movement into a lower cost environment that will inject the airline and shipping business like new blood. Energy is 50 percent of what it cost to run airline production, so they have to move testing and R&D forward to proven choices. This can follow or be parallel to automotive efforts because of risk adversity. Energy may move an industry, but actually Air transport can move the market by doubling or tripling air speed, at equivalent costs. (Not immediately).

Venezuela: The US saved its last state review with Venezuela, its toughest American relationship despite being 40 percent of Venezuela's oil exports and having good exports to Venezuela, especially autos. The relationships with socialist Venezuela have been volatile, with the late Hugo Chavez's claim the United States' CIA was always messing with their politics, and Venezuela voices its displeasure. The United States knows Venezuela has one of the largest oil reserves in the world and is friendly with Cuba, Iran, et al., and is a member of OPEC. Despite reserves, the United States produces more than three times the oil, making Venezuela appearing to be under producing. (Or under resourced), is really under resourced to refine their heavy oil. Yes, *96 percent of Venezuela's exports is oil*, but just don't see opening their economy (yet).

The dilemma is Venezuela's economy is in chaos, with inflation at about 1000% and they've long ago nationalized many private (US) companies. Their government refuses support from capitalistic companies although they need it because it takes resources to convert their heavy oil to a more commercial use. Although their reserves are greater than Saudi Arabia's, the quality of their oil (heavy) needs innovative support from companies like Exxon Mobile. Meanwhile they have the USA as their primary customer and their people are standing in bread lines. They've let the courts dismantle their democratic institutions, and they are in a quagmire. This a case where Oil & Gas has put a socialist institution in un-releasable gridlocks. THE USA stands back because of history. We were to bold, or perhaps greedy, with South America, but remember, that was in our anti-communist era, 1940's-1960's. WE will show them that we've changed. Change started with Nixon/Kissinger opening China, and America's shock with Vietnam.

US President: I really appreciate your attendance given our state of diplomatic relations because we purchase almost a million barrels of oil from you daily and our trade imbalance is reasonable. You know our agenda, based on changes of energy mix throughout the world, and we seek deeper, mutually beneficial trade benefits within the Americas. I know you're a member of OPEC, but including yourself, you know that the world is increasing its outside of the Middle East oil percentage every day. Now technical innovation puts us at a crossroads.

I appreciate the fragile political situation, so this is to remain confidential between participants, and I'm empathetic, believe me.

Venezuelan President: We find it interesting, but we can see the America's increasingly becoming the new Middle East of oil and gas, and particularly gas, which we see your proclamations daily. I appreciate your empathy in our situation.

US President: But when you look at Australia, China, the Mediterranean, and Russia, it seems the dispersion of fuel is historic. Natural Gas, exporting as LNG (liquid natural gas), is rapidly advancing in the USA, Australia, and Canada. We feel that the new thrust is Water and Energy (symbolically WE), and we aim to change the mix to lower oil costs, expanded volumes, and provide a savings or a spending window for water, like saving energy costs and expanding investments in water.

Venezuelan President: That's curious and remains to be seen. But when it's all said and done, regardless of government type, we all have agriculture issues, crime problems, pollution, unemployment, and military issues. Will it ever hit a common point of satisfaction?

US President: You know I agree. But it seems to me, your oil exports are one dimensional, yet your production-to-reserve numbers are quite low. You have the Andes and I have to believe they are a vast fountain of resources. You were (historically) once close to Australia, and it must be that your mineral assets are underserved. Given that our trade seems to flourish on top of our political differences.

We could evolve with a mix of state owned and private resources. America has moved away from trying to interfere with state politics. So, we wait on you. We can and will help, but it's your move. We're here to tell you that the world is moving forward, and the march of science is unrelenting.

Venezuelan President: We'll work with you on this because then you have an OPEC member in the mix. Meanwhile, let's talk on the side some more. Just wonder this, we could have relations, but we want you to keep the CIA, or any other industrial-government interference at home. We see our potential in the Americas and the Middle East The world is getting more homogeneous, or maybe it's just telecommunications, air travel, and the Internet.

US President: It may be just me, but I see us having mutual self-interest, and I agree to keep our security considerations out of your country, unless you align with Al Qaeda or ISIS (laughing). Please consider adding a million barrels per day to our oil imports. How fast could you deploy that if asked? Maybe you could help us find a final path to Cuba.

Venezuelan President: Cuba? Maybe after the Castro family is overcome. (He hands the president a Cuban cigar.)

President: Thanks. Please participate in this if only for your self-interests. We must find a way to evolve past the last century, at many levels. And trust me, we have nothing to hide. But, I must warn you related to your current status. Only countries like the USA, Russia, and China can help you out, and quite frankly only the USA has the engineering and chemical expertise to efficiently convert your reserves, but if you continue your current direction and hope oil will save you, you'll discover you're on a lonely path. The world needs diversity in clean energy and new volumes of fresh water. To choose a unilateral choice from the last century is disastrous for citizens, because the sources of clean energy and fresh water will be so plentiful, the price of oil and petroleum will drop under $20.00 per barrel.

Venezuela President: Why so sure, so forceful in your declarations?

Us President: Because the problems of the 21st century are three: Pollution needs to be solved now; Water and Energy need to be solved, with the solutions tied to the synergy of Water & Energy; and the population explosion to nine billion plus including South America and mostly focused on the Pacific Rim, will define the winners in the 21st century and who will define solutions in Africa which will address their Water & Energy drought. Venezuela needs to be a robust partner in solutions, not be part of a quagmire in political and social disarray. We're here to help, not politically dominate, in any way. The times and experience have changed us.

Aerospace Military

(The president prepares for meetings with industry reps.) The President and cabinet members meet with the airline executives A 1, Al 2, Al 3, Al 4 (airline 1–4) M1 [military rep].)

President: Thank you for meeting with me. As you can see what we sent you, thank God for replication technology, I'm preparing, rapidly, to take American ingenuity to the next level. I am not choosing the direction, you must. But without action on your part, we will set the direction with Boeing and others.

The point is entire industries are thinking short-term profits and someone must stand up for the medium term. You and I know the current mix and supply of transportation energy must change and we can't ignore the developing nations and Americas' population growth.

We must break the cycle: challenge innovation; execution; not compromise until we are driven to war. It is clear, but our inevitability does not have to be tied to war or oil. We must evolve. But our direction is steadfast, and we must change the mix.

What did Stephen Hawking say in 2006? "In a world that is in chaos, politically, socially, and environmentally, how can the human race sustain another hundred years?"

Obviously, it is not by repeating the same patterns pretty much "short-term thinking" until we are undermined by population explosion which won't die down until 9.5–10 billion at the least. Squeeze the status quo until its run its course? Well, it has run its course. And you will see the time to change is now. The population has put us at a crossroads. The march of history is led by Asia, Africa, and the Middle East. The Middle East has had its moment in the sun, but now it's over. Africa is right next to the Middle East, so that's their opportunity. But who is there in force, China. So, location is just an obstacle to be overcome. And as we've said, we will shrink the planet once more.

Al l: I have read your dialogue with Mexico, Canada, and Israel and am very interested about the joint conference tomorrow morning. Of course, our industry has participated in and observed all the tests of biofuels with Boeing, GE, Air New Zealand, and others. The main issues are. What are truly the best biofuel sources? What is the power level compared to current jet fuel? And how can it be produced on mass scale in a consistent reliable way? It is clear from the engine companies that the product will run with certain adjustments, as long as it can be "mass" produced efficiently, and widely distributed. The most immediate question, of course, is whether natural gas can be converted to a liquid high potency fuel (LNG, hydrogen), cost effectively, or what is the best tactical direction now and in five-year increments.

We see the airline engine companies on a path to 20% improved efficiency and more, but how can we get 100% and better improved price productivity? Also, can drilling results like fracking just produce product at lower cost? Since fuel is about 50% of airline costs, this is one of if not *the* major priority. That is an international stability. And we could produce a new standard for military aviation.

The future, of course, is the 1,600 mph commercial and military vehicles, and they must be developed under and within some strategic direction. That will ensure American domestic and military airspace technology leadership for decades. There is at least another generation of change. If any industry is primed for change, it is ours. When we hear pontification about $100.00 per barrel fuel, we cringe at the thought. Twenty dollars per barrel equivalence, we are in. If you can do it without war, that is good enough. But even with price reductions, our natural gas direction is fixed. In fact, the only change would be with success in fusion, success in hydrogen conversion, and a massive energy storage breakthrough. Could you even imagine an Electric airplane, a hydrogen airplane? But that's next generation, as we see it.

President: You know the Department of Energy has been all over this for decades. Also, their work on graphene and silicon nanotubes with university and other partners is significant. We look at all applications together because if we make major inroads in automotive or heating, it causes demand reduction for oil or petroleum. If demand truly reduces due to efficiency and fuel choice, price will follow like a falling rock. Generally, though, we see the need for forward progress at all levels, because the shift must be large. We know that alternative energy is here, in Germany, and elsewhere needs a boost. Quite frankly, subsidizing price does not work, and standing in for corporate funding through grants has been unsuccessful. You know that the vast investments we make through the Department of Energy have yielded stirring results in the past years, and the university and R&D centers in America know how to work with industry to convert research to product. The success list is long. We are much more successful than the "war machine" but we all have done a minimal job showing taxpayers the relationship, including government funded innovations. It's what we do, including fracking, leveraging tax incentives for R&D and production. Quite frankly, expansion into Shale gas, development of methane hydrate, and the potential of coal to gaseous energy development, even with conservative evolution, and the electric revolution, more than satisfies world demand. The American public doesn't realize that the US has paid much for Energy research. When Japan sees, and they have developed successful tests, the potential of methane hydrate, they salivate for energy independence. But they are prepared to proceed cautiously because of Tsunami protection and are very interested in industry direction in their massive automobile business. We must step up and provide industry development and deployment innovation and execution. They are looking closely at Sun-Gas and Syn-Gas, but need USA leadership, because we are the dominant Energy user. Open the market, and the world will follow.

Al 2: You know as well as we do that it took World War I to consolidate patents that produced the first air force, and the momentum after the war exploited those patents into an industry. From what I can see, you are tired of war being the vehicle for change. I do not blame you. God only knows if we have the courage and the vision to go where we must. It is certainly not our current international direction.

President: Yes, four trillion plus dollars on Iraq and Afghanistan gives you great pause, when you consider the effect of that kind of money could do for transportation, energy distribution, water desalination and more. It is like, in the Middle East anyway, that the outcome of war seems tenuous at best. Especially since the people of those regions are sick of it, and sick of us, quite frankly. Many hate us, and that is an Energy we must contain or redirect. Of course, reconciling the wealth from the monarchs and dictators, as well as our oil and gas magnates, which almost run like governments within themselves, requires great leadership and a true vision. International voices are simply screaming at us to make whatever actions it takes to improve productivity and clean up the product and its impact of the governments of the world itself. Oil and gas somehow get twisted up in discussions of socialism and capitalism, government interfering with private business and so on, but we will leverage domestic innovation.

But governments, through "laisse faire", just let stagnation and inefficiency dominate the world condition. Socialism? My God, China, Saudi Arabia, Russia, the USA, and Venezuela alone control more than 70% of the world's oil reserves (although this will dramatically shrink) three autocracies representing autocratic capitalism, state-controlled private enterprise, and socialism—not exactly the hallmark of free enterprise. Oil and gas are, quite frankly, a socialist, cartel administered, and free market oligarchy (US, Euro, etc.) in the West. The oil-and-gas-free market has the invisible hand of capitalism in its roots. But is held in invisible handcuffs.

It is up to America to once step forward and pave the road to not only new technology and a new frontier but to a new economy. Yes, we want change, and we are running out of time. But this is for the Americas and China and India and Russia and the world. It must mean that the productivity of energy is moving forward, but it is about Water and Energy and a new world equation. Water has always been a known issue but moving to an eight billion people planet makes it seemingly impossible.

Our citizens must see this to set the stage for world economics. These changes must be fundamental. It will mean as much in the Americas as it will in Africa, Australia, and more. It must mean a new transition to more Water and Energy than we immediately need. The supply barrier will fall, and we will invest the productivity into the next generation...fusion, hydrogen, and artificial gas and oil compounds we have not even discovered (invented?) yet, and did I say Electric? We will change the mix and create the distribution system that facilitates energy accessibility in homes, businesses, retail outlets and fuel depots from cars, to trucks, to airplanes, and more. It's an economic path to refueling and a new level of efficiency—energy productivity and freshwater generation through turbine and other processes of H_2O recycling, as well as desalination mills that work with agriculture, biomass, and other chemical processes that produce fresh water as a direct or indirect product. We need to get there in stages, led by Natural Gas and Hydrogen and Electricity, if only to bridge ourselves to a new ecology. We need an economic mentality that is symbolic of war but realized through peaceful transition. I need your airline industry to get together and consider this a way to achieve change by bypassing the casualties of war. We want a determination and innovation that is symbolized by the Wright brothers at Kitty Hawk, or Commander Neil Armstrong stepping on the moon.

Between us, we have a short term "out" for jet fuel. If we successfully convert the large and small automotive market, airlines can utilize petroleum jet fuel, because the demand shift will drop jet fuel prices dramatically, due to oversupply. But the momentum will drive innovation further. That is an interim strategy that gives you the low cost you need and leads us struggling with jet fuel pollution in a focused way. Please don't default to that, because we need the momentum and focus on all transportation.

You know we have it in us; we have just been trapped in our twentieth century history, and bogged down in a century of oil, which has entwined ourselves in the Middle East and elsewhere. In an economy that must grow from Asia, the Middle East, and Africa, to the reinvigorating of Europe and the United States, the 21st century, is the century of "WE," not "ME" (Monopolistic Energy). It is time that we set new levels of cooperation and trust in the Americas.

It is time to recognize that the world is reborn through a new mix of energy production, technology, and exploration reengineering that produce as simple results, water and clean Energy supply that exceeds demand, produces massive water resources, and clocks its way to the ability to provide the food, energy, and water to support a more than nine billion population, and lift all economies to a 21st century of growth and renewal. Catch the vision, and work to provide the synergy to succeed. **Think WE not ME.**

M1 (Military representative 1) But I know what you know. These Islam nations will hang on to the illusion of infinite control and power over Energy. When you announce that oil dominance is over, you can only imagine...they're drunk with money at the top echelon of Corporations and Kings and Dictators...will they fight evolution, or evolve?

The President meets with the auto executives. They received the progressively updated DVDs right up through the airlines. The auto industry reps are as follows: **AR 1, AR 2, AR 3; Auto Nat-Gas Rep 1**

AR 1: I appreciate the openness of your DVD and can see how you are melding the ideas. For us, this is maybe as stark as the original introduction of the assembly line. If we pull it off, it will reshape the world. Obviously, we are very tenuous on how it will reshape foreign policy and foreign markets. I think that we, as a matter of business, will have close collaboration with China, Japan, Germany, and South Korea. On one hand, it could result in a strong bond between the Middle East and China. But when we look deeply into China's planning, a dramatic reduction in the cost and cleanliness of oil, or should I say energy, coupled with an abundance of fresh, clean water, would have a profound impact on their domestic potential. If they could impact their cost and their **pollution,** it would be transforming. But their history is to believe in the tangible-short term. If you had 1.3 billion people to raise up, you'd feel that way to.

President: We have had these discussions before, and they are the being strengthened by our actions. They should consider that if they did not follow our lead, how would their progress compare to ours? We believe this is an opportunity to seize the world stage. That is why the American people must embrace this as if it is a surge of leadership and commitment. There are risks. But our leadership is based on solid progress in fuels and technology to drill as well as the progressive performance of the FCEV and EV.

AR 2: Yes, but the profound impact is on the Middle East.

President: And Russia...and Brazil, Venezuela, and Argentina. But even more so on Mexico and Canada. You must brush away the cobwebs of the twentieth century. Really! The solution must allow transition.

Yes, China leans to the tangible that is why we must push ahead. When they see our competitive advantage, they will act, in self-defense, as well as more self-reliance. But their real assurance is that Russia and Australia will be able to buttress their supply. What they really need is the path to use water (or liquid CO_2) in fracking but have a real direction in desalinated freshwater generation. But really, we will convince them with our own production and conversion. Remember, their massive conversion to automobiles hasn't really started. They must take the obvious option: cleaner, cheaper, and more available. If they don't, their economic climb will be stymied. Our commitment stuns their reality because they can't be on the wrong side of energy productivity and desalination. They will evidence this by our actions. Of course, if a practical method can convert seawater to hydrogen and fresh $H2O$, then the doors open to real progress. We have all spoke of the sea representing 70% of the earth's surface, now consider depth. Seawater probably is 98% of the world's organic capacity. (Note: People measure size in linear terms but consider depth of the oceans).

AR 3: As you know, we are on this like those fearing their survival, but we have to have a clear image...for example, at the rollout rate of distribution, what the real role of biofuel and/or natural gas/ hydrogen is, and how deeply and long will the nat-gas be converting. When does Hydrogen take over? Right at the start? The biggest issue I can see is how will Nat-Gas prices go? How can you prevent massive escalation in price?

How to control the tiger of Oil and Gas?

President: Yes, NG needs to stay under $6.0 natural gas is currently $2–4.00 plus, because that will be huge in winning the battle with coal, which oil and gas wants. If oil and gas want to win, they have to keep gas prices low. The question can coal effectively creates a coal to liquid or gas/hydrogen production and remain competitive? It's up to them, and India and China will contribute substantially. Or will we/ just sell our/their product internationally? If the world follows the United States, and they will at 100-150 mpg, coal's international market evaporates. China must deal with their pollution and water shortage. If they align only with Saudi Arabia, it is their demise because our plan will work. They must see this. And I say humbly, India and China will dominate the future (3 billion people strong). But EV and FCEV improvements raise the productivity engineering and improve the efficiency of Hydrogen and Electricity and resulting Hybrids. The elements of change are before us, and moving to an 8-9 billion population makes the shift mandatory, with or without us.

AR 4: If they want a future, they must have a cleaner strategy because once the balance of supply and demand is broken, and understood, then innovation will take over. I think we must consider this carefully, for the purposes of this meeting, and beyond, of course. One area we must consider is the progression of the internal combustion engine (ICE). This is huge, but innovation will reign supreme. I know there are major R&D efforts underway, and a gasoline Hybrid is still viable if it can consistently produce 100-150 mpge. That's the key, and quite frankly it's guaranteed, unless the forces of the status quo drive us to darkness and ultimately, collapse maybe I'm forecasting the end of the ICE.

President: I would not stop that at all, because with all you have invested, you must decide what are the factors that can give you early wins? Also, you know of the several competitive engine design innovations at play. I personally favor choice, but if someone developed a one hundred mpg internal combustion engine (ICE), why not go for it? Innovation and conservation must press on. An extended battery brings you right there. There is no question, however, innovation in energy store is the game changer and we (that is the government) will invest heavily. After all, if we achieve three to five level of density improvement, the game is over, and I've heard it. It will cause a surge in electric cars, note India's announcement and China's investment. With all the applied technologies like graphene and carbon nanotubes, and innovations like aluminum-ion storage in play for the electronics business, electric could have its day. I think the magic is about a 600-mile range with swappable boards, as my advisors tell me. Solar recharging stations will boost direction and the electric engine is so mature, an EV engine less than one hundred pounds could rock the planet. But distribution of fuel depots must be pervasive. And the weight reduction would allow for more weight and space for nat-gas, hydrogen, and more. With Hydrogen, the most available element in the universe, and proven EV engines weighing seventy to one hundred pounds, the opportunity for drive train efficiency is almost unbounded.

The dream is the fuel cell electric vehicle (FCEV). Start with Natural gas, convert it to Hydrogen, convert coal to hydrogen, convert saltwater to H_2O, drive an electric engine, and improve

Hydrogen generation and battery storage. That is the vision. Mercedes, BMW, and Toyota are already there. And the FCEV emissions are Water. The end-state can be created and then the fuels can be evolved into spectacular performance, reliability, maintainability, and most importantly, "energy productivity and clean water." WE (Water & Energy) are the future.

Clean water can be obtained not from the FCEV emissions but from reinvesting part of the savings from energy productivity to desalination. But many paths to freshwater will be developed.

AR 3: Yes, I can see how your opinion evolved...the key is to break the supply and demand imbalance. Once fuel depot distribution is available, energy productivity at the equivalent of 100-150 mpg, and unit cost of clean energy is down, then every idea is back on the table. We have needed to come up with a battery/storage investment that would exceed $25B, $50B, 100 billion or more. The payback is huge almost any feasible, practical plan should be employed. Don't throw money at it, but the ROI, given what we know is happening out there, is certain and a priority. It's the best military defense we could consider. Commitments must be built to work in a Hybrid form and plug-in stand alone, like Tesla or Bolt/Volt, Prime, or Leaf, that can get you from LA to Vegas or NY to Boston or Washington DC on one tank of fuel with fast recharging or swappable energy boards would change the world. Put a stake in the ground to show us you are committed to a breakthrough toward real change but be specific and insist on a short-term best choice. We did it building the A-bomb (the Manhattan Project) and going to the Moon, we can commit to a Water and Energy (**WE**) project. Low-cost energy and fresh water must be approached with a warlike mentality and get the citizens to know what is at stake. Our very future, that's all.

President: Therefore, the Nat-Gas discoveries are so relevant around the world. They are stepping-stones to the next level, but a pure efficiency. On one level, who cares if nat-gas has a cleanliness deficit? They knock the hell out of coal, environmentally, and an auto/air/etc. progress is better than oil, with FCEV and EV success, so they can be the step to all the innovation that will follow. No matter how much advertising coal does, the oil companies see the blood. That's why they just preach home heating and air and cooking. Coal is like a good enemy target. But automobiles aren't discussed. Energy productivity, you must be serious to see the obvious?

Now let's get carried away with the next step. The key is that it not be monopolized, that path to convenient refueling, and distribution (refueling) will be pervasive (bio alternatives, hydrogen, even fusion should be given a chance, but we know it's some distance away. Hydrogen is just waiting for the obvious to be seen. When we win the price battle, even with improved ICE productivity, the boost to the world economy will be great. So, China needs to be very cautious about what they want to pay for oil and Nat-gas. And their own shale discoveries are awesome, except they need a water or liquid CO_2 strategy. Like converting coal to methane. Add methane hydrate and coal to natural gas or hydrogen conversion, and we're all flush with energy, including enforcing a near zero-defects methane drilling strategy (fracking, hydrate). Once the eco-model turns, once clean supply exceeds demand, it is all over. I am not saying it is easy, I am saying it has to happen with a fervor that is at least as ambitious as a World War. This is what the American public must learn about a true bridge to clean water and energy. Now that's the 21st century. It's this simple, the USA sells less than twenty (20) million new cars per year. India and China are projecting a billion more. If we don't step up and help, we'll be driving India and China cars and proclaiming, "What happened?"

Think and act **ME to WE**. A simple idea that even amplifies the importance of trade.

And believe me, with a worldwide projection of 2.5 billion autos, the transportation business is at the heart of change. It's the turn of the century all over again, hopefully without two world wars and constant embattlement, and depression…but population keeps rising…It's time for a change.

AUN1: Given your goals and what we do, what can I show but excitement? As we watched the price of Nat-Gas stay consistently around three (3) dollars and we began to wonder, is this chance to really become part of the automotive mainstream? I know so. With the continual improvements we are making in safety and performance, I know we are ready to be on the main stage. We definitely have to reconcile with the green movement. They hate natural gas because of the tactics they have taken to reduce regulation in drilling and extraction and it's not purely carbon free. They even produce movies about it.

President: I agree. Part of that solution is to stop assaulting EPA and let's commit to zero-defects methane containment. Yes, there have been problems, and occasionally a chemical factory blows up or there is a train wreck. That's the war, and US manufacturing is the hallmark of clean engineering. We must open the books and show massive success and where we need to improve. We don't need hooks in energy bills to bypass control and quality assurance. We need a priority to regain the productivity and safety; we need to boost our and the world's economy. Ask yourself, why did the automobile industry all start producing Hydrogen cars?

AUN1: We look at the amazing results in the central United States and around the world and we know it is real. I know we can become main stream with trucks and autos and the opportunities we see in the air with liquids. But the real opportunity is in cars, personal automobiles with 100–150 plus mpg, low emissions, and safety: Just let **refueling distribution** go mainstream, give incentives to have hookups at home, at the workplace, and in refueling depots, and it will be transformational. Five + years from now, Hydrogen will have been declared a success and with battery density augmentation, you will see performance and price/performance beyond your wildest dreams. If worldwide Natural Gas reserves, methane hydrate, and coal–gaseous conversion are what have been predicted, the bridge to zero emissions, self-sufficiency, and productivity is set. We will be clean and water efficient because we insist on safe energy productivity and a water and energy strategy.

Just invent a 10x high density storage answer and it's over.

Understanding:

To not realize that natural gas fits right into the four cycles of ICE: input; compression; power; and exhaust; that the gasoline engine basically compresses gasoline to a gaseous state and then ignites the gas. We just drop into that post compression cycle and we are ready to go. Fire and ICE. We are more efficient, and we burn cleaner. The fact that the world is given forth these gaseous discoveries is a sign that we are just part of the evolutionary cycle. But most people don't know the benefits of

FCEV and EV engines, it's real and it's here. Imagine if we really focused.

Imagine, within a few years, the Americas and then the world could be weighted to the supply side: clean supply. That will provide the time and the resources to take gaseous and electrical power to the next level, and drive prices down so we can address water. The reason this is so important is that we need productivity to boost the economy, not just compounded high investments. The key isn't let gasoline prices rise to expensive biofuels, quite the opposite. Drive prices down on the road to green. If you have the sense of urgency you're talking about, this is phase one, the stepping-stone to green. I know the competition will be tough, but even the evolution of ICE will be there. The key is across the board energy productivity which will extend the life of fossil fuels. I also see that we are only a few science steps away from significant enhancements to batteries. The combination of gaseous plug-ins to gaseous hybrids can put 150 mpg equivalents within the near term. When you invited us to this meeting, I knew our day could be near, but now I feel if you can inspire a new change-the-mix attitude, our mission has arrived.

AUN1 (chuckles): Don't get too enthusiastic. You know we have been supporting this technology around the world. Quite frankly, Mr. President, we are ready to step up just to obtain change. We're war weary, apparently for nothing.

Just get the Natural Gas distribution adapters in people homes, apartment complexes, and business places as well as refueling depots. The convenience will be awesome and then we have a reason to reengineer. If you could have low-cost natural gas to hydrogen converters at the end of the natural gas cycle, we could rapidly move to hydrogen, FCEV, and zero-pollution emissions. Just think hundreds of millions of nat-gas to hydrogen converters. Use the natural gas network of pipelines and convert to hydrogen at the end.

President: And as we do it, *gasoline prices will drop like a rock*. And do not worry about China. They will see this as a godsend. And that will make everyone else more competitive. Just imagine, if we could avoid another round of war, private and public dollars for advanced R&D will just be there. I think there needs to be an international dialogue that takes everyone to the next level. And there is plenty of room for the Middle East. As you said, with newfound reserves, it will just kick-start the next level of energy usage: energy productivity.

The key is that the energy business must keep natural gas effective pricing below coal's effective price. This takes the long view and the winning paradigm. Coal needs to be repurposed!

AUN1: If Fusion is the ultimate solution, wouldn't the distribution systems of electric be the right direction? Why create a hydrogen distribution system?

President...Yes, this is the first question. Perhaps Natural Gas and hydrogen and biofuels should focus on heavy trucking and airplane fuels and focus automobiles and light trucking on electric systems. I believe that we should enable energy credits for a distributed refueling capability "gas stations" simply would enable Hydrogen, Natural Gas, and Electric refueling "outlets". Then the market would decide based on consumer choice. Admittedly, the efforts of Tesla and others have put recharging on the table. Comprehensive competition, maybe the best choice. What is needed is congressional approved tax credits for refueling depots, which begins with a build estimate. Networking would be estimated by each sector, electric, natural gas, hydrogen, distribution systems. We need to open refueling distribution...Note that most gasoline refueling is trucked around the world. This can be an incentive for electric networking and solar systems. But let the markets decide. Tesla has already estimated comprehensive changes in the US. Let's lead, not react.

The Joint Meeting

(The president makes sure everyone has the last group recordings of one-on-one sessions and then brings everyone together).

President: I know it is a challenge, but please keep these communications out of the press. I must meet with our Middle Eastern partners, and the EU, China, India, Australia, Russia, and more. I know you need to spread the word but tell the press to wait until we play this out. I know it seems impossible to keep this story quiet, but we will get this behind us in about a week. A week, please. I am not going to take this much further. I thought we would get together so you could see my agenda and then communicate it back to your organizations.

In the next week, I will talk jointly with NATO, China, Russia, South America, once more with Canada, Mexico, and then jointly with our Middle Eastern friends. I will make sure my communication to our citizens is parallel with worldwide announcements. You'll get further meeting briefs as we travel.

What you need to ponder is the threat to the US dollar as we work through a kind of realignment and you'll see that a new economy is being presented and the Americas will lead the world. You see the 21st century must break the chains of the twentieth. The past doesn't want to let go of the accomplishments it made; we're not denying the good, we just want to reinvent the opportunities going forward. Each major war has some of that in it, but we need to try without quite so much bloodshed. We have to make way for a ten-billion-population world.

The President meets with the energy companies—a tough audience: En1, En2, En3, Nat-gas 1, and Nat-gas 2.

President: Thank you for meeting with me on such short notice. I have provided you with my secret discussions, so you know who I have talked to and what has been said. You know that this was spawned by the instability in the Middle East, but, at the end of the day, our decision is to go with the facts as they are to forge a direction. You know the realities that are coming from our own national resources and what you are discovering through the world, so you are not surprised. Maybe surprised by my resolve and my call to action?

En1: am sure you know, we are a little alarmed by your numbers. As soon as you announce this, the world will react to the numbers at your recommendations core, market-driven at $20 per barrel of oil and $1 per gallon targets (equivalence) for oil and gasoline, presented as an opportunity to reinvest in water and more. Those are equivalent prices and the public will get used to them because they'll see their cost per month decrease as their mileage increases to 100-150 mpg. I am not a prognosticator, but simple math is appropriate using a reduction from a nominal $85-$100 per barrel to $50, at 6.72 billion barrels per year equals $336 billion reduction in income annually, gasoline consumption at $1.50 per gallon, savings= 32.627 billion gallons at a 30 percent reduction from

106,758,582,000 gallons per year equaling $48.941 billion per year reduction in revenue at the gas pump.

President: Yes, but here are the real numbers that are relevant to the United States. (He shares the following graph.)

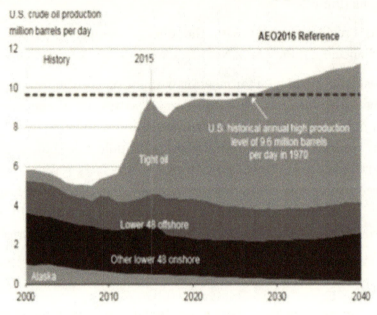

US Gasoline consumption

US EIA Dec 2017

In the last ten years consumption was flat, yet crude and gasoline prices went up 400%. Now, your natural response is that's because of worldwide demand. And my answer is, if we would be driving Natural Gas or Hydrogen cars, not only would our citizens be saving $48 billion a year, it would be double that ($100 billion) because their effective mileage would be more than double. You need to recognize that it's the dawn of new discovery, new combinations that drive a productive society. It's the Pacific Century and we must take a leadership stance or be a footnote to the 21st century. It's time to believe.

Note: with the airline industry doubling their profitability, there would be a huge increase in airliners sold, commercial air traffic, and business and recreational travel would soar. The economic kick would be worldwide and touch most segments of industrialization in the world. The key is not only the US making a stand, but China aggressively and simultaneously following suit. (Chinese courage instantly transforms them to a leader) If we don't step up, why should they? Their impact is bigger due to their use and population. The real question marks are how much undiscovered natural gas is there in China, Russia, and Mexico. Even bigger, with hydrogen at the core of mobile transportation energy, how many opportunities will open with the most plentiful element in the universe? And how will the earth reward us for restoring the oxygen/hydrogen balance? And how will the transition from silicon-based electronics to graphite and carbon-based innovation take in a world not only filled with low cost-clean energy but with a vast energy storage facility around the world? You have to believe it's beyond 1975–2000.

You see, this revolution is just normalizing the aberrant price growth since 9/11. We are normalizing the excessive profit taking. This is very natural yet uncomfortable, and a commitment to reinvestment into food and water is the core of a vast intellectual explosion.

En1: It would take a rapid buildup to reach those numbers, maybe five to eight years. Given history, that's really the ignition stage. You must see us doubling agriculture output.

President: That is why the meeting, we start by restructuring our suppliers from the all over the Americas, with Canada and Mexico augmenting as added suppliers from Saudi Arabia, Iraq, and a few others, while we ramp up our own production from our shale, oil sands, and other discoveries. But that's the transition, not the revolution. At the same time, we would be supporting the rollout of distribution of nat-gas, hydrogen, direct electric and biodiesel to the trucking and auto industry and aerospace. You know that, simultaneously, the markets will respond with at least a 25 percent reduction in oil and petroleum prices, and I do mean at least. The world is weary from a decade of unstable prices, at the end of the day, caused since 9/11. The United States played right into Bin Laden's hand.

En2: But I do not think the Chinese purchasing and Russian production would step up enough from the start to offset OPEC pressure. OPEC will respond irrationally.

President: Within a year, US imports would go down enough to provide more capacity from the Middle East and elsewhere, particularly North Africa, sub-Sahara Africa, and South America. OPEC must reconcile the fact that 60% of oil is outside of OPEC-Middle East and that disparity is growing soon to 70-75%. It's a geological fact that the Americas will exceed Middle East production. It's a fact that soon following, Russia and the

Russia-China-Australia strip will outpace Middle East production. This is the real change, and the key is how visible and involved China will be. You will learn a key factor on how we will be resilient and ready for prosperity/ Australia will be. China must consider Russia above them and Australia below southern Asia-India, Indonesia, China, and more. And Japan, still the number-two or three economy in the world, must pursue its opportunity in the name of Asian equilibrium. China is already deeply committed to Russia, and that's fine, given their needs. The west is still absorbing a simple yet important set of facts.

> 1. China and India represent seven (7) times the population of the USA, with all that implies.
>
> 2. Their top quartile of people (achievement, intelligence, education, and more) is twice the entire USA population.
>
> Note: All enhanced by the USA led PC/Internet/ distrusted intelligence (google, etc.) systems.
>
> Given # 1, their intellectual resource (#2), will be hard at working on amending pollution, cost of energy, and availability of Fresh water and agriculture. They have no choice, but we think we do. Too many people think its 1955...no it's the 21st century and time to change.

En3: It seems to me, besides assuring your American supply base, you need an absolute picture of how the OPEC nations will react. You know, in the past, Saudi Arabia has shut down production very rapidly to affect economic pressure. You cannot politically allow a repeat of 1973 to occur.

President: We're already preparing our strategic reserves for that eventuality. You see this isn't a poker game in the Wild West; this is an action plan that our citizens will assist in. This is the process of redefining the paradigm of Energy in the 21st century. We need the energy companies to exert a positive effect on this, not a quarter by quarter price per share view that uses lobby actions to slow the process down, a transition, one that shows the Middle East that they will do everything possible to give the transition a positive spin. The Middle East will need cooperation to alter their distribution of oil and ramping up their natural gas production and examining hydrogen, even as a gasoline or oil to hydrogen conversion. Also, we feel that, under no circumstances, should energy users not know where the support is coming from.

The worldwide energy companies must vote their strength toward effective expansion, or they will be the railroads of the 21st century. And China massively seeks for more, when the United States and China need a different mix of Energy productivity; but both clean.

RAILROADS have a fine place in America, but it's as different as we saw with trying to detach from horses in WWI.

The real shock to the Middle East is the reality that more than 60 percent of fossil fuels (projected) come from outside the Middle East and that disparity will continue to grow, guaranteed. And really, places like Russia and Venezuela are way below their energy generation capacity. The Middle East has known this, but now they feel, as the world switches to n=Natural Gas, Hydrogen, and pure Electric, they have to dominate something that has already left the starting gate. The status quo is hanging on to the present, which is in reality is the past. And the American oil and gas companies must decide who their country is. The world market seems larger than the US market, volume-wise, or is it because the United States sees the potential of population? Change will happen, and the United States is still the Master of Engineering, if not vision. Venezuela has almost more reserves than Saudi Arabia, but they can't quite leverage their advantage. The United States and Venezuela quibble over "government styles," yet the United States consumes more than 40 percent of their output, including oil; go figure. Now Venezuela is in chaos.

Will oil and gas be the next railroad or horse-driven wagons suppliers? And are they always ready for the US military to intervene? Or do they realize the revolution will come from within their borders and the Americas.

Nat-gas 2: This is all music to my ears, but I should make some comments about continuing to aggressively move to the next level. I am not sure where wide use of hydrogen is expected or when FU–line. For years I've been hearing fifty years. I think you need to invest in the next generation ASAP, because the true transformation of society is when finding new volume is not the task. It is distributing it worldwide and transitioning to "different". Can you make us ready to leverage growth? Did you really think that our science and engineering wouldn't secure out how to break seawater into H_2O, Hydrogen Fuel, and Oxygen, efficiently? Wake Up, America.

Secondly, the excess power needs to be there and pushing worldwide water desalination. The world needs to decide to control population through a natural evolution, feeling secure about life in general, but the green movement is really about the oxygenation of the planet and not letting food become a victim of the weather and pure lack of water (climate change,). I think Nat-Gas will have its place in the sun for Energy, but a shared set of energy resources is key, until generation and storage of electricity becomes "unlimited", so to speak. Water and energy, that's the point, short-term battery longevity, Nat-gas, and hydrogen with petroleum prices plummeting due to real competition. Can you achieve it without war? If you can't, America's values are second class to the almighty dollar. Shame on us.

President: For us to make the right moves are critical, but raising the productivity of energy, in such a way that it is accessible and clean, is our objective. You see water demand, ultimately will drive our priorities. You need to confer with your associates and have them acknowledge that this is not just change and profit management, it is societal transformation, that resistance is the way to failure and poor results. Think about it 7.3 billion to 9.3 billion people.

Yes, and we see the clear transformation by supporting Natural Gas to Hydrogen conversion, the path to the fuel cell electric (FCEV) and the hybrid FCEV (augmented by batteries). Add to that Hybrid gasoline and Direct Electric. All supporting ICE's front ended by Hydrogen and Natural Gas input adapters as well as gasoline input adapters, already in service in Pakistan and Iran for Natural Gas cars. Embrace it like the fulfillment of a necessary transition step to a new level of opportunity. We have not begun to imagine how many ways the earth can be more hospitable. After all, we finally use the universe's most plentiful element hydrogen. Even the Middle East must make its way out of the desert. Remember, Israel is not even in the energy quest and they are doing fine. This is the beacon that the Islamic nations must seek: "life after oil" or life through oil transition, as well as ramping up in gaseous fuels and getting into the solar cycle (Saudi Arabia is already working on solar desalination-the World's number one user of desalination)

En1: With the exception of the top tier of users, I imagine by participating you are opening yourself to a lot of second-guessing, but I am sure that a lot of the future will be carried on our shoulders over the next couple of years (decade?). And the key is how we balance concerns of life and the reality of a nine to ten billion people with concern over money. When you shake $50–100 billion profit out of a resource, really trillions of dollars in stored wealth, be sure that the respect of the change process on the people is the number one priority. False or misleading steps will give the threatened power brokers all they need to stir up a hornet's nest, blame the United States, and/or promote Armageddon. No, change is necessary, and the market is wide open for those who want to participate. Why would we? We could be the best, that's all.

We need Yeltsin/Gorbachev/Reagan leadership, but we have kings, tyrants, and revolutionaries in the halls of the Islam power structure, so if you pull it off without Armageddon, you will be in the history books. You do not want the alternative history. Just take this public and you will be in the forefront of history, one way or another. Oil's role isn't accumulation of wealth, its funding opportunity out of a desert, and its fundamentally time to reinvest in change.

Remember the difference between the collapse of the USSR and this is that trillions of dollars of oil power are in control of people that are not all rational. The USSR was a massive military empire that had decades of discipline with weapons of mass destruction. The Middle East has a different mentality and for the last 50 years or so has the perception that they had the magic elixir of control, oil. Perhaps what Bin Laden did was show the world that assumptions and traditional flexing of military and financial power was just an illusion. In a brief few hours, Al Qaeda took the technology of the day, the commercial jet plane, and after a few months, they were trained to wreak havoc on the United States to the extent we invested over four trillion dollars to seek revenge on those who would dishonor us and the image of security we had over our citizens and to a large extent, the world.

At some point relentless efforts made us realize that earth's resources had at least, one more iteration, vast quantities of natural gas, to let us modify our energy structures (shale, methane hydrate, and possibly coal/petroleum conversion to hydrogen, now electric). So now it is up to our will, to stand up and redeploy. With all we are gaining in nanotechnologies, quantum science, graphene, and other revelations, the ability to have the quantized power, storage/memory, and computer speed to transform and deploy new energy sources is at hand. We just need a bridge to that level, and I believe Fracking and horizontal drilling are the tools that built the bridge, with just some more focus on making methane leakage a zero-defects target. But I think you are not just unleashing the resource, you are telling us to fulfill America's needs first, thereby controlling the international distribution. How the use is manifested between air, trucks, and automobiles cannot be dictated, per se. But far beyond any of our primary concerns are, how the Middle East reacts, how Russia and Europe react, and how China reacts...not to mention stories like Venezuela, Mexico, and the like.

This seems like too many variables.

President: No, multitasking is our discipline, our secret weapon. I think we must know that this is the right time. That's why we have selected a strategy that is...let the consumer decide: Offer tax credits at the pump to support nat gas, hydrogen, electric and gasoline refueling. These would offset the enormous tax credits the O&G industry gets for oil & gasoline. I know the consumer will, over time, make the right decisions. Opening the market will create enormous innovation. **Without refueling, there are no alternatives.** The green movement or the clean movement have no future. The home heating market will continue its transition to natural gas and hydrogen, atomic energy will self-justify, and in the future...timing is everything, so they say. I believe you must act on the hand that was dealt to you, and you know that all this discovery of fracking, horizontal drilling, avoid war, and such and delving into the nooks and crannies of our earth to find methane hydrate was not just a timely coincidence. We have been at it for a long time and the forces of the last decades, maybe since 9/11, have been in high gear due to the negative oil marketplace, war, and hatred that has manifested itself over the last decades. The United States is sick of it, the world is sick of it, and I happen to have the baton currently. We are recording this and all the sessions, so I am asking you to share the message with everyone that matters, but please for a week, limit this message to the necessary few until we release it. You know how at risk we are right now, so please, let us not have this on the Internet next week, please.

Regarding your concerns, yes, we must consider it all. My position is even without natural gas, we have to reprioritize our pursuit of the source of our oil and petroleum. We must break the cycle. I should say that this being dictated a recession by cartels and conglomerates is no longer acceptable and I am going to ask our citizens, to pursue this change like they were bundling down for war. The eras of pretending to afford our ventures in order to pursue less than adequate results are over. We must stand strong for our positions. Americans are ready for this as an alternative to lingering weakness, propped up false values, and I am afraid to say, lies. This is what is needed to restore the middle class. Trillions are sitting on the sidelines looking for real change, real direction. This is it, energy stability, and freshwater creation, which will lead to massive agriculture growth. If we will be forced into war, the perpetrators will be sorry. They grossly underestimate the power of a growing economy. We are so used to complacency and weakness, they forget about our resourcefulness, an asset waiting to be unleashed.

Nat-gas2: Well I am glad someone said it. Now we must do it.

Joint Meeting- All Participants

President: We have shared our conversations, and I appreciate your first responses and your willingness to listen to our views. You know that I am driven by things that became clear in the last 24 months first there is a new level of oil and gas, emphasized all over the Americas, and the world. It is very clear that between the United States and Canada discoveries and some outstanding indications in Mexico that the Americas are the largest source of oil and gas in the world. And that includes Venezuela, Brazil, and all around the South American coastline. The USA is number one. The Americas are the new Middle East, because of what is going on in not only the United States and Canada, but also Brazil, Venezuela, Mexico, and elsewhere. They're held back because of price. No, the world is held back because of the cost to humanity.

I should point out that our science community, based on geological similarities around the world, sees that the upper third of the earth has vast amounts of oil and gas. This makes Russia, Scandinavia, and upper China and Manchuria probably equal or better than the American reserves. Given the success of offshore drilling in Brazil, there is reason to believe that both coasts of South America are bountiful. That is what our geologists have indicated. So, the boom is also in oil and gas. This issue is how to use the "mix", or should I say *"change the mix"* i.e. how we use the resources and for what purpose? Importantly, the availability of natural gas, including methane hydrate, exceeds the oil deposits, so we must rethink our strategies, short and long term. Concurrently there is significant headway in energy storage and progress in hydrogen and fusion, actually even fission will see another window opening in five to ten years. We no longer can let the high cost of energy depress our economies and feel: with the emerging economies; BRIC and their neighbors; and opportunities in Africa that our energy policies have to change. I share with you this extract from the US Energy Administration, April 2011:

http://www.eia.gov/analysis/studies/ world shale gas/

The use of horizontal drilling in conjunction with Hydraulic Fracturing has greatly expanded the ability of producers to profitably produce natural gas from low permeability geologic formations, particularly shale formations. Application of fracturing techniques to stimulate oil and gas production began to grow rapidly in the 1950s, although experimentation dates back to the nineteenth century. Starting in the mid-1970s, a partnership of private operators, the US Department of Energy and the Gas Research Institute endeavored to develop technologies for the commercial production of natural gas from the relatively shallow Devonian (Huron) shale in the

Eastern United States. This partnership helped foster technologies that eventually became crucial to producing natural gas from shale rock, including horizontal wells, multi-stage fracturing, and slick-water fracturing. Practical application of horizontal drilling to oil production began in the early 1980s, by which time the advent of improved down hole drilling motors and the invention of other necessary supporting equipment, materials, and technologies, particularly down hole telemetry equipment, had brought some applications within the realm of commercial viability.

The advent of large-scale shale gas production did not occur until Mitchell Energy and Development Corporation experimented during the 1980s and 1990s to make deep shale gas production a commercial reality in the Barnett Shale in North-Central Texas. As the success of Mitchell Energy and Development became apparent, other companies aggressively entered this play so that by 2005, the Barnett Shale alone was producing almost half a trillion cubic feet per year of natural gas. As natural gas producers gained confidence in the ability to profitably produce natural gas in the Barnett Shale and confirmation of this ability was provided by the results from the Fayetteville Shale in North Arkansas, they began pursuing other shale formations, including the Haynesville, Marcellus, Woodford, Eagle Ford and other shale.

The development of shale gas plays has become a "game changer" for the US natural gas market. The proliferation of activity into new shale plays has increased dry shale gas production in the United States from 0.39 trillion cubic feet in 2000 to 4.80 trillion cubic feet in 2010, or 23 percent of US dry gas production. Wet shale gas reserves have increased to about

60.64 trillion cubic feet by year-end 2009, when they comprised about 21% of overall US natural gas reserves, now at the highest level since 1971.

The growing importance of US shale gas resources is also reflected in EIA's *Annual Energy Outlook 2011 (AEO2011)* energy projections, with technically recoverable US shale gas resources now estimated at 862 trillion cubic feet (tcf). Given a total natural gas resource base of 2,543 tcf in the *AEO, 2011* reference case, shale gas resources constitute 34% of the domestic natural gas resource base represented in the *AEO 2011* projections and 44% of lower 48 onshore resources. As a result, shale gas is the largest contributor to the projected growth in production, and by 2017, shale gas production accounts for 62% of US natural gas production.

Practical methods have been discovered to directly convert Natural Gas to gasoline, (S. Africa), meaning that the Middle East oil is, for all concerned, a footnote in the 20th century. Creating hydrogen and numerous other clean fuels has been dampened by dominant oligarchies and cartels holding back on progress.

This hindering of energy evolution led directly to less progress on fresh water initiatives and as a result food production.

Of course, population growth should be curtailed, you may think, but China's efforts have resulted in a projected 50,000,000 more men than women, due to cultural biases, showing that governmental efforts to control natural selection can lead to unimagined consequences. The answer is to raise living standards and people will self-select lower birth rates which has occurred in almost all western democracies, worldwide, Japan, and elsewhere. If you are going to wait for Africa or the Middle East, you've got a long wait coming.

The successful investment of capital and diffusion of shale gas technologies has continued into Canadian shale as well. In response, several other countries have expressed interest in developing their own nascent shale gas resource base, which has led to questions regarding the broader implications of shale gas for international natural gas markets. The US Energy Information Administration (EIA) has received and responded to numerous requests over the past years for information and analysis regarding domestic and international shale gas. EIA's previous work on the topic has begun to identify the importance of shale gas on the outlook for natural gas. It appears evident from the significant investments in preliminary leasing activity in many parts of the world that there is significant international potential for shale gas that could play an increasingly important role in global natural gas markets.

You can see by this map that the Americas are dominant and Russia has begun to be explored. We cannot ignore these realities, and we intend to quickly communicate about this around the world. This is an Energy revolution.

Given significant discovery in places like Argentina, Brazil, South Africa, China, and Australia, we pretend the world hasn't changed. These statistics are 2009, 2011, and ultimately 2013 and actual findings to date imply vaster reserves. In fact, unproved natural gas reserves are approaching billions of cubic feet. The point is that solutions to our energy resources have to support multiple vistas including enhanced battery/storage, natural and artificial gas, shale oil, biofuels, nuclear, and even enhancements to petroleum and internal combustion engines. The mitigating fact is that the gaseous choice is so significant

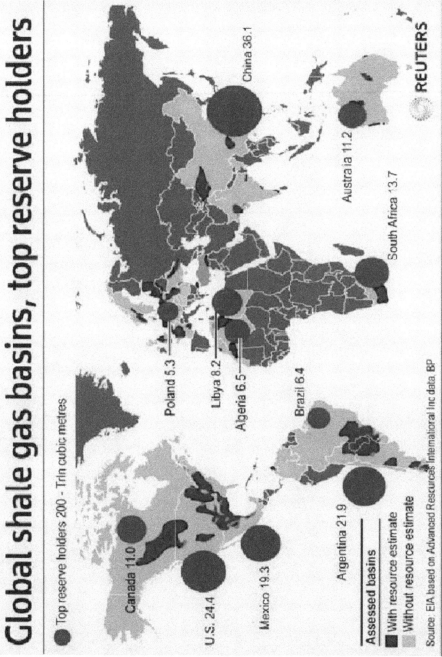

that there is no risk in providing government tax incentives for nationwide distribution, including cars. The marketplace must know that multi-fuel distribution is available where there are vehicles that need fuel. This will unleash sidelined capital.

1 Sources: Dry production and consumption: EIA, International Energy Statistics, as of March 8, 2011.

US data are from various EIA sources. The proved natural gas reserves number in this table is from the US Crude Oil, Natural Gas, and Natural Gas Liquids Reserves, 2009 report, whereas the 245 trillion cubic feet estimate used in the Annual Energy Outlook 2011 report and cited on the previous page is from the previous year estimate.

Author comment:

Russia, Central Asia, the Middle East, Southeast Asia, and Central Africa were not addressed by the current reports. This was primarily because there was either significant quantities of conventional natural gas reserves noted to be in place (i.e. Russia and the Middle East), or because of a general lack of information to carry out even an initial assessment.

One particularly fascinating thing is that, as it turns out, Europe does have significant energy resources apart from coal, and these are liberally spread at that. The list runs from around 8 trillion cubic feet in Germany right up to France (180 trillion cubic feet) and Poland with an enormous 187 trillion cubic feet. But even for heavy gas consumers like the UK with around 20 trillion cubic feet projected, it will mean more than doubling what is currently still available from North Sea resources.

The EIA table shows recoverable resources on a mind-boggling scale around the globe: China, at a staggering 1,275 trillion cubic feet; Argentina at 774 trillion cubic feet; *Mexico at 681 trillion cubic feet;* South Africa at 485 trillion cubic feet; Canada at 388 trillion cubic feet. Algeria well, you get the message.

And who knows just how much Shale Gas or Oil lies beneath the still un-assessed Middle East and Russia?

We could do it the sensible way–understanding that "Fracking" and SAGD (for oil sands) processes are tried and trusted, no matter what the long-term objectives are–start drilling and save billions of dollars on unnecessary oil and gas imports. Comprehensively, we reduce emissions on the road to zero emissions. We are tired of high prices and low expectations. And yes, we're tired of lobbyists always promoting loopholes in legislation that results in low quality drilling and extraction efforts, and yes, potentially contaminating water sheds. This type of legislation is over.

There are and will be lots of stories about reserve estimates and more. Some (whiners) say the volume is 98% overstated. Don't fret over this. The short-term availability of numerous sources of clean energy and near unlimited capacity is what defines the 21st century, if we want cost reduction, a clean environment, and fresh water. We just must face up to the inhibitors of change.

Yes, there have been numerous problems associated with Fracking documented on Television and Movies. But what's not shown is when EPA controls are adhered to, the track record is unblemished. The Spector of the Fracking/horizontal drilling going on, now all over the world, and recognize that government and mining have been, and are a partnership that can lift the world out of its "recession like malaise" by doing what we do best...managing technological science and engineering like we were at war. And it all goes down the drain when you consider "sun gas", artificially producing hydrogen fuel out of water. No studies on the hazards of Chemistry!

So, you must be very clear on this point. This is not anti-anyone or pro-anything, we are simply resetting our thinking based on what the discoveries and innovations are providing us. Remember, once the marketplace for gaseous automotive is provided, the opportunity of methane hydrate, even just from the permafrost; excluding the ocean floor while its safety is assured, is yet another significant source of methane. The point is opportunity clearly outweighs risk. And the concerns over methane leakage can and will be addressed.

It has been estimated that the available methane hydrate on the frozen ocean floor and permafrost exceeds all fuel sources on earth combined. Initial tests in Alaska and off Japan say one thing that is also true for shale: disciplined and safe practices need to be redefined for near zero defects mining, pipelining, and deployment production process that makes exploitation and efficiency right in line with an effective environmental strategy.

With an EPA and energy department and industry integrated strategies, we can reinvigorate the United States and world economies. Therefore, we need to elevate the stature of energy productivity. Also, environmental concern about methane leakage in natural gas mining must address three factors:

> 1. Methane dissipates in the air faster than CO_2, so true environmental impact is not estimated. Also, if natural gas replaces coal, leakage should be measured

against the reductions in emissions from coal. But more importantly, American engineering will adapt a near zero-defects mining and delivery strategy. Yes, I know that zero defects is not possible, but a high quality mining process is what we can do. The era of the energy loophole is over. We now deliver to change the world with economic, clean energy productivity.

2. Natural gas and hydrogen are a bridge fuel maybe for fifty years. It could speed the transition away from liquid fossil fuels and provide the deployment infrastructure for change. A zero-defects commitment will be made. If natural gas can be converted to hydrogen, what are the environmental benefits and the benefits of converting from ICE (Internal combustion engine) to FCEV (fuel cell electronic vehicle)?

3. But the real game changer is the emergence and evolution of what we call "Syn-Gas" and "Sun-Gas" the actual creation of energy from air, water, and sunlight in a way that meets all our objectives: low cost, pollution free, and infinitely available. Totally within the scope of the USA, Germany, China, et al this is the world direction: No drilling, no spills, and no fighting over the best "location", no environmental conflict, and a manufacturing/ engineering paradigm that allows distributed hubs around the world. Solar, wind, or other energy sources convert water to hydrogen gas. Power to gas or fluid fuel with exhaust h 2.0 or other clean byproduct. These products are well underway in

California and Germany. Sun-gas is available in Ontario, Canada. Since 2015, some automobiles are with hydrogen engines. It will take several years for set up distribution, costs, etc. but the inevitable will soon be clear. Fuel costs to manufacture have been rated at 1.28 per gallon. That's before the effects of hybrid technologies and enhanced batteries are considered. Hydrogenics and several sun-based companies are gearing up, one advantage of sun-gas is the creation of distributed energy centers cutting the need for national pipelines. Sun Power corp. (SPWR) and Hydrogenics (HYGS) are on the move. You may ask, why isn't this frontline news? What is front line: War.?

Remember, the US heating or electric natural gas source will soon be 50% of electricity generation, and there are already 14.6 million cars running with natural gas on the planet. Have you heard of massive methane releases? No! However, the importance of controlling methane leakage or release is a necessary part of a zero-defects natural gas/hydrogen strategy. Although few, there have been some/too many mistakes in methane drilling, period. This is the point that we don't have to have a tsunami-type misjudgment. THE POINT IS YES nat-gas isn't perfect, but hydrogen is, so let's move forward and evolve from Nat Gas to Hydrogen, if Fusion doesn't intervene. I believe time is on our side American engineering says, "Do It Right the First Time" (DRIFT). Taking on these types of challenges is what we do. We just need a moonwalk level international project, and a strong EPA. EPA just needs to keep getting better, they, however, must endure.

Transportation productivity would be greatly enhanced by electrical battery storage improvements in less than ten or fifteen years. So, the relative impact has to be measured against marginal progress in petroleum and oil fuels over the next ten to fifteen years. Progress has to transition, and a productivity war between petroleum and natural gas and hydrogen. We welcome it. Hydrogen and batteries can only spell lower cost and cleaner, more efficient products across the board. And remember oil from oil sands is still in upward discovery mode (including defending carbon quality) and methane hydrate and coal to gas are our assurance of excess capacity. So, with excess capacity we can be aggressive and careful.

You may ask, why not just wait for Elan Musk to re-invent change. With his resources, why hasn't he just produced a 1000-mile battery? Admittedly, it should all be over. The answer is it's hard, and there are scientists all over the world struggling. Remember, Fusion is another 50-year project. The answer is a billion people are just 10-12 years away. So, I repeat, what do you want War or Change. When millions die per year because of pollution, it's time for a change.

This is the key strategic point. We have four sources, each enough to power the automotive and airline industries. So we can choose the easiest and most efficient to acquire, or manufacture, safely, and know we will never have a shortage. Generally, we can acquire energy from all US sources, and many parts of the earth can do the same. Supply is no longer an issue. Supply > Demand. You just want to have it.

The key has been to bring forth energy credits for fuel stop distribution, which is already in bills in congress (for nat-gas)... It is also clear, by China's recent action to acquire Canada's Nexin Inc. for $15.1 billion is a clear indication that they need to assure energy availability and diversity and the engineering disciplines to make it successful.

Shale gas—which is trapped in rock formations and is plentiful but difficult to extract—provides a potential solution in the eyes of Chinese officials. China recently set a target of producing 6.5 billion cubic meters a year of shale gas by 2015 from virtually zero in 2010 and hopes to produce between 60 billion and 100 billion cubic meters a year by 2020. The US Energy Information Administration said last year that China has an estimated 1,275 trillion cubic feet, or 36 trillion cubic meters, of technically recoverable shale-gas reserves, making it the largest repository of shale gas in the world. But it has no water strategy to enable it. But now liquid CO_2 is being considered (perhaps a residual of coal to NG or hydrogen creation) to fill caverns left by drilling to prevent the earthquake trauma that now s apparent in Oklahoma (although at low levels, places like California must be seriously aware.

<u>This is the enabling point that a joint China-United States strategy</u> for freshwater creation could set the baseline for the 21st century Water and Energy (WE) strategy of "changing the mix".

The US President knows, despite competition and everything else, if China knows that the United States has made a stance they must consider and evaluate it. The point is that the United States, once again, has invented technology, in this case for shale gas extraction that is rippling across the world stage. Now is the time to leverage this and to use this leverage to change the balance of supply/demand in the world by adapting a wide range of transportation solutions around gaseous fuel, as well as raising the ante on advanced Hybrid, standalone batteries and hydrogen, so that the productivity of fuel is back in line with other expenses over the last 10 to 20 years, actually the last fifty years. But a tri-fuel strategy of shale, methane hydrate, and coal to gas, including a priority to hydrogen, will result in the rapid acceleration to a low cost, productive fuel, and a redeployment of resources (money) to freshwater generation. And hydrogen/FCEV emits H2O as its exhaust. And now I must repeat...Sun Gas? What is stalling the most massively obvious direction which could also fuse with fresh water creation?

US President: We have decided to travel West with stops in Japan, China, Australia, Russia, the Middle East, and Europe over the next seven days. Please contain your communications and expect that we will be conferring in Washington with Congress, Mexico, Canada, Venezuela, and Argentina within ten days, and then to the American people. Please be sure that you will all get direct feedback as we travel through this web of change, and feel free to communicate through our state channels in any way you see relevant. I know this seems dramatic, as is all significant change, but it should be looked at in a very normal way. The mix of energy sources has changed and we are adjusting our resources to achieve economic, environmental, and strategic benefit, with the full awareness of the world dynamic, so all segments of our global marketplace can achieve productivity through restructuring of energy supply and demand. The calling card is to "change the mix".

(There is a pause.)

Let's pause to go over three factors:

- We must focus on methane extraction that must succeed with minimal leakage from fracking.

- Or hydrate drilling, which to date is okay, and natural gas supports 14.6 million cars.

- But we will excel in zero defects. That mentality will transfer to methane hydrate extraction, and all gaseous choices. It is mandatory.

We have to let fossil fuel oil productivity compete. The real goal is *low-cost water and energy, and high mileage gasoline still produces ecological benefit*. At 150 mpge, a 2/3 reduction in pollutants. But we're still adding millions of cars to the world, so we must overcome oil and gas as the primary goal. The FCEV, EV, and ICE will compete until the FCEV performance transcends petroleum sources, which admittedly is expected, and true right now.

We should find a way for coal to be productive. If coal can effectively create natural gas or hydrogen, it is okay, because, until methane hydrate is widespread, we still need oversupply and guaranteed supply greater than demand. And methane hydrate needs to be mined very carefully. The coal industry will be functionally dead with gaseous displacement, so it's up them to reengineer and offer clean powerful alternatives including hydrogen strategies. Many countries around the world are converting coal to hydrogen.

The path of least resistance is transferring natural gas to hydrogen which can be done on many levels, even a small converter in your garage. This is important because of the distribution system into homes and apartments and industry that is already in place. Now think again, all of our investments in young lives and treasure in War. With that kind of resource, FCEV vehicles can start out with zero emissions except H2O. I don't know about the collectivity of H2O for other purposes, but the synergy is beyond belief. The more hydrogen used for factory/electrical applications, the more H2O by product will be created. This can't just be incidental to our needs. It would be the water and energy strategy the world needs, at least until fusion or something similar evolves.

What we have:

energy productivity—an excess of natural gas from fracking/horizontal drilling, plus advanced hybrids methane hydrate more volume than all fossil fuels combined hydrogen, which will produce the desired clean and can be extracted by from coal the EV and FCEV engines, which bolster productivity investment into a battery density goal of up to 3-5 x (at least).

Tax credits for diversified refueling (Nat Gas, Hydrogen, electric, gasoline) must be done.

Very importantly, the more successful battery density innovation is, the use of all energy sources makes even petroleum more successful. Once 100-150 mpg is the norm, the door is wide open.

> 1.0 Conversion of coal to natural gas/hydrogen
>
> 2.0 Distribution of choice through tax credits for fuel distribution 3.0
>
> 3.0 A near zero-defects mentality no methane leakage/spills promoted by all the excess we will have in methane and hydrogen and petroleum.
>
> 4.0 The ability to create hydrogen fuel and convert NG to gasoline, a proven ability from South Africa. (This eliminates any potential "blackmail" from detractors.
>
> 5.0 Sungas and syngas massive investment worldwide.

6.0 Switch over to all electric grid. The problem is transformation. (Problem? Nah)

As previously indicated, the real question is how long it will be when we can create hydrogen fuel such as "Sun-Gas". What you must recognize is science has learned to create "element reconfiguration" to create applications such as hydrogen fuel, fresh water, and more. You have to understand; in 11-12 years the world has to accommodate a billion more people and civilization has not matured enough to rapidly change societal behaviors in Africa or Southeast Asia. It will happen, tomorrow. Society must accommodate food, fresh water, medical resources for an 8-8.5 billion world that can thrive, not survive. And at the same time, we don't want war with countries that have not learned to foster a stronger and larger middle class. Even China and the United States are in a middle-class growth quagmire. We must change the fundamentals in energy productivity, eliminate pollution, and increase profits in order to restore GDP growth potential. The operative word is change.

Wait a minute. Is the world our responsibility to fix? You've just been given a signal-EBOLA. Think of a world with plus one billion people mostly in Asia and Africa. Where are our troops and Navy carriers? It's time to reconsider what the hell we are doing. Did I mention world market opportunity?? The USA S&P 500 already receives 40% of its profit overseas. We are less than 5% of the world's population.

Is the right strategy nationalistic isolationistic embargoed trade, or open up the market with Water and Energy (WE) initiatives.

Initiative: Japan, China, Australia, Russia, the Middle East, Europe and the United States.

The president's entourage shifts gears and establishes a Western loop around the world, trying to show respect for the massive world codependency, population, and production base he is impacting. The President realizes he must sell two ideas:

First. Americas' strategy is steadfast because we know the resources we need are at hand. The technology expanded and aggressive priority is based on research that has already happened and really needs funding to take conclusions out of the labs and into production.

Second, the world needs improved energy productivity and freshwater generation that are tied together because energy productivity will ignite dormant resources that are standing by waiting for true economic expansion, an easily described future that is achievable in the short-and medium-term.

The keys to the 21st century are threefold *energy productivity* and availability is assured; *a clear water development plan* can be deployed for North America and, ultimately, the world; *real estate resources* can be earmarked for expanded food production and biofuels including creating freshwater availability. This kind of commitment would end famine as we know it. Droughts would be a 20th-century problem a history of the past.

The overriding factor that must be managed is the prevention of war. The President's position is clear: we have the resources and the determination; it's time to step up to needed change. The Water part of the strategy has universal application. Imagine the Middle East no longer being a desert. This would transform the export and import realities of their region, not to mention North Africa and the sub-Sahara. Imagine the consequences in every drought-endangered region in the world. That plus elimination of water-borne diseases like malaria would revolutionize the world economy. In fact, it's the only way to support a 9-10 billion person earth.

All are fundamentally provided by Mother Earth and humanity's science and engineering.

CHAPTER VI

The First World Tour

Japan: Japan's prime minister, energy czars, automakers, and technology representatives have all received DVDs of the Calgary Energy Summit one day in advance of the meeting. The president and key cabinet members fly into Tokyo and prepare for the meeting.

President: I appreciate your attendance. I believe this subject must have some clarity around the globe. It must accomplish much. My positions are clear and on the table. You should know by now, this is not a suggestion or idea gathering, it is a succinct high-level action plan. Our people are monitoring this on many levels, so you should appreciate that we are making adjustments along the way. I feel that Japan can offer many levels of input, and they have been in a steady state with us since the seventies. (Late 40's)

Despite the financial challenges we all have, Japan is the number two or three world economy. We have been through a lot—maybe three or four economic cycles, an oil embargo, and several wars. Your economy has been shaken, and we have both experienced the rise of China and India. From your unfortunate tsunami disaster, we have learned much.

I think you would agree that the major topic of the last seventy years has been energy. It is magnified by the commitment to provide energy productivity, environmental security, and risk prevention. As a major importer, you have as much if not more at stake. I know you participate around the world in Energy projects. Your expertise in Energy systems is among the best. So, this discussion is clearly a continuation of our collaboration and will result in positive markets for all of us. But you have to admit, the real acceleration of our enthusiasm comes from integrating water and energy into a Water and Energy strategy. This is done because of funding and because it must be done.

Japan Prime Minister (JP-PM): Yes, we have seen this coming and are enthusiastic players. We are collaborating with many nations and are seriously looking at our own environment. Of course, like England and others, we do not have vast quantities of real estate. But we have three powerful resources: expertise, money, and a distribution of manufacturing and support facilities around the world. We must be world partners in many aspects of Water and Energy.

We just hope the world can focus on change and transition and not conflict and military obstruction. Your proposals have been apparent for a long time. We wondered what it would take to act.

The other big factor for us is not only Shale but the presence of Methane Hydrate in our seas. This may be our one shot, before fusion, at energy independence. Of course, our tsunami experience makes drilling and extraction assurance a number-one priority. But that's why humanity built and extended science and universities. You can see my enthusiasm. Now you present us with Sun-gas and Syn-gas. Upon examination, we say of course, apply well engineered chemistry to the problem and from salt Water, we can extract H20, salt, and Hydrogen. It's so obvious, it's painful.

President: That's why we're here. We feel change is imminent. It is paramount for us to improve Energy productivity and lower costs with solutions, including fresh water, that move the ecology and economic agenda forward. I've been told you should even consider onshore horizontal drilling to the seafloor base where there is methane hydrate. It really depends the trade-offs between distance and building totally safe Super Rigs. Once again, mankind must challenge itself.

Japan President: Yes, a primary consideration, but we have considered it and concluded that both would work fine.

Japan Auto Representative (JAU1): Our automobile industry has been in the forefront of Hybrid and efficiency measures from the beginning. And we agree with you on a major issue the world needs to respond together to develop a marketplace, especially when it comes to fuel standards, distribution techniques, and performance objectives. On a competitive level, we know there will be proprietary advantages, even from us, but we are in a world market and systems and solutions need to be maintainable in virtually all countries. So we are all in, as all countries weigh in on timeliness. Like most manufacturers, we have prototypes and working cars with Natural Gas fed engines in Pakistan, Brazil, Iran, and many bus and truck solutions around the world. We are ready to ramp up when the markets open. We are happy to participate and compete in the expansion of distribution systems and fuel depot options around the world. This is all good. We just need to see that the USA executive and legislative branches are good to go. You dominate in Energy, and I believe have competing solutions that all have trade-offs. One thing about gasoline, it has had near comprehensive application. But a growing nine (9) billion-person planet, with a growing middle class, has a pollution derivative, the earth's population can no longer tolerate. Especially a planet with 2.5 billion cars. (Currently 1.3 billion). You could say, we should all be riding trains. I say, that's fine, but the markets want cars and trucks. It's a human thing, like horse ownership.

US President: Therefore, we had to make a stand. Of course, it goes without saying that we would not be making a move except for the vast Shale reserves we are discovering and with all the promising methane hydrate tests around the world, and committing to three important realities: Effective mining, refueling distribution, and the electric car This plus a positive and closely observed development and regulatory environment. We are done squabbling and will treat this without political chicanery. Manufacturing versus the EPA will have died with the 20th century. The American people and Congress are ready to move forward with warlike vigor. We want a mix of sources, so we can overcome any unforeseen dilemma or event. We have this well in hand, but it seems we can create large scale and small-scale delivery systems and open the door to a lot of creativity and innovation.

JAU2: I must admit the frequency and vast amounts of reserves being discovered daily is inspiring, yet alarming. Mother Earth spent four billion years preparing herself for vast amounts of organic fuels, perhaps giving the environmental bridge we need. But we are somewhat skeptical, if I may be blunt, about the chicanery aspect of your government. Perhaps more important than the next election, that'll be a first.

US President: It's enough to make you zealous at least toward mother earth and heartened toward getting a flexible approach that works around the world. The resources are abundant if everyone can see the big picture. And we're at a moment that can drive energy productivity and provide resources to feed the plant, the car, the truck, and airplanes. The condition of life is that we transform through many species in a way that creates combustible resources, perhaps all leading up to this time. That's a summary of four billion years till now. Somebody must be taking care of us. And as I look at Australia...I just say wow. A new Energy frontier.

JAUR2: That's a good way of looking at it. We just are here to prevent becoming dinosaurs and part of the turf residue of history (everyone laughs). We, along with our science colleagues, are excited by the many near solutions there are, but boy, are they hard to complete. So, when new angles on Natural Gas were discovered, it is almost like a necessary bridge to give us time to let quantum solutions manifest themselves, like easily produced hydrogen, new fission ideas like reuse of fission waste, and of course fusion. At the rate that computer chips are accelerating, and subatomic particles are becoming manipulative, I am filled with hope and optimism.

But you must admit, what we are experiencing, to a large extent, is caused by population growth. It is the pressure of health and wealth issues that are causing consternation. Efficiency is a modern concept since the industrial revolution, although really since the containment of fire and the invention of the wheel.

US President: Our innovations will catch up, and we need to break free from an economic energy trap, without war. We should proclaim a UN edict supported by Japan, Germany, China, the United States, the European Union, the Middle East, Russia, Canada, and others. We will reenergize and hydrate our societies and perform the transition without war. If we stand together, the detractors on the top of the money mountain will have to see this as inevitable in our time. **The enemy: pollution.**

Japan Tech rep 1 Jtcr1: But I see history constantly stomping on our attempts to catch up to restore the optimism of the seventies and 80's, and the collapse of the Soviet Union. The world is a fragment of thousands of years of history. Technology and global commerce have built opportunity, but also makes the disparity become frightfully visible, whether by national comparisons, or within small towns. As you know, what is going on in computer processor and storage technology, as well as the mobile phenomenon, keeps bringing scale of everything faster, cheaper, and smarter. If we could just overcome the energy bottleneck and water shortage, we would all be on the road to massively improved economics. How did you come up with shale gas and fracking? Is it just a twist of good luck?

US President: Hardly We have known about Shale gas since 1841 there has been a push since the seventies at improved drilling and the proponents of Natural Gas have been teaming with government for more than 20 years. Tax credits, department of energy (DOE) grants, and private initiatives have worked together. We developed diamond drill bits relating to coal mining. Horizontal drilling and many government-supported initiatives have been at play. There were breakthroughs in 1998 where the cost effectiveness started to become possible. This kind of innovation is a tribute to our diversity.

Finally, a few years ago everything came together. As Edison said, invention is 10% inspiration and 90% perspiration. Those in industry kept focused on it and government support came through many times. That is often the real secret to success, *perseverance*. Quite frankly, the initiative in the private sector has been supported by government assistance and tax credits, which has worked more often than advertised. The point is it's inevitable and ready for prime time. That's why we do it.

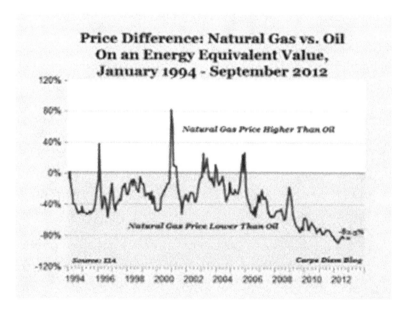

Emissions have plummeted 7.7% since 2006. Aside from the recession, the clear reason is the switch from coal to cheaper and cleaner natural gas, which emits 40% less carbon dioxide on average than coal. The use of Natural Gas to generate electricity, notes David Leonhard in the *New York Times*, has jumped 25% since 2008, while prices have fallen more than 80%. After much trepidation, I said it is time for the United States, and most emphatically, with the support of Japan, the UN, et al, *to step up and evolve.*

We know Nat-Gas is only a partial solution. But it moves the bar forward and **we know Nat-Gas to Hydrogen conversion exists** and only Nat-Gas has a major distribution system available. Now consider a Nat Gas conversion system with a billion systems in the world...with Hydrogen conversion...very low cost. Direct electric with a nat-gas energy system converted to hydrogen at the power centers...I'm starting to see green with a built-in distribution system.

Where did all this cheap gas come from? A concerted public or private effort dating back to the mid-1970s to cheaply extract gas from shale is the primary source. But simultaneously, there has been an investigation of methane hydrate and the conversions of many hard fuels to Natural Gas and Hydrogen. The victor: energy productivity. On one level, the constant threat and disruption of oil has energized the movement to find different answers. So, when kings, military czars, oil and gas magnates, and the status quo look at this in dismay and wonder, I hope someone can rebuff the noise simply by saying, what did you expect? We would just let a billion more people on the planet with no answer for them. That thinking can only lead to war! If O&G is the answer, then why didn't you improve it? The answer is the question of humans. When will greed be tempered with humanity-based actions? China has 4,000 people per day dying because of pollution. What we see as a problem, China is engrossed in a human disaster. In major cities people walk around in masks.

You can see how Natural Gas is already having positive influences on the environment. You know that government R&D funding has propelled semiconductor innovations, cell phones, the internet, and much more. The United States spent $166.5 billion dollars on foreign oil in 2016. We are now going to change the cycle through a process that excludes no one. This is the type of expense that can pay for US national healthcare, when fully extended.

J-PM We know all about it. Believe me. The world needs a turnaround, but we do not need more war. The veraciousness with which China is acquiring energy sources clearly shows the world what they need to raise the standard of living for their 1.3 billion people. You need them on your side in this. Yes, their priority is finding more *when they should be seeking different.* Leverage what we have with a change manifesting end.

US President: I believe what is holding the world back is simply belief. Belief that the volumes required can be met at low cost and preferably cleaner. We also have been caught in that dilemma, but we came to realize if the market moves just to balance its energy sources by a positive percent, it will shift the supply/demand balance and cause a natural reduction in energy costs across the board. We would not be stepping out like this, if we did not see the clear view. Unfortunately, Russia and China are caught up in support of Iran, Syria, and growing relationships with Saudi Arabia, when all this is over oil access the ever-daunting issue of *more*. And during all of this, mother earth projects *different* to scientists, geologists, and engineers.

What the Middle East is observing is that their dominance in oil is slipping to 35% and then lower, Change is the engageable resource, not oil, I know electric is part of the answer and now China builds more electric cars than anyone, yet their quest for oil is unfathomable. The resources are available in the Americas and around the world. What's going on in Australia is mind-boggling. The United States is better positioned with pipelines and such to accommodate increased volumes. But the key is to commit to a direction. Coal must decide whether it can efficiently convert coal to gas, or does it just want to die on the vine as last century's fuel. Canada and Mexico will buy into the paradigm at some level, and China must decide whether to turn toward the vast discoveries, it has recently made. The United States will support nations with its technologies, because the time for change is now. It may not be perfect, but we have done the math, and we know by turning the direction we set in process the new paradigm which will diminish the rise of petroleum demand in a world, while energy demand is increasing. Once our business sector has seen that change is immanent, watch the innovation take care of the rest. That's speaking from the fountain of two hundred-plus years of capitalism with oversight and regulation and even recent autocratic capitalism, which in its own way is praying for the wonder of the invisible hand and free enterprise. I said free enterprise, not the socialist/ oligarchy-ism that has become the energy business.

J-Pm: I agree. But there is one point to be reconciled. How are you going to keep the cost of gaseous fuel low enough and prevent the takeover of the natural gas economy by the Saudis and all others that control the oil and gas markets? How can you fix the cost of natural gas to be declining?

President: Let me say this. Our job is to control what happens in the United States, and the action you will see from us is the enforcement of anti-trust laws and the emergence of "Sun-Gas" and "Syn-Gas" market actions that will revolutionize the fuel markets. But also, the conversion from coal must be sustained and the growing potential of methane hydrate has to be considered. Our projections are that plentiful supply will dominate the "gaseous fuel" environment for at least forty to fifty years. During that time, you will see, and participate in, the improvement of transportation productivity like never. Yes, natural gas below three dollars will not stand, but it will grow by less than double. At those figures, there is lots of profits to be made and it will stimulate more mining and R&D. The target productivity is the equivalent of 100–150 mpg at today's oil prices, but many think it will be much greater than that. This is all we wish for, the cost of energy reverting back to the general level of inflation, or better, 1962–2012, about 7.5 times the value of the dollar in 1962. Our target is $1.00 per gallon equivalent or less. At 100-150 mpge. Personally, I think that's high, but it's a good working number. In a world that is economically recovered and growing, all markets would be satisfied, even the Middle East. Why, because of the increased growth that would occur at those cost levels. Remember, on September 10, 2001, oil cost $31.00 per barrel. Without all these findings, innovations, and chemistry. Remember in 2001, we thought we were running out of fuel!

Of course, our real targets are far more fuel efficiency than that, but now we're talking about fusion, etc. The other potential is productivity in the engines. This could happen in more ways than I can count, but the real need is to increase battery storage by a factor of three, then five. It's been proven many times that FCEV and EV exceeds ICE by a factor of three easily canceling out loss of product from converting natural gas to hydrogen or coal to hydrogen, and more. Once that happens, the world will be in a new paradigm, the age of the electric engine and the super-hybrid, all producing water as its exhaust, exactly the other aspect (food and water) of the world we expect. Not that we'll use auto exhaust to fuel water needs, but "energy productivity" can provide funding for freshwater expansion by using less than one-third of the savings from energy productivity for water, so everyone wins. If Iran doesn't agree, why are they supporting two million of these cars in their own country with natural gas?

Quite frankly, if oil and gas tried to raise short-term prices to affect oil prices, they will be swept away. The Middle East will soon recognize that they no longer control the oil business. Science and engineering do. We know it will happen. So, we must move forward. And we haven't even discussed the profound impact on the environment. I can't contemplate the reduction in disease and the improvement of health, but it is all part of it. This is the undeniable truth that even China can't hide from. China is trying to corner the gold market, but they must recognize that the true economic shift is **Water and Energy. (WE)**

J-PM: And our second issue is the dollar as a reserve currency. Please keep it stable. Remember we are the number two external purchaser of T-Bills, China being number one.

US President: World support of the dollar as a reserve currency is perhaps the difference between peaceful evolution and potential war, emphasis on the word potential. Our underlying answer to stability is massive productivity and profitability, and growth. Japan and the USA have learned that Real Estate speculation is stupid, and maybe the USA has learned that war is stupid, but now we still must reconcile the 21st century and its reality, to the 20th century.

You must realize, though, that the real strength of America's dollar is the strength in its economy. And it's our ability to be resilient. Our actions will immediately find positive response, and with our people understanding how it all fits together, our resilience will once again shine through. Now, whose stability is assured, a robust and growing economy, or those grasping the energy and water mix of the twentieth century? My vote is for the 21st century.

Consider what you need to change your economics and aggressively support the automobile market around the world to drive toward energy productivity, fresh water, and the support of nine-ten billion people. When the world sees our economic benefit, the dollar will be fine and America the safest, securest investment. Don't get me wrong. The 21st century is the Pacific Century and monetary stability will change. That's why we all need to change our Water and Energy paradigm. It should be all good for Japan, if we can avoid war.

The President's team departs to Beijing, China. In attendance: ten members of the standing committee of the central committee of 25 members. The general secretary (GS) and nine central committee members (CCM1–CCM9) They've received all the DVD and recorded input since Calgary, including Japan.

GS: Good afternoon, Mr. President. You'll find that a number of our committee members are engineers, so we embraced your DVDs quite handily. It's amazing that even Japan could be handily convinced. We are interested that you opened your communication it appears nothing is hidden.

President: You will find that this will continue and that there is nothing to hide, no hidden agendas. We just find ourselves analyzing history and carefully acting accordingly. The more this occurs, particularly with the United States and China, the more our actions will be a collaboration on issues as important as war and peace.

I often hear that your strategy is you'll try everything which is great, but we know that certain investments or should I say bets, take a while to unfold and longer to move away from. We also know that when compelling change is visible, there is also tremendous momentum in the wake of what you're building toward.

GS: These times are full of invention and change. You know we have been very dominant with coal in our industrial sector and have invested significant amounts to produce cleaner coal production than the rest of the world. Yet concurrently, we are discovering more than one terabyte of cubic feet of shale gas, and we've only been looking for a while, and we have invested significantly in Canada.

It is somewhat unsettling, particularly with the volatile Middle East situation, and the seemingly, in your terms, unnecessarily high cost of oil-based fuels. We agree that something must temper the insanity and bring clean supply into dominance over demand. What we see is unsettling to say the least. We've absorbed your discussions to date and are absorbed to say the least.

President: On one level, even though our per capita consumption is leading the world, something must change. In 15 to 20 years, you will probably be holding the burden of economic leadership, so it is not only important, but I think essential to see through the eye of the needle together, even though our tactics may vary. But we need to step back and see the parallels of our mutual vision. It is clear from what you can see that we expect to significantly address transportation fuel by unleashing natural gas and hydrogen in conjunction with battery enhancement in conjunction with fossil fuel productivity in such a way that we achieve 100–150 mpg equivalence and cleaner fuels so that the fuel oil productivity equivalence is under $20.00 per barrel and $ 1.00 per gallon under our tax structure. (i.e. the cost of oil is tempered by the mileage (mpge)). We see you cornering the gold market, and that's fine, but the 21st century will be defined by Energy, Water, and pollution or lack thereof.

GS: When we do that math, achieving those parameters would be awesome for us, so we're listening closely, but have many questions. We think the coal versus natural gas in electricity generation is a lively topic, but let's stick to transportation for now. We can go back to address industrial fueling.

President: We know that to make a real commitment in transportation, we have to believe we have the capacity to handle real growth for decades, consistently and with backup. We believe the convergence of resources and technology is at hand. We also know, if we lay down major commitments in distribution and engine technology, we must have deep knowledge of all the possibilities that could happen. We also must believe that new innovations in other areas, as we've discussed. Our advantage is the USA public loves new cars and innovation.

Suppose OPEC just let the price per barrel of oil drop to $20.00 per barrel or lower? Saudi Arabia has done it before to corral Venezuela. Our answer is multilevel. First, we believe the price of oil will come down in that range. We welcome it. Secondly, we know shale gas discoveries and methane hydrate's success in the Americas will continue, not only in the United States but in Japan, Canada, Mexico, South America, Europe, India, Australia, China, Russia, and more. Natural gas, shale gas, and methane hydrate will grow to support electrical generation and a large segment of transportation. We believe the FCEV is unbeatable, which says the EV is unbeatable. We think the norm in the future will be diversity at the pump including electrical, through swappable batteries with three to five times, initially, battery storage capacity; hydrogen with the booster of Syn-gas, biofuel ultimately led by algae derivatives; the conversion of the coal industry to liquid and gaseous energy; and within ten years the emergence of methane hydrate in large scale. Let me reveal something in this area. The president distributes a snippet he extracted from the EIA.

According to one conservative academic calculation, Earth's conventional reserves of Natural Gas hold 96 billion tons of carbon. Earth's reserves of oil contain 160 billion tons. Earth's reserves of coal contain 675 billion tons: Taken together, 931 billion tons of fossil fuel. But Earth's methane hydrates contain three thousand billion tons of carbon, or more. Methane hydrates are found at larger and larger volumes the deeper you drill. ConocoPhillips drilled 830 meters for its field test at Prudhoe Bay, Alaska. At this level, you calculate the reservoir of methane gas in the hundreds of trillions of cubic feet (tcf). Drill deeper and you calculate reserves in the thousands of trillion cubic feet. Drill deeper still and you calculate reserves in the hundred-thousands of trillion cubic feet. Earth's reserves of this resource could theoretically reach millions of trillion cubic feet (tcf).

Citing the first prolonged release of gas from methane hydrates, previous US energy secretary Steven Chu celebrated the "enormous potential for US economic and energy security" of the new technology. The United States has reserves of 2,600 tcf of conventional natural gas. The Gulf Coast alone holds methane hydrate reserves of 220,000 tcf, nearly 100 times as much. For the next technology trial, the partners will head to the Gulf. The Arctic trial began (with drilling) on February 15, 2011. It concluded on April 10 (when the experiment was arbitrarily ended). In the interim, the partners "safely extract[ed]" a steady flow of natural gas from methane hydrates for thirty consecutive days the first-ever test of a technology that uses CO2 to capture the cleanest of the fossil fuels. (Using different technology in 2008, a Canada-Japan trial produced a continuous flow of natural gas from methane hydrates for six days.)

Methane hydrates are hunks of porous ice that grip natural gas molecules as they rise naturally from deep reservoirs under the Earth's surface and grip them tightly, under pressure, in cold waters. In the successful test this spring, ConocoPhillips used CO2 to relieve the pressure, causing the ice cages to open and to liberate the trapped gas.

Why trade CO2 for methane gas that, when burned, releases carbon dioxide? And isn't methane gas especially dangerous? In Conoco's revolutionary technology, the CO2 not only replaces freed methane but simultaneously disposes of CO2 waste product from conventional oil field production. This isn't zero sum. It's net gain, which is why Energy Secretary Chu, a celebrated environmentalist, champions it. Mr. Chu says, incidentally, that methane hydrates could cut the price of natural gas, already cheap, by one-third within ten years. But that was before the invention of Sun-gas and South Africa's natural gas to gasoline, which are synergistic, from a pollution reduction point of view.

Now we know that the exploitation of methane hydrates needs to be very cautious, initially from the permafrost, but ultimately from carefully crafted extraction methods with fallback to prevent any large-scale methane release.

The point is we understand the challenge and have the engineering know how to effect zero defects extractions. Certainly, mass economics prevail when compared to disparity and war. This is not a problem because the other factors over the next ten years, particularly battery storage density will take the performance of both hybrid and plug in to levels that push productivity of fuel from between 100–150 mpg. The combined effect of all these factors means that the continuation of LNG and natural gas-powered trucks, buses, and automobiles assures its viability and continually decreasing unit cost and increasing energy productivity. And with the productivity of petroleum or alternatives like LNG, natural gas costs driving down quickly, we can translate this to economically justify significant investment in hydrogen technologies, which all will do very well over the next five to ten years. Keep in mind also that methane hydrate around the waters of Japan will transform their ability to be largely self-sufficient, as Sun-gas, as will battery enhancement. And integrated options like onshore integrated horizontal drilling into the seas can make storm resistant zero defects drilling a clear choice. Of course, those operations have to be in places and with technology that can secure against tsunamis and more. Additionally, with the Americas becoming self-sufficient, the use of lower cost petroleum and natural gas from the Middle East and Russia will support China, India, and more. Quite frankly, what we hear from Australia is significant, but you already have an expanding relationship, and we welcome it. There are very good reasons to believe that Africa and Russia and India will also greatly benefit from shale gas, methane hydrate, coal to gaseous conversion, and importantly the battery density revolution which we and perhaps you should, actively achieve.

Let me emphasize that we don't really want to hurt markets in particular, but the discovery of new alternative Natural Gas, Hydrogen, and Methane resources and continued investment in technological enhancements like nanotubes and graphene for electronic efficiency, along with the next generation of computer chips, will get us close to the world of quantum computers which already are in a positive escalation of R&D. In fact, as science sees the breakthrough of efficiency tiers it moves on to the next level, which is *quantum science*. And this Nobel prize-winning compound graphene was identified by two Russian scientists in Manchester, England. The serious short-term point is that once the supply/demand for fuel sources move to the clean supply side, this will unleash a period of innovation stronger than the 1980s or '90s. This is what I call the era of WE, Water and Energy where we, the human species, learns how to supply the water and energy needs of nine to ten billion people, causing an unmatched level of economic improvement. Keep always in mind that the underlying driver is population growth, can best be mitigated by security, health, and education of women. History has shown that these natural forces always produced the desired result and artificial enforcement always fails, note your population mismatch.

I have mentioned four ways that transportation energy could be fully supported: shale gas, methane hydrate, coal to gas or hydrogen conversion, and hydrogen including Sun-gas.

Competition and innovation make hydrogen fuels the viable step up. Now consider the WE Project of the 21st century: battery density and diversified methane, hydrogen, including artificially, and gasoline, always with a hybrid design: this is the game changer, let the citizens decide. Choice, it's the peaceful path to change.

GS: You have given us serious reason to be careful about our plans. I can see no matter how we address electrical generation vis-à-vi cleaner coal versus nuclear versus natural gas, and the other maybe most-significant challenge we have is the car. This is a huge issue for us because of what we expect will occur over the next 25 years. I believe this is an area where the United States, China, India, and the EU should collaborate at new levels. I know your next steps are with Russia and India and the Middle East, so we'll be watching with significant interest.

You know your pursuit of this direction means that, the Middle East will converse with China at some new level. Let's be sure that this isn't misunderstood by the American people and elsewhere. China knows we must have a significant shift in strategy before we are overwhelmed by the rise of the car market, worldwide. You can see our cooperation with you with G.M, Apple, McDonalds, and the Movies. We hate to hear all the misinformation and political rant, but you see our bottom line. Remember China's estimate of 2.5 billion cars from today's 1.3 billion. As was true 100 years ago, the car and the airplane, are at the forefront of change.

Yes, this all will drive us to public transportation, which large populations will make that the ultimate choice.

And we know our real challenge, beyond cost and capacity, is pollution. But on a certain level, you can see our people have chosen "the American way."

Just understand one fact, India and China, reaching to three billion people, will dominate Asia, and this is the Pacific Century, which the Americas are certainly a part of. But recognize that in the age of telecommunications and transportation, no part of the world is left out. What the world must understand, issues like Water, Energy, and pollution are not academic, they are issues we will solve now and in the next ten years. So, we hate being brought up with issues like war. When was the last time, we were mentioned with war, outside the USA.

US President: We're anticipating that. That's why it is so important that China and India are very cautious about the next steps. India has already made their first choice, the electric car. At the end of the day this isn't about any one nation or idea. The fact is, over the past fifty years energy use has doubled and the cost of energy, has risen 10–15 times. This disparity of what we can call clean supply and demand is clearly the path to economic recovery of the planet and the rise of Africa, and many places where the introduction of electricity is necessary to raising their standard of living. Likewise, addressing the creation of fresh water in conjunction with all steam turbine power applications must happen.

John F. Kennedy said, "If we could competitively, at a cheap rate, get freshwater from saltwater, it would be in the long-term interests of humanity which would dwarf any other scientific accomplishments." We know the Americas and China have many deep issues when it comes to water for energy, agriculture, industry, and life itself.

Water is the elixir of life and energy is the elixir of modern society. Making Water and Energy available at low cost will energize civilization.

We cannot fall into the trap of fighting over energy. Remember, it has been at the center of conflict for decades, even the underpinnings of WWII.

Consider one thing. If you spend the next 25 years building gasoline-powered ICE-based cars, you will be out of step with the rest of the world, who will have better productivity and clean exhaust, even with gaseous fuels from natural gas and/or hydrogen, at a minimum. And our battery technologies will revolutionize not only transportation but all forms of industrial tools and motor applications, even the wireless buildings with battery backup.

This is our chance to rise above the 20th century and redefine what the actions are that place the 21st century above the warlike tendencies of the past. And believe me, our actions may be on Natural Gas, but our clear direction is the FCEV, which is really an EV with a different longer-range fuel option (Hydrogen). You can imagine all the ways that will be discovered to utilize Hydrogen, the most plentiful element in the universe, not the least of which is the ocean. So, EV vs FCEV is a customer choice and a competitive opportunity.

So let this discussion lead with one idea. If the United States and China and India could find a way to leverage our codependency, we could separate ourselves from the twentieth century and redefine the planet's short-term future.

GS: Well put. One of our cultural problems is when we are rendered speechless by American sales and marketing. Remember, we are experiencing the introduction of thousands of McDonald's and Pizza Huts. So let that be a sign of Chinese and American interdependency. It's not smart to declare war on your business partners. We will support you and confer with you about the actions of the Saudis or Iran, who can and will clearly see this in a different way. Keep this thought about Syria, replace their current regime with what? A quagmire that we agree with Russia on. It may be ugly, but it's not ISIS. We just must remind ourselves that changing the oil supply or demand paradigm is essential to the efficiency of China's growth. As well as the strength of the Yuan.

President: Sorry for the enthusiastic sales pitch. Sometimes we can't help ourselves. We have one more discussion. We are committed to continue to see the monetary reserve currencies evolve.

We know the BRIC and Iran actions are moving in a different direction. With the tremendous business volume between our BRIC countries, and our potential of working together, on this and many other mutual interests, we want to assure the dollar's stability in the world market place. That's why we are aggressive about trade and fairness. We need to engage Russia. Our three nation productivity actions are an assurance of our economy's resourcefulness and resilience. We understand your backing of the Yuan with gold. That's good, but the future of world and currency stability is Water and Energy. (WE) Don't let short term focus cause delay on the real subject: Plentiful clean water and fresh air.

GS: We see this as very important to both our countries. You can see that we believe the world sees financial stability in terms of gold, and India sees it the same way. We would ask you take actions that reduce the tension between the United States and Iran, and assuredly Saudi Arabia. That's the path to financial security. And we need to keep the Chinese Yuan as low cost as possible. But the world needs to see the Yuan as stable and unflappable. So, we all have common interests and compromises to make. We both know that strong dollars and Euros can only be good for us. The more commonality in our endeavors, the better for all of us. We understand it, but it is a complex world, and neither of us wants to be embroiled in war and must refresh our resources on a continual basis. Knowing your traveling directions, good luck with Russia.

President: Remember, this issue of Natural Gas, Hydrogen, Electricity, and Atomic Energy is where China and the United States could change the world. You must admit the ability to cut your energy costs by more than half, could really help to transform your people. After all, your and our preservation as a government is around that simple fact, our people's trust and happiness. And your success in the world is largely based on your ability to raise your people's earnings so you can sell your products to your own people on an increasing percentage, like we do in the United States. So, let's not wage war over the Middle East. That is like warring over the past. Their future is dependent of changes that we and they will have difficulty making, like the "monarchy problem" and their religious and cultural intolerance. That will interfere with their own ability to have stable, military might. We will never be weak over Israel, and the shrinking role of Middle East over energy is the reality of the 21st century. Like you, we must find energy productivity, freshwater, and economic resilience.

But the American direction is based on solid and excess resources plus technological advancement in the near term.

GS: Know this, we are changing and will change our sourcing of fresh Water. As you know, the key is lowering the cost and dramatically improving the cleanliness of fuel, well to wheel. You know our people and country need clean, low cost, power.

The President's team exits and moves on to Australia.

Australia background:

While much of the local focus has been on Southern Australia's (SA's) role as an emerging uranium powerhouse, Australia and specifically Southern Australia are set to benefit from predictions *global energy demand will increase by a significant amount* in the next 25 years.

As recently as 2006, United States natural gas production was in decline but drilling technology advances have allowed United States companies to commercialize gas found in deep shale's fragmentation, which has caused the country's gas production to rise sharply to the world's leader.

Natural gas from shale is now the fastest-growing contributor to total primary energy in the US. Only a few years ago, the US was planning to import gas from other countries. Now, it sees hydrogen and natural gas as a new energy mix that will be applied to transportation and take the reliance on the Middle East for energy off the table and produce energy exports.

The Southern Australia shale industry is still in the early stages of development, but many people think the state is very well positioned to capitalize upon its shale gas resources on a large scale.

The US Energy Department in 2011 estimated there was 396 trillion cubic feet of recoverable gas in the Coober Pedy basin with enough gas to power Adelaide for 6600 years. That's Mid

East level resources. That must fit in with India's and China's growing demand.

Southern Australia is clearly set to play a major role in Australia's emergence as a global energy superpower. Australia's commitment to LNG plus numerous projects in shale R&D should assure their role in the Pacific Century. It should guarantee their role in the Pacific Century.

Australian now has $170 billion worth of oil and gas projects currently under construction. And this effort appears to be grossly understated. That means they have the wherewithal to attract hundreds of billions of Capital to Australia.

Australia was on track to unseat Qatar the world's leading supplier of liquefied natural gas by the end of the decade. Remember Australia has only been considered a fringe player. Australia has three operating LNG projects and another seven LNG projects worth around $170 billion currently under construction.

In just 12 months, four LNG projects have been given the go-ahead representing an investment of more than $90 billion. There are also tens of billions of dollars in other Australian LNG projects currently awaiting sanction. Strategically located right below the Asian population boom, the quiet sleepy continent is about to become an awakening giant.

The United States and Australia meet.

Aussie Prime Minister AUPM: We appreciate your coming down under in what appears to be earth-shattering news about the world's energy platform for the next 20 to 30 years and beyond. You know we are well into exploring potential for shale gas and many other resources. Realize, we really haven't seriously considered methane hydrate, which a positive for us.

With Australia underneath Asia, we are well positioned to support the emerging Asia and the amazing population projections. We've experienced some overzealousness in America and several energy companies have taken write-downs due to plunging gas prices in the United States. But now we see overwhelming projections and now this. Meanwhile, our Coober-Pedy project is unfunded, because of the drop-in oil prices.

President: We know there was an overly aggressive asset valuation, but when you look at the potential shift in transportation, asset values will spire upward to highly competitive prices. As you can tell by what we sent you, we see an integration of technologies and an abundant supply to enable strong progressive productivity improvements around the world. From what I read; you have potential all over Australia that will challenge your water resources. But this is the perfect example on how you can turn a constraint into an opportunity. Take your energy game and include in it a fresh-water creation axiom and you will position Australia with population potential that you can control. The 21st century is the century of Water and Energy, a period when thoughtful investment can allow support of a nine to eleven billion world population. And the one thing that is currently the largest unexploited asset is Australia dry land. Why you are as big as the continental United States and only have fewer than 25 million people. Australia plus water equals unfathomable opportunities. Recent consideration of liquid $CO2$ used in fracking makes exploration in Australia viable virtually anywhere. Extract seawater for desalination and create hydrogen and liquid $CO2$ for Fracking. Make fresh water a target and open up vast amounts of land for farming.

We can move from a world in strife over resources to one that uses low cost water and energy to ignite economic growth. We see Australia as an emerging economy due to exploitation of its natural resources and management of its environment. Our own assessment is that over the next 20 years, we will move into hydrogen, nuclear fusion, and quantum technologies that will enable us to harness energy for a thousand years.

AU-PM: We're cautious, but onboard. We just hope the fossil fuel community does not fight the transition. The amount of money accumulated and flowing in the oil and gas industry is awesome and scary, especially in your country and of course, the Middle East. But really, it is all over the world and the balance of price and potential growth needs to be properly understood. I think China is so deeply into this and India is at a threshold that they need clean efficient energy to move their economies upward, and Australia needs to see itself in a model that will change with the direction of the world. If somehow, we can channel Africa correctly, which is clearly a task, then we have both the economic and health paradigm will be clearly redefined. The ability to meet the demands of a 9–9.5 billion population's world in terms of water and energy is at hand and it will take the US, Europe, Russia, China, India and Australia to turn a problem into prosperity, with or without the Middle East, but it is up to them, to meet a 50% productivity target. This means the industrial world will have markets that, quite frankly, I cannot even fathom. Now if we can do this without a World War, the planet and all of us will be grateful, but can we really hope, given the experience of 2001–2018, that we can put the ways of the 20th century in their place? The first decade stinks, I should say, and is clearly 20th century hangover, thanks maybe to Bin Laden.

Yes, a direction largely derived out of fear.

I am onboard, but be careful, because you know Australia will, at least until this point, follow the United States down the path. So be cautious and bring the power of Europe, the United States, Russia, and China into a resolve to reach all your goals, even Russia. Remember, we are the markets where money will flow, so somehow the middle class has to exert its voting power into the right direction. We will make sure that this message will flow from Australia to all those markets above us and try to create the balance. You know I look at Russia and what they did in 1990, with relatively little bloodshed, and say to myself, with courage, anything is possible. But is it?

President: Yes, if only they could see their own courage, Russia, that is, and apply it with wisdom over Iran and Syria. We can only hope, and with that said we will move on to Russia.

AU: PM well we are engaged with China and the US over Coober Pedy. Obviously, we need billions of dollars to support mass mining and extraction and distribution.

President: What about your findings about the carbon footprint of cattle?

AU PM:

A recent study by researchers at James Cook University in Queensland, Australia, has found a certain type of Australian red algae that can significantly inhibit methane emissions from cows. Led by Professor of Aquaculture Rocky De Nys, **researchers found an addition of less than 2% dried seaweed to a cow's diet which can reduce methane emissions by 99 percent.** The study was conducted in collaboration with the Commonwealth Scientific and Industrial Research Organization (CSIRO), an Australian federal research agency.

Methane is about 25 times more potent than carbon dioxide in a 100-year time span, and a single cow releases between 70 and 120 kilograms of methane per year. **Burps from cows account for 26 percent of the United States' total methane emissions**, and the U.S. is only the world's fourth largest producer of cattle, behind China, Brazil, and India. There are currently approximately 1.3 to 1.5 billion cows roaming the planet.

President: Wow! Therefore we need diverse participation. Australia needs to consider itself a major player in the world energy game. This will transform the Pacific. You must make China see that the world is transforming away from the Middle East and towards the Pacific. And that the timeframe is now.

The success of your University efforts endorses the value of a free and open economic system...and sharing science. The President's team moves on to Moscow, Russia.

The cabinet consists of the following members meeting with the US President's team: Chairman (CM), Prime Minister (PM), Minister of Energy (ME), Minister of Foreign Affairs (MFA), Gazprom (GP exec)

CM: Welcome, Mr. President. We viewed with great interest your DVDs of your global trek. You know we are somewhat skeptical of the cost of shale gas mining and fracking. And Australia can't go unnoticed. We have such enormous reserves of natural gas that we are studying before we pursue drilling. That being said, we are very interested on the other hand, in your pursuit of more natural gas-powered vehicles. You and we know our potential for energy mining is vast and growing. Getting the most out of a field is high on our agenda. Where we clash, I think, is on projecting the cost of energy downward. We still see the generic growth in the Asian continent and Africa, causing the demand on resources to pressure the market prices, maybe upward? And we haven't even started with methane hydrate.

President: Quite frankly, we realize the cost of energy must decrease to free the markets to move people and goods in the econo-sphere. We think all aspects of the global market have to be freed to prosper. You know, for example, Europe is paying $11.00 per thousand cubic feet versus for our gaseous state natural gas. Now, this is a moving target, but as sources grow and delivery is refined, we see the price of natural gas below $5.00 and LNG $8–9.

Further, technological initiatives will prosper and make the improvement of battery storage capacity significantly improve gas mileage we think the entire sector is in upheaval because of the price of oil and petroleum. This, of course, is also being impacted by oil and oil sands, which continues to be on an upward spiral of discoveries, although the prospect of dirty energy is troublesome. We cannot let the status quo persist, at least in the United States and perhaps the Americas. We know Mexico and South America, and really Canada, are largely undiscovered meaning the opportunities exceed the aggressiveness of exploration currently. So, we have to ask whether this format has the legs when the world embraces gaseous or electric fuel in transportation. It would certainly get your attention. When we study this matter in depth, quite frankly we cannot ignore the implications of even partial exploitation of methane hydrate. Our tests so far are extremely positive, especially with the injection of CO_2 in the permafrost or on the ocean floor. Having an application for storing CO_2 raises the prospect of other energy conversion. If the United

States and China, together, recognize that conversion of coal to liquid or coal to gas, is commercially practical, well...

Quite frankly, our people see your vast northern slope, and project your potential as large as the Middle East. And Arctic waters as the greatest source of shale gas and methane hydrate in the world.

GP (interrupting): Are you saying China will go this way? They have gone so far in cleaning the output of coal.

President: Yes, it is a major paradigm shift, and no, it has not settled yet. But consider they are getting ready to raise their economy enough that there will be a major growth in cars and trucks. I am sure their aspirations in air travel will be significant. So, the need for clean liquid fuel, or its gaseous equivalent, is a major agenda item for them and they also have a major water agenda, as should most of us. Look at your wheat statistics. We believe that since we are all scrambling over energy, and America's consumption has decreased slowly, which has changed upward because of a dampened economy, it's to all interests to fix the problem. China must reconcile one clear reality, if Europe and the United States do not rise out of their weakened state, China's biggest purchasing partners have weakened buying power. So, I believe the Euro-United States-China link just needs more partners especially the BRIC countries. I think we all have to recognize three facts.

If the price of energy decreases significantly, the level of energy use will increase substantially.

Something must be done to shift the paradigm as clean supply exceeds demand. WE need the capital and productivity strength to raise the production of fresh water. We need it in our west and Midwestern breadbasket. Canada needs it. Mexico needs it. The Middle East needs it. China and Western Asia, including India need it. Australia needs it, and Africa needs it, and yes Russia needs it in their grain belt. **Climate change is real, but as I've repeated several times...our real near-term challenge is global "warring", not global warming,** China's GIANT issue (perhaps in terms of American awareness), is the overwhelming problem of pollution. With the noteworthy progress they have made in "clean coal", it's not making a dent on pollution, in real terms as opposed to statistical progress. They must transform their energy direction, with the agreement that the USA will transform theirs. The USA should lead the way, by example.

While we address this problem, the availability of clean water at significant levels must be addressed not as a theory, but a practical matter. What should we do, go to war? Russia should look long and hard at the 20th century then decide which parade they wish to follow: into Armageddon or into a robust, clean future. As the population grows to eight then nine billion, considering worldwide discovery, outside the Middle East, our direction and guaranteed success will become a bellwether that can't be ignored, that is if you want your economy, pollution, and yes climate change to be addressed. And yes, Russia, more than any other nation needs to rebuff the signs of major war. Looking at the problem this way tells us the United States and China have significant parallel interests. I see Russia as another player in this equation. It is clear to our scientists that Russia easily could be another Middle East. Your geographical place clearly means your potential is greater than the United States, China, and many others. You must see your opportunity as great. Quite frankly, with European dependency on your gaseous fuel, the way it is, you have an overriding agenda to assure that energy does not stop flowing and that your own sources need to expand so that pricing is not a barrier. I believe our agendas are not significantly beyond the cold war yet, and all eyes need to stop trying to fixate on high prices of energy is a good income stream versus competitive energy costs will serve all expanding markets. This will never happen unless supply exceeds demand and the mix of use of that supply changes. Keep in mind, we are just reacting to the fact that new resources plus drilling technology, as we see it, is an opportunity to move the reality of change forward. And you know the NG market is growing competitively, daily.

You can see that the Americas are economically improving because of the availability of the technology to "unearth" energy. But their ability to truly upgrade their economies will require a paradigm change. The Americas will respond to this opportunity, but we know that the world must continue in the 21st century knowing we cannot simply revert to stage where the only way to reconcile differences is through war. I say this as both of us arm small nations with the power to engage their neighbors with military intervention. The one thing both of us know about each other is that, if forced we will engage, and we will persevere at almost any cost. The world has misjudged the United States on that level, time and again; I think the same is true about Russia. So, we need to engage on a single focus: water and energy. That is the story of potential for this century. And it is not if, it is when. If it does not happen, we can measure the march to World War III. Nobody wants that except for "Armageddon's believers." Remember, Russia larger energy resources than the Middle East.

If not yourself, then with China and Australia and the combined Americas have larger energy resources than the Middle East. The fact is the era of Middle Eastern energy dominance is over.

And the US and the world needs to restore the economy. The key to that is Water and Energy productivity. Its importance exceeds gold manifestly.

Now, what about water? What about next year's wheat projections. I believe you must look at the future. China, Russia, and the United States need to reclaim history for our mutual prosperity.

CM: Well said, but you speak from the vantage point of one who wants to preserve their wealth, and quite frankly, you want to assure your political viability. If I can be so bold.

Russia chooses to try to understand at a surface level, USA politics. No matter who the President is, our joint agenda is Syria, ISIS, Oil, Russia's role in Crimea, European Natural Gas, Iran, and more. We don't want to take down Syria because we don't want a more perilous leader to take over Libya, Iraq, etc. We had enough with Afghanistan we don't interfere with other nation's elections. For the USA, it would be foolhardy. Who is more adept at Cybercrime? Angelina Merkel's email? Even I couldn't figure why you would do that? The point is the cost, politically, of spying. We literally had nothing to do with that and your public is considering whether you should go to war with us. Can we compete with Silicon Valley, even 10–20 years from now? We should use trade, no? We have no relationship with President Trump, his businesses, his Bankers, Relatives, none whatsoever. You watch too many James Bond movies, where the Russian are always the bad guys. We don't want a nuclear exchange with anyone. You don't think we understand the USA's military power? We are a nation that is developing our democratic methods and values. I know you think we have a KGB mentality, but I can show you have your CIA or secret service driven history including funding the Afghan response to

Russia, which, in effect was funding Bin Laden, who led the defense against us. By the way, Bin Laden took his efforts to the Saudis and they chose the USA over Bin Laden to defeat Hussein in Desert storm. That put 500,000 troops in Saudi Arabia. That led **directly** to 9/11. My point is I can use your involvement in South America, and more, like the Shah in Iran, to say your attempts at government building CIA based methods put you where you are today. If Kennedy wasn't assassinated, you would have not had the Vietnam War, Nixon, and more. Although opening China was a good thing. Although having Henry Kissinger was probably the real genius. Imagine if GWB had him instead of Cheyney, not as VP, of course. My point is I understand history and the many mistakes that the USA and yes, the USSR have made regrettable errors to end up with where we are today. So, we're not part of the axis of evil, we are a nation that made dramatic history in the 1990's, but we also were a major partner of WWII, and Israel, so let's find a way to evolve out of this terrible mess, together. Yes, we're part of the Oil and Gas society, and we see the obvious changes in Europe, India, China, and more. Look at what India is doing. We know that we both want to move forward, and we understand that "Cyber terrorism" stands in our way. Maybe, like what's occurred in nuclear treaties, we need to join in a Cyber Pacification agreement. We want to build relationships, not go cycle after cycle, back to yesterday, pre-nuclear agreements.

President: I say do the math. We know, within the next 20 years, China will most likely be the world economic leader, although their per capita economics will hopefully still be rising. Likewise, India will have the largest population on the planet. The 21st century is the Pacific century, but the paradigm of world trade and water and energy supply along with the vast incursion of computer technology and telecommunications will shrink the planet so the notion of defining the world around the oceans leaves everyone with the opportunity to grow. You will also see Australia as an energy leader and Cypress will emerge as a natural gas exporter. Just the notion of BRIC nations, Brazil, Russia, India, and China show that emergence crosses all continents. So, our agenda is to play the cards we are dealt, but under the keen awareness that we are now in a global village. Yes, we all have border issues, and the challenge of reconciling the post–World War II era, and in your case, USSR disillusion, but I implore you to step back and recognize your goals from 1990 on and the enormous opportunity you have just by strengthening your energy position and your role in supporting the upgrading of the world's economy. I won't propose it today, but China-Russia, United States must look at our geographic synergy, the advantages of technology sharing, and common water and energy needs. We will succeed in a water and energy strategy that will change the world. We know your support of Syria and Iran, and we respect that. But Mother Earth and science and engineering have moved the equation around. Please study this very carefully, especially with China. We need to fix what is broken. And to the world, what do you want Russia's water contribution to be? Understand what the next 20 years will provide in terms of energy growth, water and energy productivity, and transportation transformation, It can't be ignored. It's the 21st century.

Russia should be rethinking its strategy as a true world participant, not as an adversary.

CM: Yes, but I am very interested in how the Saudis and your own corporate holders of the energy resource adapt to the changes you suggest. You can be sure that we'll support the genesis of your ideas, but please increase our communications going forward. This is no time to mistake bravado for policy actions. As you know, managing bravado is the underlying challenge of political leadership. With your attacks on money interests regarding political influence and decision making, we will be very interested in the noise we here from within the corridors of Washington. And we are very interested in China's gold moves and it impact on the dollar, if any.

That seems to be the one major issue. What if China just seizes the moment and compromises with the Saudis in return for dominant relations with OPEC? OPEC trades in Chinese Yuan and the US dollar collapses. You must plan against that scenario.

President: Yes, you have identified the real challenges we face. But remember, trying to understand American politics from the Beltway is like us trying to make sense of what goes on in the Kremlin. The American system is taunted by the same fundamental problem as is Russia, too much money in too little hands. The one thing that is universal in our new global economy, the profit numbers in the top one percent of our citizens are way too concentrated. We must overcome, or should I say quell the voices of too many billionaires. Fortunately, we still have many that appreciate what it took for our constitution to give them the opportunity and the political stability for them to create wealth. When we talk of energy, we are confronting as many people at home who want it to continue as is, as we are at the top of many nations. It's up to us, who chose to grapple with the power of politics, to look very clearly at the future, and know when it is more important to solicit change than to let the potential create more havoc than our people want or deserve. We certainly are accountable for too much of it already and I feel that *it is time to harness the beast of destiny* before it is too late. The true enemy of us all is **pollution** and its sources.

Remember, America *always* finds a path to resilience. And so does Russia. My God, you just woke up one day and said the system you were ready to risk the world for doesn't work. Most don't see it, but I believe that is unprecedented in history, and you are still berthing what you can become. Leverage your natural resources and become a player. Again we (Americas) are a W.E. Country and we'll get energy under $20 per Barrel equivalence, and you can be with China, India, Japan, South Korea, and Australia. Those five along with Russia are the new center of the energy economy in Asia. But more importantly, no one is against the Middle East. Resources and technology, including drilling, are shifting the mix of how energy is used, and fresh water is created. That's the next three quarters of the 21st century.

And yes, we have reconciliation with OPEC and the Saudis, which must be achieved, and we will. Their dilemma is much worse than either Russia or the United States. We have vast environmental resources and engineering. With slackened demand for oil, what do they have? How will they address the water crisis? When will they see that the genesis of change is around the Pacific Rim not the Mediterranean? Are you prepared to ignore the needs of the next billion people? Note that China prepared itself with diversity. What has Russia done?

CM: I can say amen to that prayer and will give you a call if we ever see the beast losing control. There is no question that both of us get direct feedback from different levels. Just make sure Israel deeply considers before they act. The idea that you are, at some level separating yourself from the pressure of the Middle East could make them feel they have to take preventative action.

President: Likewise, there is more than an equal chance Islamic nation feel they have more latitude without as many financial ties of the United States, Europe, or elsewhere. We are crossing into the territory of new horizons and uncharted waters, so we both must be more sensitive. Israel will not be threatened by nuclear missiles. They will destroy any threat. There are no ifs! Let us just keep the channels open and clear, no matter what. Remember, both of us know the power of "abstinence" or should I say national perseverance. World War II, post-World War II, Europe and USSR and United States created Israel, and we will never falter our support. Never! This should be clear from the United States or EU point of view. If we must stop the world for ten years or so due to Middle Eastern ignorance, then we will. We will never default on our commitment to Israel, and neither will the EU, and quite frankly, neither should you.

CM: No matter what, just remember what we learned. Sometime religious fervor in government produces unimagined consequences. This is what Israel is haunted by every day, I assure you. But consider this equation Syria–Bashar al-Assad=ISIS. No? Then who? Right, you have no idea. By giving quasi support to the opposition, who is really the cause of all the death? Hope without resolve, sounds like the whole Middle East.

President: If action is required to support Israel, even if it takes these plans 10 to 20 years to come to fruition, it is simply not a problem for the United States or Europe. The rest of them? Let's work on it.

The presidential team goes to India and meets with the Indian prime minister. **India** President (IP), Prime Minister (IPM), Council of Ministers (ICM).

IP: This estimating of our potential for shale gas has created a large disparity. But the facts are clear; we have enough to make it commercially viable for a long time. If it is six hundred trillion cubic feet (tcf), it is enough to make a market. We feel that the productivity of this kind of drilling will expand with volume, so we are all in for massive exploration which can result in hard numbers. But, like you, we are observing China, Australia, Poland, and several others, and it all seems positive. But America is gaining the expertise at a higher rate than everyone else. So, you have our attention. And we have serious investments to make in the car business. And have committed to the **electric** car. So, we have the same directional investment issues as China, and both of us will move forward. And we are aware of Australia.

President: We have already been working with you on this for some time. As a great ally, we will keep you heavily in our production support. I know you are working with ConocoPhillips, Exxon-Mobil and others. You realize my next stop is the Middle East. I just want you to understand that the world is rethinking energy, especially concerning transportation. But our step outward, out of the box, is for the expansion of fresh water. Its time has come.

Natural gas cars

Worldwide, there were 24.5 million natural gas vehicles by 2016, led by China five million, India 3.045 million, Iran (4.0million), Pakistan (3.0million), Argentina (2.05 million), and Brazil (1.78 million). The Asia-Pacific region leads the world with 16.8 million NGVs, followed by Latin America with 4.6 million vehicles.[2] In the Latin American region almost 90% of NGVs have bi-fuel engines, allowing these vehicles to run on either gasoline or CNG. In Pakistan, almost every vehicle converted to (or manufactured for) alternative fuel use typically retains the capability to run on ordinary gasoline. **USA has 160,000 active NGV Vehicles mostly government buses**, We are the largest active car user in the world, but limited refueling for electric, hydrogen, natural gas. No refueling = no sales.

http://www.iangv.org/current-ngv-stats/

You can see that leadership on these grounds are not the Western nations, although the United States, Japan, and Germany are already producing small vehicles with Nat-gas as its fuel, around the world. It's clear, nations are shifting to Ng cars, and energy is projected to be in excess.

IP: We know the markets, but have decided to concentrate on Electric cars, because it's easiest to deploy in India. Commercially, we will support all markets.

US President: The point is that the West is about to step up with a vengeance, and we need your attention and support, including deep understanding of why the paradigm is changing, and why, although a bridge, this fuel will reorganize the supply and demand formula as a result of a relatively small penetration into the petroleum market. You may ask why Iran leads the world in natural gas for cars. It's simple. They found it cheaper to have natural gas in cars than invest in refineries for oil. They sell oil at a high price and use natural gas for people's transportation, something we haven't acted on. Once our direction is clear and visible, many will join us. Someone had to step up. I know you are deeply committed to addressing fresh water. So, you are on my front page. Recognize, we are opening with diversity, due to the vast diversity of support for Nat-gas, hydrogen, electricity, and yes gasoline. We will let the public set our direction, with guidance on productivity and efficiency (mpge).

IP: Thank you for sharing the DVDs in almost real time with your trip. I can see both the rationale and the issues. I am really interested in your next trek vis vi Israel and Saudi Arabia.

President: It's as important as it could be. We also need you to reconsider your oil agreements with Iran and commit to us about purchasing oil with dollars. Although it seems like there will be some slowdown in their politics, although they should not be foolish about Israel.

You know about the Iran situation and the BRIC agreements. I can just say we are considering these matters very carefully, and change is relatively simple, although its implications profound. But we can't interrupt our oil flow, it is not an option. Although, as I've said, we're going electric. Our infrastructure for over a million cars has not been built yet and we're not building it twice. As you say, "Energy is the elixir of society", so lift the ban on international transactions with Iran. I beg you to reconsider. You're painting yourself into a corner. We must keep our energy doors open and find the best way to get massive fresh water. With over a billion people we can't compromise our flow of energy. Make your decisions carefully, as we will ours.

(The presidential team heads for Saudi Arabia.)

Saudi Arabia

Saudi Arabia is a monarchy supporting and supported by Islam. The government is headed by the king, who is also the commander in chief of the military. The king appoints a crown prince to help him with his duties. The crown prince is second in line to the throne. The king governs with the help of the council of ministers, also called the cabinet. There are 22 government ministries that are part of the cabinet. Each ministry specializes in a different part of the government, such as foreign affairs, education, and finance. The king is also advised by a legislative body called the consultative council (Majlis Al-Shure). The council proposes new laws and amends existing ones. It consists of 150 members who are appointed by the king for 4-year terms that can be renewed. The country is divided into thirteen provinces, with a governor and deputy governor in each one. Each province has its own council that advises the governor and deals with the development of the province. Because Saudi Arabia is an Islamic state, its judicial system is based on Islamic law (Shari'ah). The king is at the top of the legal system. He acts as the final court of appeal and can issue pardons. There are also courts in the kingdom. The largest are the Shari'ah Courts, which hear most cases in the Saudi legal system.

Source: Saudi Arabia embassy, Washington DC.)

Attendance at the meeting: crown prince (CP), energy minister (EM), Aramco exec (AE), various ministers.

President: I have communicated with you via DVD files transmitted from all the meetings until this point in an attempt to provide everyone an open forum.

CP: We appreciate that. However, we ask that you not use that approach with this meeting: we want an open discussion, but the king feels we would have a freer dialogue without that. We of course will record the session for our ministry using our built-in system.

President to his staff: Turn off the recording the staff complies. I will report back to my Congress, and I will provide you a copy of my report. But this meeting is essentially confidential, and we will only share what you transcribe as mutually acceptable.

CP: Thank you. I want to take you through a sordid but open view of our relationship, as honest and as skeptical as I can and then weigh your direction against the realities. I asked you to not film this because it is too skeptical for Islam. In many respects, we aligned with you along this path when we rejected bin Laden's request to let us hire his military experience from Afghanistan against the Russians to take on Saddam Hussein, who at the time had the largest standing army in the Middle East. Your agreement to bring five hundred thousand American soldiers onto our soil and successfully execute Desert Storm was both a stop to Sadam Hussein who clearly would have moved next to Saudi Arabia if we had not asked for your intervention. You know that the relationship of Iran, Iraq, and Saudi Arabia has been trouble for both of us, ever since you supported Saddam against Iran, to some extent is the result of the overthrow of the Shah in 1979. You supported Bin Laden in Afghanistan and Saddam in Iraq as our relationship evolved. And it evolved, to our mutual benefit because of oil. I am setting this up but let us go back to the beginning.

You have always known that Saudi Arabia was an Islamic state with a deeply conservative Wahhabi sect, as conservative as the Taliban, if not more. You know our culture respects God over society, and that what you call freedom we call subordination to society's whims and liberalization. It also took us time to accept that fifteen of the nineteen perpetrators of 9/11 were ex-Saudis, by nature or birth, but we had cast out Bin Laden, long before 9/11. Presumably our choosing the United States over Bin Laden to fight Saddam Hussein was the underlying cause of 9/11. I am saying this, this way, to reflect our king s request that, undocumented, we have a rush of candor. And you should admit, your invasion of Iraq was somehow tied to this chain and to oil. It is also true that the last ten years has shown widespread strife and the rise of the cost of gasoline went from about $1.11 to $3.64 and higher, gold from $228 to $1,600 per ounce. I think we both should admit that all these steps had much to do with the state of the world economy. But let us go back to the beginning.

Oil in Saudi Arabia can be traced back as far as the eighteenth century, but its strategic importance was recognized by the Nazis and the allies during World War II. In fact, with tanks and airplanes, recognition of the strategic importance of oil probably began there and also the logical conclusion by the allies to kick Hitler out of Africa and the Middle East.

Around 1971, the United States began importing oil because its consumption of oil had finally passed your own production levels. Along with the problems between Israel and Egypt, it was the time where our relationship was escalated. When Iran was taken over by Islamic leaders in 1979, both the United States and Saudi Arabia had issues, especially since Iran was dominantly Shiite and we Sunni, the two branches of Islam with roots in Abraham, the historical leader in Judaism. In the eighties, we sent missionaries all over the Middle East to promote our deep Wahhabi message of conservatism. Remember, the Middle East and Islam in general is largely Sunni, maybe 80–90 percent, with the exception of Iran and to some extent some of Iraq and Syria. Of course, our numbers are worldwide including Indonesia, the United States, and much of the "istans". We were unhappy with the Iranian direction, as were you.

But since 1979, our embrace of the United States was largely rebuffed by our own Wahhabis, and many, including Bin Laden, who saw the buildup of troops due to Kuwait, as bringing in the infidels into the Middle East. As you know, we have a broader world view and even have many Western communities in our nation. Nonetheless, we have had high stress since Desert Storm. And you know that historically, our culture resisted radio, television, and the Internet, but we have evolved. The mobile culture and social networking of the Internet and the Arab Spring has further stressed our relationship, much which has been due to the cost of food. But, unlike how we have been depicted, our women have Internet access and are allowed international travel, despite the fact they do not drive cars. Our women dress so conservatively because how your dress is a product of your society. Clothing is a slave to society. The Islamic world is 1.6 billion across Asia, Africa, Europe, and the United States, certainly attributed to a conservatism and religiousness in the world. Our small country is about 34.5 million compared to 330 million in the United States and 1.3 billion in China. For the first time, we send less than a million barrels of oil to the United States, *and more than one million barrels per day to China*, a shift perhaps relating to the Pacific Century you speak of.

We appreciate your support in Yemen but recognize the difficulty that has caused you in the world.

What is true about the 21st century, including your activity, is Saudi Arabia is losing or has lost control of the supply and demand balance. This also has considerations for OPEC and many nations. You need to recognize, we are back to sending more students to American universities than since September 11 and are creating more sectors that are hospitable to non-Muslims. We may be conservative, but we are certainly growing into the new century. We also lead the world in saltwater desalination, with 75 percent of our freshwater being manufactured through desalination plants. We are a desert, but we are addressing the long-term interests of our people. And you know a lot of the work is being done with American companies, even IBM, taking a systems approach to using non-oil sources to power desalination such as solar and other utility functions. You know we are leaders in reserves of natural gas, and I assure you, the shale deposits that exist definitely will be tapped. Please note that we are leaders in the water issue and have encouraged the Middle Eastern nations to follow suit so we can evolve out of being a desert. Recognize that this puts on a path to transform our economy, by 2030, to not rely as much on Oil & Gas as our primary economic driver. It's an active guaranteed direction, but it's not overnight.

President: Thank you for such a broad look at our relationship, as we say in the United States, warts and all. We have been through a lot together and that fact will enable both of us to endure change. And I say endure because there is no significant change without pain. What we are discovering that the developing of natural gas and artificially created gas is growing in leaps and bounds. The United States is now the leader in worldwide Nat-gas and oil production, something no one would have considered merely five years ago. These efforts are also producing more oil through the new drilling techniques. I think strategically, what you need to consider is this. The unit cost of energy must go down and the shift in how we use oil and gas is shifting somewhat to the gaseous side, and electric. This is also a big factor in how coal will be used in the future as a fuel source. Our huge coal reserves must change because natural gas will take over the energy generation business, and very quickly.

The real factors that describe the future are these:

The economy of the world cannot really reemerge without lower cost, through low-cost clean energy.

Once that accelerates, the use of energy will grow significantly in a short period of time. We advise you to understand how much you can grow with lower cost. We think if you dropped prices to perhaps under $20 per barrel, we suggest the markets will take you there anyway, that would not change the paradigm being set for the next 20–30 years: the Middle East is losing its dominance over energy, and the marketplace will become more gaseous and pure electric, a trend driven by innovation, population increase, and discovery, nothing more.

But during that period, massive changes in energy storage and the efficiency of biofuel creation will occur. America is not only pursuing technology and resource excavation around the world but will begin to harvest freshwater creation out of the energy producing changes. Something you know very well. You and I know of the intensity growing around fusion and reemerging regarding fission. And all this emphasis around gaseous and LNG related infrastructure build has a lot to do with the emergence of hydrogen fuel, and importantly, the raising of the storage capacity of batteries, eventually, three to five times. When you look at population trends in India and Africa, you can only imagine the impact when their economies emerge. India, I believe will be more self-sufficient, but when you consider

China's growth over the next 20 years, it will be overtaken by India over the next ten and then there's Africa.

China is certainly building its own path to commerce. Of course, they have become such a central source of product manufacturing that they can feed their trade expansion along with energy consolidation. This, of course challenges the Middle East to expand its product categories and synergy with energy delivery. When China gets control of its own energy destiny, which they will and are doing, they will face one simple fact, environmental cleansing is just how the energy choices will sort themselves out. As you can see by their conversations with us, raising the income level of their citizen's is a strategic balance between exports and internal "customers".

Remember that Japan was like this in the 1970s, but their overenthusiasm created a bubble, interestingly largely real estate, and a debt challenge, they are still recovering from. And Russia: our scientists and geologists say they alone are larger than the Middle East. Well, what are we going to do about it? Are we to just carry on and fight another 20th century type war? Should the United States engage Iran on the battlefield? Will that change anything? Really? It will change nothing because technology and discovery is perhaps preparing the world for a 9-10 billion population. To not leverage and address that is self-destructive.

AE: The way most of us see it, Israel will bomb Iran's nuclear facility as soon as they deem it a real threat. And quite frankly, Americas shift in energy policy, as we see it, will be a threat to Israeli security, prompting Israel to feel that they must go it alone, at least to some extent. They must deal with bad assumptions caused by global change.

President: Let me interject. The United States is a supporter of Israel, Saudi Arabia, Iraq, Turkey, and others, and regardless of what is said in any tactical discussion, we intend for that to be guaranteed for at least the century. You know that the Islamic Nations on one level or another have wanted United States military dominance to leave the Middle East. Your king has made it clear that even within your own citizenry, there is skepticism about us. Well quite frankly, we are just acting with the hand we have been dealt by Mother Nature and our own science and engineering. Keep in mind that we have been at shale gas, as an example, for more than 20 years. We just do not stumble on things and then forget the past. Our point of view is based on three important factors: Our economic and social prosperity; the world's economic and social prosperity; and some sense of fairness, balance, and mutual respect.

But you must understand that methane hydrate is right behind shale gas, and it's easier to mine and vastly more available than all sources of fossil fuel combined. We can't ignore the realities of mother earth. Our economy must adjust to the inflationary cost of oil, and its downward direction. We will move very carefully with methane hydrate, but early tests make me convinced it will happen. And to, that countries like Japan it's a godsend, although admittedly, it's Trumped by Sun-Gas.

If this were not the case, we would not be providing our technology and experience around the world. It is good business. The reason we were traveling around the globe before going to our citizens, is we cherish the trek of the last century and the importance of openness and communication. And Saudi Arabia and Israel, now Iraq, and historically Egypt, are important allies, even who do not see eye to eye with each other, but who needs to recognize that the winds of change are upon us, and the world must snap out of this economic malaise and into the positive agenda of this century. Remember many of our R&D efforts, including shale, were motivated by 1973. That has nothing to do with any subsequent history.

And real change won't happen without the improved productivity of Energy. You can afford to absorb desalination, we can't. And we must have desalination and other water creation activities. The benefits of USA agriculture are felt all over the world and we benefit from agriculture all over the Americas. So, we take steps to achieve our goals. You should always expect that from us. We refuse to be suppressed and will always find an answer. And trust me, innovations will be forthcoming.

AE: Pardon our candor, but it looks like the objective of productivity is coming out of our hides, and the hides of emerging nations in Africa, South America, and around the world. Just at its surface we are looking at revenues in multiple hundreds of billions of dollars, including your own energy companies.

President: I think the adjustment you must make is to look at 2002–2015 as a 10+ year energy bubble. The fact is, as I have shown, the dollar in the last 50 years has inflated by 750 percent, in terms of value while the energy sector has grown by double that. Meanwhile, the energy reserves have increased, US consumption has been flat, until recently, for the last ten years, and we have experienced a tripling in prices, all circumventing around unrest in the Middle East and our willingness to engage.

This was very much instigated by September 11, which your historical brief covered very well. But on a certain level, this is not even about that. The facts are that decades of research and development have opened one of several expected energy breakthroughs over the next ten to fifteen years. And a world grasping for growth is hampered by energy costs. China is at the cusp of creating a better economy but is choking on energy policies based on 70 percent coal and is at the threshold of becoming, along with India, the leading producer of automobiles. So, no matter how they differ politically with us, our success will offer them the best chance of achieving their goals. And given the implications to the world market, any country that cares about their own future, could see that streamlined profit margins will result in massive long-term growth. The problem with bubbles, whether real estate, Internet, stock market, or energy; they all get lazy and protective of the status quo, which makes them pop every time. This is market realities, if you wish, free enterprise.

They live in enough of a state of denial that one way or another the market reacts, and the bubble bursts. This is the story of the last 20 years: the Internet bubble; the real estate bubble; the stock market bubble and now the energy bubble. True economic technicians can line up the charts and show you the trends and the results. It's as sure as death and taxes. And how about this? Apple Computer now sells more cellphones in China than they do in the USA. General Motors sold 3.8 million cars in China in 2016, more than in the USA, and that is why they have greater profits than in all their history. McDonalds is proliferating stores all over their country. We have stabilized our currency, so it doesn't interfere with trade. China's movie business is staggering. This is what's known as a trade relationship. Note that Nigeria, which in 2050 will probably equal the USA in population, is selling "Nollywood" to its people and has massive movie productions. The point is, our culture is proliferating.

That's the result of your trade policies (of the past). The point is synergy works and will continue to work.

The problem with the energy bubble is that there is massive information about how it stymies economic growth. And when you have an answer at hand, which only requires that your people and companies clearly see the adjustments necessary to turn your world around, you either act or declare yourself part of the malaise, and that is not what I was elected for. What is important is that we recognize that our own security and economic issues and work together to assure peaceful and careful initiatives toward results.

We keep checking and rechecking assumptions and results of tests and initial mining, as well as worldwide investigations, and conclude that the only hindrance is if a nation has no pipelining infrastructure and is unwilling or unable to establish same. Other than that, there is evidence after evidence, that the results forecasted, are greater than initial projections. Our price-point, say under $20 per barrel, is not artificial, it's the result of when clean supply exceeds demand, and consumers have a real choice. Real choice. To some extent, it's the whole world reacting to energy inflation at a time when the world is depressing and polluting. The world has no choice but to act.

Now that the reality of "Syn-Gas" and "Sun-Gas" is upon us, how can we avoid Acting? It's like us demanding to stay with coal in 1900. We recognize that only Saudi Arabia took advantage of their wealth of oil and desalinated your state. Where were Iran, Iraq, and the others? I'm sorry but the era of oil dominance is over. Now we need to consider how to feed the next billion people on earth and part of that is low-cost energy. So, without cooperation, and squabbling with Israel over nothing, the Middle East is doomed to return to its pre-oil existence when it should have used its wealth to create a green belt and eliminate famine. Of course, besides the Saudis, the Middle East has to adapt to change because the next Billion people will be here in 10-12+ years, and that will change the world.

CM (of crown prince): Please keep us aware of all considerations that could affect us. We obviously are considering actions at many levels. You and we must reconsider our military assumptions, troops, purchasing power, and more.

President: Remember my point. This is a change that I would call "inevitable". And our continuity of military superiority is not only good but accelerating. Remember, we have the military resources and the electronic resources to excel. Drones are an excellent example of synergy. We are already developing the 1,600 mph next-generation airplane, (early stages) and it will shrink the world once more. Our economic resilience will respond to this energy productivity and our world focus, as well as Mexico-US synergy with water, will show that the United States has reemerged, again. So clearly understand who you want to partner with for both energy and internal security. Regardless of wars even ill-considered or ill-executed, the United States focuses inwardly and at the world and then rebounds. We'll meet again soon but be sure to look at world involvement since World War II, and then consider our relationship during good times and bad. We're the best friend Saudi Arabia has had, and energy must change, and water must rebound under the umbrella of a population increase ten or eleven years. Forget the last ten years since 9/11. That was twentieth century overhead. The 21st century began in 2015, almost like the nineteenth century ending in 1917. I appreciate the meeting.

The US team moves to Israel.

Israel: The president will confer again with Israel and then attend a parlay with England, France, and Germany, and then head back to Washington. He provides limited distribution of the transcript to the Europeans, the Senate foreign relations committee, back to the Saudis, and to Israel on a confidential basis.

Attendees include the Israel president (IP); defense (ID); energy and water resources (IEW); and strategic affairs (ISA).

IP: I always knew these days were approaching. The pressure of world economies and the impact of the citizens versus the financial stakeholders, I guess you call it the 1 percent, has been growing. Someone had to step up for the 99%. The dilemma we see is that we are in a culture that in many ways is hundreds of years from maturing. Based on the confidential transcript you had with the Saudis, which I assure you will not be shared or disclosed, I think I see a tiny bit of hope, hope that the last 40–50 years meant something that sticks, for peace in the Middle East. Of course, you know our position on Iran and perhaps Syria. I think in the back of their minds they can reinvent Persia and with that reestablish an Islam empire that we have not seen since maybe the Ottoman Empire. Perhaps I am rambling a bit, but we have to consider the worst and prepare to defend against it. Quite frankly, we have to deal with regimes that are a century or more behind in governmental maturity, people who do not really understand the WMDs of today's world but are willing to create them. So, we ask whether your actions will invoke their questionable side. We need you do something that makes it clear that you may appear to be withdrawing from the region but are just switching fuel vendors and class of fuel. But you have so many treaties and food related and military grants, will they rush to Russia or China and try to build more firepower? If you have no strategic value in their oil, how long will your citizens let you expend billion-dollar military grants? In return for what? This realignment with China, who will trade anything for a good oil price and guaranteed flow of product, is perplexing to us. When people or nations get conservative, they often revert to what they feel was the rule of the past. It seems to me so essential that the United States prove it is still in the region, and perhaps in the market. But then we ask ourselves again, why? What would we do when we had a new answer for energy?

President: These are the same thoughts that go through our planning, so we are open to suggestions. But look how we are responding to the skeptics, that our and the Euros response to skeptics are unequivocal, if you force us to delay our energy rollout plans because you didn't believe what we said or wanted to test us, we and Europe are willing to waste 20 or so years and you can assure your own self-preservation, because our alliance with Israel has nothing to do with oil politics and never has been. So please spare your own self-doubt caused by infantile, emotional acts and lack of foreign relations experience, by some.

We would hope you would continue to respond that way. I know you have not taken this lightly, of course. But the one thing that will just jump out at the Middle East oil states is the loss of several hundred billion dollars of cash flow/revenue. If they preempted your offer and just lowered their oil price to fifty-dollar s per barrel, I am sure they would still make money by the billions. But then as you proceeded to continue your path to the new paradigm of clean supply exceeds demand, they may want to threaten China with the potential for lost suppliers or just cut you off like in 1973.

They are going to do the opposite and try to capture China's attention for the long haul. But China needs the United States and Europe as customers. This is a part of the reality check you have well considered. What good is cheap energy and low cost, if you do not have customers. China is too early in its maturity to think of themselves as their own best customer, like the United States. You can always sell inward. But I suspect that in today's global economy, that option is not too profitable, especially when your global companies need their world markets. Just think of Apple computer with 116,000 employees in the United States, but *a million* essentially outsourced workers in Taiwan. These problems are probably to the advantage of the United States. Apple could go away tomorrow, and they would be absorbed by Google and/or IBM. GM already sold more cars in China than the USA. And the world's getting ready to buy a billion more cars. That means that the world is more than a Global Village. If you're a good producer and have only 5% of the world population, unless constrained by war or inward nationalism, the way the world perceives you, is your own problem.

That's the effect of capitalism and a free, unchained, invisible hand, that you're trying to restore in energy and find a way to expand fresh water, and in turn, agriculture and food in general.

This is while we will work with companies to assure production sources somewhat split with countries like Thailand, Vietnam, Indonesia, and such. Some already have as a common business practice.

IP: But what we really must concern ourselves with is what spurs Iran to more aggressively pursuing nuclear weapons, and what happens with other countries like Syria. Or what does it take to sell their oil in a down market and how will they be able to sustain their economy without excessive oil prices. Just more reasons to get mad at the United States and/or the United States' closest ally, Israel.

President: But we did not create higher prices, or did we, to the benefit of Exxon/Mobil or Chevron? Note that a big problem we have with the Middle East is the vast resources we have in their countries or supporting their efforts in oil and gas around the world. Our expertise does mean something. American companies are all over the world exploring for shale gas and oil, or just production support like Nigeria. We have already supported other company's abilities to frack for oil. Canada, China, and others are buying into companies with that expertise. The magic has spread so fast, it is like wildfire. In spite of the opposition, properly managed, shale is an energy revolution. Coupled with energy storage, it's a world revolution, including hydrogen and dense battery proliferation.

IP: As you know, the real issue is how threatened do the oil producing countries feel that demand will diminish, and or prices will drop. And how will Exxon Mobile, Chevron, Occidental Petroleum, ConocoPhillips; Koch Industries Inc.; Marathon Oil Corporation; Sunoco Inc.; and others react to serious momentum away from petroleum and toward natural gas, hydrogen, and electric?

Will the Presidency and Congress stand strong against the lobby money and pervasive hands of manipulation and control? And it is much deeper than that: the military industrial complex, Israel's powerful lobby, the energy producing countries in Europe and South America, and how will China behave with those nations with great producing power in the Middle East, northern Africa, Brazil, Venezuela, and Argentina. You saw what happen when you took on the medical establishment. That is nothing compared to the world energy, military support, and manufacturing infrastructure in related states, even China, India, and more.

Since we are not an energy producer per say, we should reduce the challenge to one thing. Will the whims of the United States cause a military confrontation in the Middle East, and will the traditional arbitrators, whether within the OPEC nations; NATO, or the United States show any signs of weakness or disinterest in the short-term alert caused by an extreme United States announcement. How will Russia or China try to turn this into benefit to their countries? You could just do it and not talk about it. But it's too late for that.

President: We see it quite differently. How much longer will the great oil-consuming nations put up with high prices, threats of disruption, and the constant drag on their economies when they know oil is at a record reserve level and prices stay high when consumption volume is consistently at a flat line level, overall, or slightly increasing at best? Well, corporate and support infrastructure must recognize when the era of shortage scares on energy is over. We consider downside scenarios and concluded that all the internal "big issues" take precedence. Cause we are on a path to world war, if we just ride with the status quo. And of course, we won't let that happen.

Recognize, at one level, this isn't about oil, but the struggle between citizens and the dominance of lobby's and bribery money over the United States' democratic values and personal freedoms.

Our great scientists and engineers have provided us a way to maintain the status quo; we see overlapping progress in natural gas, electric, energy storage, and biofuels and feel that success in our country alone will spur activity around the world. We feel pricing has, within a few months, tapped out. We expect to have significant incentives to span out refill/distribution and are lobbying heavily with trucking and air transport to openly commit to switching to natural gas, LNG, and/or CNG, Hydrogen, Electric, and biofuels. Part of this cycle is all the internal US mayhem, which is where I'm going next.

I'm caught on one point: if hydrogen is so plentiful and is in water, and the seas are 70-98 percent of the earth's surface and depth, why do we not boil seawater for energy and water. It's so obvious, it hurts. Currently, it takes too much energy to boil water. That's, I suspect, the most important aspect of the **WE project, cheaper energy to produce water.**

I don't know. I just think ideas like that will change the world, and we need to unleash that kind of thinking. That upsets a lot of the status quo.

Just let me emphasize, the USA and NATO will never let Israel down, despite politics, changing Oil and Gas direction, and more. We will never forget WW II, the battles of the 1970's, and beyond. We also note your discovery of natural gas in the Mediterranean, as well as Cyprus's.

Nigeria

Before returning home, the presidential team visits Nigeria, the largest nation in Africa. With Over 200,000,000 people, Nigeria, is projected to grow to 392,000,000 people by 2050. They are among the poorest nations in the world, yet have a rich oil supply, with the lowest extraction cost, matched by Libya and Saudi Arabia. Like much of Africa, they are challenged by 250 ethnic groups, 500 languages, although religiously, they are 50%

Muslim, and 40% plus Christian, the rest indigenous religions. Seventy percent of their people live below the poverty line, eighty percent live in "cities", yet 70% are employed in agriculture. Life expectancy 55.5. 75% of people on the internet, with smartphones, and use social media. You can see the opportunity and see why they have serious problems with terrorism. They consider themselves a democracy, and recently had a peaceful election. Side note, they have a successful Movie business, called Nollywood, and 75% are on the internet, with smartphones. Literacy–8%, and your official language is English. Aids affects 36mm people, significant corruption, especially around the oil business and female gentile mutilation (fistula) is significant. The above description highlights the significant challenges surrounding Africa. At the same time, my bean counters tell me that Africa, in 50 years, will have half the planet's population, over four billion people, and by 2050, Nigeria will have US size population. 2050 is tomorrow.

The Nigerian President (np) welcomes the US president and his entourage:

I really appreciate you including me in your trek. I've been following the DVD's you've sent me, and it shows me the pressure the world is putting on itself.

US Pres: Well, it's appropriate that you absorb this, before you do your part in participating in blowing up the world. Quite frankly, I had a mind opening, eye opening realization that it's time to adjust our direction, and especially including Nigeria, the world must clear the air, so to speak. All our community of nations seem to act like we're on our own island, and even thou we have the north pole melting around us, we hope the planet, society, and the earth will self-adjust.

The U.S., which consumes 25% of the world's energy, is leading this self-dilution, so we must change. When you absorb this, please remind yourself that our target of cutting our energy cost by more than half, dramatically increasing fresh water supply, eliminating pollution, and improving the world economy, is a direction we all have major roles in. Nigeria can't continue to have 4.5 children per family and continue to accept poor quality air, and limited freshwater availability. Please, we understand that your society is your business, but the world is changing. I'm just trying to be open. This conversation is heartfelt and genuine.

NP...I appreciate your straightforward, dialogue. I know you know that oil is a huge part of our economy, and we need to be part of a **Water and Energy (WE)** evolution. We understand that culturally, we are at a stage that is behind the West, even Japan and China.

President: In our mind, we are allowing our worlds to adjust, even though the physical world, apparently, is tired of waiting, with China losing 4,000 people a day to pollution caused disease. Africa is threatened by massive drought and world challenging disease. On certain levels, Nigeria is under greater pressure then the USA, although our underpinning of war builds daily...Iran, Russia, N. Korea, Israel, and the threat of terrorism confounds us. Surely, the Muslim/Christian strife is a daily issue to you, I think you can see why I'm pushing our agenda so hard. It's time to change.

The US team returns home.

CHAPTER VII

The President and Congress

Upon returning to Washington DC, the President calls a joint meeting of the leadership factions of the House and Senate, including the major committee heads. They meet at 10:00 the next day.

For simplification, we will designate the parties as Dem 1, Dem 2, etc. and Repub.1, Repub. 2, etc. in the conversation.

President: Thank you for meeting so early, and I hope you have all viewed my DVD sets and the confidential brief with Saudi Arabia and Israel. I'm relieved that we've been relatively silent in the media, and that says two things: You understand the implications:

You know the enormous impact of what I will present to the American people tomorrow and the fallout, and, I am sure, the ultimate acceptance of what I am saying.

I present this as a world war, not a military one, but an economic and ecological war pitting democracy and energy productivity against poorly directed short-term money. You must maintain silence as Americans who are determined to break the gridlock. I've made it simple because besides the fact that I know we'll succeed, failure will hand you the presidency and the legislature. So why would I do that?

Why risk affronting the status quo? The answer is easy. I refuse to add any more firewood to the World War III shit storm we've been brewing since 9/11.

Repub. 1: We understand the importance, and obviously, this confidential meeting needs to be as open as possible.

Dem 1: Yes, let us let our hair down and forget, impossible as it seems, our loyalties, and most importantly, our financial contributors.

President: I believe this will go down as a key moment in American history. If you take it that way, you will be one of the patriots of our history, no matter what your position. But this gamesmanship has to stop. I should have done this four years ago, but we are under the thumb of the wrong people, and it is, quite frankly, disgusting. Now, I am under the thumb of the voters and history will show you I'm right. So, you decide...your citizens or your money interests. Either join me in the takeover or sell your souls, because it will be obvious who is enabling who.

I will provide you with the transcript at the end of this meeting, and implore you to maintain the confidentiality, which will be distributed to the media and the Internet before tomorrow's speech

Let us begin. You should know that during my trip, I had numerous confidential discussions with Americans all over the world. My assistant recorded my conversations my personal historical records. I know I should not start with detail, but for your own research, know this: a few things that are important to my conclusions have become clear over the last few months.

The EV (electric engine) and the Fuel Cell Electric (Vehicle) are far more efficient and maintainable than the internal combustion engine (ICE) by a factor of three. The simplicity of engineering and its light weight are major factors. Switching fuels, from natural gas to hydrogen, for example, generally reduces effectiveness by 25 percent. So, the math is easy. Three times the efficiency at 25 percent is .75 x 3, or 2.25 x better. And then the equation is enhanced by hybrid technology by x 2, or 4.5 x better. As battery density rises the numbers get better all the way to the EV and delivers about 200mpge, (e meaning factoring in (adding) the cost of electric recharging). If you recharge with solar energy, the efficiency numbers go through the roof, arguing that with solar panels and battery storage in the facility, the power of solar is unleashed, reducing the night and cloud cover factors.

The advent of shale gas is the inspiration, but when even small incursions into methane hydrate open the door to vast, and yes, potentially dangerous, energy capacity or we convert coal to say hydrogen. We have excess abundance, so we can carefully roll out a mix of quality product.

This leads to a discussion of battery power and mobility, a requirement of transportation. The progress that science is making at MIT, LBNL, UCLA, Princeton, University of Colorado, Minnesota, and other department of energy research affiliates (Partially listed at the last page of this book) we have moved beyond speculation. All the work invested in hybrids and EV's in the USA and China, Germany and elsewhere will pay off astronomically.

Additionally, in China and the United States in particular, the future for coal should be considered because, even with loss of power through energy conversion, this can be trumped by the electric vehicle (EV) and FCEV superiority over the internal combustion engine (ICE). Even with a power loss of up to 50 percent, the EV comes out close to three times better than the ICE, when you consider the net productivity of 100–150 mpg equivalence. And then science and engineering can spend decades enhancing the conversion and the performance superiority.

It is clear to me that the future of transportation is diversity, meaning the power suppliers and auto companies need fierce competition to maintain low cost, low distribution cost, and opportunities for innovation. So, we, the executive branch, need to not allow lack of access to results in powerful companies using monopoly power to generate higher prices of energy or equipment. We need the kind of revolution that, in terms of relative change, sparked the equipment revolution evoked by the breakup of AT&T. Of course, globalization of the economy has made this even more complicated because of the perception that size matters. But look what sprung out of Silicon Valley from say 1979-1995, just by separating the equipment aspects of telecommunications from signal, (AT&T breakup). That's who I'm aligned with. Remember, China and India may dominate the low-cost automobile market, so we need to dominate with innovation and change. Note that Apple Computer, with seventy thousand employees in America, and a million contracted workers in China is now one of the most valued (in terms of stock asset value) companies in the world and Samsung, in South Korea, a vibrant competitor, and vying for leadership. Then we have Google, who acquired Motorola mobile and the divested the hardware to China, poised as the intellectual leader who complains that the Telecom companies are not keeping up with the data streaming opportunities with gigabyte transmission speeds. So, they set up their own network in San Jose. My God, with what Google and their competitors have done, this should revolutionize any notions of higher learning, and probably K–12 not only here in the United States but all over the world, simultaneously. All the "lowliest" country has to do is join the telecom network, give its people PC's and tablets, then build and distribute some wireless towers, educate some teachers and students, and they are enabled. They could probably get it done with foreign aid and gifts from Microsoft, Apple, Intel, Dell, and Hewlett Packard. And we'll add Peace Corp workers and teachers for free.

So given all this, the world is facing a severe water shortage and an energy quagmire, at a time we are growing at an accelerating pace of one billion people every ten to eleven plus years, there is only two choices:

War at a level that will be greater than all the wars and genocides in history combined.

Change our water and energy strategy and implement "sun-gas" equivalent technologies for water and automotive fuels. NG and EV strategies can be part of the solutions around the world depending on the rate of change including battery density acceleration and dealing with low-cost NG and drilling leakage prevention progress. Further, ICE proponents will offer advanced Hybrids and offer very competitive solutions. The free market is wide open. To accomplish this, all we had to do is provide tax credits for refueling depots. Compare that to building security walls to keep out aliens.

This is what you must feel in your bones, so get onboard because I believe we and China get it. Canada and Germany get it, Japan gets it, India gets it, and on and on.

We are frustrated with the conflict of the old ways versus change. I see a new alliance with Russia, China, India, the Americas, Canada, Australia, Japan, S. Korea, and Europe, for starters. Russia will be the hardest, because they haven't spent decades providing their people with diverse manufacturing skills, compared to others.

Rep

This sounds great, but I have two issues, under the umbrella of openness of discussion. Major change will shake the foundations of our "lobby-driven" republic.

And a Middle East that operates still under World War II chieftains and money power assumptions.

In the Middle East, when a king is not in control, the army is. Both these appetites are severe and want to be fed and probably feel they can manipulate Asia, Russia, and et al., back through their supply and demand power structure. (Perhaps the army reference is widespread?)

President: Thanks for the honesty. You have keyed in on two of the primary issues. Maybe they are the most important ones.

That is why I want you to go back to your swearing in documents and remind yourself that Madison, Jefferson, Hamilton, Adams, Franklin, and others actually lived in a moment when they, with all their own prejudices and realities of their time, rose above them and tried to blend the history of England, France, Rome, and Greece and countless others to create a new paradigm of government, which is the best in the world today, as corrupt as it is.

Now I know we have messed it up a bit, but we are still in control. Except for one thing. Every ten or eleven plus years the earth adds one billion people while water resources are diminishing, even right here in the good old United States. Why have we not fixed the problem? Because the energy costs of solving the problem are too high. I understand that India spends one-half its energy supply on finding and pumping water, and they are about to pass India in population, and they still maintain a caste system. I know you may see it as a flaw, but I cannot shrug and say: "Well, do we need a world war with casualty counts in the billions? This will resolve the problem for the next hundred years, if the pandemic rising from a billion deaths or North Korean atomic bombs doesn't kill the world.

The Ogallala aquifer, spanning eight Midwestern states, is responsible for 30% of the water in the United States used for agriculture: it provides drinking water for two million people and is projected to risk being dry by 2021–2030. (Opinions vary). Ninety percent of the world's fresh water is used for agriculture.

Nature would take six thousand years to refill the Ogallala aquifer if we let it. Meanwhile, 70% of the earth's surface is saltwater, and Saudi Arabia gets 75% of its freshwater through desalination. Why? Because they have the excess high-cost energy to make it happen, and even they are researching solar with IBM to free up oil consumption.

Now, you know why I am presenting the case as I am. This is our time. Remember, Jefferson and Franklin did not sit around worrying about lobbyists. They, in an environment where the colonies barely had a semblance of cattle production and butcher shops, did not worry about the NRA not allowing us to pursue gun shipments to Mexican cartels. Goddamn it, it's time for a change. We don't want street corners to be the O.K. Corral. I'm sorry, our schools haven't taught that for 150 years. Before we act in partisan ways, please say this to yourself every morning. This is our time, perhaps the biggest moment in our history.

(The President's aide hands out the speech, and they all take a break, grab coffee, and read the material for about half an hour.)

Dem2: Like the way you are always asking to free up free enterprise? The real challenge is how we can present a solution that prevents Corporate America and the Middle East from buying the next energy and water solutions.

President: Because we in the executive and legislative branches won't allow it this is your challenge, as well as mine: remember where we came from, in 1789. I believe we need a constitutional amendment to make potential candidates' electability overcome world money. Remember, if we and China, etc. do not solve this problem, it is our fault because we now have the resources that can support change, without bankrupting us. We must overcome a lot in South America, and we cannot push Mexico and Canada around. China and the United States must reach down and meet both our needs. Why am I so confident in China? I simply don't feel they are letting us distribute McDonald's, KFCs, and Starbucks all over China so they can nationalize them, or do they have a motive to tie their best customer to an irrevocable partnership, including our worldwide dominance in mobile technology? Last year, we sold more GM cars in China than in the United States. If we don't lead the problem, I assure you Asia will, this is the Pacific Century and the three problems in our face are population growth, Water, and food. Besides food, Asia's number one priority is pollution, not weapons of mass destruction. We know it and China knows it, and India knows it. And those two countries alone are soon reaching three (3) billion people.

Rep 3: We certainly hope so, but we must go one on one and be sure.

President: That's exactly what I've been doing, and I tell you, the time is now! The way to start that is to confidently begin a change that can only benefit them through cooperation. This is because, with trust in us, our people will unleash innovation and entrepreneurial spirit that have been bottled up by our, quite frankly, self-interests and the wrong perception of where the power of America really lies. It is not by making the voter go along with our business-as-usual paradigm. Remember, we spent more than four (4) trillion dollars in war in the Middle East. How did that fix our problem in the Ogallala aquifer? Asia is ready to lead; do we want to be follower whose claim to fame **was** we spent more in military than all the world combined?

I won't say it publicly, but if someone asks "why didn't you fix this gradually?" I'd have to say we were spending all our excess money fighting or preparing for war, and the status quo didn't want change. They adjourn the meeting, which reconvenes in front of a national audience and the Congress the next day at nine p.m. EST.

CHAPTER VIII

The President Speaks to the American People

I have come to you today because I want to address our great Energy challenge with a new breath of honesty that you see as not only important, but as a line in the sand as we step toward our future. Since the 1960s and over the last 58 years, there have been several times when the executive branch of government has not been as forthright as it should. Case in point, Vietnam and Iraq both started on premises that were highly suspect: the Gulf of Tonkin in Vietnam; and the search for weapons of mass destruction in Iraq. The United States wanted a fight. We were not clear to the citizens when we supported Saddam Hussein versus Iran in the 1980s. After all, we hate them for ousting our partner, the Shah of Iran, and we supported Bin Laden against the Russians in Afghanistan. After all, he was fighting the Russians. He was against Russia, and that was good enough for us. We sacrificed our soldiers, our future, and our principles time and again. Is this just World War II hangover, a seeming brashness that ignored on-the-ground realities? What's hard to swallow is the truth. If JFK wasn't assassinated, we wouldn't have fought in Vietnam (so its speculated), and all our history would be VERY different. Cultural and economic partner shipping is replacing economic dominance, and is expanding with India, Indonesian, African, S. American, and other growth, quickly. Wake Up America!

We pursued a "guns and butter" campaign in the 1960s and early 70s that ultimately gave rise to inflation and interest rates up to 20 percent. Since 9/11 we allowed deficit spending and "lose money" policies to pay for Iraq and more, and that led to the economic mess we are now in. Of course, we spiced it up by repealing the 1933 Glass-Steagall provisions separating investing and banking. That went well, didn't it? If you recall, World War II, a credible war, was supported not only by our troops and money but our citizens experienced rationing of food and domestic goods, and for a time no commercial cars were built and more. Citizens supported the war. Yes, we built up war debt, but paid for 2/3 of it by selling War bonds to our citizens. Today, we still have the spirit but not the committed objective, and a 20 plus trillion-dollar debt we owe to China, Japan, and our own people. (And many others)

We have new challenges, which have not been clearly explained for you, and I am going to change that. You know I have been traveling around the world talking about energy and why it is time for a change.

You know we have been struggling with oil since the 1970s, but since 9/11 prices have tripled, from about one dollar eleven cents for a gallon of gasoline to three dollars and sixty cents to four dollars and fifty cents per gallon, while our consumption, largely due to our economy, until recently, has gone down. Our excuse is that it was largely because of the energy growth of China and India. But the profits soared in the American and the world's oil and gas companies. Since the 70s, when we could no longer use only domestic production to meet our needs, we have evolved to 45–50% of our needs being met through oil imports from Mexico, Canada, Venezuela, the Middle East, South America, Nigeria, and more.

One of our best exporters (to us) is Venezuela, about one million barrels a day. Our prices have increased largely due to uncertainty in the Middle East, and lack of will to change. Meanwhile reserves have grown, even though United States production rates for oil have been flat, until recently. Last year, for the first time, Saudi Arabia sent more than one million gallons of oil per day to China and fewer than a million gallons per day to the United States. Remember, most petroleum in the world is settled in American dollars. In the last decade, we produced shale oil and gas, through horizontal drilling and Fracking, and took over world production leadership in NG, and now Oil. Inflation is raising its head through food prices. Treasury financial "kick the can down the block" called Quantitative Easing (QE), funding bonds and pushing our deficits down the financial highway is suppressing the real impact of deficits. If this doesn't define a bubble, I don't know what does. Yes, we simply buy our own treasury bills, (which already is a government loan), and float bonds to some future date. We already have trillions in these bonds and were floating more to the tune of 850 million a month. Although this is diminishing, debt accumulation hasn't. More than a trillion dollars per year are interest payments. In2018, we boosted our debt by 2 trillion dollars to improve our performance and lower taxes.

This is a subject that bewilders most Americans. In the months ahead you will learn a lot about this, for the wrong reasons. Much of world trade occurs in dollars, because the currency is not volatile, including about 76%, although rapidly declining, of oil trade. You know we have 20 trillion dollars in national debt and have been operating with an unbalanced budget. This is called deficit spending. We sell treasury bills (T-bills) to the world at a current rate starting at 1.5% interest. Don't you all wish that was your credit card rate? Nations buy it because they need dollars to support their trade, because they feel we will not let the dollar become volatile. If we cannot sell T-bills, we have to make loans or stop spending money. So, a strong dollar supports lower T-bill rates. Another factor is that the US military supports the trade world it seemingly "secures" our stability. If your tankers are intercepted in the Pacific, our navy will come to your aid. The trouble spot has been pirates in Somalia, and our fleet is all over it.

Well, this is under attack, and the implications of the dollar not being the world's reserve currency is potential of massive inflation, some predict, beyond 1980, that was 20% interest rates. I have said enough on that for the moment.

You and I knew that a lot of the drag on the American economy is led by the cost of energy, and particularly, oil and petroleum. It has almost destroyed, in the past, the airline industry, and has hindered transportation, and trucking throughout the world. Energy presses on the cost of manufacturing and retail supply delivery and is the biggest single factors behind our depressed economy, and in fact, the world economy. *As I mentioned, we also see, at the same time, record profits in the oil and gas companies.* They seem to avoid the recession/depression, depending on whom you ask. It's not their fault, they just leverage the system we built for them. Yes our Shale efforts have reduced our gasoline costs substantially, but OPEC meets often to figure out how to limit supply. This is capitalism? Oh yes under the Sherman anti-trust act, its illegal, but we just "take it". That's because we believe in our shortage even though it no longer exists.

There has been significant drought in middle of the United States impacting agriculture, and corn (remember Ogallala Reserve), which feeds our meat (chicken, beef, pork). Much of the dismay in Libya, Egypt, and the Arab Spring was that although oil prices were high, now reduced because of shale, with reduced profits to their governments or kings, the cost of food for the everyday person was skyrocketing. The USA exports $796mm (2017) of agriculture to Egypt. Sixty percent of Egypt's food is imported. Corn is the staple diet for hogs and cattle including dairy cows, and more. Livestock consumes 47% of the soy and 60% of the corn produced in the United States. Some governments supplement food costs, but that did not solve the problem, they just trade oil profits for keeping the peace at home.

And it did not work. Agriculture's problem is water. With seven billion people, food and water must be stable commodities. Imagine with nine or ten billion people. How are we going there! *The United States' population went from 183 million in 1962 to 330 million in 2017. The US expects to be at 450 million by 2050.* A large amount of food exports to North Africa come from the United States, and other countries.

We must change, and I am sure you are dismayed at our seemingly unacceptable choices. Despite what you have seen and heard of as *stimulus*, economic progress in the United States is still marginal at best. One thing, after 2008, that should have been clarified by all of us, in government, is that *two-thirds of stimulus was really stopping of the economic decline.* After all, supporting police, fire, teachers, and more does not stimulate anything except the status quo and preventing a depression. I believe the American people were led to believe we were investing in growth, not anti-decline. For that I apologize for us; not for doing it, for communicating poorly. Government is too frequently afraid to be honest, and it always comes back to haunt us. That's why we want more money to stimulate growth. You hear a lot about bridges and tunnels, but we keep cutting back on government revenues.

Supply and Demand. Did I mention supply exceeds demand...something we haven't heard for 75 years, yet OPEC talks about reducing supply to raise the oil price, and we, the American people, take it. If you don't think that as un-American, you're living in a dream world. Go back to sleep, I'll wake you up when the next war starts.

So, we spent more than four trillion dollars on war in the Middle East. We let our banks invest in poorly underwritten loans, which shook our financial stability, and we absorbed tripling the cost of our transportation energy and more, even though, as I said, *the United States' consumption of fossil fuels declined in the last ten years (until recently)*. Think about it: China is buying some of our debt in T-bills while GDP growth in China persists at more than 5.5–7.5%, and that is why our transportation energy expenses have tripled. That is insane. Countries are buying our debt in T-bills, so we can secure their energy at triple, now double the price. That's insane for them. We need energy independence. Not the words, the reality. We are spending many billions of dollars extra per year so we can pay foreigners interest on our debt. And how many trillions have we spent securing the delivery of oil around the world? This is upside down logic.

Therefore, the paradigm of *demand exceeding supply* must be permanently reversed with clean supply and we need the support of the American people to change it. When energy supply is properly increased, prices will fall, it is as simple as that. We can do this quickly. Therefore, I am speaking to you today, so you can understand the dynamics of change, and what we together, are going to do about it.

This is a commitment as secure as our commitment to World War II, where the end state is practical and achievable. We had to stop Hitler, and now we must change the Water and Energy supply and create a different mix of heating, cooling, and transportation fuels, with clean supply. Most people don't realize that in 1940, Germany produced 40% of its energy artificially…no progress since 1940?

Most politicians leave things unsaid so as not to be cornered one way or the other. You know this but I am trying to open up two examples that have major relevance.

Republican (conservative)

Healthcare (Author's opinion): They believe in personal accountability. Funds can be borrowed from your job or family to help to pull yourself up by your bootstraps, it's ok to ask your family for support. It's not the role of the government to provide certainly not the role of government to provide permanent assistance. In disasters, such as floods, Tornado's, etc., its ok to provide temporary support, even block grants. But Obama care, providing so much subsidized benefits, only promotes dependency, and it's the job of family to take care of themselves.

The Dems would argue that businesses get so many tax breaks, that industries such as Aerospace, are merely corporate welfare.

So, when health care changes are proposed, the more conservative lawgivers want to cut the dependency chain, so personal accountability is restored as the American way. Of course, since the Dems created Obama care, switching to the Republican way seems to put 15-25,000,000 people unprotected.

The Republicans would say "it's ok", just change your life and everyone gets paid. Also, if you or your family raise the money to afford healthcare, and the lower premiums for all, make the care more affordable for all. The conservative opinion won't change, so finding a compromise solution is impossible. The Repubs. Would say that the Dems way institutionalizes non-accountability, and that's the problem. Meanwhile, despite all the business tax loopholes, poor people are out of luck, so the Repubs, say the Dems set poor people up by passing a law without massive consensus. And the Dems point out that all free market economies pay for citizen's healthcare, except the USA, the wealthiest country on the planet. The Repubs say USA care is better, the some say the AMA and Pharma are monopolies and have huge Lobbies that fund elections, but action is silent.

Democrats;

When social security was introduced by FDR, in the 30's it was a self-sustaining program. President Johnson, in the 1960's, with Congress, made it possible to borrow excess funds in the social security coffers to be borrowed by other budget "partners". Although all the funds were paid for at T-bill rates, this borrowing helped fund things like the Vietnam War, which ultimately drove interest rates to 20 percent. In the late 20th century, we invented "quantitative easing" to push deficits to the point where we now have over $ 20 trillion in debt. Now consider this:

Most people don't realize that in WWII, 2/3 of the cost were paid for by selling War bonds to the American people. Imagine if we asked the American people to buy Vietnam bonds or Middle East bonds. WWII bonds were like invest $18 and in 5 years, we paid you back $25. That was an honest deal where everyone was paid back. No long-term debt.

Maybe if we asked the American people to pay, we'd have fewer or shorter wars? One thing for sure, our methods since Vietnam (maybe since Korea) now has us approaching bankruptcy. The government needs to be honest with its taxpayers. After all, at the time of WW II, the government asked its people to support war, and we did. Were politicians aware that a controversial war may not be supported? We were only recently made aware that JFK was actively considering withdrawing support for Vietnam (before we lost 55,000 and the Vietnamese lost 500,000+).

In hindsight, it's easy to see how JFK, and George Bush Sr. had a more tempered view of war, since they were part of WWII. Remember it was Bush Sr. who refused to close on Hussein, because it was not part of the UN mandate. All the following leaders, Johnson and Bush Sr., had a legacy to live up to. (Perhaps even Trump with his, now volatile, military cabinet). What seems clear is, with JFK, had he lived, we would have a completely different history, although our addiction to oil dragged us to the negative.

You'll see the relevance later, but we can't lie, the Facebook and tweeter world are upon you, which I guess means our leaders speak to you, unedited. Now, the Russians have exploited the new media to disrupt our elections. Let's turn a new leaf, and lead with the truth.

One of the great things about America is the government and entrepreneurs often invest in change, and the public benefits: computer chips, the Internet, cell phones, satellites, and much, much more. This has been going on at a steady pace since World War II, and in fact, much of basic United States baseline technology has department of energy funding involved in many of our universities throughout the United States. In many cases we, (the tax payers) own the institutions. You have heard a little about Shale gas and new discoveries of Natural Gas that have made the United States the largest producer of natural gas, and now oil, in the world, a distinction previously held by Russia and Saudi Arabia. This was not a *discovery*. Politicians often argue that private enterprise is more effective than government, but don't point out that we've funded energy research since WWII (1945). I should point out that this surge occurred during President Obama's administration. He couldn't deny the advantages of "self-reliance."

Our history with shale oil and gas goes back to 1821, with specific grants and tax benefits flowing to natural gas partners since the 1970s. It turns out that in 1998, the diamond drills, the art/science of horizontal drilling, and hydraulic Fracking came together so that effective mining could occur. Much credit for the investment in shale oil drilling is given to Mitchell Energy in Texas. In the 1980s and 1990s the company pioneered new technology for *horizontal drilling of shale for natural gas (ng)*. This technique, combined with hydraulic fracturing of rock, makes it possible to economically extract natural gas and oil from shale rock formations. The new approach has been widely adopted by the gas industry and spawned a new gas boom in North America. The Potential Gas Committee estimates that US recoverable reserves will last 118 years at current production levels assuming the current mix of use.

Extracting from shale rock is rapidly spreading to countries outside the United States. Some consider Mitchell's innovation important in the context of energy security, making the United States less dependent on foreign sources of energy. Mitchell Energy Development Corp. was later acquired by Devon Energy. Prior to this, natural gas was in decline, and the forces of **government grants and tax allowance** together with entrepreneurial market proponents made the research and experimentation happen. We now lead the world in natural gas, and oil.

For the moment, allow the evidence to show that hydraulic Fracking can occur without endangering water resources in our wells. The fear is that gas will flow through the shale and into the watershed we drink from. Give me that, for the moment. It is manageable, and it has been certified by the EPA in Pennsylvania (July 2012) a continuing process. Yes, risk must be managed by the states and EPA. The United States and individual states make testing and certification a priority, despite Congress exempting companies involved in shale on a wholesale basis. (The USA Energy Act loophole.) We will show you that regulation is important to the credibility of our mining efforts. (Author opinion) This type of legislative chicanery is, in hindsight, failure to see the big picture at best, although the big picture includes our ascension to be the world energy production leader.

The story is much bigger than that because all over the world, and in particular in China, India, Canada, Mexico, Argentina, Australia, nations have discovered many large deposits of shale oil and gas. In fact, it is big enough to call it "an energy revolution".

To really forecast a revolution, however, you need to see that the resource can overcome risks, such as the analytical models being to zealous, or careless processes causing methane leakage. However, there has been decades of research on methane hydrate, another capture of methane, in the porous ice at the bottom of the ocean and on land in ice in the northern permafrost. According to one conservative academic calculation, Earth's *conventional* (including shale formations) reserves of natural gas hold 2,331 billion tons of gas. Earth's reserves of oil contain 160 billion tons. Earth's reserves of coal contain 675 billion tons: taken together, this equals 3,186 billion tons of fossil fuel. But Earth's methane hydrates contain 3,000 billion tons of carbon-based methane; and more. Methane hydrates are found at larger and larger volumes the deeper you drill. ConocoPhillips drilled (tax deductible) 830 meters for its field test at Prudhoe Bay, Alaska. Prudhoe Bay Oil Field is a large oil field on Alaska's North Slope. Earth's reserves of this resource could theoretically reach millions of trillions of cubic feet.

(Source: EIA Annual Energy Outlook 2011, followed by massive growth of shale gas and Methane hydrate.)

In other words, the forecasts of shale gas do not stand alone; they are augmented by the potential for methane hydrate, the largest fossil fuel source on earth. Then if the coal industry became a producer of gas and liquid hydrocarbons that would also play into the paradigm *supply exceeds demand*, demonstrating low cost and high use! The forecasted volumes are in excess of what is needed to transform the paradigm of energy transportation, electricity generation, and heating in America and the world. By keeping natural gas prices low, the oil and gas industry can take over United States power generation from the coal industry. So, coal could choose to change its objective to produce gaseous and liquid methane to guarantee our capacity to generate all the natural gas we need. Even shipping coal to say China will rapidly diminish. The national and international focus on natural gas and hydrogen as a strategic resource can cause an energy revolution by causing energy productivity to cut our costs in half. If China provides its own focus, together it will cause an energy revolution and an economic upturn around the world. And now electric cars and hybrids are dominating planning all over the world. China is now the largest manufacturer of electric cars with Warren Buffet as a contributing investor.

Remember, you often hear congressional complaints about regulation like its government overhead hurting productivity. But October 2008 recession happened because Congress and the executive branch passed laws to loosen regulation and oversight. So, the financial disaster occurred because we reduced regulation (and common sense) and began making loans to people who couldn't pay. Why? USA Congress, big hearts, no brains. As soon as interest rates rose, the house of cards came down. So, we need regulation, and efficiency is desirable, but America doesn't fare well when the balance of power is usurped by people who don't understand deposits and loans. That's why more than 97% of banks didn't make these loans' they were smart, and the 3% of so-called super-banks insisted on making bad loans and protecting them with investment instruments that bet against the loans. To be fair, many of these loans were from acquired S&Ls and the government pressured the Banks to acquire them. But the government had nothing to do with the packaging and selling the loans worldwide. This is what anyone with sense calls "conflict of interest" investors betting against lenders. **(What–from the same institutions?)**

The answer was to lower regulation. That's like playing Russian roulette. If it doesn't kill you, add three more bullets and try again. That's what happened on October 2008. We filled up the chambers and pointed the gun at ourselves. We had fixed the problem in 1933, but now we have computers, which led to a higher volume of stupidity. That is Congress's definition of efficiency.

Now we have Dodd-Frank, which makes it tough for small institutions, while the too big to fail syndrome persists.

The primary issue with natural gas is not volatility or fear of explosion. This is addressed. It is when converted to compressed natural gas (CNG) there is a loss of efficiency. In natural gas's natural state, it is extremely light, but its physical size makes compression desirable in vehicles. With natural gas selling for about $2.30 per million BTUs, its energy equivalent price for a barrel of oil would be $13.34, or 87 percent below the price of WTI oil (at $103/barrel, now at $50.00, so oil is only three (3) times more expensive). When measured on an energy equivalent basis, natural gas has never been cheaper than it is today. As to cost equivalence:

Price difference nat gas and oil
Source EIA: Price Difference Natural Gas versus Oil

Forbes reports that major oil and gas companies Chevron and Exxon Mobil will continue drilling for natural gas, even with record low prices, with Chevron planning to double its production in the Marcellus region. Why? *They are winning the war with the market.* This is an opportunity market for oil and

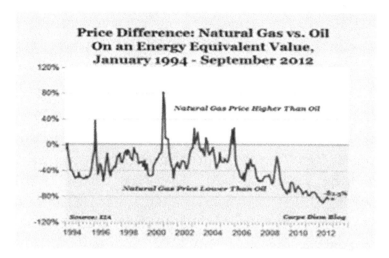

gas to have net new business. It is happening rapidly, so the coal industry has to re-strategize. They spend millions on advertising for a lost cause. But Americans must see this as a clear opportunity.

Remember, we are not necessarily looking for the ultimate answer such as atomic fusion or even energy creation (sun-gas), we are looking for a sustainable bridge. This is not wishful thinking; it is hardened research, backed by your tax dollars. And the industry is looking at solar recharge units spread around the travel centers and freeways that could recharge batteries in a half hour for free because they are solar-based batteries. In high-volume applications, car batteries should be swappable like a high-tech barbeque (propane tanks). This can only be done with massive density improvement and weight reduction, which adds to my refueling scenario. But the real impetus behind *natural gas* is innovations in efficiency. Here is an example, which I am providing to show you how dynamic the alternative fuel market can be. Natural gas, when converted to fuel cells that operate from hydrogen, can make the case for a bridge to hydrogen over time. The big question on natural gas vehicles is efficiency. But innovation is the solution. For example, what is the best use of natural gas for transportation? Pardon my detail, but you must see that the key to real game changing decisions is realizing the opportunity of a competing innovation like this.

Is it better to burn that in an internal combustion engine, natural gas vehicle (NGV), or is it better to decide that natural gas can make hydrogen for a fuel cell electric vehicle (FCEV)? Converting natural gas to hydrogen is the clear winner for two reasons: less natural gas will be required to travel a given distance, and hydrogen in a FCEV will create less well-to-wheels greenhouse gases than burning the natural gas in an NGV (natural gas vehicle). First consider efficiency. The steam reforming process to convert natural gas to hydrogen is approximately 75% efficient on a lower heating value basis, meaning that 25% of the energy is wasted in converting natural gas to hydrogen.

But a FCEV is up to three times more energy-efficient than an internal combustion engine. This is equivalent to 69.1 mpg of gasoline on an energy-equivalent basis. Now add hybrid technology. It's so easy to reach 100 mpge.

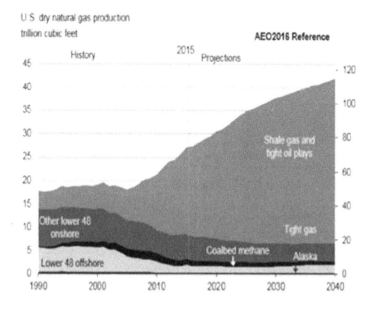

This logic would also apply to converting coal to hydrogen and compensates for the inefficiency lost in the coal conversion. The reason is a fuel cell vehicle is essentially a converter of hydrogen to electricity, and the electric motor is far more efficient than an internal combustion engine (ICE). So, you can have a fuel that is less efficient then say gasoline, but the motor is far more efficient than the ICE. This is because electric motors lose very little power from friction, they also make more torque at a lower rpm than gas engines, they also require little maintenance, and pollute less. With hydrogen fuel, a FCEV is more efficient, more reliable, and cleaner burning than an internal combustion engine. Cleaner burning? I repeat, its emissions are water. Why don't we switch. **There is no place to refuel (gas stations). Acquired data from the oil and gas industry.** Keep in mind I just showed you three sources of fuel, each large enough to efficiently power cars, trucks, and airplanes. And we haven't *even* discussed biofuels. Look at supply, and you immediately see the NG/hydrogen side of the picture. Airplanes can spend time to optimize, if we take care of cars and trucks. This is especially true given that Asia and others will add one (1) billion cars over the next 20–30 years.

For any of this to be true, you must decide to invest in both the technology and its distribution system. A natural gas distribution system can front end the natural gas to an FCEV system supplying both alternatives. That is until innovations on the FCEV make the NGV or the ICE obsolete. Simply tap your home heating gas and convert it to hydrogen in your garage. Every night or so, plug in your natural gas/hydrogen converter and fill up your vehicle. And then there's the electric car! Tesla is feverishly creating recharging stations, but a comprehensive refueling strategy is necessary. Given this path with variable innovation time, *the solution is to convert to hydrogen through natural gas vehicles and fuel cell electric vehicles. FCEV's are electric cars with hydrogen fuel tanks.*

So, with all this opportunity, what are the main barriers to moving forward? There are three.

We need an expanded distribution system to make compressed natural gas (CNG) as accessible as petroleum. Further, we need to be able to tap home, office, and retail pipelines to make a superior pipeline system for cars and trucks. The system must support multiple fuels and battery charging, including the adaptation of a FCEV converter (NGV to hydrogen already exists). It just needs to be priced for the next billion cars.

We know there will be plenty of retrofitting of transportation systems to integrate safe natural gas vehicles in our world. Fortunately, there are already 25+ million vehicles in the world running on natural gas. The United States is using only several hundred thousand NGVs. You've seen them increasingly as local buses, airport taxis, and many commercial applications. Now electric is presenting itself.

We need the American people to see this large view and recognize that the key factor for the first years of this century is that supply of transportation energy has to exceed demand, as opposed to the current state where (cartel imposed) demand exceeds supply *by design*. This is not the ideal green solution we have been looking for, but it is a bridge to our goal with immediate environmental benefits (e.g. replace coal with natural gas and significantly expand the use of natural gas or hydrogen or pure electric in trucks, automobiles, and yes, airplanes, or step toward clean with natural gas hydrogen converters for cars).

It may appear suspicious to step to green with a fossil fuel. What is needed is a government that assures the public that it won't loophole its way to quality extraction e.g., the "Energy Act loophole"—the clean air act exempts Fracking/horizontal drilling from inspection, i.e. mining and extraction regulation.

Remember: Any time we wanted, say, thanks to our friends in S. Africa, we can manufacture gasoline from natural gas. Yet our political actions are upside down. Why?

We should be ashamed, because it proves lobby money rules and the public be dammed. This is probably the first time you heard of this. Now ask, who does your representatives work for? Next time you hear them quote the constitution, check their voting record. They really vote for the status quo to ensure the cash for re-electability, which must be addressed, i.e. lowering the cost of elections. Of course, if our total GDP and productivity grew, we may be able to see more clearly. (Sorry for the diversion, but it's complicated and that's why we need Congress people who are supposed to pay attention.)

Now let us look at some other benefits.

Lack of military support will be assured for our energy supply. This is United States product, so think about the immense savings of cost and lives. Think of how many times we won't have to compromise our values to support a foreign supplier whose allegiance might change? Think of our independence.

The multiplier effect as the world changes with us would clearly lead to a march to clean and save our real green-*money*. Given a comprehensive approach, 100–150 mpg equivalence mean our energy costs would be cut in half (at least). We could invest $50 to $100 billion in raising the storage capacity or density of batteries to assure maximum productivity benefits. Don't worry, this is just an "option". An open system would clearly create funding.

And a cleaner environment at lower cost with significant progress toward a clean planet and economic recovery tied to lower cost fuel and the massive, reduced emissions. (Clean water and air). Think of China's health benefit.

We are tired of the debate over global warming. The real concern you should have is over global war. We have made more than four trillion dollars down payment in war. It is too expensive and ineffective. Many Islamic leaders want us out of the Middle East. Nothing has changed except for more unrest in the Middle East. Quite frankly, since and including Korea, we haven't succeeded in war since. In a codependent and vulnerable society, war doesn't work, except almost bankrupting the USSR when they cried uncle. That was a Reagan strategy that hopefully will work, given the tenuous state of democracy in Russia.

Now take 50% of the benefit from lower energy costs and apply it to freshwater generation. Fifty percent energy cost reduction, 25-50% water reinvestment applied across America or the world, and we have our green revolution financed by Energy productivity. Reminder, Asia says it needs a billion more cars, worldwide.

A 10% share is 100,000,000 cars. What if it was greater?

In 2016, 17.55 million cars were sold in America (all sources). A USA target of 100 mm cars in Asia would be a fair goal!

Now there are other larger questions to be answered, so let us consider...What about China and India.

Will China and India leverage our action into deeper relations with the Middle East? We think the market for oil and gas is a viable market. The suppliers have to be price competitive in an open market of supply and demand. One of the new terms you have to absorb is paradigm change, a change in fundamental understanding, like when automobiles began replacing horses.

This age is a *new paradigm,* where CNG and LNG and other nat-gas or hydrogen fuels become the dominant source of electricity and vehicle fuel. Petroleum will earn its way back into competition through efficiency, cleanliness, and price. What you need to understand is that energy supply will transform over ten to fifteen years, and that is okay. But right up front we will begin progressing, with supplies exceeding demand. This means the goal of expanding distribution (for example, alt. fuel depots) is of the highest priority. And we have source agreements in America to handle the flow of oil and petroleum right now, if we greatly reduced Middle East imports, to compensate for not buying fuel from the Middle East.

Fracking is also *increasing oil supply* from Canada, Mexico, the United States, and in a few years, Australia. As a rebuff, the Middle East could lower prices by half. Let them, we will march forward at lower cost to assure continuous long-term productivity and emission reduction through higher gas mileage. The expected revamping of energy storage will raise the productivity of gasoline ICE autos. But as the benefits of FCEVs, EV's, and Hybrids will quickly manifest themselves; consumers will evolve out of ICE and gasoline. With only 50% conversion including a commitment of trucking, the savings and productivity will dramatically lower oil consumption and price and reduce pollution.

We may ask what about Israel? America and Europe are and always will be strong supporters of Israel. Israel is not a major energy producer, so they get no downward impact from revenue loss. Beyond that, the United States is their strongest ally. They knew this paradigm shift had to happen. After all, does anyone think we would accept $100–$200 per barrel fuel costs for a sustained period? *You see, 2002–12 is what we call a decade of an energy bubble, which was bound to pop.* With the American people behind this shift, Israel knows our steadfast support. It would be very foolish for a country neighboring Israel to think the West is not resolute in its support of Israel. We back our resolve with blood, money, and military power.

And just to be clear, this support has no limit. We trust our ally, we supply arms to our ally, and we respect their security and wisdom. If Iran attacked, the United States, along with NATO, would respond with full force. If they resort to stupidity to save oil, we will evolve faster.

The real issue of Israel is layered, but its roots go back from the Crusades to World War II. Underneath it, the Middle Eastern Islam countries have been slow to provide the diverse economy they need, and the culture defines the role of men and women differently. This is anathema to the west, but the solution over the long term is education and political change. You have to wonder whether the Arab Spring will influence that. Since it seems clear that Sharia law will dominate, we can assume that their "democracy" is not what we perceive or would like it to be. Islamic countries do not believe in separation of church and state. Israel, to a large extent, is a country of immigrants from Europe for the most part, and Middle Eastern Jews. It is a western state physically in an eastern culture. Their biggest threat is that they are physically small and their population is 7.8 million people, about 15 million Jewish people worldwide. Islam in all sects is 1.6 billion worldwide. Israel cannot even consider the idea of a nuclear explosion in their country. Israel could fit into Florida eight times: 263 miles long, north to south, and a width of nine miles at one point and seventy-one miles at another (east to west). So, they will not let nuclear weapon capability exist anywhere near hurling distance to their borders, including short-range missiles. It is that simple and it is irreconcilable. Meanwhile, economically, their country thrives even with no oil and gas industry.

I should note that Israel has discovered deep reserves of gas in the Mediterranean, as did Cyprus. So the only real hope is economic prosperity within the Islamic countries, which has to move beyond oil and gas. With lowered pricing assured, the only hope of Islamic people is the better distribution of income from the petrol business into emerging industries and education. No matter how you turn it, this is the only bridge to the reality of peace and prosperity. Meanwhile Israel will persist and defend itself vigorously, and the West will defend Israel's independence and freedom. This is very clear to the West and there is no compromise. If the Middle East wants Armageddon, it will be contained to the Middle East. In other words, radical Islam can be self-destructing if it chooses, but the west will disengage from the oil business if it has to. Of course, the preferred solution is for the Islam nations to use their oil and gas profits to build a new social structure and economy. Let Saudi Arabia lead you in massive desalination and begin to evolve.

Peaceful Islam should be a brotherhood with the United States, Europe, and Israel, for that matter, not manipulated oil policy. They could use our help in water initiatives and education.

What about Saudi Arabia and Iran? The Saudis have known for a long time that this type of action would occur. The world energy consumption is rising, and improved cost effectiveness will make US energy consumption rise with our recovered economy. Air transportation will boom with profitability, and all forms of economic transportation and leisure travel will excel. The Saudis, besides having huge gaseous reserves, will leverage their position into the improved economy they serve. Now they have to compete on price, cleanliness, and efficiency. They have already used their profits to provide 75 percent of their freshwater through desalination. They should lead the rest of the Middle East out of the desert.

They, of course, will continue to strengthen ties to China, but China cannot let the United States dominate the lower cost, cleaner fuel paradigm just when China is growing their power consumption with coal, oil, and gas. They need these efficiencies as much or more than we do! With four times our population, they could achieve over four times our benefit:

population plus economic improvement which leads to more energy consumption. China can't ignore pollution and its market ties to Europe and the United States, their best customers. Upon reflection, the United States, Russia, and China have real synergy and common problems. What can tie them together is a Water and Energy strategy. Leveraging all three nations' geophysical differences, we all have common water problems relating to food production, the real definer of the 21st century Water and Energy relationships. China and Russia can't ignore it. China has a big question. Do they want to build out a million plus automobiles with obsolete ICE technology with high pollutants? With their needs, they have to change their demand for more, into a quest for different, and they can't do it alone. They need to invest their real needs into Germany and the USA. An impossible marriage? When you see the alternatives breaking down to war, it's a real choice.

Iran has to reconcile their position as an energy provider and a robust business partner. We will no longer have an energy embargo on them because supply of oil energy is no longer a limitation in the world. Iran needs to realize that this market action is inevitable. If they progress to nuclear weapons, Israel will destroy their nuclear manufacturing capability. If they care about their people and their history, they will change, or their people will revolt. However, the current embargo placed on Iran by the allies is being circumvented by direct sales to India with Gold and Rupees and sales to China denominated in Yuan. The United States currently settles under 76% of world oil in US dollars. But this is rapidly declining. But the United States' and the dollar's future can truly be guaranteed by a booming and robust economy that works with its Asian partners. The water and energy strategy will ultimately tie the United States, Russia, China, Europe, and the Middle East into a Water and Energy economy, part of the Pacific century, with lower cost fuel and abundant fresh water in every port on the Pacific Rim: the Americas; Japan; Russia; China; the Indo–China nations (Korea, Vietnam, Laos, Thailand, etc.); India; Indonesia; New Guinea; Australia; and New Zealand. This is the return on the recognition that Water and Energy are intimately wed; and it can only occur with clean low-cost energy and an integrated Water and Energy strategy.

Aggressiveness with Iran may very well be the catalyst for the whole United States oil house of cards coming down. If the United States loses this, the motivation to buy US T-bills is diminished, and it could spur interest rates beyond the 1970s. So our entire money printing exercise over the last ten years collapses and the United States faces financial catastrophe that could exceed the depression of the 1930s. With that in our sights, the alternative is war. Note that the problem with food costs is then spurting out of severe inflation, Quantitative Easing 3, the last hurrah of the old school. Later you will see that we can address this.

But a robust water and energy strategy across the world will stabilize currencies and lead to an integrated currency pool. It's easy to fix once the key players "change the mix" of Water and Energy. It is the hallmark of the Pacific century. The US can adjust to this if we have a robust economic plan, led by a workable Water and Energy plan, meaning lower cost and higher clean efficiency.

Likewise, all dominant energy users will respond to the economic uplift from lower priced and cleaner energy. Energy suppliers will adjust to new pricing dynamics which will still produce profitable returns due to the rise in consumption. For example, most people do not realize that oil is extracted out of

Libya for about one dollar per barrel. Nigeria and Saudi Arabia also have easily "tap able" reserves; maybe not that inexpensive, but with plenty of profit margin. *The point is that profitability is not under a major cost constraint for the Middle East,* obscene profitability is. Additionally, in the unlikely event OPEC should drop their price to under $20 per barrel for oil, market pressure would keep the cost of natural gas or derivative energy sources low, *so the winner is the consumer and consumption. That is the goal for citizens and business.*

You can choose to use petroleum and an ICE. Who knows, maybe oil will drop to $20 per barrel and $1 per gallon. Over the post–World War II period, the median for the domestic and the adjusted world price of crude oil was $20.53 at 2010 price equivalence. However, if the market price was $20 per barrel, obviously Saudi Arabia, Iran, etc. would consider every possibility to raise the price, since they don't accept the free market. The only choice is to let "lack of demand" leave them no choice. US oil and gas companies also would have to believe that the markets are in control. That is the point. US citizens have to choose alternatives that they believe are the right, price and environmentally sound, and didn't impact the food markets or cause a reduction in water.

So, step back and realize what's happening. Success is augmented by three factors:

Methane Hydrate, equal to all fossil fuels combined, with only a partial implementation would assure that a strategy of natural gas, hydrogen, and methane hydrate would oversupply demand resulting in the first time since 1973 **that clean supply** exceeds demand. The implementation of a battery density project, already underway, would grow capacity by 3, then 5 current levels. This would foster, through hybrid and electric cars at a minimum of 100–150 mpg, that even with gasoline, reduce carbon emissions by 2/3. The multiyear target would be towards hydrogen, producing these and simple evolution.

But now with Syn-Gas and Sun-Gas., it's time to rewrite the 21st Century. That's because we can make hydrogen fuel out of water H20 two parts hydrogen and one-part oxygen

This strategy would phase out the coal business *in its current form.*

NG presently is absorbing 50% of the fuel fired plants, expected to displace coal anyway in the next 20 years. Coal can create a liquid and/or gaseous fuel, hydrogen, which again would harmonize the objective of reducing fuel to a clean fuel and costs to under $1.00 per gallon or under $20 per barrel.

China's GIANT sub issue (perhaps as a reminder), is the overwhelming problem of pollution. With all the noteworthy progress they have made in "clean coal", it's not making a dent on pollution, in real terms, as opposed to statistical progress. Wearing gas masks in their cities is now commonplace. It was recently noted that they are losing 4,000 people per day to pollution. That's an Iraq war every day and a half, in USA casualty terms.

This trifecta would revolutionize the productivity and effectiveness of fuel, even with only a 50% penetration, but would follow with China, the Euros, Japan and others following and would result in the success of the clean energy movement in less than 20 years. The key to success is the using ½ of the 50% cost reduction in supporting a worldwide fresh water initiative, e.g., desalination and other initiatives, which would support the billion–person population increase in the next 10–12 years, and clear the world agenda to eliminate famine, drought, and pollution, and boost all economies by reducing cost of clean fuel. We could double our agriculture output.

The United States is not acting out of any anti or pro anything. We just are recognizing that, after years of government supported business research and development, we have harnessed multiple sources of gaseous power and are creating a strategy that includes coal, natural gas, and or pure electric EV. WE chose to provide choice to allow states to set a direction, an evolution, if I may say so. A paradigm is a model that forms a basis of something, especially one that forms the basis of a methodology or theory like how to power airplanes and automobiles. Support natural gas or hydrogen for transportation and your energy costs will drop and the economic or environmental impact will be vastly improved. Then aim of energy productivity savings, in conjunction with solving the fresh water challenge, would be a rebirth of the 21st century.

The competition herein will ignite the kind of innovation from one single fact: the United States will invest in expanding the transportation fuel distribution system, so the baseline for natural gas/ hydrogen/electric innovation is set. Just watch our innovations soar. You just need to follow through. We should be proud when government supported private-sector pioneers see the opportunity and choose innovation. I know I'm not supposed to say it, but you get big returns on your tax dollars, and likewise from your elected representatives. Next, follow solar recharging of electric batteries or swappable battery "sleeves", it will energize electric cars and plug-in hybrids and leverage the fusion age, where electricity is king. In other words, we can evolve without rebuilding again.

What about the oil and gas industry in the United States and the world oil markets? The great American and international companies are behind this initiative, and in fact they are participating in shale oil and gas exploration all over the great nations of the world. Remember, oil and gas have been advertising about their role in leading edge research and development for alternative energy for decades. Our positive results in shale and methane hydrate are with their deep involvement. If we the people decide to embrace change, oil and gas either competes, innovates, and responds, or it become the consumer railroads of the 20th century. It's time to reinvent themselves, at half their unit cost, and more than double the volume. That's market dynamics, which exists for committed players.

This is not the first time we went through major changes. But we are in a global market and we helped create a global village. So, the world is now in a time of energy change, once again through the work between the Energy dept., University partners, Industry, and countries like Canada. China, Germany, Japan, and South Korea we are ready to lead the world out of the energy doldrums and into the Water & Energy era of lower cost, low pollution, and the clean planet. Success IS WITHIN OUR GRASP'.

The companies that embrace the change will have a world market to embrace their expertise and a new basis for innovation. In the 1970s, there were about 170 million cars in the world. Now there are more than 1 billion, and it is expected to rise to 2.5 billion cars by 2050. That is staggering growth that electric vehicles, EVs, FCEV, and hybrids will have to address. Yes, we should all ride trains, but the projections are what they are. How many cars and trucks do we sell in the next billion? In the olden times, if you acquire any wealth you probably would buy a horse, now it's a car. The year 2050 is less than forty years away. You see, the oil and gas companies believe in low-cost natural gas, because with it, they can take over the coal based power plant business. They did not see, however, that it could be the fuel for the entire transportation business and ultimately drive the entire FCEV, hydrogen revolution and the EV (Electric vehicle) revolution and by reinvesting some of the savings, funding the entire water desalination business. Gaseous vehicles along with high-density energy storage will change the world, spur our and world economies, and provide a basis of water and energy change around the world.

Instead of 2.35 times the fuel productivity of natural gas converted hydrogen in FCEVs, let us hold it to 1.5 times better and invest .85 of the improvement, in desalination and water reconstitution...Change the world. Ah yes, call water and energy a dream, but it is civilization we are saving. It is not a dream but a requirement. And our own innovation is the basis of reengineering our energy, freshwater, and farming, and support of our increased populations.

If African population growth is reality, failure to change can only lead to pandemic disease. History has shown us (AIDS, EBOLA, etc.) That Africa's "rich" climate, plus forthcoming massive population is a great place for resources and pandemics. They need to join and anticipate with the modern world. And they will.

The transition between NG and hydrogen is about the effectiveness and economics of converting saltwater to hydrogen and fresh water. Probably dependent on wind and solar power and the ocean as a conversion resource. What about too much salt? If that was our only problem, deal me in.

Remember, these realizations are not just some lucky find. The federal government and private sector have been at the center of this discovery for decades. In fact, the United States, in the last five years, has become the largest natural gas producer in the world, and thanks to joint efforts, huge findings in China, Russia, Australia, European nations like Poland and England are all in the forefront of natural gas discovery. US companies are spreading the revolution. The major constraint of a country is if the country has no pipelines to move natural gas and cannot afford to establish pipelines. LNG (liquid natural gas) conversion provides even more options. Additionally, oil sands drilling is expanding United States and Canadian oil (with a clean energy mandate). In the Mediterranean, Cypress has a gas find that could pull them out of economic depression and challenge Russia for the European natural gas business.

Capitalism with social security is not socialism. It is our attempt to provide a safety net to both senior and citizens in general services such as healthcare, and a base level of living standards that smooth out the ripple effect in a "free" society. The USA formula is freedom is our dominant personality, and our leadership in World commerce with clean Water and Energy (**WE**) is our direction. The realization is that economies are not perfect, and life is not perfect, and humans are not perfect is worth some financial security for our people, perhaps a contribution of our Judeo-Christian moral history. The only question is how much, as balanced with our need for personal and societal accountability.

Simply stated, if retraction from the world marketplace is our strategy, we are participating in the worst strategy since shying away from using fire as a positive resource.

And, by the way, we approve the Keystone XL pipeline with safety provisions. You see, expanding oil is no longer a threat to energy, clean and green. It just adds to the rapidly declining petroleum prices once supply of clean transportation fuel is greater than demand. And it must be clean. We recognize the problem of oil sands is "dirty oil". It will be cleansed. The pipeline will serve as a southern pipeline as we create Liquid National Gas (LNG) for sales in Europe, S America, and Africa. And else ware while we transition USA fuel mix. And while we fix that, offer Venezuela help with their heavy oil. I'm also speaking today for a special announcement. Several years ago, we engaged the US Air Force Office of Scientific Research (Princeton University lab) and the US Dept. of Energy to find a true way out of this fuel and environmental quicksand. They simply knocked on the doors of major research labs across the country and asked scientists to develop their own prototypes to help speed up the process. After a decade, they have secured several ways to convert solar rays and water to hydrogen fuel and Natural Gas (NG) to gasoline. The list of participating labs in Minnesota, Colorado, New Mexico, plus the work in MIT, LBNL California, Northwest National Laboratory, Washington (state), leads to one conclusion. We are now able to transform many fuel resources by reconfiguring their elements for a specific purpose. This allows us to harness sun, wind, and other energy sources and convert them to hydrogen fuel and then store them for future use. A breakthrough to all partially available (wind, sun, etc.) energy sources. Hydrogen fuel is designed for Fuel Cell Electric Vehicles (FCEV) leaving only H20 as an exhaust. This will create a true strategy of a clean inexpensive fuel that will meet our economic and environmental objectives. We have discussed this world wide and have Canada and Germany as global partners. **We will** present this over the next year and start unfolding a **Hydrogen. Pure electric or denser battery, and ecologically positive strategy that we call a WE strategy** (Water & Energy) meaning we will use this science a cost reduction to address the fresh Water and agricultural shortages worldwide. Get it? Save money on Energy and spend money on desalination- a direct net savings that also fixes the planet.

We just knew, as the world's largest energy consumer, we needed to step forward so that the paradigm shift would occur. We would not do this without careful consideration of all the impacts that change has all over the world. But we really cannot ignore the facts. Our earth, our science, and our entrepreneurial efforts were rewarded just when we needed a boost: one that will lead to cleaner, lower-cost energy and allow us to continue our evolution to a clean and energy rich nation, as well as improved world economics. The market will decide the efficiency of natural gas to hydrogen or the rapidity of electronic battery storage density improvement. The United States will fund the progression of R&D along with private enterprise, and the innovators will win. Once we commit to natural gas distribution, the forces of innovation are unleashed. American innovation is back in the forefront. You, the citizens, are back in charge.

The equation for energy evolution is simple: **clean supply > demand.**

The other subject I felt I must discuss in depth with you is water. You know that the effects of climate change, whether permanent or not, leave us at the mercy of droughts and other natural disasters. This is another global problem, but we are using this change to leverage technology to address a series of options, wherever possible. Here are some of the related actions we will address. What if, for example, natural gas or hydrogen fuel was only 1.5 times efficient and the difference was invested in freshwater for agriculture, biofuels, fracking, and expanded living choice?

From this point forward, all energy and chemical initiatives must determine if there is a water adjunct. That means because our incoming assumption is to drive the cost of energy downward, most generator projects will include a steam capture and recycle aspect so that water can be produced as a by-product. This has a lot to do with the coal to gas initiatives with power plants and any nuclear plants. As we convert from coal to gas, we want to create desalination wherever possible. This is funded through the leveraging of some of the savings in automotive fuel. In other words, from the outset, a Water and Energy strategy is an integrated strategy that considers the value add of desalination or other water creation initiatives. It varies from project to project but is really measured by the degree of agriculture, biomass, solar, and, in effect, water needed. This, for example, has to be jointly measured by a green strategy for both sides of the southwest United States Mexico border. Think WE and it will be better for US (A).

Now excess CO_2 can be liquefied and enter the debate on how to make Fracturing safer, and less water intense. Of course, we could choose to keep high prices and pay dearly to combat pollution and create fresh water. Think about it. Will the current trends lead to war, or should we open the door to a new future? Obviously, we think we should change.

We have talked to China, India, and other countries that are deep into coal, and we will share R&D and investments where practical. The primary role of coal, once displaced by natural gas, will be to develop a low-cost coal-to natural-gas and/or hydrogen process and feed the local hubs of natural gas or hydrogen collection. By design, natural gas will fit into an array of small to medium-sized companies, as well as the natural gas arms of the oil and gas conglomerates. We will ask all related chemical and gas and thermal producing organizations to consider opportunities to consolidate or reuse H2O in their plans, buoyed by tax incentives. We will ask our attorney general to propose a legal model that permits competition without mass consolidation. In general, we are to be very rigorous about evaluating and assuring that the oil and gas business has no cartel involvement and operates to assure the evolution of the water and energy model. You may say, why a global strategy? The answer is we're good at it, and a trustworthy partner, if we keep out of other countries affairs, and control our weakness to greed.

We recognize that eventually fusion operations as well as hydrogen could require large organizational structures, but will let the marketplace decide, yet under strong anti-trust enforcement. Shale, as with any other energy initiatives, requires water, or apparently liquefied CO2, so the integration of a water action plan is part of the new paradigm (e.g. water used for Fracking is recycled and purified so we have more efficient capacity. We will also assure, by law, that Fracking chemicals are not permitted in the drinking water stream and are purified. We don't fear this challenge, we know solving it is our core requirement and competency we have. **Of course, if sun-gas is that effective, we can just stop mining for fuel. But this solution provides evolution without disruption and high cost and proven results.**

We will reassert the Sherman (1890) and Clayton (1914) antitrust acts where required. It is imperative that the energy costs go down and some savings are re invested. A Water & Energy strategy (WE) think of what innovation followed the breakup of AT&T. One provision was to separate the networking business from the equipment business. The rest is history. Just think of it, break in up AT&T in 1982 produced the handset revolution, worldwide, driven by USA freedom and innovation Electric is the simplest, if we have a clean way to produce it, and hydrogen the most plentiful if we can control its volatility. Oil is powerful and dirty and has become unacceptable in a 7+ billion population earth. Our enemy is not nations, per se, its inefficiency, pollution, and greed. Likewise, we will assure that drilling, Fracking, or whatever will be cautious about earthquake or any potential intersection with the water supply. This is especially sensitive along the west coast but has applications in all regions. Part of the answer is to let carbon fill the holes created by Fracking. And liquid CO_2 could replace mining caverns. Carbon and CO_2 will be a big part of coal redeployment. Texas and Oklahoma are racked by small earthquakes, so minimizing that is top priority. Of course, the issue of safety and methane containment are primary objectives; you will find that industry and the EPA already has that well considered, but proper regulation and testing will improve the effectives of a water and energy strategy. The point is the problem of EPA and industry infighting will be redirected to an efficient zero defects model in mining, drilling, extraction, and transportation model. We are good at it, and can step up to the next level, efficiently. Maybe new resources like graphene can make a strong, pliable pipeline infrastructure. At any point, the foolish attempt to create loopholes in our water and energy policies is over there are series of endeavors going forward, an agenda for Congress, some of which they ready have initiated. I would like to share a couple of them at this time.

We know of existing legislation to provide tax incentives for the creation of methane distribution, electrical standards for batteries, and upgrades to refueling sites for multiple petrol choices at gas stations. We will follow through on this a.s.a.p. We also will encourage and set up tax incentives for converting natural gas to CNG and hydrogen in homes and office locations at very affordable prices. Distribution and access will not be an issue in a very short time. But it's a mandate.

We will ask Congress to create legislation to put significant emphasis on funding R& D and implementation funding for extending battery density and recharging with improvements, incrementally if required, to five to ten times current storage levels for the purposes of supporting the electric car and hybrid enhancement. At least fifty billion dollars, we estimate, but the amount can escalate with the goals and objectives. We also will encourage any innovations to augment the productivity of the internal combustion engine or alternatives with the goal of achieving gas mileage or equivalent price performance of 100-150 mpg through hybrid efficiency, ICE/FECV innovations, or alternative motor and/or fuel choices, including natural gas to hydrogen. These are well within reach. Recognize that the electric car revolution is full on, although only Tesla has committed to the real challenges...Battery longevity and recharging on the road. China now builds more electric cars than all nations combined. All manufacturers have been selling electric cars and hybrids for years.100-150 mpg is already a given, what's needed is range (600 miles) and distribution/must (refueling).

Someone must commit, and the USA is ready.

But you must acknowledge the already accomplished reality:

Manufacturer	Efficiency range (mpg)
Toyota Prius Prime	110-120
Toyota RAV4	115/107 city mpg higher than highway
Tesla model S	120
Hyundai electric	120
IONIQ 5	114 Faster Charger in 5 minutes+++
Chevrolet Bolt	119
Volkswagen Egulf	119
BMW I3	110-113

Hydrogen cars (small sample)	
Toyota Miraa	67
Honda Clarity	67

This is buffeted by announcements of the targeted end of the Internal Combustion Engine in Norway and India. China has selected several major cities where all public transportation is/has going electric. Norway accomplished great wealth from oil in the North Sea. Yet they had the audacity to look forward.

Understand that Hydrogen cars have not announced hybrid versions and that they're pure end products. Electric systems are backed by nonelectric electric generation sources. Not a problem, once you are committed to change.

But this momentum is before any comprehensive refueling systems are in place, although Tesla and others have vast numbers of refueling stations. The point is that if the free market was backed by tax credits for refueling additions, comprehensive market expansion would proceed the list goes on and on and I haven't even included China, the declared largest e-car manufacturer in the world. The auto business is currently backed by an international Monopoly energy (ME) cartel, but we're moving to an open Water and Energy (WE) system. It is what the US Congress understood in the late 1800's, with the passage of the Sherman Antitrust act- monopolization freezes the market and suppresses innovation. Now our entire system is at stake, subject to world momentum that must go forward. Why? Because the world has to change.

At this point, I want to share with you the triangle of our lives:

Economy

Energy   Environment

This triangle tells you that our economy is held at its base, by energy (heat, electric, transportation) and environment (food, water, pollution free). Please grasp these directions, because they are part of the pyramid of *this decade. The subject is exponential growth.* You tell me what is wrong?

India's population of 1.2 billion will surpass China's 1.3 billion in the next five-ten years, marching toward three (3) billion (combined) people.

We know that population is targeted at 8.5-9.5 billion in 2050. It is supposed to level. Really? In thirty-eight years? And that's + one billion people in ten years. Who has discussed the population solution? In the 2016 Democratic and Republican conventions was it even mentioned?

The Ogallala Aquifer (8 states) has *30% of national irrigation* and is expected to be drained by 2021 to? This is the American breadbasket and it includes the drinking water for 2 million people. This is the water infrastructure behind the American bread belt (wheat).

United States, large exporter of wheat. It takes a thousand tons of water to produce one ton of wheat.

The planets use of freshwater (last ten years) peaked and world production of oil peaked in 1960 and flattened around 2006 at 75 million barrels per day. We think this has been eliminated in the last five to seven years by oil and gas discovery and mining innovation, and now sun-gas, an open clean and expanding platform with a future.

I know you may be asking, what have we been doing for the last 10–20 years? The answer is we've been focused on Kuwait, Iraq, Afghanistan, Arab Spring, Al Qaeda, and the Islamic State. We have been fighting wars over a paradigm that is no longer fact based. We just must change our use of energy.

I present this case to you because we know it is time to shift our Water and Energy policies. We are proceeding to Congress and will surround our budget, foreign policies, and domestic priorities with "warlike" focus. This is dramatic, but it can happen rapidly and without economic uncertainty until the next drought or economic collapse. It is time for all Americans to say it is about time we faced the challenges at home and abroad with purpose and vigor.

Over the next few months, you will see our focus is around the cooperation that will magnify in the Americas: Mexico, Canada,

Brazil, Argentina, Venezuela, and all our friends on the two American continents. We will also spend much time with our allies, as well as Russia, China, the Middle East, and all of Europe, Asia and Australia. These countries recognize this not as a United States problem, but a world problem. Now you can clearly see a United States' energy policy, I mean a Water and Energy strategy. **(WE)**

I am presenting this agenda and recognize that change can occur very effectively with your support.

I have one more agendum to discuss with you. As part of this initiative, we are redeploying some troops and working with Mexico to resolve our border problems, another supply and demand problem, particularly with drugs.

We are going to migrate some of our troops around the world back to the states and join a hard drug initiative to stop illegal immigration and combat drug movement in the US. We have already discussed this with Mexico and have assurances that we have a mutual objective of shutting down drug cartels and eliminating the business of crystal meth and cocaine trafficking and stop the heroin trafficking from Afghanistan and elsewhere. We expect the focus to be beyond our borders but will add funding to or augment current local and state law enforcement. We expect to eliminate Mexican cartel entrance into our cities but basically stop all hard drug trafficking, period.

We will use our existing law enforcement to stop drug trafficking in our cities, augmented by our national guard. Tell your children that hard drug availability is over.

We will ask Congress to legalize and decriminalize marijuana at the federal level for individuals older than 20, maintaining severe penalties for sale to minors. But we need a modern-day Elliot Ness, and we'll find him or her.

Additionally, we will have strong initiatives to assure we can track gun sales to end-users and stop the sale of American weapons to drug traffickers. Mexico has agreed to work with us on stopping the trafficking of guns from Russia, China, and elsewhere, as long as we develop a comprehensive approach to inhibit guns from flowing from our manufacturers through third parties and into Mexican cartel hands. This will have no impact on our personal gun security laws and freedoms, but it must be done, period.

If the near future, you will get a lot of feedback from lobbyists and spokespeople regarding the status quo. I am getting your attention because we know this will and needs to work. I repeat, *we know this will work!* But you must understand these objectives and any possible short-term considerations. This is a moment in US history as significant as World War II. That is a bold statement, but you must know this is right, and the time is right, right now! I am not overstating it.

There will be a lot of second-guessing, but you must know this is a prudent action that will work, on a positive path to a needed green economy. It is forward progress that will be visible in the short term, and you will see many actions, reactions, and overreactions, but Europe, Russia, China, Japan, and others will quickly have parallel or alternative plans. And that is okay.

I know you are tired of actions or inactions that do not move the agenda forward. These actions will do more than move the United States forward, water and energy change will be the step that improves the economy, prevents war, and causes the greatest peacetime world cooperation in the last hundred years.

What are the risks? The downside is simple: We have to assure extraction and transportation methods have no significant leakages of methane. We also have to find the fastest path to pure electric. Although it dissipates faster in the air, methane is a denser greenhouse gas than C02. So deeper insight needs to be developed over leakage risk and cost of prevention, and the risks associated with the creation and distribution of hydrogen, which has a greater greenhouse benefit in the long run. Don't worry, we can use all the time we need. But understand, this plan includes the reengineering of coal as another methane and/or hydrogen source, so the long-term benefits of coal pollution reduction, plus the creation of carbon and C02 stores have additional benefits.

The work currently being done to convert carbon as a replacement for silicon in electronic chips and graphene's and aluminum ion's and other's role and timing in denser lithium battery storage or other media, must be realized. The point is, though, that when we make this decision, we begin what is necessary for a new paradigm change. For example, phase one can be enough distribution capability to impact the trucking industry and then geographic evolution of gas stations to fuel depots over a longer period. The other choice to isolate is airline fuel, although once cars and trucks are addressed, the cost of airline fuel will drop. The US electricity is about 36 percent coal (rapidly declining), 36 percent natural gas (rapidly increasing), and 18 percent nuclear (the rest being hydro, thermal, renewable, etc.).

Once our commitment and action are seen by the world, the real impact of true paradigm change will occur. If China and other nations join us, the impact on world ecology will be substantial. If they hold out, they will do so at the detriment to their own people. Quite frankly, once the methodology, mining, distribution, and safety concerns are addressed, Asia should respond. The amount of effort around the world, particularly Japan, will create a new market for technologies that improve the process and safety. Remember, there are already 25+ million cars running on natural gas. In fact, Albania has 75 percent of its transportation running on natural gas. This is not a fledgling industry. It is a proven industry that must address scaling up. *This is what we do.* The United States scaled up for World War II and we will scale up for Water and Energy change by committing to a needed strategy and incremental time frame. What is needed is commitment to not only cleaner energy but improved quality of extraction, pipelines, etc. Remember, we are already deeply committed to the extraction and use of natural gas, with more than one-third of our electricity, soon rising to more than 50%.

The issue is transportation. This is all done in close coordination with China, our Middle Eastern allies, Russia, Japan, Australia, India and Pakistan, Indonesia, Saudi Arabia, and Europe. It will strengthen our dollar and keep the dollar as the safest and most stable currency on the planet. China and India have almost insurmountable demand and resource problems, including water shortage and pollution. They know that the mix of water and energy must change. China also knows the United States and Europe are among their best customers. If China doesn't change, the detriment to their people will be very visible. The all-important second downside is if/when the United States loses the role of the American dollar as a world reserve currency. Understand this has massive potential of inflation and high interest rates. This is caused by our massive 20+ trillion dollars in debt, covered by T-Bill sales all over the world. The T-bill rate ties to our prime lending rate, and importantly, many variable rate loans. This has a lot to do with our strife with Iran and recent movements with the BRIC (Brazil, Russia, India, and China) nations and others.

China has captured the Gold market and will soon announce their plans to solidify the Juan as a world currency. (Not **the** world currency).

Our strategy is to let the dollar to be the most stable resource in the world market. If no one wants to buy our T-bills (8-9 trillion dollars) we will acquire the assets and assure our T-bill rates are not affected. The United States will lead the effort for Water and Energy (WE) productivity. This will stabilize the world's economies and prepare for the next billion people by lowering costs, increasing water and energy production, and assuring that domestic and international food supplies are in line with an 8–9 billion population.

What will change the world is a worldwide Water and Energy strategic and tactical plan. To address the tactics and flexibility for the world, the United States and China must make a historic energy alliance. One that leverages, with other world leaders, a redistribution of clean electric, heating, and transportation energy, a fresh water strategy, and an anti-pollution strategy that assures that clean supply continuously exceeds demand. So, ask yourselves an important question. What is the alternative? After conferring with the world's leaders, I am pledging to you that we are going forward. China, Russia, and the Middle East must decide how to frame their energies in the 21st century, this mining and technology bridge was built to be crossed and reflects the bridge to the clean energy and freshwater targets the world is ready for moving a new paradigm forward.

Sounds hard? No, establish a tax credit to add Ng, hydrogen, or electric fuel or gas stations pump stations to existing fuel depots or facilities such as apartments, retail outlets, hotels and home adaptations for electric and NG or hydrogen conversions. Some facility needs to provide incentives for creation of ways to deliver fuel through a network of sources. Open the door and American and International Industry will respond. It will respond to an open market. It's big, but that's what we do. Stand off and Asia will work with whoever wants to own their part of 21st century.

This is foolproof but needs our leadership.

Not only will we improve quality and efficiency, but we will also reassert ourselves in energy and economic leadership around the world, and with the dollar as the world's **stable** currency, among an array of strong currencies throughout the world.

Thank you for your attention. It is time to consider how we can assure that this agenda will be successful. That is water and energy (WE) will lower our costs, clean up our environment, and provide fresh water for agriculture, food and drink. You will look back at this and decide that you were fortunate to be alive when the people of the 21st century overcame the energy bubble. The bubble did not burst, except for the energy created by dismissing the quagmire created since September 11. We took care of Bin Laden, and now we are going to participate in the courageous act of moving the water and energy challenge forward. We know a paradigm shift will soon embrace the world and address fresh-water generation and pollution, particularly in the United States, with its volume of water and energy use, and Asia with its emerging water and energy consumption, current over reliance on more coal for electricity, and massive water quality issues. This momentum will speak for itself around the world. And at home, we will protect the Ogallala reservoir, the source of our mid-western breadbasket, and set up targets for freshwater increases. The Ogallala water reserve and the Mexican border are two visible targets for increased farming and irrigation capacity in America. These targets will be instead of war, if our detractors don't make us do what we will do if we or our allies are threatened. We have the technology and resources to change. We must reclaim or economy before it is out of our control. We must prepare for a 9.5 billion population, 450 million in the US, and this is our strategy.

The second risk is the pressure on the dollar as a reserve currency. This risk exceeds all others. The problem is the assault is already happening. In 2002, Saddam Hussein departed from selling oil in dollars. In 2004, we invaded Iraq, he was hanged by his people, and Iraq went back to selling oil in dollars.

I would like to underscore this direction with two points. I am not sure the impact of these actions will have on the lobby money in Washington or the states. We aren't anti-lobby, just anti-graft. We will assure absolute transparency in this world, so we ask our business partners to respect the dignity of positive change for the United States' and world's sake.

Remember, the issue of excessive lobby money is the underlying problem regarding the relationship between the president, Congress, and the citizens we serve. Our goal is to serve the citizens, not finance elections. Somehow, we have forgotten that. The quest for a new Water and Energy paradigm is a challenge for WE the people. We have to prioritize our spending this way. For a long time, you have been lobbied those biofuels, etc. are great, *as oil prices rise to the cost of alternatives. This is not true or acceptable. We've already demonstrated the disparity between all costs and energy costs over the last 50 years and especially since 9/11.*

We have been overpaying for oil and gas for more than 15 years. We will make it a clear choice that fresh water and clean energy supply exceeds demand, and you will pay less for clean, efficient energy. You can thank focus from government and private enterprise for that. This requires teamwork with one objective: a strong and resilient economy forged through energy and freshwater capacity and productivity.

The market can compete for the best delivery system, but in order to achieve change, natural gas, progression toward hydrogen, and greatly increased battery density, are at the solution's center, and at significant cost savings. Now this is the center of a paradigm change.

There is only one way to realize that dream: *provide the low-cost energy source and the integrated strategy to make Water and Energy the core of our economic upturn.* The Water and Energy paradigm is the necessary turn of this century. It is the point that we take back the economic momentum and innovation from world history and rewrite the playbook of this century. This is the path of an "earth walk" to humanity's future.

If you doubt the clarity of this necessity, remember, *we wasted more than one trillion dollars on invasions of Iraq and Afghanistan.* Yes, with the lives and refugees sacrificed, you may think this as harsh and unfeeling. You may think this root cause of our economic breakdown is unfeeling. We hate it, but it dwarfs the impact of not recognizing the world pyramid scheme. The danger is the scheme is unintentional, but real.

In 2006, the late Stephen Hawking, noted British physicist, asked Yahoo Answers, "In a world that is in chaos politically, socially, and environmentally, how the human race can sustain another hundred years?" One of the brightest minds on the planet was dismayed. That was because he couldn't imagine how we could do it. He felt this way because of the difficulty for mankind to change. Well, it's massive but simple, provide tax credits to add fuel outlets for ng, hydrogen, electric, and gasoline to our filling stations. Provide the mandate. Industry will decide whether or not to play. I assure you that networking solutions and industry niches will rise with trillions to invest. Wake Up America!

The five elements of entrepreneurship **are honesty, instinct, imagination, discipline, and persistence.** The world is ready, and the need is way overdue. It's our time. Sell this lyric every day at breakfast, and we will prevail.

The road to clean, economically efficient, and safe Water and Energy are joined together. *"WE" are the solution. This is one giant leap for mankind.*

Energy strategy

Focused plans to move forward, such as commitment to a phase in of enhanced batteries, and EV vehicles, commitment to a shift to NG and Hydrogen FCEV vehicles, all hybrids, with focused adaptation of trucks choices between algae, and other bio fuels, and hydrogen, with all in solutions, hybrid, and all–electric options considered. Congress needs to incentivize a free market. Provide the incentives and step back.

The same mixes should be made for airplanes, with the option of fossil fuels until a transition plan is adapted...all targeted for zero emissions. Besides a battery plan...a sun-gas solution should be prioritized, and a plan to produce

NG/Hydrogen/electrical fueling stations should be planned. The "WE team" which will include at least Germany, Japan, S Korea, and Canada along with the clear USA players as designated by the Department of Energy, and perhaps the Military (US Air force, etc.) should be created. Of course, China, Russia, and more should contribute but the phase 1 study should be limited. If thus is too traumatic, just form our team and offer Germany, Canada, and Japan a seat at the table. (Germany should become a strategic ally at an unprecedented level). Selected companies with expertise can be drawn in by the team as required, with at least Tesla participating. There should be a ten-year plan, with directions established in two years. None of this would prohibit anyone from introducing new products. If all this is too status-quo shaking, move the project into secrecy and evolve. Water initiatives should be addressed including Chemistry based solutions that reconfigure "element mixes" to produce H20. I say this because "Sun-gas" makes element reconfiguration ok. There must be a way to get passed boiling water.

I must admit I will keep bringing up Germany. Maybe it's because Chancellor Angela Merkel is a Physicist/Chemist and her Country leads the world in alternate energy 'Maybe it's because Daimler invented the Internal Combustion Engine (ICE) and was investing in US Tesla, until they had to start their own electric car division. Maybe it's because Germany is importing solar solutions that should lead to Sun-Gas. Maybe it's because Germany, more than anyone, can separate itself from the 20th Century. Maybe if the USA chooses a union of change, we could evolve us out of the mess we've put ourselves in. Imagine the USA, Germany, and Japan (with the help of many) reconstitute the 21st century with China, and free the cloud of pollution, despotism, and focus on our real priority: Water and

Energy (WE) in the global village. But alas we can trade Trumps thwarted World trade, USA isolation, uni-culture to the robust trade leadership, world market, and diverse participation that is meant to be. Meanwhile, Europe spun into Brexit and nations spread the anti-EU rhetoric which is really about Syria and that EU policies temporarily 1 stumbled border protection. A real issue, but the real problem was how to solve the Middle East "problem.

So, let's divert a little…trade…because Germany is among the best traders in the world… (Superior products?)

What about trade deficits and should import fees be established? The Reagan, Bushes, Clinton's, Obama etc. spent decades upon decades opening the markets to our products and services. Just say hold on…stop?? No, adjust agreements until the doctrine of fairness and equity is realized but recognize the dynamic of world trade that we (and Europe, India, China, S Korea, and Japan) created.

Here is the kind of stuff we created in the last decade or so:

Apple, in 2016, is now selling more **I-phones in China than in the USA Apple has 116,000** employees in the USA and 1,000,000 contractors in Tawian, all, by the way in Taiwan. Their dividends are increasing every quarter, with all those USA shareholders being paid.

General motors is now with the highest revenue they have ever had in all of history…They have sold 3,800,000 vehicles in China in 2016 and their revenue increase is directly tied to China sales. They sold more vehicles in China than in the USA. Now Ford wants to accelerate their relationship.

A large percentage of IOWA's corn exports is sold to Mexico. Yes, Mexico provides us with a trade deficit, but our Mexican business has expanded **tenfold** since 1994.

The list is awesome and pervasive...40% of the profits from the S&P 500 comes from overseas:

Company examples:

Percent of international revenues

McDonalds	66
Exxon Mobile	45
Intel	85
Boeing	31
IBM	64
Ford	51
Amazon	45
Apple	62
GE	54
Walmart	26
Dow Chemical	67
Agriculture (all)	33

The list goes on and on. Trade is pervasive and it defines America in the 21st century, a global leader, with great products and services, and wonderful people to do business with. That leadership defines what our potential and posture should be.

We need to focus on the real issues of drug cartels and gun running while we assure our trade agreements are fair. We've allowed the American based Mexican Drug Cartels become the 1920's Mafia of our time. When states like Vermont have a Heroin epidemic and opioids have addicted our states, it's time to focus on the real challenge: how have monopolization ruined the world's commerce and is threatening our health and safety? We don't need "walls", we need Elliot Ness, and the guts to eliminate illegal cartels and monopolistic drug companies.

Trade agreements must be equitable, but not diminish our most powerful weapon, our manufacturing and multinational world footprint.

I believe that most of the import/export losers are in states, whether rust belt or agricultural, diminished our desire to be a world competitor. We need to provide the enabling education and jobs to spread this expertise, not suppress it.

In a couple of years, India will succeed China in population. We created the outsourcing market with technology from companies like CISCO, who made worldwide telecommunications like calling the next town. We enabled our nation's business outsourcing. With our leading technologies and expertise, we are an enabler of efficiency, quality, and mass production. So, let's promote it, not diminish it. With an Open Market, that's what we have been and are doing.

What you have to anticipate is the two largest nations on earth could pool their power and become the leaders of the free world...both consumed by the quest as being the most productive. So, we must decide are we competitors or are we collaborators in making a 9.5 billion planet world. This should be our quest. Understand that northern Europe (Scotland, Denmark, Norway, and Germany) and Canada (Hydrogenics Inc.) are transforming energy as a utilizing water and wind and sunlight to create a prolific hydrogen fuel that can diminish the need for fossil fuels. Norway announced it will stop using internal combustion cars in less than 10 years...Yes...that's Norway, who is rich because of oil and gas, but also have witnessed what wind and powerful seas mean, resources that they have a premium of.

Meanwhile, Saudi Arabia says that by 2030-50 it will transform its economy to not rely on Oil & Gas as the determinant of its economic power. Yes, that's Saudi Arabia who also gets 75% of its fresh water by desalination of the ocean and is considering how to do it with solar power.

The list goes on and it's staggering.

By the way, why is the business community, who makes the decisions about labor and manufacturing is not held accountable? After all they outsource or offshore source manufacturing and labor. The USA promotes worldwide product and service expansion. **Retraction in a global market is asking for reduced market share.** The world is shrinking, and USA's innovations are a primary driver...If we retract our initiative, I assure you India, China, and others will fill the needed gap, because they have to.

Why did we go this way? What was our goal? What should our going forward strategy be?

Simply, USA has 4.6 percent of the world population which means as the rest of the world economically improves, the potential markets for our products and services grow. The reason China is such a great market is they have a burgeoning Middle Class! I assure you, Germany, Japan, South Korea and others are eager to expand. Do we want to allow the world market to leave us behind? Or should we invest in the now and the future.

USA is among the leading world's exporters of food (and crops). The population of the world is expected to grow by over 1 billion in LESS than 10-12 years, mostly in the Middle East, western Asia, and North Africa (and I'm sure S America). The USA is expecting 400-450 million populations by 2050. Countries **without** strong immigration history. Japan, Eastern Europe, etc. are facing population declines and resulting recession. We need to expand agriculture, keep prices low, and provide expanded service worldwide. Fairness, product quality and cleanliness need to be our brand and like Germany, nations want our products. So how should we act?

Most of the Arab spring was caused by mostly rising food prices...caused by rising costs from countries like the USA and worldwide drought. This is what we should be working on! Both sides of our borders should be teeming with agriculture.

My question is simple...Why hasn't there been exposed documentaries on trade policy and the other major...issue...Drain the Swamp? Everyone knows that Lobbies and money rich leaders have taken over our congress and the price of elections has skyrocketed. The answer is "everyone is paid...Dems, Republicans etc." Lobby expense has risen from $1.3B to $3.5 billion per year in the last decade or so. Let's start with Oil and Gas and energize the world economy, and deal with lobby domination of our Congress and the Executive branch, and while we're at it, let us add term limits and campaign financing limits!" That will invigorate the political parties or replace them with responsive representation. Let's reenergize an emerging electorate.

The fact is that gasoline should cost about a dollar a gallon and the stagnation of that market is an underlying problem in the world, causing funding of terrorist war, pollution, and more. True alternatives are available now and growing...but action is needed to change the paradigm. Failure to focus on the real issues is self-defeating. In today's world, massive excess profitability means that competition is lacking and is suppressed, that is the definition of our Energy business. Clean, low-cost food, water, and energy will expand world GDP to new levels. Let's drop the labels and reinvigorate competition and commerce.

For 75+ years we have convinced ourselves we were short on supply of energy sources, gasoline, etc. Now we have an excess of clean supply, but need to expand distribution, places to refill our energy choice. Failure to recognize this is ignorant and stupid. It's this simple, Oil and Gas is simply 20th century and the 21st century needs more clean robust choice. Now who will provide it? Germany, Japan, China, India, EU, or the USA? We are at the forefront of innovation in this area, but monopolies and cartels are stagnating our leadership...all to preserve existing market share. Large is not evil, look at companies like G.E. There are plenty of models of win-win in our society. And obviously Africa must intensely participate.

The world is ready to expand natural gas, hydrogen, and electric into a new generation of hybrids. Gasoline can now be converted from natural gas. Chemistry can change water and sunlight to hydrogen fuel, and fresh water. Did you ever hear of Sungas and Syngas? The US government (DOE & Air force) has funded millions into these technologies and they are being suppressed, not jailed, but not prioritized. But Media, don't feel free, you're paid by oil and gas and other lobbies as you chase the ratings bubble instead of the actual news...Oh no? tell us where are the expose's?...Will someone pay CBS's 60 minutes and or HBO's VICE to do a thorough expose of this obvious phenome...Lobbies, competitive competition suppression, and the abuse of power?

That's the news we need now, expanding our world markets, not withdrawing from them, with high tariffs. Trade is such a poorly understood issue, it's pathetic.

A slight diversion, HBO's Vice has shown that American fast food is spreading out in the Middle East and China it's a clear sign that American culture (pop culture?) is highly accepted, the way it did in the late 80's and early 90's signaling and supporting the collapse of the Soviet Union. With all our trepidations over fast food, maybe we just accept the power of video over branding.

BY the way, years ago, it was forecast that the 21st century is the Pacific Century meaning world growth will be centered on countries around the Pacific Rim. So, our solution is to pull out of the Pacific partnership? Don't tell me you don't know this, President Trump! If you don't, you should! In light of all this, the Supreme Court announces (Citizen's United) that corporations can make unlimited media contributions to causes/candidates without disclosing the participants. How can they do that? They simply have gotten to the point that they believe money is King. They can't conceive that in a world where 1% of the population owns as much of the wealth as 90% of the masses, that this could drive a person or a company to do whatever is necessary to secure that wealth. In other words, the Supreme Court couldn't see that the power of the 99% to overcome the 1% (the money holders) has been subordinated because the Supreme Court decided that people have no power, Money has the power. And of course, lobbies are the manifestation of money power over our entire constitution. The Supreme Court merely says it's the executive and congress to set direction. That's why we elect a billionaire to challenge the system, simply desperation of the masses.

What is missing is with emerging middle classes in India, China, Indonesia and elsewhere, is the USA answering the worldwide demand...clean water, clean fuel, food, and technology to amass communications, electronic education, and access to solutions which of course represents the key to advance healthcare. Imagine a world where all the attributes of true democracy manifests itself in a nine billion population earth. It can't even be dreamed of in an oil/energy and insufficient fresh water paradigm. If you noticed, the world is adapting fast food everywhere. This seems strange to us, but it's true. The world also loves Hollywood, so let's embrace it.

We better expand our Middle class, because China, India, the rest of Asia, and Europe will so we need to expand our leadership why will the middle class rise? Because that's what is needed! This is the 21st century, enabling what's needed, not the status quo.

America's dilemma:

Understanding the population challenge worldwide and America's (and Europe) inward focus, i.e. nationalism, must be understood considering the Middle East's and Syria's creation of refugees and immigration, all resulting with or from terrorism. Anyone must admit this is the root cause of the EU's shaky condition. Arming is not the answer, although obviously we need to defeat Islamic Terrorism. The solution is to change the Energy Paradigm, so clean energy and fresh water dominates our actions, and open markets spell economic freedom and innovation.

The 21st century is the "Pacific century" centered around China, India's, Indonesia's and all the Pacific Rim's rise due to population and to international trade and technology' s worldwide proliferation, particularly in product, telecommunications, and the internet. This results in a rising middle class (in those and other countries.) The worldwide population will rise by a billion people in 10-12 years particularly in the Middle East, North Africa, and western Asia, very dominated by Muslims. It is forecast that the Muslim religion will exceed Christians by 2060. Pollution and water deprivation are the underlying detraction, and related food shortage (including north and central Africa) which is forecast to affect 20-30 million people To America, this should spell opportunity, which is the antithesis of the inward focus of "nationalism" and the world market we and all dominant countries created. Don't retract, respond to the secret of our success, freedom and persistence.

Consider this: about 25% of all society's populations are the top intelligence, productivity, and creativity of those people. That means that China's top tier, intelligence and personal productivity-wise, is about equal to **all** USA's population. China and India's top tier is close to all north and South America's population combined. Furthermore, the proliferation of computers, the internet, etc. with tools such as Google, the potential rate of expanded intelligence is awesome. America's cultural advantage has always been unrivaled **belief** in unlimited opportunity. This has been our **problem and our blessing.**

We've been living under a cloud for the past 75 and more years that "we're running out of fuel". Understand that that problem is over. Keep repeating it to yourself. It's over. If we embrace this opportunity, we'll, again, will lead the world in innovation.

The answer is the government must open the markets by providing tax credits for the enhancement of **refueling distribution,** expanding gas stations and many alternatives by adding hydrogen, electric, and Natural gas fuel to the pump alternatives. Don't worry about networking. Once the marketplace knows the market has opened, solutions will appear. Imagine converting your home gas lines to hydrogen in your garage and refueling at home? Crazy? If you want the USA to lead the world in massive GDP growth and open more markets for USA and European products (and China, Russia, and everyone else), simply massively create **CHOICE**. Don't worry about fossil fuels. Consumer choice will take care of that problem, because the product alternatives are already here... clean, inexpensive, and robust fuels and we will continue to improve.

The world is ready. **Without distribution, all claims of alternatives are lies, or at best, ignorant.**

A personal note (not an ad): I drive a 2017 Toyota Prius Prime and recharge daily...delivering me a 70-100 mpge (including the electric cost) and a 600 mile range. And I rarely use backup gasoline, dramatically reducing fuel pollution. I also have solar panels on my home roof and if I recharge during the day, the electric cost is free because my solar creation of energy exceeds my daytime consumption, meaning my actual "mpge" This issue will disappear with solar battery storage.

Even gasoline hybrids could get mpg close to 100. That means regular gasoline is also a pollution reducing player! Pakistan and Iranian cars run on natural gas or gasoline, and they don't build the cars.

If the government doesn't enable the open market, we will continue to use war, high cost, and pollution as the true price of expensive polluting gasoline. Warren Buffet bought into one of China's electric car companies (BYD), but he's just America's greatest investor. **China sells more electric cars than the rest of the world, combined.**

Or you can get behind one of our paid off politicians who would rather see our children and grandchildren fight wars in the Middle East and elsewhere, or do we want expanded GDP, world economic expansion, and support of using this technology to enable fresh water expansion, food production, and fresh air, worldwide? We are America! Embrace this Dems and Republicans, Independents, et al. Forget labels, our children and grandchildren need our courage, initiative, and results. If the existing parties can't get it together, get the problem solvers together. They are ready.

But hasn't the world leaned to the electric model? No, it must step up to refueling, or it will lose. Don't think the world will wait for us. We must lead, not follow opportunity.

Final point!

How to Simplify this?

To see this through the long term, understand: there are two basic networks that can be exploited.

1. Electricity

An electric grid, all homes and offices have electric connectivity, you can connect through a 240 kHz line in your garage or elsewhere and plug in. If you had a swappable battery, you could swap your battery, and then recharge the backup offline. When density was improved, you could have both batteries in your vehicle, and recharge the backup on a regular basis. This "ultimate" solution would be a generation 2 experience, once the right battery has been invented.

2. Natural Gas or Hydrogen

The gas grid exists for all offices and homes have a gas line for natural gas. This natural gas line could be run into your garage and hooked up there. The ultimate solution is to have a black box you run your NG line into, and convert NG to hydrogen, so you could have A FCEV car receive fuel from the black box. This idea is being pursued in many labs. This could also be a 2-phase project-first NG, then Hydrogen.

I'm not oversimplifying this, but if you knew you were going to need millions of these Black Boxes, the scale economics would be different. Of course, you could have these hookups at a filling station. And the economics of a conversion box may improve.

The point is the networks already exist and could co-exist as they do now. These ideas have existed for a long time. We the people have decided to invest is war machines and mining projects and we've invested trillions to pursue availability of

Energy, before the inventions I noted as this book began. Tesla has many plans for an electric grid, but they need someone with the commitment and understanding to stand up. Of course, we can just use war and trillions to continue the pollution and high expense path, we are on, and not to mention all our men and women we will sacrifice, over and over again.

America, down deep, you know where we are going, and it is not pretty. That's why we invented democracy, to enable change. Freedom, Capitalism with a social security. Diversity is the world order. The offered alternatives are bullshit.

Green new deal? It's the junior congressmen's plan to put Trump back in the white house. Understand Capitalism with social security and Freedom's open door to innovation. The answer.

Recall: We spent trillions to continue the old way, the usual way, yet for castors see us planning for more of the same.

CHAPTER IX

The President and the Lobbyists

The next day the president meets with his cabinet, preceding a meeting with ten lobby representatives of energy, Pharma, military Industrial, education, agriculture, automotive, airline, NRA, and a few others.

This is a very important confrontation, because the lobby system is imbedded in the congressional process and often funds and supports legislatures and the president to a total of more than three billion dollars per year for political action committees (PACs), parties, and entire constituencies (unions, corporations, individuals, and other groups.) Because of the Supreme Court's "Citizens United" decision, there is now no limit to what can be spent, and contributors are protected from disclosure.

President: Thank you for meeting with me today.

Energy Lobby (EL 1): I am coordinating input from oil and gas and many related fields like gas stations, refineries, and related upstream and downstream delivery systems. On some level we just do not get it. We have been financial partners with the executive and legislative branches for a long time and are not sure where to place our bets. Or should we say, we are not sure where our legislative partners stand on this.

President: Well, I've made it clear that we are done with trillion-dollar wars, unless there are direct threats to NATO or Israel, or other nation states we are close to. We need our industry lobbyists to take a long look inward. We need all the support we can get, but in this sorting out process we want the oil and gas industry to recognize when a paradigm change is before us. We believe that when all is said and done, you are Americans first and this is a time when the past processes are behind us, and a new approach is at hand. We want positive steps to improve the productivity of the delivery system, lower costs, and fund water initiatives that will enable the United States to cure the illnesses and negative impacts of the pollution, droughts, that plague the United States and the world. We see that it must be done to prevent world social deterioration, war, and address the impact of adding a billion people to the world and a few hundred million people to the United States. You see the planet, you see the unrest, and it is time to change.

EL 2: But you cannot think we will witness a reduction of oil prices to half when we saw the pressures of demand taking us to say $200 per barrel?

President: That's the very point. Your industry, with our support, has created new resources and technology for the way we do business. I expect your deep continued cooperation in natural gas and R&D regarding hydrogen, desalination, solar, battery density, and more, as well as to enable a smooth transition to cleaner, more robust alternatives. America has been watching your industry commercials for a long time and sees you defining yourselves as energy companies moving to a new paradigm, not just oil and gas. Well, innovations invested in by the United States and oil and gas and the United States' dept. of energy and the university systems around the world, have finally developed bridges to the future. So, we are recognizing the fact that you are one thing more than anything, American companies with unquestioned patriotism and committed to support us through this change, almost like a war, so you can be part of the huge growth in demand that will accompany clean water and energy. That is why this is like a Defcon Four situation, where government direction is not only supported but embraced by all. After all, the United States is not just real estate in which private company owns the space. This is the equivalent where eminent domain (United States), compulsory purchase (United Kingdom, New Zealand, Ireland), resumption/compulsory acquisition (Australia), or expropriation (South Africa and Canada) is an action of the state to seize a citizen's private property, expropriate property, or seize a citizen's rights in property with due monetary compensation, but without the owner's consent. Maybe that overstates it, but when the threat of balance of power is before us, we have to act, and those companies that want to be strong on the other side of this new paradigm will see the reality and adjust their plans. The threat of near Armageddon is before us, and we are approaching water crises that cannot be solved without lower-cost energy. Our mandate is clear. After all, all good US citizens know our survival is predicated on the system supporting the people, not the people submitting to the system, not just status quo.

EL 2: I'm not sure the Supreme Court will buy into that. We may have a constitutional impasse.

Resident: No, there is no impasse. In fact, we are going to be putting forward a constitutional amendment that clarifies the election process and the role of citizens and companies. If we must declare war we will, but it will be quite uncomfortable in listing who our enemies are. We know from what we have seen and heard after yesterday's manifesto that the people are ready to take back control of their destiny. What oil and gas and related companies have to realize is that the people want us to do anything we can to reinvigorate all that has made us great? From great companies to the realities expressed in the Sherman and Clayton antitrust acts. The power edge is out of sync with the world emergency on water and energy, and it is government's job to take on prudent actions. This is why we have been providing tax credits, investment credits, and related R&D investments for decades and decades. It is payback time.

It is our job to be sure our people are at the core of our objectives and they are properly being served. I believe that we, in government have taken our eyes off the citizens and that the primary goal is to get reelected, even right after election. The second goal is to stop progress so you can blame it on the other party. We are not just policeman making sure that laissez-faire business activities are just safe. Many do not like it, we know, but back when corporate smokestacks endangered health, we were elected to do something about it. We often ask ourselves, not frequently enough, what the writers of our constitution would say about the increasing role of government to assure the health of our society. I am sure that they would go as far as taking over the industry, but which is largely in public hands today. And if energy companies refuse to be part of a new paradigm, we could take that over too. However, we are not saying that we are saying that change is necessary, and corporate and private citizens act in the benefit of the people. Note, 67 percent of world oil is owned by governments. In fact, this challenge we have is in the interest of creating a newfound freedom of commerce and innovation that will be a second coming of our exercise in intellectual and industry freedom.

EL 2 But we are at peace, not war.

President: We just spent more than four trillion dollars in war, and we recognize that we did not hold our government accountable, save the soldiers and generals who we sent abroad, by creating debt and unacceptable loss by pushing the financials into the future. Well, the future does not like that approach anymore and it is time for a change. Sure, we will reduce our government footprint cost, but when we clearly see that our oil and gas expenses have tripled in ten years while our consumption declined. That's quite frankly, the opposite of the way markets has to act. We have found we have a choice, and by God, we are going to act. So, if you want to be run over by history, go for it. 330 million people growing to 450 million are accountable, not accumulations of increased wealth in one percent of the people. It's time to step up to America's potential.

LM 3: So, this is class warfare, is that it? You have unveiled your disdain for those who worked the most for what America represents?

It's true that even at the Supreme Court level, corporate money takes precedence over the will of the people. No. You really forgot that Jefferson and others believed in the power of the people? Curious. But you should remind yourself, you did well and were paid...but it's time to change' **the new ME is WE.**

Please, we have been socially and politically engineered to turn our system of government into a state where wealth pays us to assure conformity and congressional representative re-electability. I'm sorry, you and I know what bullshit is, and this is bullshit. The fact that our Supreme Court thinks that money is voting power (Citizens United) would make Madison and Jefferson and Franklin turn over in their graves. Every generation must reignite itself, not by war, by innovation and persistence.

We are changing that by enabling our free enterprise system to burst our energy bubble, we will use our entrepreneurial edge to reestablish our water table. This is not socialism; oil and gas are closer to socialism, or an oligarchy-socialism to preserve the status quo. It is a reestablishment of our principles of freedom as we saw them in 1789 and 1890 (obviously except slavery and women's rights). What I hope oil and gas sees that the green movement is not about grass, it is about money. We need an adjustment, and we have to let the forces of freedom recover what has been manipulated out of control: their health, and well-being. And yes, I know that we are on top of the economic ladder and the production ladder, but there needs to be an adjustment, not in our principles, but our actions.

Don't get me wrong. I do not believe government can do better than private enterprise in finding solutions. But we must balance short-term interests with what is clearly going on, and free our people to act. My God, we borrowed and spent more than four trillion dollars for what? To get rid of a dictator. We simultaneously prop up kings and military juntas to put us in a position where nations see us as neocolonialists. (Which is used by autocratic leaders to manipulate us.) It's all backward.

Meanwhile, an economy by dictatorial committee, China, which is now called autocratic capitalism, is instilling free enterprise in their people to unleash the power of the invisible hand. Now we know that our system of balance of power, although pressed too many times, constantly makes us review what we were given by Jefferson, Madison, etc. Quite frankly the success of the global market, which was spirited by: the United States, Europe, Japan, Germany, Korea, India, and China and escalated by technology mostly originated in the United States, have made the numbers too great. We are being screamed at by world society that it is too close to the edge, so it is time for a change, once again brought in by American innovation.

Remember, the critical population number is plus one billion people every ten to eleven years. We could say we are not responsible for Asia and Africa, but we are active participants in raising their economies through our deployment of technologies into their societies, their grateful provision of low-cost labor due to our view of international free enterprise, and opened gates of almost free enterprise. I say almost because we, the world, still protect agriculture and many niche products. But we are in the precarious situation largely due to agriculture and the mismanagement or illegal control of supply. But that, we see, as a problem caused by global warming, or save that debate, the reduction of fresh water due to drought. We look at China and India with their increased demand for energy but blame them for the reason their demand raises our oil prices. It's sick.

We have to recognize that 70% of the earth is covered by saltwater, and we have treated water as nearly "free" and have serious conservation issues, but we have to recognize that desalination is not working due to the cost of energy to provide it. The fact that Saudi Arabia gets 75% of their water from desalination because they have the energy resources to do it should be screaming at us. We need to lower the cost of energy and we say let the free market fix the problem, so we are about to do it. Despite the trillion dollars plus we have spent in Iraq and Afghanistan, and despite of the terrorist attacks of 9/11 and elsewhere, we have to change the paradigm. Government is stepping in, as we have done before, not to control the market but to assure the market is free and our enterprisers are freed to innovate. The US has decreed that it is illegal to monopolize an industry. Yes, with tax credits, and yes with incentives, which imply we are setting direction. When we see the advent of war and massive drought, we will act within the strength of our constitution, including amendments, which will make this all possible.

We will not set direction, but our scientists will team together because our nation is going to rise with a common purpose. We have just forgotten how to lead and how to ask, and the difference between want and need.

We have not had the strength of will or character to say that since 9/11 we have an energy bubble that must be deflated. That deflation will finance our recovery, our water initiative, and a new century of world and local growth, and yes, peace.

EL 2: Yes, but it seems like you're deflating our profits to reinvest in initiatives.

President: No, we are allowing a market-driven readjustment of our energy costs because we have allowed greed, manipulated taxation, lobby money, and a war mentality that defined the twentieth century; distort our purpose and our progress. Do not get me wrong, we are not going to weaken our military posture. But we are going to redeploy wasted resources. And NATO, the Middle East, and Asia and Africa can be sure we will revert to war if we have to. That's the readjustment the world has to make. We won't start wars, but we can and will end them, if required.

This is a moment in time when China, Russia, the NATO powers, Japan, the United States, and most definitely the Middle East recognize that we do not want to war over energy, we want to "change the mix" of water and energy cost and deployment and fix greenhouse gas content, and we have to do it together. Just recognize that 2002–2012 was an oil bubble, and it is time to fix the problem using the tools oil and gas gave or should I say we own by constitutional mandate. We the people declare that enough is enough, and we will reorganize industry to distribute the wealth through entrepreneurial effort and competition. We are just exercising the limits of assuring free enterprise.

EL 2: I understand what you have said, and we will consider this very closely here and abroad. We, quite frankly, do not see how China will not seek, in the short term, to gain opportunity with the Middle East.

President: We will work very closely with China and they must recognize that once our transformation emerges, they would sacrifice their own costs and health by not embracing change. The Americas will see the big picture, that lower cost and cleaner water and energy, and it will energize their economies and their future. The transformation will be in full activity within five years. Once the paradigm shift is clear, and the distribution system is rolling out alternatives, and we obtain most energy supply in the Americas, the future will have to react. These opportunities I discussed and the investments all are visible, and the people will decide if it is to the benefit of mankind.

Trust me India and China's challenge is so great, active nations should collaborate and participate.

You must know that if the direction is set and the people are behind it, this will happen with a personal vigor not WE, (Water & Energy and lack of direction). *And it cannot change without a new water and energy paradigm.* Ten years from now we will look back and see the world GDP rising because of the courage and foresight of water and energy spurned by the good old US innovation, supported by a responsive government. Remember, we are not creating anything. We are focusing and responding to United States innovation by the oil and gas industry. If the cartel/oligopoly tries to stop it, what does that say vis-à-vis the Sherman antitrust act? But let us hear from more of you. Remember WE, (Water & Energy) (WE) are at the core of needed solutions.

Automotive Rep (AR 1): We see it. We see the motor as defined by Tesla motors is among the needed attributes of electric motors. It is powered by an electric motor, a 3-phase, 4-pole induction motor, producing a maximum net power of 248hp (185 kW). Maximum torque is 200·ft-lbf, obtained at 0 rpm and almost constant up to 6,000 rpm, a common feature of electric motors and one of the biggest differences, from the performance point of view, with internal combustion engines. The motor is air cooled and does not need a liquid cooling system. These motors are designed for rotational speeds of up to 14,000 rpm, and the regular motor delivers a typical efficiency of 88 percent; or 90 percent; 80 percent at peak power.

The point for this detail is that it has attributes far beyond the ICE It is light, powerful, and simple. And yes, put in the framework of a FCEV it has the attributes of efficiency and cost that is great and can be driven by battery power and hydrogen. The whole point of hydrogen is mobility and refueling which we agree is desirable unless batteries had a quantum improvement, which remains to be seen. (So don't stop trying), we also agree that natural gas can play into that and the sources you mentioned: shale; methane hydrate; and coal to natural gas or hydrogen are good for at least seventy-five years seemingly good enough until hydrogen and nuclear electric creation (fusion and even enhanced fission) solve the problem for good. It seems like this scenario is within reach, as long as the nation invests in distribution; at homes, offices; and shopping centers; as well as fuel depots (gas stations), and solar recharge-like stations across the applicable highways and freeways (preferably evolve to swappable batteries for convenience).

Believe me, we would love to have Élon Musk, founder of Tesla, to solve our problems by inventing a perpetual battery. Even he knows that teaming with Japan and Germany are a big part of the innovation puzzle. Yes, the USA should lead an effort, but Japan (battery leader and squabbling with China about Sea drilling rights) and Germany (Invented the Internal Combustion Engine (ICE) and is deeply committed to be under Russia's NG price point, are committed to move energy to the next level and will help redefine the 21st century.

Most of all, insist that the end result will not be static, but a continuum, i.e., "SYN-GAS" and "SUN-GAS" creates a new fuel paradigm, and probably fresh water. Thank God for American science and engineering, fostered by free enterprise and close partner shipping with government.

We also feel it is imperative for the R&D on battery life be raised to the level of deployable engineering from its current research state. This is critical because hybrid and plug in vehicles can make ICEs, NGVs, and FCEVs, and EVs reach those higher levels of efficiency we are aiming at meaning that gasoline, natural gas/hydrogen, and electric vehicles running at least 100–150 MPG. We also feel that major brands around the world are already deploying various brands of NGVs and have prototypes of FCEVs. We think the smart short-term play is to major distribution points along the highways and freeways and focus on trucks. It would be a major advantage if we could bridge the natural gas/hydrogen part of the equation if it could be done in a couple of years. Meanwhile all government agencies, the post office, etc. could be moving to natural gas while private competition focuses on large/smaller vehicle solutions.

We also see the necessity with water and energy and we will play our part in the new paradigm which we believe should be conservation and alternatives: natural gas, hydrogen, electric, etc. With agriculture consuming 90 percent of fresh water and population growing at ten billion people every ten or eleven years, the need is obvious. We know the UN has been working hard on these issues for years, and fairly successfully, but does not have the consensus or the cooperation to find a low-cost desalination. They are in the invisible handcuffs of (free?) enterprise i.e. cartels and oligarchies. No, we will reinstitute free markets, if necessary, by downsizing or breaking up monopolies. Just the way the AT&T breakup separated the telecommunications business from the equipment business and revolutionized an industry, perhaps the world. If we have to separate industries by liquid, gaseous, or electric from liquid/gaseous power trains. Whatever is right we will produce the answer and cut our energy costs in half and then reinvest in freshwater supply, giving the majority of benefit back to the consumers. Together water and energy will reshape the 21st century.

Obviously, your announcement is trying to push world action forward.

President: Yes, my next stop is the UN, but we still feel that the United States should address the world by solving its own problems because we consume 25% of all energy on the planet, and provide agriculture all over the world. Water and Energy will allow the spread of agriculture through distributed aquifers as well as giant mega farms.

America produces about $136 billion in agriculture. (Actually about 1.1% of GDP. As China and Asia increase their economic wealth, their consumption of food soars and in particular, chicken and beef. The water and energy movement will enable distributed and economic sources of food and water.

From 2001 to 2011, consumption rose from $697 million to $3.1 billion. A large percent of the United States' agricultural exports go to developing countries. The success of our agriculture has within its accountability to not only ourselves, but to the growing customers in Asia and Africa. We need the world to see that our water and energy policy and tactics not only has critical export or revenue opportunities, but a responsibility that America, yes even the Americas, can leverage to the benefit to the emerging world. That is why it is critical we exceed not only in energy policy, but water policy. Ninety percent of fresh water goes into agriculture. We as a nation that leads the world in the realization of freedom and democracy. We have an opportunity and a responsibility to prioritize our efforts. The solutions needed in the 21st century must lead the world growing to 9.5 billion people. And in fact, if we solve our border problems with Mexico by expanding cross border farming through desalination efforts, we can overcome the immigration problem and the drug problem. The real drug problem, though, may have to be fought in the streets of our cities. The fierceness of our resolve and actions will lift both countries to be the steady, dependable supplier of agriculture that must dominate the world. This mentality will serve Africa as well as Asia and is the hidden agenda of our resolution of the water and energy crises. So, this new paradigm is one that needs to be embraced by the Americas and China. There is also a huge potential for Japan, Africa, et al. Although Japan is still the number two or three economy in the world, it is still, even before the effects of self-sustaining energy, gives them the equal footing to compete.

Surrounding Japan's islands are deep reserves of methane hydrate, so very careful evolution of their opportunity can lead to their energy independence. I emphasize careful, because their experience with Tsunamis and nuclear power is a foretelling of the need to carefully extract Methane from the sea. On one level, they are the most energized to succeed in a proper way, because the realized the results of not respecting mother nature enough. Once they see hydrogen distribution is a standard, what do you think they will do? Tied to their success is the opportunity to leverage their expertise round the world. The point is that America can pursue Methane from multiple sources, including coal, to our own and international benefit, as a way to steer the course for a green ecology, eliminating drought as an agriculture concern, and therefore strong economic benefits to the emerging 1 billion-per-decade population increases in Asia and Africa for at least the next 25 years. Hopefully, population stabilization will work as people learn to sustain families with near zero growth. But we know that comes with wealth and female education.

The 21st century is the Pacific century and it is clear to me that Asia, Australia, and Africa will all participate. The USA is redefining our role. But it has to all come from a culture of the 21st century. This is why I implore you to not fight the future but to build it. That is the power and opportunity you have. If you don't, you will follow other obsolete transportation delivery systems, wood, coal, etc.

And please, we do not have to talk of the obvious need for population control in Africa and India. It has to happen, but China can tell you about the dilemmas of cultural bias (e.g. boys-only births), which led to a projected 50 million too few women. We have to let societies take measured steps. The best step is improved wealth, health, and education. That will spurn a new concern, not enough population growth or more correctly, government can't rule over the natural order of things. The fact is when people feel financially, physically, and emotionally secure, they have smaller families. It has been referenced that the number one way to control population is to educate women. Think about that and you'll recognize the world-wide challenge. Some of the world is miles from the starting gate.

Agriculture (Al): This all sounds great, but how can it all happen without low prices, something that current policies are clearly able to not favor, energy or agriculture? Yes, there is distress, but farm prices are the highest ever, and we live year to year.

President: Do you want to be the proud leader presiding over deserts, or do you want to expand volumes beyond your wildest expectations, and with security of unlimited water and therefore, agriculture, including biofuels, fertilizers, etc.? Even the creation of fertilizer requires fossil fuels. This is the kind of national focus, and international focus that America, and the Americas, and the world require.

AIR 1: We can see it. We are among the largest of beneficiaries, and our efforts will ripple throughout the world and continue the progress of closure realized by air travel, and now the Internet and global easy to access communications. Yes, it is a paradigm that surrounds three elements of WE: water, energy, and we the people. What about the Middle East? How can they see the forest for the trees?

President: The Middle East is a virtual desert. If they cannot see the benefits of W&E, it is sad for them and the world. The answer is quite clear. Solidarity between the US and China, reinforced by the EU, Japan, and Russia will have to come together and look the future right in the eyes. Look at Russia's land mass and northern location. As an American, with those resources, it would be all opportunity. What we need first is solidarity in the United States, and I see your groups as key players in change. And quite frankly, if you do not, you will be swept aside by constitutional amendment, history, and the American people's commitment to reclaim control of our destiny. These moments in history come and go, and it's here.

The nation with perhaps the greatest energy potential is Australia. With the momentum of their energy discoveries and the prospect of water wealth, they have to decide what kind of country they need to be. Australia is a land mass like the United States with fewer than thirty million people right below the largest population in the world. I wonder. Look at a map, it jumps right out at you. After four billion years, how much methane does the world have? The discovery of Methane Hydrate is an indication of its pervasiveness, and that discovery is greater than all fuel sources combined. Remember, when the earth started; it was a mass of swirling energy. So, as it solidified, it left a molten or gaseous center.

Military Industrial Rep (Mil): When you look at this case of grim recognitions from a military perspective, my conclusions and reactions are all over the place. Where do I start? The Mexican border?

On one level we all want to resolve this problem but find it hard to believe we have the will, the resolve, to not compromise it into a problem. The problem will be clear. First, the criminal cartels will try to drag us over the border to create an international incident. Second, they will find ways to go around us. Third, the NRA will protest on any controls regarding tracking gun sales to merchandisers. And fourth, the all-important goal of peaceful transition. If the Russians can do it, the United States can do it. But can the Russians continue to do it?

President: I never said it would be easy. We will work closely with Mexican authorities to close both sides of the border. The New Mexican regime needs to show their people that they will get it done. Mexico is not Pakistan. They will see that cartel heads sitting on Mexico mountaintops plotting against United States children is unacceptable. Unacceptable! Honestly, it's hard not to think of drones, but I think we'll resist that, unless Mexico wants to buy our technology and our expertise and control.

I know you have seen weakness in resolve before, but this will be different. We will make this highly visible and will allow the right groups to see our actual and honest intent and results. We will make our citizens see the extent of our anger over hard drugs and our new legislation over marijuana. We will clear our police, courts and prison system from soft drug issues. Since we cleared our illegal import problems with Columbia, the pressure moved to our Mexican borders, Venezuela, and more. Stagnation at the border is over.

Mir 1 Now as to our presence in the Middle East, we both know that Saudi Arabia agreed with us to have us physically protect their oil fields. If they turn to China, its physical presence must result in a changing of the guard and has to result in trading oil in Yuan. The impact of that on United States inflation could be devastating. We will look like we are stepping down in our leadership and inflation could rock our currency. This would not be true if our debt was not so steep, but it is what it is. The way to solve the problem is massive GNP and profit growth. So why would the United States not leverage water and energy to stabilize the dollar through profitability. You would not make us pay for all those past regressions. Free markets and competition will rapidly clean up our economics.

But at its core, we have to reduce our cost of energy by a half. And the plan we have will accomplish that. Understand and prepare for change, opportunity, and a new world order.

President: Of course, I knew all you just said, and maybe more. Maybe I just know something more. One thing is for sure, you will find out very quickly. Remember, the continuation of the weak economy is our enemy, and the solution is to insist on energy productivity and inexpensive water generation. WE (W&E) are the solution.

So, I did not bring you here for us to exchange the obvious. Your lobbies, I should say, your sponsors are used to working the system, the execs, the Congress, et al. I need to tell you that all of that would be fine except the pain thresholds have been exceeded. In the past, we would just blame the other side and go to war. But that is so last century. We will not make decisions based on lobby money. That period is over.

The first ten years of this century have been ugly…All the forewarnings: wars, depression, drought, recession, near genocides, religious venting, and on and on. You need to tell your sponsors that either they find a way to see the big picture, which is a growing global economy where the markets will exceed 100–trillion-dollar GDP and the opportunity is not based on suppressing the 99% or controlling product to the extent it is anti-capitalism or anti-competition. What was supposed to happen will innovate your way to the next paradigm, not delay your way to short-term profits, no matter how many trillions of dollars, or how many lives.

In the last 50 years, the world has evolved to growing a billion people every ten or eleven plus years. What is supposed to happen, as financial growth and health stabilizes, families shrink, and the earth stabilizes at about 9.5 billion people. The United States has grown primarily through immigration, because everyone wants to catch the dream, the hope. But with China, and India, and Africa and more, the disparity is too great. History and their cultures have not caught up. But they want the American dream they have to see a new light on the hill, and we need to deliver it. And we encourage immigration because it's good for the economy. Look at Japan and the effects of lackluster immigration. Look at the United States and consider the effort it takes to welcome all cultures. This is our dominant culture, appreciating our special experiences, and accepting the need for fairness, honesty, and morality.

It takes time and effort and science and patience and less greed to dominate so that the pursuit of happiness is a real experience, not words in a bad history lesson: life, liberty, and the pursuit of happiness, as long as its actions don't restrain energy profits? I don't think so. Catch the new dream, robust expansion through open markets and clean energy supply exceeding demand plus freshwater expansion. Now we have that opportunity, maybe just this once. So, you tell your sponsors that we have to struggle, sacrifice, and endure. If you want free enterprise and small government, the people in power, the people with the edge, the gift, you must look around and make sure wealth is not an enclave, but a bubbling spring. I know your history, the pain of suffering, the uncertainty of real competition, because is the natural of affairs. And by God, if it is not understood, we will adjust the system till we get it right. Not a welfare state, but a state of reliability that the democracy will adjust to if it gets too big, too powerful, and yes, too wealthy. This isn't a wealth issue; it's a free market issue, including the use of money to drag the economy for the benefit of few.

Now, recognize what we, the earth, have become a global village with differences that allow the equality of men and women, knowledge transfer from old to young, and the experience to want families to endure. We also know that there are elements in our village that just do not want to put in the time, the work. Well law and order must prevail, and yes, rules that certain societies have to evolve to: women's rights; eliminating caste systems; different religions; and different customs; all challenges that must evolve. No matter how much we think our way is best or more moral, if you do not see the preeminence of peaceful coexistence, then you will get the unfortunate alternative. And that goes for all sides.

Now my job is to do my best to not let all the history, and all the distrust, prevent peaceful change to take place. Remember, the USSR recognized they had to change. Now they must realize that they have the power to have lasting security, lasting opportunity, and evolution. Russia needs to see its destiny as an aggressive competitor, yet a peaceful democracy. They are at bat, and they are not steadfast in democracy quite yet. Their focus needs continuous evolution. The problem with Russia is they haven't done what Saudi Arabia is doing...understand that they must reinvest and transform them from industrial might and good fortune into new enterprise. If they don't, Russia will try to muscle their way to the future. If Europe keeps the EU, and they should, they will transform their energy resources to electric, Nat-gas, and hydrogen fuel and transform their societies...this is the call of the 21st century.

Mir1: How can you claim that energy can be provided for $1.00 per gallon?

President: Numerous studies have shown that energy can be provided with fuel cell electric vehicles (FCEV), which is rated 2.45x more efficient (factored down 25% by conversion, e.g. NatGas to hydrogen) than the Internal combustion engine (ICE). When added to hybrid technology, mixing electric with liquid sources (Nat-gas, hydrogen, gasoline), (e representing inclusive of the cost of electric) brings you to **at least the equivalence of $1.00 per gallon.** Now add three special factors. With clean supply exceeding demand, the supply economics will plummet the energy price downward. Added to that, the improvements added to hydrogen, batteries, solar, wind, sea and other fuel sources (sun-gas, syngas, etc.), will push the equation to another level of price performance. Finally, the environmental impact of clean energy will produce new levels of health benefits and more, not to mention, the dreaded (to naysayers) air temperature and reduction of melting ice. Now consider the reduction of military support to fight the impact of energy stress. By leveraging the technology to reduce the cost of energy, we can transform our resources and technology to create massive fresh water, because the primary factor holding back desalinization is the cost and availability of energy to produce fresh water.

Never forget, without massive volume projections, the cost of change is grossly misrepresented. Mass acceptance of flat screen TV's, cars, computer chips, cell phones, and anything that went from new to mass acceptance Add to that the stimulation of innovation led by minimizing the density of stored energy, will exceed all the above invention. Think of all the "residual enterprise" created by the internal combustion engine and the jet plane. Quite frankly, you can't even begin to imagine the impact of excess clean energy on the earth's population, but in a 9 billion population earth, it's not only directional, it's inspiring. Now consider a 9 billion population, two (2) billion cars (currently, over a billion) and clean Water and energy where supply overwhelms demand.

I believe in 100 years, we will laugh over how we struggled to dig wells even beneath the ocean...how we learned to recycle and reenergize our waste, and how we distributed good health. The recognition of the discipline it takes to prevent sickness and how much cheaper it is to work with nature instead of trample all over it, including our bodies. Well, it will not be easy, but your group has a lot to say about how painful or peaceful it will be. This is your moment of change. Do it or lose it.

Guidance

Don't let the saber rattling in the world distract you. Supposedly, China and Russia are planning space armaments to disrupt or disable our space satellite network. China would have to think about that for one second before rejecting something so absurd. The war mongers just won't quit. Always looking for funding the next project. Our, and the world's enemy is **pollution, limited fresh water, and high cost, polluting energy.**

This will be replaced through a Water and Energy (WE) strategy. Societies need to address population growth and the elimination of drought and poverty. If detractors want to stop both needed and achievable progress, do it on someone else's planet! We have the answers, the funding, technology, and finally, the will and courage to change. Dreaming up superior weapons is so 20th century, although sophisticated drones are very scary. What is needed is the willingness to live peacefully with diverse cultures in an eight to nine billion citizen planet. We are embracing the 21st century, because war and terror doesn't work on a planet with our scale of citizenry. So, let's move and act in a positive direction.

Running a country is not a game show, and tit for tat is not a popularity contest, where we measure success based on poll numbers or crowd size, it is real people, facing real challenges, where outcomes change the world. That's what Water & Energy **(WE)** is…real solutions, just when we need them.

Thank you.

CHAPTER X

The White House and Camp David

The President wakes and informs his staff that his family is going to Camp David for a few days and will consider the last month and respond to world leaders, industry leaders, and Congress on an informal basis. Of course, the cabinet is in full engagement considering all that is needed to go right and what could go wrong.

Saudi Arabia asks the president for the king to have a meeting ASAP in Vienna, Austria. The President considers and then schedules flights to Beijing, Moscow, Paris, and Vienna. All the DVDs and reports from the last loop around the earth are provided and the meetings are scheduled, starting in three days for about a week.

Day 1: Camp David

President to the First Lady: Today, I am lying low. What I need to accomplish in the next couple of weeks is, if I must say so, historic. Tomorrow, I have set up phone conversations with the prime minister of Australia, Israel, Mexico, Canada, Brazil, and England. They know I'm looking for not only guidance but a sense of relevance and timing.

First Lady: I have reviewed all the meetings, and the only question that stands before us is: Is the world ready for change, ready to embrace this century?

God, the last ten years has been a foretelling that maybe the world is still captured by all the wars, genocide, and revolutions of the 20th century. Are we, the global we, ready to insist on change? How many ways and through what techniques can our citizens both embrace positive change and stand strong against the tide of the status quo? I know you would not have done this if you did not have a sense of not only the mandate but the ability to engage the people in momentum. You do not need to address it immediately, but you have to think how we can embrace the Internet through Facebook, Twitter, and social sites around the world.

President: This is the history that tells me to do it. I would not consider it if it was not for the Arab Spring, the notion that for the first time in history, billions of people are accessible. One hundred thousand Americans could create a swell that would result in tens of billions of positive contributions taking place. In fact, maybe all this experience in blogs and social networks are meant to create an unparalleled communication, if we can handle it. Facebook's base of 2.3 billion compares to USA population of 330 mm.

If we could stop militarizing everything and focus on the science and engineering for clean, efficient water and energy, we'd be better off. People must see inevitability of it all and know that they can insist on the necessary changes.

Honey, this is a challenge I will pass to you. Get the best people you can to develop a plan with an irreconcilable Internet force, all with existing sites based on user site members and activity.

Go to the major companies, especially Microsoft, Google, Yahoo, and look for innovators like Facebook, Twitter etc. Have a plan in a month and deployment steps ready when I return, okay?

First Lady: I will be talking to the top people and distribute it so they can ripple the process through all their points of communication. Please give me a guidance letter to open doors for me. I will take no action until you approve it.

CHAPTER XI

The United States and Australia Speak

Two days passed and the President is back at the White House and makes a series of phone calls to Australia; Israel; Mexico; Canada; Brazil; and England.

Australia PM (A-PM): I appreciate your call and I am, quite frankly, dismayed by the actions in the last five years. In fact, to be open, Bin Laden and Saddam Hussein in death have wreaked quite a dilemma on the United States and the world. What I am sharing with you is blunt, but it will not be distributed so it is confidential. You know Australia has followed the United States down the road to war ever since World War II: Korea, Vietnam, Iraq, Afghanistan, and now what?

In this 21st century, the openness in communications is something that I think any of us truly does not understand, but the public is more informed and opinionated than any time in history.

You can see by the chart that since 9/11/2001, oil has been in an energy bubble, and I think it is about to burst. Before your trek, everyone was speculating about oil at $100 per barrel, primarily because of things like Iran and concern about the Strait of Hormuz, for example.

One of the key reasons the United States has yet to experience a sovereign debt crisis is that the world reserve currency status of the US dollar supports demand for the US dollar and for US federal government debt. Through 2011, the vast majority of world oil trade settled in dollars, but markets have been projected to change as early as 2019-20. The US dollar is in the process of gradually losing its world reserve currency status. Global trade is fragmenting into increasingly autonomous trading blocs defined by currencies and trade relations, such as the BRIC nations together with South Africa as of March 2012. Further, Iran is settling with China in Yuan and India in gold and rupees, as of July 2012, in violation **of the embargo, which apparently, with China, you approved.**

Having taken a decision to act unilaterally against Iran, regardless of the UN actions, the United States may be forced to resort to more extreme measures, if the world reserve currency status of the US dollar begins to break down even further.

Of course, the United States does not control the oil trade solely through financial means. With Israel as a close ally, Iraq and Afghanistan occupied by US forces, close ties with Turkey, Saudi Arabia, Kuwait, Qatar and other Middle Eastern countries, Iran is surrounded by more than 40–US military installations.

Historically, trading in US dollars was done for two reasons. One, the stability of our currency, and two our military force protecting oil fields all over the Middle East. With China, you approved.

Of course, the United States does not control the oil trade solely through financial means. With Israel as a close ally, Iraq and

Afghanistan occupied by US forces, close ties with Turkey, Saudi Arabia, Kuwait, Qatar and other Middle Eastern countries, Iran is surrounded by more than forty US military.

I wouldn't rely on that visual. It's suspect. Recent pictures are much less comprehensive...The point is quickly is not the answer in foreign affairs.

A successful invasion of Iran would eliminate the largest US dollar oil exporter, delaying the breakdown of the US dollar's status as the world reserve currency. Although a war with Iran would cause a spike in oil prices and Iran would increase the supply of oil available for purchase in US dollars, which would bring the US dollar toward stability.

This is what I see, not necessarily how the United States will act: A preemptive military strike for reasons of monetary or economic policy would be politically unjustifiable and morally unacceptable.

Not yielding again in the absence of evidence, it's another matter entirely to have a military strike to secure the world against the horrific specter of a rogue nuclear state, one that openly challenges the right of the nation of Israel to exist and that might eventually be able to put nuclear devices in the hands of radical Islamic extremists.

Are nuclear weapons being to Iran what WMDs are to Iraq? So, you'd better be right this time. We are both students of history. The only difference is if we do nothing, it is a certainty that Israel will destroy the Iranian nuclear sites. So you have to ask, who should intervene.

I say again, on March 2012, the BRIC nations and South Africa signed an agreement to not trade in US dollars anymore, but in their own currencies. They are even working on creating their own bank for trading between each other and to handle the currencies, besides lines of credit in the currencies. BRIC nations account for half of the world's population. And Saudi Arabia is having China build them an oil refinery in their country. Just a few months ago, China's oil shipments exceeded the United States' for the first time in history. High oil prices have diminished the United States' demand, but China still grows at 2-8 percent per year.

President: We have and will continue to restore our growth in energy. It is projected that United States' population will reach four hundred fifty million by 2050. So, in some respects, we are like Australia. But as a society, you are young. Further, you are the size of the continental United States but have only about 33–million people. You have been discovering more and more key geo-science minerals, and now a Saudi-sized shale oil field in South Australia (although stalled due to funding). China is now your key business partner. And your numerous shale findings have been remarkable.

Pres AU: Yes, with the exploitation of mining enhancements like your horizontal drilling, we are optimistic. More importantly, any work you do in converting coal to methane, and of course desalination is critical to us. Imagine if all the money we both spent on war in the last ten years were in exploiting water and mineral innovation and mining. When I consider your compelling writing on population growth, we wonder if somehow the economics of desalination could be achieved faster and cheaper.

President: Therefore, we need your support. The US, China, India, and more need to recognize that, especially the growing population regions in Asia, all aspects of water and agricultural enhancement is a world priority. China must realize that the key is not to just getting energy but achieving low cost clean energy productivity is the goal. And the path to that besides fracking, oil sands, and such, is the switching of a large portion of transportation to advanced hybrids with deeper battery density, and NGV/Hydrogen, with FCEV and EV engine expansion. This is what we need from our allies focus on the larger scale.

A-PM: Yes, if only the world followed Jimmy Carter's warnings in the 1970s. We know water is the key to our future. We still struggle but need a lift from technology, and as what you say, low-cost clean energy.

President: And the key is to focus on nonpetroleum transportation and water conservation and desalination. *We call it Water and Energy. (WE)*

We know, as the largest energy consumer on the planet, we have to lead to the new path, and our direction will be emulated.

A-PM: Without the oil producing nations crippling you by going off the oil-based dollar, you are to a degree handicapped by the sins of your past, particularly your debt and T-bill demand caused by a negative budget. Just as your path to the future could lead all of us out of this gap between supply and demand, you could be challenged with near hyperinflation. I think the answer is increasing your price productivity in oil and your earnings growth will fill the tax revenue gap, as long as you draw the line as a welfare state.

President: Now you know why we need your support. We cannot be backed into a corner. Maybe your own discoveries can back us through the realization that the new century is a worldwide event, not just the United States. We have the resources and the will to secure our economy and maintain a very stable dollar. Thank you, and I will keep you posted.

The President works his way through his phone list and gets his support message out but hears the combined message of support with concern over the dollar as a reserve currency, war with Iran, and how China and Russia play into this challenge. China does hold a lot of US dollars and US Treasuries, around one point three (1.3) trillion dollars, but those are denominated in US dollars and cannot be converted into Chinese Yuan overnight. If those two trillion dollars in currency reserves were magically converted into Chinese Yuan, then the Yuan could start competing against the $ US 9.7 trillion-dollar reserves held by institutions around the world. But there are other factors to consider.

The Euro may collapse, making the financial world more conservative and the dollar stronger. This, however, won't benefit China or the US.

The Chinese economy is dependent on the United States and Euro economies. We know you are changing that. It still does not have enough "in China" consumer purchasing power. The American consumer is still the strongest buying power in the world. If the US economics was pushed down by acts of China, the United States and its citizens may discourage Chinese product. China needs to yield but to also pursue clean energy productivity.

The US still could exercise military power in Syria and/or Iran, especially since Iran is bypassing the embargo on oil sales by exchanging oil in other currencies. This is what Saddam Hussein did before America invaded Iraq. But this is a time to learn from our mistakes, not repeat them.

These uncertainties are in the President's briefcase as he travels once more around the world Beijing, Moscow, Paris, and

Vienna. The president faces an interesting challenge with mostly grim alternatives:

Succeed in brokering a stalemate while the US reengineers its energy delivery system around natural gas, hydrogen, and electric. The president may have to compromise XOF for: OIL: Oil Import Latency (something that is latent exists but is not obvious and has not developed yet) for example, continue current oil arrangements while reengineering US supply and demand and let the market control price.

Wait for Iran to create a nuclear weapon, and then invade and control its oil fields. Note an extreme idea to most! Or let Israel act on its own, and then NATO supports an air war. This assumes maybe an active rebellion as in Libya or elsewhere.

Make a deal with Saudi Arabia and China.

The United States is vulnerable because of its deep budget shortfalls. If we did not have a national debt of $20+ trillion dollars, we would not be subject to fiscal blackmail. About $5 trillion on the books of oil exporters; $1.6 trillion to the BRICs, of which China is owed $1.169 trillion; and $254 billion to other oil exporters. That is the governments of more than half the people in the world; pushing four billion, which more than the entire world population fewer than fifty years ago.

Realize that the US government itself is inside the inside owners of our public debt. We hold T-Bills in: Social Security $2.67 billion; Federal Reserve $1.659 billion; savings oaths and related instruments $1.102 billion; pensions $903 billion; mutual funds $798 billion; state and local governments $444.6 billion; Medicare $324 billion; and more. In other words, we can never default, no matter how much interest rate escalates. We have to meet any interest rate requirements of T-bills and stave off the ripple effect. But the American economy is accelerating and reducing its debt. That is really our opportunity to continue to increase our profits, and debt shrinks away very quickly.

And about five trillion dollars must find new investors and/or lenders if we lose the faith of our oil exporters. The good news is that the United States is the only superpower that has endured massive challenges, militarily and financially, even simultaneously, and who has always followed through. In the next 20 years, who is Saudi Arabia going to invest in, China? Only the United States shows time and again it can bounce back.

If the United States or Israel attack Iran at any level: nuclear reactor elimination, air support to eliminate air strike potential; or invasion by troops; that is the end of the current Iranian government. That must be understood by everyone, especially Iran.

But quite frankly, that's not why we're talking. I want to sure you understand the implications of Coober Pedy. Australia is soon to become a Middle East, in concert with China and Russia. Your wealth will expand, but your role in World leadership, could be a major factor in the Pacific Century. You must carefully grab the reigns for your people and the people of the world.

Aus: But private enterprise must lead, The Coober Pedy opportunity was paused because of World conditions, i.e. the impact of shale on energy prices.

President: and we're here to tell you: we've got your back.

CHAPTER XII

One More Trek around the Globe: Beijing; Moscow; Europe; and Vienna (Home of OPEC)

The trip commences.

The President and four cabinet members arrive in Beijing and prepare for the next day's briefing.

Beijing

The President knows a high degree of communication is the only methodology that means anything. This meeting has to be handled as if the future of both countries is on the line.

They arrive at the offices of the Ministry of Foreign Affairs of the People's Republic of China (CP). Also attending is foreign relations minister of China (FRC)

The meeting coalesces.

CP: We appreciate the meeting because the agenda of water and Energy is perhaps the focal point of the 21st century and is our mutual concern, as is the nonproliferation of nuclear weapons.

Our relationship with Iran, Syria, and Saudi Arabia is the soil that must be sowed. Saudi Arabia has asked for a deeper relationship, so we both need to openly and mutually put everything on the table. We have more to gain from mutual discussion, and we recognize that the EU and America are our best customers.

President: We are where we are today, in this meeting, because we have found the opportunity to shift to greater use of gaseous fuels, which we hope you could see also, given both our vast coal and natural gas resources. You have read or seen all our dialogue on these matters from our distributions over the last months, so I will not repeat it, but it is clear to say that we must evolve with our current Middle East partners; in fact, we are here because of the directions set by the OPEC organizations. Of course, this is also in context of Syria and Iran, and all the other oil-producing nation states, for that matter. And all of that is also in the broader context of highly successful relationship in mutual commerce. Yes, we have trade differences and points of view, but the size of our business is both remarkable and still filled with opportunity. In fact we both know that our manufacturing support, particularly in electronics and telecommunications and our proliferation of retail restaurants and the automobile business in China shows, at some level, a deep trust in our mutual objectives, both in employment and use of the products and also in the implications of our codependency, which I am sure we both see the peaceful dividend.

America also recognizes your need and desire to evolve your commerce to a prosperous inward focus as well as in international commerce. We also recognize that China's progress will soon make her the number one economy in the world, so our need for cooperation and the spirit of free enterprise enjoins our spirit and actions. We were probably here, in one sense, because Saudi Arabia oil exports are now greater in China than the United States, probably a significant milestone in history. You also buy more than a trillion dollars in our T-bills, making you a deep investor in the United States. The point being, our relationship will continue to get even stronger over time. We support the evolution of the Pacific Century, and we are also partners, with India and really all of Asia, and remarkably Australia. We particularly look at the 9.5-billion-population planet of 2050. As strong and powerful as we are, this should give us pause. If the rate of change continues for the next fifty years, we cannot even imagine the challenges of growth. But, we have to contemplate three responsibilities:

1. The Water and Energy program will be well underway.

2. We will have averted a war of major consequence.

3. Economic uplift will be worldwide in a way that also will have reduced nuclear threat to a figment of twentieth-century history. Not that this will be easy, the rogues of war will fight this if they can. But the benefits of challenging poverty will be the millennial result.

The consequences of avoiding a Water and Energy massive crisis are in many ways greater in Asia than anywhere else, except Africa, although our agenda is certainly full. What is true is we have had to resolve the nature of agriculture across the planet and within the United States, which implies we have solved the water problem. To not place all other issues in perspective is to deny the future. We see it as usurping all other issues.

The proper word is evolution. You must believe in a few things. First you have to believe in the opportunities in and around natural gas and hydrogen and pure electric energy. You must believe shale gas is available to a large extent around the world. I believe your discoveries so far are clear signals. But you must reconcile the use of Water and liquid $CO2$ in that agenda. And yes, you must believe that clean drilling regulations are enforceable. Second you must believe in the opportunities coming from methane hydrate. We believe that even if we stuck to mining the permafrost around the arctic regions, this would be enough. But Japan has to seriously consider methane hydrate. Although these findings are in the early stages, they add to the prospects that the automobile could switch to NG and hydrogen with little risk we can't deny that Sun-gas and Syn-Gas opens the door to true energy independence. We must admit that hydrogen from sea water is assured. This is a scientific reality. It is Japan's one shot, before fusion, at energy independence. The third is seeing that converting coal to methane including burying the $C02$, or liquefying it for Fracking, would more than compensate for any shortfalls. Our opportunity for peaceful security far exceeds our last fifty years, if China sees and follows the vision. The vision we see for all is not just more but different and more efficient and pollution erasable. That is there are key reasons pointing to need solutions that at the outset reduce pollutions and they need to be taken very seriously.

As we convert the trucking industry to natural gas and/or hydrogen, and/or electricity, it would be enough to relieve the supply or demand imbalance. Then there is air travel. We believe if the pressure is not so strong for a single solution, such as exploiting biofuels from algae, for example, it could fuel the airline business. We see two things occurring.

The freeing of airlines from the cost pressure we are under would stimulate the airline business for massive growth. Has China truly seen its potential if its economy rises and air travel costs decline? Especially since you're already moving into airplane manufacturing!

The new 1,600 mph engines we're working on at Boeing have precise and achievable goals, but is still out there, time wise. We will create a level of travel and military jet that would shrink our planet even more. This must be incorporated into a strategy. And you need to be on friendly terms with us. We just want you to be sure, it will happen, and we see a China-USA relationship not only synergistic, but a necessary part of a free world.

But what you must see is that China and the United States going down the same path would tip the supply and demand balance so greatly that the cost of gasoline would spiral downward. We are prepared to help you prove that you have the resources within reach to assure breaking the 9/11 bubble and reducing the cost of energy in half. Now add to this hybrid and electric motor battery densities at three to four and then five to ten times more storage capacity, and gasoline and natural gas and hydrogen can evolve together. Now add the evolution of the FCEV and hydrogen from natural gas and the evolution is so strong that we could take one hundred years to develop fusion, and it is okay. But it will be sooner. Have your scientists spent time in England and at CERN in Switzerland? But we must progress now. Stop the pain of unconscionable oil cost and pollution and our economies will bloom again, and in your case, even more. Clearly you can see...

The point is that it's time to stop pollution as a 21st century problem. We must honor China's reality as our own. That is 21st century thinking.

FRC: Yes, these are the major opportunities before us. We know when we look at our challenges with water pollution, the need for more water for industry and agriculture, and the population we have driving us forward. The problem is each time we decide to build more coal fired energy plants, or strike strategic oil deals, there is a certain let us say concern about America's actions. We clearly see the 9/11 oil bubble and see the price of oil tripling, and in many respects pointing to China and India for the surge in demand. But the realities include Desert Storm, Iraq, Afghanistan, Libya, the Arab Spring, Syria, and now Iran sanctions all with a US footprint behind them. I want to discuss this further and confidentially, so I am a little concerned given the audit trail of previous meetings.

President: Let me momentarily interrupt and assure you this meeting is meant to be open and critical, so we are not recording this in any way. We see this as something you should document and decide what is publishable and what not. This is because we want to talk about Iran, Israel, Saudi Arabia, and Russia in such a way that there is no doubt of our mutual direction.

When I step back, you must decide whether you are to invest in a million cars with unproductive engines producing half the efficiency of the FCEV. I can see you moving to electric cars on several fronts. Please participate in our energy research. It will be productive and will push all our goals forward. We see that one of our leaders invested in your electric car. That's good for you and us.

FRC: This what we want, so take our comments as idea generators or clarification points because I believe in your science and your humanity, despite positioning statements, but the impact of commercial and political pressures is something else. We must overcome that, both of us.

We see your relationship with the Saudis as pressurized as it has ever been. The Sunni and Shiite divide with the Saudis and Syria and Iran is something we quite frankly cannot reconcile when it comes to anti-American presence or anti-Israel concerns. When Bush was in power, he was running around spouting off about democratic nations, but his actions were based on oil and the dollar. Almost immediately after Saddam Hussein started trading oil outside the dollar, you invaded Iraq. You had a lot of excuses, WMDs and such, but you were very sensitive to that issue. You know that we are building a refinery in Saudi Arabia, and yes, their concern for military protection of their oil fields has come up. You know that the BRIC countries have agreed to settle oil outside of the US dollar and there have been discussions with others. You know India is settling with Iran in gold and rupees, and China–Iran in Yuan. It seems all of our issues are surrounding the dollar and let us call it "energy security". You have said energy is the elixir of society. You can see through the bypassing of the of the Iran boycotts, that nations can't risk an oil shortage. You have to see that with our and India's population, we can't risk energy embargos, it's unacceptable for China and India. These aren't strategies, they are hardened realities.

President: The issues of debt and purchasing our T-bills is meaningful to us because the actions we are taking reduce the cost of energy as a paradigm that no one seems to talk about. You have pressures to internalize your growth and the infrastructure build-up you are under is commendable but also very expensive. But you can't keep building unoccupied cities. You have to internalize your wealth and that takes clean water and more productive energy. We are on the edge of an inflationary spiral and need to take correction action in a significant way. Our solution is to strengthen our economy. Apparently, you wish to strengthen the Yuan by cornering the gold market. That's well and good, but if you don't address pollution and continue to pay twice what you should for energy and don't address the freshwater impact for the next billion people as well as your aging population, your short-term strength will willow away.

We see the dilemma this way. We, and you, quite frankly, need to change the energy paradigm not only to lower costs but to do what must be done to produce more fresh water. Conservation and tactical improvements are important, but there are three salient points: Saltwater covers 70% of the planet (98% including depth); the limiting factor on water desalination is the cost and availability of energy to generate steam; and **China and the United States have the same problems: clean water, pollution, and the fact that 70-90 percent of fresh water needs to be used for agriculture.** You know what spurred the Arab Spring was skyrocketing food costs while the people's government were awash with cash from oil. This is an unstable economy because too much of the wealth rises to the top. As you know, when the issues of core living are at stake, people lose their sense of humor. When we move forward, we advise you to have your plan in place because our plan will succeed.

You see the opportunity in natural gas or hydrogen, but Fracking implies using large quantities of water to free the gas from shale. You need an integrated approach for food, water, and energy. We see the application of liquid CO2 in the shale initiative, we just suggest you join the hunt for viable Water & Energy. It's clearly the time for a WE strategy.

We see 2019 as a moment in time when we decide not to fight over energy, but to fix the problem. Imagine a progression where you knew the cost and availability of clean, fresh water and energy was on track and costs were declining. Yes, we think there is strife in the Middle East because they need to be doing more for their people, as Saudi Arabia is, but they did not use enough of their profits to make their economies more diverse. Quite frankly, their revenues could be cut in half, and they could do more for their people and still have great profits. The world is being driven by one single fact: in in slightly more than twelve years, another billion people will inhabit the planet, mostly in Asia and Africa, so our solution is to buck the status quo and provide effective alternatives and make energy more productive.

World War II had a lot to do with the struggle for energy, and now it's Water and Energy. China has just caught up with the pressures of this moment. Two countries, the United States and China, can resolve the issues, with no winners or losers, just winners.

It is time to reject the old way: the 20th century way, the way forged by dominance in military power. To an extent, Russia's recognition of that in 1990 was a signal. But it put us in the place of world policeman, which we will not abandon per se, but we need to evolve from. We have proven many times we can outspend and outlast anyone militarily. China and the United States need to mutually establish Water and Energy as the real challenge; lower our pollution outputs; and increase energy efficiency and the supply of fresh water. Then we will have changed the history of our species, and most importantly, the financial opportunity for our people.

The EU, Japan, India, Pakistan, the Indonesians, South America, even South Korea, Australia, Russia, and the Middle East have a lot to say about what can and should get done. We decided to change because we felt it is in our mutual interests and is something we could realize near term. The population clock is ticking, and it's in our interest to lead. And believe me, Germany, Japan, and others see the handwriting on the wall.

The crises in Syria rolled into Europe, and that virtually guaranteed, they will adapt a Water and Energy strategy. The Middle East can clearly see that instability will cause the world to change the world sooner. The tide has turned towards clean productivity which is now required for energy.

Confidentially, if we cannot resolve our problems with Iran over nuclear weapons, we may have no choice but to act. You should know that the small nation of Israel cannot abide with a nuclear blackmail, so either Iran solves the problem, or NATO solves the problem, or Israel will. We will be sure the oil fields of Iran and Iraq are friendly with the NATO powers, and oil trade will be settled in perhaps an IMF (International Monetary Fund) currency. We will sustain any change because our economy will be braced by productivity. Our solution, like yours is a rock-solid monetary base.

This should be clear. Now do we want war? Can we afford war? These are the times when you experience the resolve of the American people, and of course, China, and yes Russia and the EU. Often, countries have mistaken our internal and vocal tribulations as a weakness. No, it is a strength backed by our military power and the resolve of our citizens.

Unfortunately, Iraq got mixed up with our energy agenda. For China to be the significant player it wants to be in the 21st century, it must move beyond the current energy paradigm. Yes, we must be assured of supply, and in time over the centuries the same could be said about wood, coal, and oil. But this century is dominated by technology that not only find and extract fossil fuel and leverage natural resources, it replaces the paradigm with higher energy productivity and ample freshwater.

Ask yourself, do we really want to fight over water and oil? No we want to expend resources to enhance our peoples' way of life. Frankly, we should be racing to assure that agriculture can feed 9.5 billion people. No one admits it, but it is a China and United States problem, amongst others. Despite our rhetoric, we are world traders who just want a fair deal.

That is why our countries should move together to set the framework of the 21st century. Not in lockstep but in direction. The model for the first ten years of the 21st century is not only ugly, it's one that follows the pattern of the last one hundred years. We are approaching the stress of the last decade by supporting a model that supports greed instead of truly solving problems. In a world of seven to ten billion people, the casualties could be so great that the trauma from the numbers alone will shock the world for 50 years. Our prospective is that when the needle passes 8 billion, there is no room for miscalculation. When Africa sees itself as being half the world's population, the real threat of worldwide pandemic is before us. Look at AIDS, Pneumonia, TB, and measles all flaring in Africa, the bio-lab for humanity. An 8–9 billion population planet is a petri dish of possibilities. If we are driven to war by the Middle East, we will end it quickly, and it will be ugly. Don't ever think that the support of Israel from the US or the EU will ever waver. If we are forced to pause for 10–20 years, we'll do it. But the consequences to the Middle East will be very terminal. I'm telling you this, because I know it will never happen. Count on it.

Just consider: World War I had fifteen million deaths; World War II fifty million deaths. For World War III, will there be...a billion deaths? Remember the population and the weapon power and financial power of today are awesome. None of it makes any sense when science and engineering has proven answers.

None of us want that, but we can easily see the possibility. Think why removing nuclear weapons from North Korea and the Middle East is a primary goal. I know it is hard to say this when we have forty military bases surrounding Iran, but I am asking China to join us on a new page of world history. We can posture to temper our constituencies, but man to man, we should be in lockstep.

FRC: We both must consider our near-term actions very carefully. It is easy for you to see, we hope, that aggressive actions will not brand you with another couple of decades of neocolonialism. That era must be proven finished by the USA.

President: No, we are paying the price in debt for our choices for the first 13 years of this century, but we and you need time to reconcile our books and produce low-cost fresh water and clean inexpensive energy must be a part of the reconciliation of our debt. Not for any retribution, just providing rewards for productivity. Neo colonialism is over, and your point is well taken, and agreed to!

We feel we are setting our financial house in order, but in many respects, many see us as the standard-bearers for free trade that are creating the opportunity for another round of world GDP growth. While we carried our old role, many, including China, prospered. The allies played at major part in the resurgence of Japan and Germany and China, so you should know when it is all said and done, the world is evolving upward. We saw that and thanks to Mao, President Nixon, and Henry Kissinger. We are also in actions together that will enable China to be a leader in this century and we are just asking you to look to actions that move our world forward, not just some tactical eco-plays or power plays. In the 21st century, in 8.5- 9.5 billion planet, middle class direction will upwardly grow on all continents. We don't need war, we need clean W&E, and cooperation with common goals. You can see by both our actions that we can coalesce, with distributed answers. Even our actions in the USA must spawn diversity with an under-structure of fail safe. The one variable is breakthrough in Fusion, battery density, and delivery efficiency. My promise is to keep you advanced in our innovations, and only ask you reciprocate.

It is becoming clear that the paradigm of "more oil" is a 20th-century mindset, and the new paradigm is fresh Water and clean, lower-cost Energy. "Change the mix" is the new world order. There is room for a robust community of ten billion people, all progressing in wealth, health, and international codependency. So now China has a major role. But they must look beyond today and tomorrow to a world that works together.

FRC: Well, good luck with the Russians and the Saudis. We see it, and these two countries can be difference makers. We will take this into deep consideration. But we both must work on the

Saudis, the Israelites, the Iranians, and the Russians. Access to Russian energy is critical for us. Do you get it? We do.

Let me depart with a personal revelation. It's history. When the black citizens were enslaved, they were selected based on their personal characteristics Result the NFL and the NBA, and more. Also, if a Negro was caught reading a book, they were killed. But they could sing and dance. The Result...the entire American music culture is dominated by the Afro-American culture.

The point is that the human species has thrived based on its ability to exploit what is in all of us. Whether Chinese, African, or American, etc. We limit ourselves through culture and discipline, or lack thereof. The reason the USA is innovative is we promote freedom, and education. China (and Asia) has two advantages, a high degree of discipline and a huge population. Your limitation is a rigid culture that programs hierarchy. So, as we progress together, we must increase discipline and you need to open your society. So, let's see if we can all evolve in a 9.5 billion person world. And figure out how to prosper in piece.

Moscow the US team flies in the next day. They meet with the Russian chairman [RC] in the Kremlin.

President: Thank you for meeting me again on such short notice. I am meeting with the Saudis about our relationship, and I felt it was important we meet first.

We are not recording these meetings and will not release a transcript without your approval. It is important that we are as open with each other as possible. I want to get your input and address your concerns.

Russian Chairman (RC): I appreciate that. We have a lot of issues. And we will be open about them. We think United States concerns about Iran relate to the fact they have moved away from trading oil in dollars. Of course, the boycott leaves them no option except complying with the UN mandate. The compromise has opened up SWIFT (Society (for) World International Funds Transfer) that had stifled their world. When Iraq stopped settling oil sales in dollars in 2002, a decision actually made in 2000, the United States invaded Iraq in March 2003. In 2002, the US debt was $6 trillion against a gross domestic product of $9 trillion. In 2012, your debt was $15.8 trillion, going to $20–plus trillion. Global economies have, since World War II, captured dollars to service foreign debts and accumulated dollar reserves to sustain the exchange value of their own currency.

The world's central banks hold dollar reserves equal to their currency in circulation. Oil and import/export settled in dollars, puts enormous dollars in circulation.

Dollar reserves can be obtained by buying United States' debt in T-Bills. The more pressure to devalue a currency, the more dollar reserves are required. This makes each nation's economy dependent upon the US dollar. It is known as dollar hegemony, constructed partially by oil in other words, oil producing nations historically only accepted dollars, until the Yuan or other suggested currencies are needed to counter a US oil-based dollar, what other smaller countries seen as neocolonialism. Debt to GDP is now bouncing over to 100.

To be honest, the world is concerned that debt growth will force inflation to burst through your "quantitative easing" efforts. It already has for food. This instability would damage the prospect of settling oil transactions in dollars. So, if we preempt your efforts, as we are doing with the BRIC nations, the lower dollar circulation will reduce our purchase of T-bills. If that occurs, you are swept into interest rate increases to meet your demand for debt servicing. It seems inevitable if your country continues to increase your debt, and that can lead to your doing things to increase profitability.

Now how do you balance that inevitability with a shift to natural gas, hydrogen, and electricity priority in electricity, heating, and transportation? You are a little trapped. From a near hyperinflation perspective, it may be cheaper to buy $100 per barrel oil. So, we see your efforts as reducing our income, reducing demand.

President: It's time you see what would be called a broader perspective. As nations' economies grow, their use of Water and Energy grows by a larger amount—for example, the use of air conditioning, automobiles, etc. Simultaneously, consumption of beef, pork, and other meat grows. But in today's world, where agriculture consumes 70-90 percent of freshwater and populations need more food and water, something has to change. The economies must get more efficient. Look at China, circling the globe making any energy deal they can find. Population growth is supposed to be slowing down, but it is still accelerating, now one billion people in less than eleven years. We need to work together, with China. China says she needs Russian energy. We say yes, we need a trifecta.

Russia, with its vast northern regions as you grow eastward, must have significant natural gas and oil. Meanwhile, we are obtaining more technology to not only drill more effectively, but allow engines and equipment run at higher levels of efficiency. In a world growing to nine to ten billion people, economies will only rise with more low-cost clean water and energy. China, as a perfect example, is trying to become more inwardly focused, where consumption is by their own people, causing less reliance on exports. But that also impacts their labor costs. (A circular problem)

Yes, that represents more opportunity for us and other countries like Japan and Germany. But that makes the system work. Countries with lower development reach up. It is not evil but evolution. Certainly, Russia can see that. And I repeat the most important reality, as income rises, people's consumption of meat rises significantly- all that points to water.

In all this growth, there is another challenge to overcome: pollution of air and water. With 70-90 percent of freshwater being used for agriculture and the climate impacted by global warming, we need to expand access to and creation of freshwater. The world of ten billion people must achieve more productivity in energy to afford desalination. Even Saudi Arabia is looking to solar to create water from desalination. Even though they are the most desalinated country on the planet, they see energy as too expensive for that process, and even with them, they see oil as a diminishing resource. They are looking forward. It's a good thing. We know climate change is a mixed bag, all northern regions, especially Russia and Canada will benefit from global defrosting.

Well, in America, we are experiencing drought and challenges to our agriculture, *as are you* with wheat production. We already are feeding much of the world. Our increased costs for vegetables and livestock are affecting the world. You know a lot of the Arab Spring is about accelerating food costs, even though their governments have been making more money due to high oil prices. Meanwhile, Iran and OPEC see high prices as an inherited gift from their land. And they inhibit growth to prop up their income from an ultimately diminishing resource. They need to deal with the fact that people at the top are obtaining more wealth at the expense of their population. Yes, we have the same problems in the United States, the Euro-zone, and even Russia. When we have increased amounts of natural gas, we are going to exploit it and so should you. Your natural gas is well positioned to supply China, especially since you have more water for Fracking.

But you must see, with shale oil and gas and in time, methane hydrate, there is a new standard of supply waiting to be embraced by transportation energy needs. Add science with energy storage or battery density, and we have an *energy revolution* and a bridge.

From our perspective, diversification of our economies is the path...Saudi Arabia sees it, northern Europe sees it.

Yes, I agree that we all need to develop more distribution of wealth. This is a prime motivator for us, and I hope, Russia. The world is changing because of population growth and technology. We see transportation cost at one hundred plus mpg being commonplace. Yes, unit/per gallon revenue decrease, but the opportunity for volume is much greater. The problem at the increases I am talking about, oil and petroleum will be exhausted. How does that serve the Middle East? Do they have a problem if they do not diversify their society to manufacturing and services? Let me ask, do you? Your major advantage, even over the United States, is you have vast regions with opportunities in energy and minerals, and a relatively low population over a huge region.

Look at Australia with as much land as the continental United States, and only 25+ million people. Their problem is water, so low-cost fresh water from efficient desalination is their future, but they must prioritize it. They are lying right below the massive populations of India, China, and Indonesia. You cannot see that their opportunities in agriculture and land development are enormous. And now what, vast discoveries of oil in shale, and soon to be the world's number one LNG provider, eventually overcome by the USA and Canada.

You see, we must grow and get more efficient. We have water crises, an agriculture crisis, and pollution, even before talking about global warming or climate change. We are just asking Russia to not fight change but to exploit change. I think China and India, who are desperate due to population, at the end of the day, will see this, especially as they see how quickly we are successful. If anyone on this planet should be tired about war and its costs in human suffering, it is Russia. You know what World War I and World War II cost you. You know what Stalin cost you. I am not criticizing; we know the price of colonialism throughout the last two–to three–hundred years and more.

Remember, the United States' birth was through anti-colonialism. We will recertify our positive position in South America, the Middle East, and Asia.

But this all must change this century, because the population factor makes the consequences of more war much more devastating. Surely you know that. We need Russia to help the Middle East recognize that short term gain will diminish, we guarantee that. We are still developing more military systems, and so are you. But that must change, and you know it. Do you really think we want to use it? Like you, we must evolve our World War II and cold war mentality. The world must be more peaceful. But we all must see the need for energy productivity, to power our civilizations and the creation and transport of freshwater.

RC: Meanwhile, what are we going to do? We are all caught in the cycle. The Middle East sees the world from their history. They think oil is a gift from God and meant for them as a holy people. How do you fix that?

President: Israel is part of that. What seemed to be a given about Mid-Eastern Oil dominance is soon to be rendered 20th century and now the new century brings us hope in Water & Gas. GOD HAS A WICKED SENSE of HUMOR. Clearly you can see that Israel, with fewer than seven million people and fifteen million Jews around the world are flourishing with no oil business to speak of. Now they are finding natural gas off their shores in the Mediterranean. They are a Western culture in the middle of a Middle Eastern time stamp. I do not know how to describe it. It is perplexing. There are 1.6 billion people from the faith of Islam. How can 1.6 billion accuse fifteen million people of anything, but being highly results oriented? We, including Russia, participated in developing the state of Israel. And quite frankly, the United States and the EU will fight to the death to preserve that commitment. We cannot allow Iran to have nuclear weapons and will destroy any attempts they have to obtain them. Russia needs to join the Western position. China needs to join and lead the Western position. Our three countries are at the center.

Look at our prospects considering the growing world. Is it change and adopt, or is it war? Just like people have questioned Russian resolve over the centuries, so have they questioned United States' resolve. But both of us know differently, right? It is also part of Israeli resolve. So, are we to have a Middle Eastern Armageddon, or are we going to adapt and evolve? You tell me. You know, if anyone understood this in our world, it should be Russia. Beyond political positioning, you must understand one fact. The Middle East position as a dominant energy player is over. It already is a declining percent, probably reducing to 35% of world production, or less. And Russia's future is a growing piece of the energy pie is unprecedented. But you need to move to lower cost and higher volume and clean energy. Like us, you must race to grow. If Australia can do it, so can Russia.

What you did in 1990 was unprecedented. We were facing a global cold war and you announced an end to communism. That is unprecedented. Likewise, in the world wars, your losses were unprecedented. We have a long way to go, but you know change is required. And you have the advantage of almost limitless natural resources and the need to evolve your economy. You are in a powerful position to impact the fate of the world.

You need to let us evolve out of our fiscal circumstance while you do the same. We have about a 20-year window, and in that time, the United States, the Euros, Russia, and China can see the new century for what it can be. We're the first to admit we have not done well over the last decade and a half. We were shaken to the core by 9/11 and reverted to 20th-century behaviors...that is when under stress unleash our armies. Now we must unwind, but not at the expense of Israel, and we hope not through war. But, like Russia, we will do what we must. Never underestimate our resolve. Inflation, although undesirable, is just something we will fix, all the way to war. If we had to, we could turn to the American people and get 7-8 trillion dollars, through floating a bond.

I'm sure Russia learned about the limits of power in Afghanistan. Occupation of a country is a dirty word. Yes, and we learned in Iraq and Afghanistan, and we're both learning in Syria.

RC: You know we are vehemently opposed to violence in Syria and Iran. They have a perspective that is hard to digest, but they are trying to get ahead like everyone else. We feel many of the outcasts look to Russia and China as nations who could support them in times of strife. But we see cost reduction difficult in a near term. We can't grow our countries internally and support other nations through their difficulties unless those countries are unified, and inside the Middle East they have many factions each wanting their piece of the energy pie. But meanwhile, the energy opportunity is independently growing outside the Middle East and self-sufficiency is the new order. We know in a turbulent society, you can't just get rid of a dictator, because factions like ISIS are waiting for a sign of government weakness. Without control, undesirables will move in. From Iraq, you know this.

President: Believe me, we understand that, but to have as part of your doctrine to destroy another nation and its way of life? You know that in our worst of times, we both respected our history and have worked together in the worst of times. Someone must tell Iran and Syria this is the 21st century and the world is coming together, differences and all. You know that your nation could be the next Middle East from an energy standpoint. If you work with the allies, there is nothing but positives ahead. You already are the major source of natural gas for the Europeans. You also know that sources of massive natural gas are being discovered off Cyprus and Israel in the Mediterranean. The USA and Canada, and Australia are preparing LNG for export. It never ends.

RC: And isn't it time for Russia to join NATO? You know our acceptance in Europe is historical, and the USA…you know the answer.

President: And maybe it's time to turn the book of life...maybe with the Pacific Century, NATO should become

WATO...World Alliance Treaty Organization. The shrinking planet needs to address BRIC, the USA, China, and the Middle East together. But Russia has to prove its intensions by not interfering in elections, poisoning diplomats, etc. The path to NATO must be peaceful one.

And life and the future are defined with energy diversification.

You know about our Apple Corporation, which is now amongst the value leaders in all world stocks. That company has about one hundred sixteen thousand employees in America and contracts more than one million employees in China. Now that upsets Americans, but the reality is cultures and economies are increasingly co-dependent. We are opening a thousand McDonald's and a load of KFCs in China. General Motors is building and selling great quantities of cars in China. The point is, we can cooperate and compete knowing our mutual interests are at hand. At the same time, China and the United States have differences in trade tariffs and the like, and we feel their control of the Yuan is hurting competitive pricing, but they are changing. Why do you think they are cornering the gold market? But believe me, they must deal with their water, energy quality, and costs. We know that by 2050 they will be the largest economic power in the world, but they need a lot to go right to get their per capita income large enough to be self-sustaining. With all that at stake, we're going to fight over energy. We need to collaborate. We see the challenges of pollution crosses all borders, even yours.

Like the citizens around Arab Spring, their people and our people and your people are demanding, "What about us?" With that, their labor cost advantage will decline. And I am sure we all will develop technology to have more of our product building and distribution at home. You may not know it, but the entire technology world is about to spin out of control with, amongst other things, the use of graphene invented by two Nobel Prize winning Russians in Manchester England. Meanwhile populations are rising, and India will be larger than China. India spends half its energy on creating water. And we all must enjoin Africa as part of the developed world. And USA citizens are demanding, stop globalization? We have a lot to do and meanwhile the world must deal with hate derived from a thousand years ago? This has got to stop.

If the Middle East does not turn its resources and profits to its people and change, they are bound for catastrophe. We have to move toward water and energy productivity, and you should feel the same way. Please, don't let 20-century trust issues destroy the 21st century. Both our great nations deserve rewards from the sacrifices of the twentieth century. I would like to look back 20 years from now and know that we achieved a greater society for more people. Don't you agree?

RC: I must admit, when an American leader has his back to the wall, he will try to talk his way out of or into anything. You said this is confidential, so I will take your word for that. What you say is compelling the questions are, what path do we have to travel, and what are the pitfalls?

When we BRICs sit together, we look at the American political system with wonder. It is like your neo-right tea party wants to destroy your country. Maybe they are right? Let the system collapse and bring it back to its isolationist beginnings. You and I know the path to that end is the dollar. Just let your system play itself out. That will tell the world for sure.

President: THIS IS WHERE I DRAW THE LINE, NOT A RED LINE, BUT A GREEN ONE. Even Russia must be concerned with stopping Chinese pollution.

RC: We think, however, there would be a strong contingent in your country that would take that out on Iran. After all you got Iraq under your shield, so why not Iran. Your motivation is not freedom or ending oppression, it is oil and the propping up of the dollar, both on the brink of faltering. After oil could easily go to $200–250 per barrel and that benefits us. If you keep your natural gas prices down, you could export to Europe and that hurts us. Of course, I admit if the world depresses then we all suffer, even the price of oil. That is our concern.

But you know the BRICS met and already agreed to exchange oil in our own currencies. And India and China have cut deals with Iran to bypass the boycott, which is collapsing anyway. So, it seems your strong-arm tactics no longer work. More than half the population of earth will soon trade oil in their own currencies. And, they say, Fort Knox has almost no gold. That would surprise Gold finger, of James Bond, if he went in and found an empty vault in Fort Knox. Now we have to decide whether we still want to buy your T-bills, which loosely translated is your debt. With fewer dollars in circulation, we wonder how to store our free cash, and whether your reduced circulation requires the support of the trading world or you should need to pay higher interest to attract free money. We are, after all, concerned about the willingness of your own people to support increasing your debt ceiling. Without that all your cards seem to tumble. After all, the sum of that would be that your economy comes down to our level.

President: High-priced oil just diminishes your growth but satisfies your financial elite. You know we have the same problem. This is true, regardless of government type or depth of reserves, or apparently, economic system. With higher energy productivity and fresh water, our debt will quickly reduce due to economic achievement. What you must get past is that energy price and it will go down due to supply and demand. The United States, Canada, the Americas, China, Russia, Australia, the Mediterranean, Europe, et al., will produce more supply than demand and change the mix and productivity of consumption. This is a natural market phenomenon. What you will see is American innovation will show a very stable dollar, we guarantee it.

I understand what you are saying, but if our economy spirals downwardly, it immediately impacts our importers. The Euro is in a turbulent state, but trade with Germany is rock solid. People have talked about the Yuan but recognize that China's leadership is not tested. In the last hundred years, they have driven people outward, but most of that occurred with China and Asia the beneficiary of World War II. I am not discounting their own revolutions, but outside of their consolidation and willingness to enter the free markets, with Western support. Their military behavior is untested. It is too early for them to challenge the dollar, especially since we are their best customer (actually the United States and the Euros). If they do, you will see we have an answer. It's peaceful and fiscally conservative. China doesn't want war with anybody. Once Energy begins to change, their forward momentum will be outstanding.

The way we see it, Russia has been acting like a "Regional Power", when its potential is being focused on maintaining the status quo.

I challenge you to say, as a global power, it's time to expand your markets and create opportunities for the Russian people and the world through a broad set of initiatives aimed at Water, Energy, and diversification. You need to enter the markets as a diverse partner. The expansions I show around the world are happening and in a short time, the world will have a billion more people just south of your Asian borders, Africa, and South America. You should partner with the USA and China to expand all economies, particularly yours. The 20th century, measured in armies, military power, and Nuclear WMDs must give way to the "Global Village." I'm sure your "silk road" analogy is totally in that direction.

RC: Maybe the Saudis' negotiation with China is a way for China to begin establishing a military presence. Syria, Iran, and Saudi Arabia together is a Shiite or Sunni compromise to protect their oil interests. Maybe if the United States pulls out of the Middle East, except for Israel, the Middle East's response is to assault the dollar. After all, the BRICs representing half the world population already have done it. It seems to me you must reassess your position. I am saying this because American ingenuity has it limits. After all you're internal policies and your decision to invade Iraq put you in the compromising position you are in. You're 20+ trillion-dollar debt was your innovation devised by your own internally corrupt political system. Lack of ownership of expense.

Now the Middle East must pay for your ill-considered positions? I apologize for this frankness, but you told me to lay the cards on the table. My God, Jimmy Carter laid out the fallacies of your position and the consequences of not addressing your energy policy, so you elected Reagan, who not only reasserted himself militarily but simultaneously took out our system. He knew he could outspend us, and he did.

Now I admit, given our actions in 1990, Reagan helped us see the impact of focusing our energies on military hardware instead of our economics, although it occurred during Bush Sr.'s realm. But Bush did not focus on your economy, and the United States gave us Clinton. Seems like we have all been churning, and no one knows how to deal with the Middle East, including our spin in Afghanistan. So, we tend to say, let the cards unfold.

I can't help but point out that President Bush said the eastern European ex- soviets would not join NATO, but soon thereafter, they did exactly that. Sorry, I couldn't resist that remark

The advent of Sun-Gas and Syn-Gas is something we need to see. Because all of your Oil and Gas conglomerates will have to reconsider their business model... I just can't see how you will do it? Can inevitability be smoothly stepped into?

President: That's what Gorbechov and Yeltsen had in mind, no? Participate and diversify. We just ask Russia to join the 21st century and take actions that foster economic buildup, not a breakdown. We will deal with Middle Eastern actions one way or another, but we will not abide with any acts of aggression, including Iran's nuclear venture, acts against Israel, or attempts to compromise our investment in Iraq. This I promise you.

Sun-gas and Syn-Gas... it's real and inevitable that chemistry Trump's deep mining.

We see Syria and the Arab Spring as a move to Islam fundamentalism or their form of democracy and Sharia law. That is okay if it is producing more income to their people. But is it? You know, like everywhere it is concentrated at the top. That's a worldwide problem, regardless of the system. Usually, Oil is nearby. Now you can see Egypt knows it can't be a theocracy, they are too integrated with the Western world, especially, food imports.

When the world rejects OPEC oil pricing, then we are prepared to reinvent the water and energy mix of energy sources and water initiatives. And that is our program. We just hoped that Russia would expand its program and prepare for a new paradigm. You need to be on the winning team. And we are pushing forward because we know we have the resources to be successful.

RC: Thank you. Ask your EU brethren. With Russia and EU becoming more interdependent, why aren't we in NATO? Keep the doors open and we will be sure you know of any changes we see or do. You know we are meeting with the Europeans to discuss this expanded energy frontier and we will be forthcoming and aggressive. And open to Ideas. Thank you for your open discussion. We do have a world view and we know we both have to expand our thinking as the world grows. We don't need war at any level. When the Soviet Union was broken up, Europe and the USA quickly got Eastern Europe to join NATO and began to put missiles in place. Is that the end of the cold war? Sounds like more of the same. Please, we want to evolve as much as anybody.

President: If you don't mind me saying–when is all this bullshit going to stop? Interfering in elections, poisoning people, etc. You want to be part of NATO, you want parity. Well, this KGB tactics should be left behind with the twentieth century. Trying to mess with Hilary, Trump tactics, etc. you can't trick your way to level the playing field. Quite frankly it's adolescent. Let's commit each other to overcome the twentieth century. We have real challenges to overcome the new population challenges. We must get serious with the 21st century. By the end of the century, Africa will represent half the planet. We need to get serious or get encapsulated in a health crisis!

President: Great, let's stop cyber attacking, both of us. The cold war is so "20th century". It's time to change, and we are.

PARIS

The president's team flies to Paris, where he meets with French, German, and English officials, including a few NATO heads: English officials (EO), German officials (GO), French Officials (FO), NATO Germany (NG), NATO, France (NF) and NATO England (NE).

President: Thanks for coming together at short notice. You have gotten my communications, and I apologize for lack thereof with China and Russia, but that was by agreement to foster open dialogue I will fill you in. We can handle this meeting with the same confidentiality because the input I get is critical. My last meeting is with the Saudi King in Vienna, which is because that is where OPEC is headquartered. Then I return to America and back to work.

We will expand the oil relationship with the Americas and reduce it with the Middle East. I am running this by you because you need to be aware of the potential tensions in the Middle East with Russia, and China. You also must plan on any outcomes in pricing etc. I want to assure you of any efforts we make in mining or drilling methods and technologies; we plan to prioritize regarding battery density and related matters.

This is beyond the ideas stage; we are going to quickly open up distribution systems to accelerate changeover to new technologies. We are doing this because we see $100 plus oil and we are tired of it. We also see the need for changes in world water policies but are proceeding due to agricultural stress for us and the third world which we serve.

What we are doing we see as internal United States policies and actions, but with United States representing 25% of the world's energy consumption, what we do impacts you. Our strategy is to move quickly to free ourselves from the chains of oil yet provide a marketplace that lets oil and gas and any other energy alternatives persist.

Our concerns are how this affects China and Russia vis-à-vis Iran and Saudi Arabia, but also Syria and Israel and everyone in the Middle East and North Africa and the sub-Sahara. China has to do deep soul searching regarding their world partners, particularly Saudi Arabia and Iran. Russia, besides those concerns, has intimate relations with you and I know you're meeting. I just want you to clearly know our actions and commitments and address any concerns. And continuing an open, binding relationship with Russia is essential.

GO: You know our automotive people have been testing all possible real alternatives. I think what you're doing is what is needed to get the ball rolling. We also see trucking as a first step but we are much heavier into diesel in Europe than you are in the states. That being said, we think the natural gas direction is a good one, except we are not as far along and we have a critical relationship with Russia. Any challenge on price is a good one and we think that even selling from America to Europe is healthy. Critical to all of us is what goes on in the United States especially with batteries. We think CERN should get into the game because success with hybrids and plug-ins is critical to any assumptions we make. Also, all being informed about what

CERN does with nuclear and England does with fusion is critical to all. Your broad look at all potential natural gas sources are critical. Your direction toward oversupply is good, but, as I said, from an R&D point of view, we need a quick understanding of battery or storage opportunity and the large-scale creation and distribution of hydrogen. We agree moving toward electronic engine is the medium-term target for sure. But we think the ICE is not over yet, especially if gasoline prices plummet. We would like to participate in any research.

But none of that really matters. How are we going to manage the Middle East? If they see a direct threat, it seems clear that they will counter by trying to attack the dollar. The BRIC countries have started the ball rolling. It seems like your Iran embargo may have increased your exposure. There has been talk about the Yuan or a currency basket, now that the Euro is in question. How can you stop that? I think the Saudis are back at center stage now that they are shipping more oil to China than to the United States. The Euro countries combined are importing more oil than the United States. It's almost a good strategy to support the Euro pending this outcome.

And we are struggling with the Russian relationship in a world where natural gas is discovered in Cypress in great quantity.

President: That is why we are here, to talk about strategic issues and this currency rift. It is all coming together, because that is the way things happen. It is also happening while the Euro is in question. That is why all this needs to be discussed. But for Europe, the parallel critical question is what about Africa and what about water and agriculture. It is time to step back and address the real issues. The Middle East's role in energy is important but diminishing. We are disturbed by the Iranian nuclear blackmail being used to exacerbate the situation. And you and I know, we, or Israel, will not allow it. I think Iran thinks we are afraid to act. If they persist, they, at a minimum, will lose their government. I don't think they realize the US and EU will back Israel all the way to a contained Armageddon. I may overstate it, but do you people think they want to reconstruct Persia along with Syria and the Saudi oil fields? The Saudis must be realists when it comes to their defense.

GO: But this Iran blockade was a United States idea. We all support Israel, but UN member countries like India and China are circumventing the blockage with Gold or Yuan. It seems like there is a build toward breaking out of the United States dollar standard. If that happens, how are you going to make your T-Bill sales, which is funding your debt, attractive? Raise rates? Where will that stop? If policies threaten oil flow or cost. Nations will reconsider their alliances; Energy is the elixir of a modern society.

President: The last country that tried to break from the dollar was Iraq. We invaded them, for different reasons. Then Iraq hung Saddam Hussein.

FO: But there is an argument that nuclear weapons are to Iran what WMDs were to Iraq. Are you going to invade Iran and then realize they had no nearness to developing a nuclear weapon? This scenario has a much more skeptical audience, given the Iraq invasion, preceded by 9/11by only two years resulted in the price of oil tripling for all countries in ten years (2002-2012). Look what oil did to all our economies. Was **Bin** Laden that smart or just lucky that Bush and Cheney took the bait?

President: Our countries had deeper problems. It was just pure sick politics and the WWII hangover, Bush following up for his father, without any participation from his father, but some aberration of destiny from Cheney plus a totally misunderstanding about how much oil we'd get from Iraq. But that's my opinion and some speculation.

BO: But the debt crises perhaps have seeded this oil problem because anti-Western forces see that our weakness can be exploited to assure high energy costs. Would America be willing to incur near hyperinflation assure a near term change in energy? The disruption and financial chaos that we would all feel would be at stake. I don't know, it's all sad. Too much history of winning at all cost.

President: That is why we need the European markets to stand with us. We need to re finance about five trillion dollars. Or at least, be prepared to do it. We know that. We have not finalized the numbers. But remember, the true weapon against inflation is "energy productivity". Success with this evolves all economies. With that in our grasp, and with a freshwater strategy, watch our debt shrink. And, quite frankly, you need to rethink Russia and NATO in light of natural gas, Cypress, China, and North Africa, in light of water shortages and climate realities. Although I think Russia in NATO is premature given the circumstances.

NATO Germany (NG): It is easy to run the numbers, you could spend a half a trillion on invading Iran, and that would be cheap compared to the cost of high interest on not only your government debt, but on business and consumer debt including Europe. You are now facing a problem with the history of Vietnam and Iraq and Afghanistan. Post-Vietnam, you had 20 percent interest rates and that is dwarfed by your debt to GDP ratio (over 100 percent) today. When is NATO meeting? I can see it coming. When I look at the map with military bases "surrounding" Iran, it is not just a coincidence, no?

Consistent direction vs politics?

I'm encouraged by your shift away from your being surrounded by hawks, and our worrying that, without you being focused on "re-election", you could be motivated to seek a "final solution", when the answer is to show strength and power through real change. That's why we fully support your WE direction. What the world needs is a power reconciliation between you and China, a war with the ultimate enemy...Pollution! If the world focused on that as opposed to short term money politics, then we finally are on the road to true peace with prosperity. A close second is supporting Africa, where cultural change, world health, and prosperity all meet, like the final act of the 21st century. At some level, African evolution is the right place for the human species.

President: That is why I am meeting with the Saudi Arabia king. We just cannot see the Shiites and Sunnis collaborating in the long term. It is against history. So is the shift away from Middle Eastern oil! But, the declining power of Mid-Eastern oil is fact, not fiction. Look at Australia and you can see that the Pacific Century is upon us.

BO: Wait a minute. Your talking at least under $20-25 per barrel oil, and only a month or two ago we were contemplating, "who knows?" per barrel. OPEC was formed over a squabble about Israel. What will they do under these circumstances? I say they would bring the United States and the Europeans down to our knees. Right when we can't afford it. On the other hand, it seems that this is inevitability.

President: Here are some numbers. By 2020, it is expected that 100 million barrels per day will be extracted, with 34 percent by M.E. OPEC members, so 34 million per day, or 12.4 trillion per year. So, if prices are impacted (increased) by $100 per barrel, it's 12.4 x 100 million. OPEC reserves are exaggerated by 50 percent, so the future is about $ 6.2(half of 12.4) 100 million. Add in another 66 percent and it gets ugly. At $250 dollars per barrel, the number staggers the imagination. Using these numbers, you can also compute what our economies are losing in lost productivity. Now consider that we are adding a billion people to the planet every 10-12+ years, and 70-90 percent of fresh water goes to agriculture. And agriculture needs fertilizers, which use natural gas or other fossil fuels to be produced for the most part. We conclude that we struggle now for energy, *but the end game* is fresh water. To get a *continuous* new supply of fresh water, we need a continuous supply of energy, like solar, wind, and thermal in order to deliver fresh water at low cost.

We could conclude that the cheapest alternative is to attack Iran and settle their shipments of oil in dollars. We are at risk to be driven to war and be accused of another WMD falsehood these are different times. We will not start a war, but we will end one. And Israel sees the issue of Iran with nuclear weapons is more than a nonstarter, it will not be allowed to happen, period. So that is what we have. Are we going to change the world and free our economies, or are we going to war, or both? You tell me, because we can come up with five trillion dollars to pay down bad debt. It will be ugly, but the Americas can do it. You need to make a deal with Russia and the Americas. You need to have a conversation with the Middle East. You input more oil than we do. If we take 20% of oil out of the Middle East demand equation, you can sit there and benefit. Will they reduce your oil prices by 20% or more, or will the price rise to $200, when they settle down to $150 or so? What is your forecast? We will negotiate, and then we will act. My position to the European community is that you have to act swiftly or be swept into their demand for an Armageddon, for no good reason. Given the post–World War II environment, you and we owe Israel our support. We made it possible to evolve a Western nation into the Middle East. There are 1.6 billion Islamic people in the world, 15 million Jews, and 2 billion Christians. Israel is not an oil competitor, and their economy is strong. I should say they have to resolve the Palestinian question.

If Iran insists on self-destruction, that is their problem. I do not believe the Saudis will object. And yes, we won't create a war, if challenged, we'll end it.

But that is not the point. The point is a new era is upon us. Are we going to step up to lower gasoline prices and invest in a new freshwater paradigm? Will our markets be free to follow the best direction? The answer is yes, you can count on it.

NATO should reconsider its relationship with Russia. It's time to really end the cold war through collaboration. Geographic separatism should be replaced with geographic synergy and needs to recognize the Pacific Century. It's also true that Russian change must precede NATO reconciliation.

I probably have not quelled your concerns. But we must go forward with courage. I stepped back and looked at the first decade of the 21st century and felt our proactive response to 9/11 may have had to happen, but it is a formula for the worst century in world history. The world equation must change. We must change because we are not going to use the formulas of the twentieth century, except for backing our constitution. We have learned a lot from our experiences from the last fifty or so years. It is time for different solutions. Please be with us. We were there for you, and we need your support. You and I know that a NG and Hydrogen strategy will work and will cut down energy costs by 50 percent. This is why I say America will treat this as a world war. A war where science and engineering replaces bullets and bombs.

BO: This is something we will all have to absorb. Let me say this to Vietnam, Serbia, Kuwait, the Soviet Union, Iraq, Afghanistan, Libya, and now Syria and Iran. We have to absorb those mixed messages. Maybe we must look at the victory of the Soviet Union arrived upon without a gunshot. Of course, they have their own history and their weapons have been all over the Middle East and Africa.

President: You need to spend considerable time with Russia. We tried to get them to look past all this to their vast reserves they have not yet discovered and their need to evolve their people's chances: The Europeans; the United States; China; and Russia. That is the fate of the next 20 years. If you think you can step back and avoid it, then you have not learned anything.

And you need to spend time with China. They have massive need to evolve as much as anybody.

President: If you don't mind me saying- when is all this bullshit going to stop? Interfering in elections, poisoning people, etc. Your problems with their 1.3 billion people. They have enormous issues with air and water pollution. Are they going to resolve their problems by making oil deals and mining coal? They must see that the time to change is now, and when they America and Europe move forward, they know they must leave the 20th century.

Will they replace our armies with China's in the Middle East? If they do, America and Europe can fly by them with improved economies and ecologies. And remember, they are trying to grow their internal economy like we all have. But their best customers are Europe and the United States. They do not need a backlash from us. They need our support, not our hostility. They do not need their differences with us to be defined by Iran, Syria, and Saudi Arabia. Russia and China need to take the next step to be our equal partners in the world. Once they see that the 21st century is before them, they will see that the Euros and the United States are on their side. Where did their wealth come from?

Never forget, China is not a superpower per se, they are a super economy with lots of near term and midterm issues. They need synergy with us, not an alliance with nations with a declining market. They can only lead with improved personal profitability. Russia went for the military lead, and it cost them communism. Once they see we are not subordinated by oil, the power game changes. Power is economic, not military.

This is what the 21st century needs to absorb. Let's not kid ourselves. The Euro and the US dollar are propped up by the Yuan. And we're China's best customers, yet they own the gold.

French Official (FO): Exactly. We are all part of this struggle. And it is a new century. We cannot let Bin Laden on 9/11 and Saddam Hussein in 2004 redefine our weakness now as their legacy. We cannot let them be the final martyrs of their crusade.

Vienna

The US team arrives in Vienna the same night. They find a hotel lounge area and set up a little bar. After a few drinks they form a circle. The president meets with SOS, SOD, and SOT.

SOS: I must say, if I have not been through it, I would not believe it. Thank you for letting us be part of this trek.

President: I had to let you see and hear it all. We've got big decisions to make. We have got a hard road ahead. The next step is the hardest. You know what we're risking. But we can't. We have to be sure. We must be, for want of a better word, guaranteed.

SOD: I would be prepared to say that, and I am not sure how to present this to the American people. We're sure this is the right direction, even if things don't work out without pain. I'm afraid it's a time in our history when without pain there's no gain. But consider this, we could have just proceeded without taking sides or upsetting the Saudis or the Chinese, so far.

President: What you must know, and feel is that the American people are sick of this state of the world. You're offering potential pain without war. The American people will invest in the future of water and energy.

SOT: We are risking the fact that about five trillion dollars in T-bill purchases are up for grabs. I'll bet if you offered "peace bonds", we could come up with it. Either you lock down China and Japan, or we probably, eventually, must significantly raise interest rates.

Surely when you presented this plan to the American people, you knew that. Maybe you must go to those who back up our plan and divide the expense. But unfortunately, the BRICs have decided to buy oil with their own currencies. Maybe that is a bond that's unbreakable. Maybe there's a showdown with Iran.

SOD: You need to find out from the Saudis where they draw the line in relationships. I think the deal they made with China means they've given up on the United States and are willing to compromise with Iran and Syria. You quoted the numbers with the Europeans. Maybe they feel that if we're so sure, we should feel the pain. Maybe they feel $250-dollar oil is their final stance. Remember, we all know the OPEC oil reserve numbers are bogus. Maybe they have a realistic number?

President: We know there is no explicit way to guarantee what the reserves are. We need to believe that the amount of oil in the sands, in the Gulf, and elsewhere is enough. But the time to produce it is years away. I cannot add to the lies from before. Maybe we should let the Israelis act and force the EU's to join us in support.

You must realize that I set this direction because the world needs to step up on the issue of water and free the energy market. There is water bond between the United States, China, and Russia, They must see that in order to attack water, we need to create energy productivity, and natural gas is the cheapest and most effective way to create money. It's a market reality, not a military reality. SOD (sec of defense): Sir, you just laid out a path to war. Maybe, two paths from Israel or the United States. What if the Saudis see Israel as an affront to Islam?

President: If that assumption is correct, they are just letting themselves believe it to try to win the oil game. After all, trillions of dollars are at stake, more importantly, maybe their kingdom. That could be a life-and-death choice in their minds.

They must rise above the fray to see their chance to win the hearts of their people and create a long market.

SOD: You must tell the Saudis that backing someone other than us will end their regime, and it could end the dictator's and/or king's control over Middle Eastern oil. Saudi Arabia knows the world energy situation. After all, how do the people of the region get the funding they need for the days when oil is not king, which you've already defined as fewer than 20 years from now? Maybe your sale of the water crisis plus one billion people was too strong. Maybe they feel their reserves are at risk. Maybe the oil peak has already happened, like many insist. But you must package it in the context of what you have already declared as fact.

President: No, the scenario I have presented is confirmed. We cannot stop the march of population. The Chinese tried and now they are soon facing a shortage of 50-million women. That is enough for them to put pressure on all their surrounding nations: Vietnam, Cambodia, Thailand, even Indonesia. They need to take actions to take their people out of the malaise of pollution and they need to provide a path to lower energy costs and freshwater. They can't deny the facts that are in their face.

The Africans have a long way to go. Are we to let the contrarians win and use war and disease to thin the population? The average person thinks this is inevitable I didn't say this, but at the end of the day, military superiority trumps many hands in many games. But the 21st century is a new game with different cards.

SOS: I agree we cannot let that happen, unless it is truly the fate of mother earth the goal is the need to feel that that kind of pressure is surer than money.

President: At the end of the day, it is about money and the power to survive. We have to find a compromise, a middle ground. If you want to lose sleep, consider Iran seeing this unfolding so they join Iraq, and then the Saudi's reign collapse. But remember, when we went to war in WWII, we went to the people for War Bonds. Maybe we could go to our people for Water and Energy bonds. If we could show China that we could raise $.675 -$1.5 trillion in WE bond, it would show our commitment and unflappability.

(The team goes to bed and sets its sights on a two pm meeting tomorrow.)

OPEC Headquarters

The US team arrives at OPEC headquarters and heads to a large conference room set up for the Saudi king. They meet around a circular table.

Saudi King (SK): Thank you. I know we have had a long, mutually beneficial relationship and in the last decade we have been through much. Our world is changing, and you have huge issues with your debt. We want energy prices to go up and you want energy prices to come down. We can talk at great length about our history over the last sixty years. We did a lot for the world. But you want change and we want incremental change. Your scenario is ten to 20 years. Our scenario is thirty to fifty years. Well, that one or two decades are worth trillions of dollars, so we say slowly down.

President: Yes, these are the parameters of discourse. But we are adding that in 20 years there will be two billion more people we have to address because the world's water sources are drying up. Even you are desalinating 75% of your water. Even you see the benefits of solar for that energy need. If you use solar, you can sell Charlie Pedersen or reserve more oil. And no one really knows the OPEC oil reserves, but many say they are overstated by 50 percent. The world needs to reinvigorate their economies, and we need a Water and Energy policy that can drive down energy costs while we drive up economies. We need relief. China says they will do anything for assurance of long-term secure source of energy. When they see real results from solid efforts in Water and Energy, they will turn within a flash. But if you think China will protect your oil fields, remember what we did over the last 10–plus years and compare that to China's zero experience in world military operations and politics over the last fifty years. Our military financial power is three times China's. Look whose technology you have and ask what we have coming in five to ten years. Our air power will transcend anything you have seen on the planning sheets. Just think what our drones will be like in ten years. Then look at Iran and what is coming for them. Look at the internal strife within China.

Do you want to be part of the future or just cater to the Shiites? If the Shiites see you falter, Persia can be reinstated with Saudi oil fields. You know, desperate people will rise in a fight for glory.

SK: I know what we have done together, but I see one limited benchmark...oil price. You are saying we must choose lower price for a high-demand product so we can sustain our fuel over the next decades.

President: No, we are saying you must consider what you have and produce the best possible result for your people. You have to consider, what is the world like when Syria and Iran are defeated. How can I be sure? The people do not want to have a derived war with Israel, when all that will occur is Iran's defeat.

Israel will take out their nuclear capability and the NATO forces will destroy their armaments and enable the people to take over the oil fields which will sell oil in dollars. Iraq will sell oil in dollars. Libya and North Africa will sell oil in dollars.

You must remind yourself that energy change is a market activity, not a military one. You're asking me to ignore the facts: sources of oil & gas are emerging all over the world; technology to effectively deploy NG, hydrogen, and electric are implemented by all automobile suppliers; tests have shown that efficiency rates can be up 100–150 mpg; new sources of natural gas like methane hydrate have been discovered and proven. These are market realities and our economies are dragging from high oil prices. If we can achieve economies from new ICE technology, then let it rip. And then there is freshwater and only Saudi Arabia is moving their country forward. We will increase oil from oil sands in Canada and increase exports from Mexico, Brazil, Venezuela, and Argentina, and they will switch back to purchasing oil with dollars. Saudi Arabia will be the only kingdom in the Middle East and their deal with China will diminish. When China sees our success, they will change immediately, with our help. Quite frankly, if they build cars based on a petroleum presumption, they will look very stupid. You will try to prop up your military arsenal with untested and out-of-date technologies from Russia and China? What if Iraq and Iran consolidate into a new Persia, led by Shiites?

Africa and the world will unite from our results in agriculture in the United States and from freshwater initiatives all over the North African shorelines. Why? Because they must.

The world will grow and evolve and by around 2035-2050, the Saudi kingdom could be a fading memory in world history. That is the outcome of not grasping on proven opportunity and results that must happen to avoid calamity from a food and energy perspective. The nine-billion-population world will be as different as Saudi Arabia was around 1960. China and the United States and Russia will be staunch allies in 2050 because they wanted to leverage the Water and Energy (**WE**) advances of 2020-2050. They will see that raising the living standards of Asia and Africa will create unprecedented GDP as well as offer significant health benefits from turning the tide of global climate change. Not that it will end, but the world will act responsively. And all Saudi Arabia really wants is opportunity, and our opportunity is to change.

SK: It all sounds great and heartwarming, but isn't there another path to the same result? Could not the West settle some compromise regarding aggregate pricing and rates tiered to higher volume? There must be some other solution that gives Sunni Islam hope for a broad improvement.

President: First, Shiite Islam must see the advantage in avoiding their own destruction. They must realize that it serves no purpose when their money is being wasted on armaments instead of social upgrading, desalination, agriculture, and education. Egypt would trade military armaments for technologies that would sustain their agriculture capabilities. Once they see success stories in Libya and Syria, their people will clamor for participation and change. They may believe the next world is a better place but taking the first seat on that trip is a poor decision for their people. And Egypt is particularly dependent on USA and other country's agriculture.

Yes, we can find a way. But surely it cannot support arming Iran or continuing with the status quo.

We hate to even consider Saudi Arabia as our enemy, or even neutral friend. It will never happen. After we secured Iran's oil fields, we look to the status of our relationship with you. What will it be? Of course, I'm not saying we have military ambitions with Iran. If they force a confrontation with Israel, the chain of events will speak for themselves.

SK: We will announce with OPEC that we see a multiyear agreement to evolve more efficient pricing while the advantages of shale and other technologies will be shared throughout the Middle East. We will resume petrol-dollars throughout the Middle East in exchange for broad energy technology advances over the next 20 years, including freshwater generation capabilities.

President: We will work out the detail over the next six months while the United States and other nations let the progression of alternative energy initiatives like shale gas, methane hydrate, and hydrogen and energy storage begin to roll out. I should point out that we will provide our people with a path out of our 6-7 trillion dollar international debt. (T-bills). Gold is a secure stabilizer in the economy, but not the path to the future. **Fresh water, pollution decline, and energy productivity are**. Remember that.

Someone knocks on the door and a US aid enters and whispers to the President.

President (to the aid): Are we sure of the security? It is authentic? (He turns to his cabinet members and then the king): Apparently, we have one more stop. My apologies.

Saudi Arabia King: Yes, I understand.

(The president's team slowly gets up and exits.

The president's entourage turns down the street toward the Iranian embassy. They get out of their cars, but the greeter informs them that only the president and the Secretary of State (SOS) are needed. They split off and enter a conference room. As they sit down, the Iran-leader (I-SL) and I-P (President) enter the room.

I-S: Thank you for meeting with us.

President: I consider this meeting an act of faith in your hospitality because we are facing critical times. You have my assurance of the confidentiality of this meeting. This is historic under the circumstances and, given our history since 1979, unprecedented.

I-SL (through a translator) our goal is to discuss the embargo and alternatives and see if there is any chance of a peaceful resolution. We've taken a big step in Geneva, and we want to evolve, although you dropped out of this agreement. Quite frankly, you raised the bar and we were compliant with our agreement. It's so easy to extend our agreement, but you, not us, acted in bad faith.

So, to begin, we're tired of the US military machine interfering with the Middle East. You are undermining Syrian leadership, you treat Saudi Arabia like a puppet, and you have backed Israeli atrocities over the name of democracy for decades. You make the world think Syria is almost free, while the three hundred fifty thousand strong Syrian army dominates the tens of thousands of rebel troops, despite the interference of the CIA, Israel, and European conspirators. Your CIA and Israeli spies have murdered our scientists while we try to provide nuclear power to our economy.

You support the existence of Israel while their European-born leadership continues as a blight on Islam all these years. Well, you have supported democracy in the Arab Spring, which resulted in the people of the Middle East restoring Islam over military dictatorships. I am sure it is not what you intended, but President Bush is getting what he wanted- democracy. You have killed the people of Iraq to dominate their oil fields while you have supported kingdom and military dictators under your sick definition of freedom, while the Islamic people suffer.

FRC any attempt of nations to reach for nuclear power is destroyed by Israel: Iraq in 1981 and Syria in 2007, and now you are going after Iran. Despite all that, your grip on the Middle East is slipping. Now your latest initiative is to destroy the oil business that is leading the world's demand for energy. You would not be flying around the world if you did not see the Middle Eastern direction supporting Islam and the power of our oil and gas.

Clearly, you can see the failure at your ability to manipulate our world. Meanwhile your economy falters, while the world turns to China and Russia for support and leadership. And we all see the US dollar faltering as a reserve currency as you scamper around trying to protect 20+ trillion dollars in your government debt, much of it realized by your interference in the Middle East.

I am here to tell you that you are failing because the people of the Middle East don't want your support, and you're wasting your time, your dollars, and your military muscle. We've been supporting Islam liberation and no matter how you try, this simple fact has assured your failure all the way back to your predecessors including the crusades.

President: I attended this meeting to see whether there is any hope for peaceful reconciliation, and I can see how you see the manipulation of facts as your weapon in an unwinnable war. You need to turn your attention to the truth- that can bring peace and prosperity to your people. Population and drought are something that only Saudi Arabia is doing something about. Believing that the world and Israel will let you build a nuclear arsenal is something even China and Russia will not support. We must tell you that Water and Energy is going through a change that will result in clean energy efficiency that Iran could benefit from, but you are stuck in the twentieth century paradigm that is a road to a diminished economy. We are trying to ascend above the twentieth century, the past, and quite frankly, we can see that a country that can't participate in a paradigm change is doomed to be a footnote in history. We won't let that happen to us, and we believe the leaders in Asia, and all the continents, recognize that we are in a moment of significant choice- a new Water and Energy (**WE**) reality.

<u>Understand that the stress in Europe and the US is because of the untenable position of Water and Energy) (**WE**) and its impact on the Middle East nations and the world, and the old way, when the world is presenting us with clear evidence that Electric and Hydrogen choice are now totally viable, no, necessary;</u>

You must accept the fact that NATO and the United States will not let Israel cower under nuclear threat. In fact, they will not allow it. And they have the delivery systems to serve their purpose of survival. History is what it is, and I assure you that the trifecta of Muslim, Christian, and Jewish presence in our regions will persist. The Americas and Europe will never change from that balance of reality. Please don't make any assumptions except the America, Europe, and others will support Israel s right to peace and freedom.

We want peace through Water and Energy (WE) evolution. The world grows by a billion people every ten to eleven years, and a new paradigm must come out of this era, energy productivity is necessary for economic wellbeing, desalination, agriculture, and quite frankly, survival. You must change to get on the right side of this, because the colonial era is over. We beg you to get on the right side of history, because what is clear, your delusions of history are the last ones standing between war and real change. That is so last century. You must know that the percentage of energy creation in the world outside of the Middle East is escalating, the growth of natural gas is changing the perspective on the mix of use, and there is a growing intolerance for the overhead associated with high priced oil. You must understand this as you are a leader in natural gas-powered automobiles. So please do not believe that American and European energy changes have anything to do with the support of Israel, because to misunderstand us, quite frankly, will result in the failure of your government, if it selects war, and, quite frankly, is a high-risk point for your people. We all carry our histories from the 20th century into the 21st. Yes, if we are forced to, we will support Israeli independence and freedom. We would like to see a Palestinian solution, but supporting Hezbollah, terrorism, and war is not the path. The rich ability of your resources should be focused on peaceful change and internal improvements in Iran, and your failure to see that will be most unfortunate. If you block the straights, your Navy will be destroyed. If you build a nuclear weapon, it will be destroyed. If you wage war or terrorism, your government will be destroyed. We hate to put it so straightforwardly, but we do not meet very often, and you must understand these are choices you have to make. There is a path to peaceful evolution, but you must understand that Israel is an existential policy; they will persist and thrive, as an axiom of the 21st century.

And the Sunnis, the Europeans, the United States, and China would never allow the reemergence of Persia, including the Saudi oil fields. That dog will never hunt, as we say. We may have cultural and historical differences, but the United States is providing a path to peace and will face aggression as required. Do not test us, others have failed. Know that we have channels of communication and access. I asked for and attended this meeting because I know we are at the threshold.

You may feel you can undermine our dollar and affect our economy, but please do not follow those who question our steadfastness and resilience. You will find that we have ample ways to strengthen our balance sheet and our financial strength is awesome. Those who have not understood this have been swept away in the story of the 20th century. Please do not become the next chapter. The last chapters included Saddam Hussein, Bin Laden, and Muammar Gaddafi. It is a cruel world with explicit exclamations. We hope our mutual path is to peace, and pardon me for being so strident, but we rarely see each other, and we don't want understatements or misrepresentations. You have to be thinking about the next billion people, not the price of oil as economies adapt natural gas, electric, and hydrogen strategies, as I assure you, they will. This is not pro or anti anything. It is change resulting from scientific and engineering evolution and discovery. Look at Australia and Coober Pedy. Mother earth seems to find new ways to support populations. The fact is when the species is threatened or given hope, the multitude will scramble. This is market innovation and evolution, that's all. Iran needs to deal with real and substantive change, as we are. We will work with you under the umbrella of harmony and peace. There is more opportunity in front of us. Let's find it together.

Please let me summarize. After the USA Germany and Canada participated in intense research, they discovered how to mix air, water, and sunlight. They isolated hydrogen fuel in liquid and gaseous form and made a formidable fuel that can be transferred anywhere at a total cost of under $1 per gallon equivalent. All major car manufacturers around the world began offering hydrogen powered cars since 2015.Don't stress over the fact that sales are minimal. When refueling is proliferated, along with electric, NG, and hydrogen, change will commence. Also, Natural Gas cars will be available, and the emergence of major electric car manufacturing is underway in China, Europe, and the USA. Further studies will produce air fuel and significant truck fuels. Our overall efficiency target is 100-150 mpg. We also have a major water initiative which will produce scale and quality soon. We wish that Iran participate in this Water & Energy (WE) initiative and join the transition planning. This is the reality of science and engineering progress-inevitability is at hand.

Iranian leader: We recognize that your moves and direction are sincere. You dismiss our attempts at comprise. You don't accept that our people like America...we have deep history. In all sincerity, please accept our actions, will always be strong, and we will never Cower. But we aren't warlike in our character, we want peace even, in times of great change. We remain open, and hope you can see that, through a very turbulent period. Remember, you cancelled our agreement, not us. Yes, your military thinks we're not trustworthy, but you imposed the Shaw on us, yes, many years ago. And your own European inspectors said we are complying with your agreement, so give us some sign of good faith. We won't grovel, get it? And we will defend our airspace. Why are you encroaching on us? You just can't bully Iran. The Middle East is tired of it. You're always remarking about our Kingdoms and sovereigns...look in the mirror, who put you in charge of the world?

The President and Secretary of State leave the meeting and head for the airport.

CHAPTER XII

Back to America

The United States team departs and returns to America. On the flight:

Secretary of State (SOS): What just happened? We go forward and let our initiatives shift volume while we work with Saudi Arabia to deploy new initiatives on desalination and we hold meetings with Iran to change the course of hostilities?

President: And much more. We will wait for OPEC to see if they change supply levels and cause a reduction in oil prices. I doubt it. When our enemies know this, we could be set up for a fall. We discussed this with the Saudi king, and he assured us this would never happen.

I will go back on air tomorrow and announce a slight modification to our plan which continues our purchase of OPEC oil and allows an evolution of volume at lower levels. Simultaneously, we will announce a general agreement with the Americas for increased supplies and a major initiative with Mexico to reconsider farmlands across the borders, with desalination supporting Mexican and US production. We will also plan the pipeline to the Ogallala Reservoir from the south or west of the Great Lakes. Yes, it can be done with a new basin feed from the lakes. And then there is pipelining from Canada. Lots of ways to fix it, we'll chose one.

Announcement to the US Public and Congress

A call comes into the oval office.

President: Hello, Robert, my freelance lobbyist and ear to the ground, what can I do for you?

Robert: I know you have an important speech to make tomorrow, but I'd like you to give Anni Cline, from Citizens against Multi-Bionics, an hour of your time. I know this is unusual but is important.

President: Multi-Bionics?

Robert: You got it. But please, you need to listen to her because this is fundamental to your honesty edict.

President: Where is she? I've just returned and I'm tired.

Robert: We're at your security gate. Sorry for the presumption.

President: I guess it's why I have people like you around. Send her in. I'll clear you.

A few moments later, Anni enters the oval office with Robert and they sit down.

President: Hello, Anni. I want to tell you I rarely have impromptu meetings, so it's clear I give Robert a lot of leeway, because every time he calls me it's important.

Anni: I appreciate it, Mr. President, and this is very intimidating to me, but with all the information that is flowing in the direction of natural gas, I pushed my way up, so you got an important aspect I've heard nothing about. You know I spearhead the anti-fracking forces to some extent. With all that happens when government has a blind eye or pushes an agenda sideways until someone gets killed or worse, I wanted to find my way to Robert and you.

President: I presume this is about hydraulic fracturing. I've had numerous briefings with the EPA and around the world. I accepted this meeting because the information on this is highly fragmented, particularly concerns often associated with the development of unconventional oil and gas resources. These concerns involve land surface disturbances associated with the development of roads, site selection for drilling, and natural gas gathering pipelines; potential impacts of water withdrawal and consumption; treatment and disposal of flow back water to surface waters; air quality impacts; noise; etc. Some of these activities are subject to other federal laws, such as Clean Water Act requirements covering the treatment and discharge of produced water into surface waters. The state and federal regulatory requirements for treatment and discharge of produced water may have a more significant impact on the industry than possible UIC (Underground Injection control)–related requirements. Other impacts related to development of unconventional oil and gas resources are highly visible and may raise more concern than the specific process of deep drilling.

In discussing lessons learned from developing, the Barnett shale industry consultants recently reported that an important factor requiring 3D seismic (imaging) is the avoidance of geo-hazards, such as water-bearing karsts and faults.

The GWPC (Ground Water Protection Council) is a national association representing state groundwater and UIC (underground injection control) agencies whose mission is to promote protection and conservation of groundwater resources for beneficial uses. The stated purpose of the GWPC is to promote and ensure the use of best management practices and fair but effective laws regarding comprehensive ground water protection.

Some of these issues (particularly land-use and facility citing issues) are beyond the reach of federal regulation, and thus, are left to state and local governments to address. New York State's Revised Draft Supplemental Generic Environmental Impact Statement is one example of a state taking a comprehensive approach to addressing a broad range of possible environmental impacts that could be associated with Marcellus shale development.

Anni: I admit the tensions between state and federal oversight and authority are being addressed with more than one hundred bills pending in state legislatures. And that just shows you the awareness and anxiety by states over drinking water and rivers and streams. But since you are promoting massive expansion of natural gas distribution, I'm here to ask you one rhetorical question and provide my own assessment.

Why was the exemption of Fracking added to the energy policy act of 2005? If you recall, you voted for this, popularly called the "Energy Act loophole" which was done to lower the regulatory cost and overhead of hydraulic fracturing, period. (Note: author notes this is highly controversial) I stress this for a simple reason: if controls are slackened, one failure could be the most devastating impact on societies in the history of modern government. It could have tsunami proportions. Remember that sites such as Marcellus in Pennsylvania, New York, West Virginia, etc. butts right up to the New York City watershed. Before you turn on the real power of Nat-gas or Nat-gas/hydrogen, you need to be sure the Frac Act and all related controls are in place. The consequences to assume safety would make gun control a footnote in the history of bad government. The profit margins and the impact of neutralizing oil and gas, the Middle East, et al., military expenditures, and the restoration of all our economies are so far reaching, there is only one issue. Do it right and be sure.

You are standing at the gates of heaven and hell, and I must ask you, how many times did we succumb to the forces of lobbyists and political agendas? The decisions were unclean: Vietnam? Iraq? Immigration? Gun control? The cost was trillions of dollars and millions of dislocated or dead people. All that is asked is that we have to make the right decisions for ourselves, and the world will follow. In about ten or eleven years there will be an additional billion people in the world. We need to fix the Ogallala Reservoir, and we need to expand world food markets, lower energy costs, and clean the environment. If we don't do it right, will we get the chance to do it over? You know the answer: World War III, or Middle East or Mediterranean Armageddon, wasting opportunity and setting the world agenda back at least ten years. Is that your legacy? Political compromise, but against the people? That's why you were reelected?

Let me make one more point. I know we are politically bashed along with agencies like the EPA. But I ask you. If you didn't have them and state agencies controlling the quest for money, what would be the outcome? Some issues cross state lines like water and energy. There are so many state issues about hydraulic fracturing and horizontal drilling because people are scared. You have, along with the states, accountability to the 99 percent who have about 7% of the new profits. These are the voters who put you in charge.

President: You had to bring up Energy Conglomerates, their role in Iraq, New Orleans and Hurricane Katrina, the Gulf oil spill. They're always around substantive change. I guess that's where the money is. You hit me right where it hurts. When I told

Robert, I'd see you I knew I was in trouble, because my passion is for the people, and I must hear it all. I know we are at a turning point and must turn the ecology, the energy business, water, and the economy around. There isn't a clear path, but the simple truth you state is to do it right! *On one level, you can't point at Halliburton because they have the rocks to stand in the worst or volatile circumstances and offer assistance.* That is an understatement. I must navigate through the green versus a plethora of competing issues. It's not simple, and $ is always involved.

Anni: **Competing issues?**

President: I leave that to your imagination. Whenever you have a magnetic issue, like green, I assure there are 1000 buts and ifs. The reason is you're promoting change. And people often don't see it. The discipline and for-thought that surrounds change is overwhelming. Let's suffice it to say that green may be about the environment, but it's also the color of money. So if you're going to invoke change, you better know what you are doing, and how expensive it is. But the reason we are both where we are, is ultimately we both believe we can overcome.

Anni: Before we finish, I'd like to point out something that should be interesting to you. I can't help but see what seems to be trends going on in the Republican party: Bush's religious initiative, the Tea Party, the birther nonsense, anti-Obama Care, the attack on some of your black religious leaders' influence, the House attempts at no negotiations, which in part led to your reelection, attempts at suppression of voting rights, and so much more. There seems to be an isolation of older white male Republicans backed by a corporate Supreme Court. Meanwhile, population growth through immigration; expanding women roles; the courting of technological sectors and young people;

and immigration reform are resulting in a solid demographic base for Democrats. **The house of representatives has fallen to the democrats.** If the Democrats embrace fiscal conservatism but support universal health care, Medicare, and Social Security, followed by a strong water and energy platform that can stimulate economic efficiency and growth, you will annihilate the Republican Party, or should I say they'll self-destruct.

President: Quite frankly, they refuse to do anything positive in my administration. I'm put in the position of dealing with that. They seem to think that's the way to get to me. So, I have to pick this energy and green issue because when it's all said and done, this is the number one challenge. The problem is most Americans don't see the tie-in between Water and Energy. WITHOUT LOW COST, CLEAN ENERGY, PRACTICAL WATER DESALINATION STRUGGLES.

The solution is simple. Provide the consumer choice at the pump: gasoline, Nat gas, hydrogen, and hyper electric recharge Very quickly, the market will respond. Much cheaper than war. Tesla has already estimated the cost of electric recharging.

The key is to turn the discussion away from global warming and towards the enemy: global warring, as displayed by Iraq, Afghanistan, North Africa, Iran, and Syria. Find a way to partner with China by forming a joint energy cooperative that causes an adjustment of clean energy costs down to pre-9/11 levels. China can lose more than a decade if they follow the Middle East toward oil. It makes no sense for them. Your challenge is to get the people to stop trading their benefits for the cost of monopolized corporate welfare (i.e., Pharma; insurance; banking; oil and gas; a rational military position; and more). It seems that you need to align with Silicon Valley as the gateway to expanded growth and productivity. The opposition will fail if you demonstrate lowering citizen costs while assuring the expanded economy and an efficiency driven government. You have to embrace fiscal conservatism, as Jerry Brown was doing in California. Our citizens are suspicious of both government and large corporate business, so you need to navigate a path to renewal. The key to it all is energy. The Republicans will never stand up to business (such as oil and gas), and we are all both caught in the web of lobby money. How do we believe change is possible? We need a clean energy breakthrough, and you need to show the lobbies for what they are: at best progress inhibitors that fail to see the big picture for America and the world. If we lead, our markets will expand. You have to show oil and gas that they must invest in America beyond oil. This is the challenge.

Anni: sounds hard.

President: You understand the answer is not to stop shale but insist on its success through near zero-defect drilling. This is what we do. This is the key to American success it's what we know. I envision what we need to with China, recognize that war is our enemy and efficient energy, and a water solution must be tied to an energy solution that works for the United States, China, and the world. It's my "only Nixon can go to China," but a path to ecological health, through natural gas and shared technology. The problem is we've acted like the Middle East has us over a barrel, when the key is more transportation options. The triumph is clean supply over demand. Corporations and citizens must embrace the future with a warlike fervor.

I feel we've let our inspiration be dampened by more than a decade of high-cost energy entrapment that has slowed the world economy and is leading into a water entrapment that is the path to decline and war.

What you must recognize is that natural gas will be the path to green. And we must ensure a zero-defects program and do it right. Believe me if we could get hydrogen out of the sea, it would be easier, and safer, so if I can force it, I will. But we have to start in such a way as to reduce energy cost, so we have the resources to engineer fresh water. If we let poor energy policy happen, bin Laden will have won. He is the product of oil and the twentieth century. We will change: expanded distribution of fuel choice coupled with battery technology and drilling technology. This is the new path we need to blaze. Our citizens must see that solutions are within our grasp. China must see it. Then they need to convince Russia because that will change the world. It kills me that we can't get on the same page with Russia. The world must see it. We need to augment competition with synergy, because the leaders of demand can provide the direction for supply. We now have choices. The timing is perfect for the world. Being under the shadow of *oil fear* is our enemy. We need to replace it with the leadership of transportation and fresh water renewal. This will lead to world economics and world ecology coexisting once and for all: a paradigm change that will underscore the 21st century. The battle is with our own commitment to purpose and belief that we can change our own destiny. Once our progress is obvious, and it already is, the world will join. The beneficiary will be world peace, finally the world acting under the commitment to water and energy. Just think what war means to a world society, including the billions more citizens joining us in the next 20 years.

Anni and Robert leave the president goes through his speech for tomorrow and jots down a few changes.

CHAPTER XIII

The President Speaks to the People and Congress

Thank you for letting me join you, again. I will update you and present some changes. From here forward we will send out messages from a major Water and Energy site we are developing. Follow it.

Soon, we will be hearing from OPEC sources that the United States and Saudi Arabia have worked out general principles to allow an evolution of oil reduction from the OPEC suppliers in concert with changes in our electric technologies from electric, heating, and transportation. Settlement of oil transactions will continue in dollars while we step up aggressive initiatives in North Africa and the Middle East to address agriculture, water, and energy initiatives. This will all be detailed throughout the year, but we will continue with our initiatives as described in our previous plan with new levels of collaboration with China and the Middle East.

Our water and energy website will provide broad plans and requests for proposals (RFPs) and the like to show our progress with Water and Energy.

The major initiatives are to:

1. Propose the short-term outcome providing, tax credits to individuals and businesses to expand fueling choice at pumps to supply natural gas, hydrogen, electric, and gasoline, and provide incentives to install ng to hydrogen conversion and fast charge electric in homes and elsewhere. We intend to let the consumer choose their alternative vehicle s and manufacturers compete, with international participation. We expect aggressive support from the clean energy community.

2. We intend to develop proposals from private enterprise to populate the country with natural gas and/or hydrogen and/or direct electric upgrades first to support trucking and government vehicles and second the auto industry and general trucking industries.

3. Leverage infrastructure to provide a network of source to fuel-point delivery systems. Private enterprise must step up.

4. Develop proposals to convert airlines into biofuels; natural gas, electric, and hydrogen throughout the United States and the world **on their own schedules**. Fix other sources of eco energy first.

5. Form a strategic initiative garnishing battery technologies, including hydrogen, between several department of energy specialty labs and universities, but especially at the whim of private enterprise. This should include CERN in Europe, and private initiatives all over the world. This is a **WE** project.

6. Understand the capacity we may have to produce a "sun-gas" type fuel, into these projects, including new

ideas. Provide a plan and tax incentive to whatever provides freshwater expansion in areas that need it.

7. Provide legislation and tax incentive plans to foster the above in a timely manner, and in stages that makes sense. Consider and estimate a proposal to solicit a citizen and business WE-bond as a funding mechanism choice. But clearly provide tax credits to promote refueling diversity.

8. Create a Water and Energy (WE project) oversight team to put together an orderly and timely rollout, keeping in mind that process #1 can quickly roll out. This is to provide synergy and enable, not interfere with free enterprise. We will restore the Iranian agreement.

I would like to add a few comments that I have derived from my trek around the globe, Industry and labor, ecology, and the economy must meet. So, as we press on to gaseous and electric frontiers, we have to do our best and do it right. Our priorities are water and energy in the global economy, but redirect the USA economy first, but assume we will respond to worldwide initiatives as required.

There is a zero-defect tolerance policy in place. It's this simple: close the loopholes and do it right. A significant mistake 20 years as footnotes. If politicians tell you regulation is needless overhead, please tell them we love our country and are not naïve about the profit motive's weak link. It's great if it is monitored on a large scale. I know fracking has ramped up to now with relatively, though important, few failures. Yet there are more earthquakes in Dallas and Oklahoma, and we are swirling around the Marcellus shale and the NY watershed. There is progress and controversy all over the states, and now the world. The answer is to do it right and keep striving for zero defects. This means we need national and state regulation and industry innovation to work hand in hand, as it already exists. Trust me, the reason we have regulation is good, if we make sure they have your support and corruption is checked, we'll protect the 99 percent. If we make a big mistake, we will shut down until we assure quality of task. But we will continue, not regress while the world moves forward. This is the same for nuclear and alternative water and energy initiatives. We are looking for a transition bridge that is built with solid engineering and will assure that our nation and the world will cross it safely. This includes protection against methane leakage at all levels. You have to understand what America best does is complex problems simplified through automation, engineering, and a quality oriented work force, especially.

We have to allow for breakthroughs, e.g. a 1000 mile battery, and will reconsider if that happens. WE assume knowledge is swift and will not let futures interfere with our goals and timeframes. But *don't look for a single solution, diversity and choice is the path towards victory. In general, we support electric and hydrogen initiatives with equal enthusiasm.*

There may be no shortcuts or loopholes, but I know we can do it and it will be transparent. Cutting edge is what America does, and mistakes can be minimized and protected against. That's why we step into airplanes, because we believe, and it is regulated. But in the case of Water and Energy (**WE**), there are two truths: Water is the elixir of life, and Energy is the elixir of society (no mass energy, no society). This is what must be engrained into our consciousness, whether it's industry, government, Wall Street, or Main Street. If we can't do it, we've failed. And we won't fail. If we transform our water and energy, we will lead the world. Remember, the largest and most powerful lobby in the world is ballot power, not money. In our system, if the elected officials don't see the vote as the real currency of freedom, then vote us out. I urge patience and involvement, because the opportunity to reduce cost and expand supply and capability is in front of us.

I have mentioned that we need to approach this problem as war. You may have heard that China is cornering the gold market and that Fort Knox is largely depleted of gold.

Let me tell you a story. Before WWII, we had to figure out how to fund war. It hasn't been discussed much but you recall War bonds in the history books, $18.75 pays $25 in 10 years. Our GDP was about $1.27 trillion in 1940. We financed about 2/3 of the 300 billion the war cost through these bonds, the rest in taxes. In todays' dollar equivalence, that's about four trillion dollars, believe it or not. But today's US GDP is about 18.5 trillion dollars, and our advanced weapons are much more expensive. So, if our trillions of debt becomes a problem, and the dollar is challenged, I'll propose $750 billion-$ 1.5 trillion in Water and Energy (**WE**) bonds with 5-10 year maturities, sold to the public, and we, America, will take care of investing in our future, if required, and finance the largest technology project in the history of man. Plus, more importantly, get our people to invest in and understand infrastructure change. The point is our financial capability is awesome, and our people and industry will meet any challenge. We must continue to provide agriculture and technology to the masses around the world and we will be part of the solution. I put this out not as what we will do, but what we can do. Money is never the issue. We won't let anyone disrupt our economy, and we will cut our energy costs in half and provide ample fresh water for our agriculture, industry, and human consumption. We will work with the nations across the continents and together we will step up so our resources and consumption are in balance together as partners in our future. This is the world of the 9-10 million-person economies with a GDP over $100 trillion, and a burgeoning Asia, the Middle East, Americas, and Africa. Projections are that Africa will own ½ of the world's population by the end of the century. If we stand back, China, *India, Russia, Germany, Japan and more will simply leave us behind. Why? Because they must.*

We really have three points we see for the WE project for the 21st century:

> 1. We will change the mix of our energy use and invest in battery density to effect, in conjunction with EV and FCEV engine technologies, a 3 to 5 x increase in density in energy storage, currently called batteries. Our goal is to cut energy costs in half with effective EV (electric vehicles) and FCEV (Fuel Cell Electric Vehicles-i.e. hydrogen) engines and gasoline run Hybrids. Key words: diversity and change.

> 2. We will convert all forms of seawater and recycled fresh water to a freshwater through a product of "desalination" that is economic and widespread, including dealing with the agricultural issues on both sides of our southern border. Wind, solar, and biofuels may fit our need to lower the cost of water reclamation. It is beneficial to provide low cost, continuous desalination. All sources of water reclamation will be considered, so seawater

conversion depends on alternatives on a case-by-case basis. (E.g. fixing the Ogallala Reservoir drought) Many, many solutions will be location dependent. But it's our priority.

3. The funding of the initiatives will be from the benefits of energy cost reduction and if necessary, the issuance of ten-year Water and Energy (WE) bonds ($750 billion to $1.5 trillion) through the participation of the American people **and companies** to invest in our fiscal self-reliance for the next 100 years. The key issue is to diversify our refueling capability petroleum, ng, hydrogen, and direct electric recharging.

Why does America have to offer investments? Because the international marketplace is stuck in a quagmire that is good for the owners, but increasingly bad for the customer, i.e. population, and propped up by war, dictatorships, and invisible handcuffs.

The WE project – 2018-2028

This would include: a demonstrator desalination project with double today's solar storage capacity, but utilize solar to perpetuate a low-cost generator of fresh water, a million gallons per day; A plan of the initiative to restore the Ogallala aquifer through redeployment or generation of fresh water resources, or plan its demise; A south-western water initiative which includes both sides of the southern US American border; Planning and implanting a multifaceted program to produce 100-150 mpg throughout the automobile and trucking industry utilizing improved battery storage of 3x, then 5x current vehicle hybrid and plug in capacity and standards including hydrogen, NG, and pure electrical solutions; and A clear plan to insure drilling and distribution safety for shale gas, hydrogen extraction, methane hydrate, petroleum, and electricity generation with adequate capacity to meet transportation needs for 50 years. All this, with a target of reducing energy consumption and cost by at least 50%, and pollution reduction by at least 90%. Remember, we only need partial transitions, but a clear direction. Methane hydrate can excel when they commit to being ready but install when we've been safeguarded. Earth's realities tell us to start shifting to gaseous for transportation, unless there is an electrical recharge. Once clean supply dominates demand, the markets will act. What's clear is diversity will only create choice and innovation.

We know the economic response will create a GDP that will pay off this investment through GDP growth in the US and around the world.

As I have mentioned, we will introduce, over the next several years, legislation, perhaps amendments, that will reduce graft and monopolization in such a way that assures international competitiveness and responsiveness from an efficient government.

I know, you must be asking, isn't this just more quantitative easing pushing the debt down the road?

Wrong, we are proposing changing the game and investing in a specific water and energy direction.

Quantitative easing has been investing up to 850 billion dollars per month in preserving the status quo. Yes, it will soon subside, except that it provides no path to change, no solution to the water crises. No direction that positions the world against drought and famine. No consideration of the billion more people that are coming in 10-11 years, no energy productivity. Get it? The issue is cost reduction, but more importantly profit expansion. We seek innovation, privately and from our University partners.

This is the mantra I wish to leave you with. When you wake up tomorrow, I know you and I will do it right. We will have effective controls and appropriate regulation. Congress will be completely involved and act as it's a massive war. This transition across the bridge of change will be done through a spirit of progress between industry, science, governments, and a committed stake by citizens who clearly see not only the effectiveness and mistakes and corrections but a clear vision of the world in change. You and I are up to it, and it's time to move forward. If you don't see that an 8.5 people world is reshaping our world, then sit back and Asia will take care of it and the USA will fester.

I don't quite know how to show you that this energy transformation is here, a form of hydrogen generation-already well understood in California, Ontario Canada, and Germany. All foreign car companies in Japan, Germany, and Korea have introduced hydrogen cars since 2015.Hydrogenics is 5% owned by General Motors, Do you think it is coincidence that Electric car company Tesla, is teaming with Panasonic to build the largest battery factor in the world with a projected 30% improvement in cost! Tesla is already talking about doubling storage density and this will put the duel strategy of hydrogen/battery and FCEV / EV engines in the right direction given the countless clean energy and fresh water and hybrid strategies that will evolve.

We expect the world automotive and aerospace industries to take this as a challenge.

The point is the forces of change are coalescing and there is only one result-change. The problem with the status quo, whether the general public, Kings, mega corporations or Cartels, they can't see what the forces of change are stimulated by–unimaginable complacency that is reinforced by political and monopolistic market dominance which won't hold in a democratic society that is stimulated by new ideas and profit potential.

Citizens, join me by entering the ERA of **WE** (Water and Energy) and this will smoothly guide us to clean Energy, bountiful fresh Water, and a peaceful society, where the world evolves from the past, and people restore their power and leadership, the way our founders intended. We will assure the doubters and detractors, it's time to move forward.

Thank You.

CHAPTER XIV

Postlude

The world GDP totals are more than $70 trillion (some percent import/export). But we need to plan a 100 trillion dollar plus economy to support 8–9.5 billion people.

In summary, how do we stop inflation, prevent war, and revitalize our and the world economy?

Commit to energy efficiency and diversity like it was a world war, assuring the expansion of clean air and water and dramatic reduction of carbon and CO_2. Do it armed with the Sherman antitrust act…anti-monopolization, but if our industry were smart, they'd learn how to survive the next century.

Continue to reduce government debt aggressively through reduction in unproductive government function and assuring of low cost of clean energy. Drive for massive profitability and debt reduction. That means a rich, productive economy.

Success in energy is the path to balanced payments and the funding for fresh water. This is not monolithic, though, it's diverse exploiting the differing resources available.

Allow interest rates to *gradually* increase while cutting corporate income taxes as low as possible and increasing investment in capital gains tax credit as high as possible. This is critical to the increase in productive capital and trending away from *artificial* government incentives (with proper regulation).

Energy productivity will ripple through a majority of personal and business cost savings. This will turn our economy and the economy of the world. Best of all it will be the giant step toward a clean society and impact climate change. So, the commitment of our nation and the world to a water and energy strategy will, through implementation, once again be a beacon of hope and change throughout the world

One more time:

It is already obvious that energy is now sourced in bountiful supply all over the world and being harvested as oil and natural gas in far more plentiful supply than the Middle East. We must break the ICE (internal combustion engine) cycle that is freezing our economy.

Also, although only harvested in tests, Methane hydrate is being discovered in quantities beyond the scope of all her fossil fuels combined. This has the potential of making countries like Japan self-sufficient. Without that, oil and natural gas is developing to capacities beyond our needs given. We will hold out on Methane Hydrate, why we leverage our bioengineering.

Australia is beginning to mine shale oil to make it a market leader in oil and gas, while it is preparing to become the largest distributer of LNG (liquid natural gas). They need to be part of the leadership of a global strategy. They also harvest methane out of coal.

These factors alone, along with America becoming the leading producer of NG and oil, indicate it is time to prepare to support NG vehicles, which is now, after India and China, led by Pakistan and Iran.

> 1. The single factor to make the USA the low-cost provider of transportation, is the success of producing a battery of 3x, then 5x, increased density. This is only part of our 21st century "WE project", but we proceed now.
>
> 2. We must race to providing energy productivity equal to ½ today's retail costs; then invest ½ of those savings in increased fresh water to solve the Ogallala Reservoir, southern US border, and provide solutions that are supportive of overcoming the worldwide water crises.
>
> 3. We should provide a hydrogen energy strategy including having a conversion from NG to hydrogen at points of distribution, thereby utilizing the NG network of pipelines already in place. This will open the door to a "full-on" clean strategy, I call it a clean strategy to discount the poor reputation of green, except for money;
>
> 4. Remember, a hydrogen FCEV is an electric vehicle with a hydrogen fuel source.

Given our agreements on 1–3, we no longer must be concerned about competing gasoline, oil, and gaseous fuels, the marketplace will take care of that, and therefore consider extending pipelines as part of a bridge strategy. The core strategy is to produce an effective 100-150 mpge, making in the short run, gasoline with 2/3 reduction in emissions, because of a comprehensive Hybrid implementation.

We need to assure ourselves that elimination of loopholes and other legal actions to solidify our production quality and is the norm in our legislation. Not over-regulation, but not a strategy to by-pass regulations through loopholes. Stop it.

We need to enact legislation and/or amendments to place lobbying in its proper place and restore our regulatory processes by assuring that human rights succeed over money dominance in our legislative and elective processes. A commitment to clean productivity is the norm. Short term let's fix clean fueling and refueling.

That the U.S. should have a Water & Energy (WE) strategy while demonstrating to China, Russia, Japan, India, Australia, the Middle East (ME), and the EU how we will share in the responsibility of an effective W&E strategy to accommodate the next billion people on earth, adequate capacity of water and food through expanded desalination with low-cost energy, and general agreement that **world priorities surround Water & Energy and not War.**

The US commitment will be such that we will go forward, and other nations will catch up when they get it. Actually, we're already usurped by Asian and other markets, like EU and Germany. We expect that all nations will, however, want to compete in our car markets, airplane markets, the wide litany of advances made due to the advances in batteries. We know that the electric market will lead the way' closely followed by NG and Hydrogen suppliers. Hydrogen will accelerate growth as efficient Sun-gas and Syn-gas solution s and electric achieves a 3x density improvement. Quite frankly, most hybrid's get 25-35 miles per battery (before requiring recharging). Rise that to 100-125, and with fast recharging, we're off to transition.

We will invite contributing nations, CERN, and other national and international interests in participating in our "WE project" for the 21st century. This would be an American led project, but contributors are invited, and results shared. None of this will diminish the drive for a fusion ultimate source. In fact, the diversification of distribution (refueling) with electric, natural gas, hydrogen, and gasoline, all with hybrid methods, will lead to a diverse development and optimal cycle of change.

Caution, Plan B

You would have to be asleep to ignore the rift about Fracking. Books have been written, documentaries made, even movies. I have seen it all, read it all, and heard it all, on both sides. Basically, it's claimed, with ample evidence, that the pipelines created through the drilling process are sealed with concrete, which not are only considered weak, but estimated to be at least with 35% failure experienced and results in natural gas (NG) mixing with water table and corrupting large amounts of drinking water. Additionally, earthquakes are significant when Fracking is contemplated, for example, around the San Andreas Fault in California, the mother of all fault zones. There will be no need to go that far until safety is assured. Many solutions, for example, filling the cavities caused by oil and gas extraction with liquid CO_2 have been considered. But anti-Fracking enthusiasts say evidence shows that concrete seals surrounding pipelines will never work, and all mining should be suspended, including "traditional" oil drilling in the seas, for example. There have been numerous federal and state hearings held and bills prepared, and in some states, legislation enacted. Meanwhile the US has now reclaimed the role of the number one Nat-gas producer in the world and we are spending billions on developing liquid natural gas (LNG) near our seaports. Meanwhile we're told this is our answer to energy independence, but it seems that we are doing the "risky mining", while O&G collects the profits, and the world benefits from our low-cost gaseous energy. Of course, if there was a major fault, like San Andrei's, it would change the history of the world. Meanwhile, Congress passes (2005 the "Energy Act loophole" exempting "drillers" from deep natural gas regulation of shale and horizontal drilling, so it is reported. You must ask, "if there wasn't a problem, why the loophole?" I think you will be responded with: it prevents the troublesome and expensive EPA from interfering. The American people, given our experience to date, should be asked: can the O&G industry be treated with laissez-faire? Or should the EPA, amongst others, be a necessary part of capitalistic democracy. It isn't socialism, it is a necessary control against corporate "enthusiasm", which has been our systematic challenge, to say the least. October 2008, dam damage claims in New Orleans, and many, many, more was the fault of deferring on controls in favor of budget cutting, or deregulation. The problem is we the people, the 99%, are bypassed in a lobby driven, loophole driven Congress. With all the research driven and technology driven world that drives the USA (and World) economy today, why doesn't the truth reveal itself; or perhaps it does, but it's lobbied into quiescence. Think about it, with all our trillions of dollars in intellectual capital, we can't seem to write a truth document that is honest and bi partisan! Victory goes to the persistent, no matter how much or little is involved.

Therefore:

Since I have stated and restated our potential for world war and drought and famine in 8-9 billion population world, we should put energy productivity in the highest priority of prevention, and fresh water generation as the highest priority "must have" project. W&E seems to place certain aspects of a "WE project" such as a foolproof pipeline (e.g. Graphene or similar flexible indestructible, composites) high battery density; and all-electric vehicles; coal to gas conversion; and yes, even accelerating viable bio-metric solutions, Water & Energy needs to be addressed in a war like status. And yes, we need a Congress not be subject to lobby money as a constraint, and a realignment of people and money as the influence of policy and practice.

Isn't it clear? America needs to look at our demons from within and break free from our corruption, particularly in politics, so we are not dragged into war, which clearly doesn't work, and pull our self out of fossil fuel dependency for good in a clean, plentiful, Water & Energy (WE) environment. WE are the solution to the problem of population caused water and agriculture stress and energy productivity. It is America's and the world's number one priority, and WE (the population) must be in control, which clearly, we are limited. The path to decreased population is not inhibition, it is improving wealth and wellness, and educating women. Given the cultural barriers, this isn't short term, so we need to plan for 8.5-10 billion population earth. Wealth and wellness will produce the desired birth rates. Also, concentration on improving in-state economic wellness, will open doors to rational immigration, instead of war enabled fleeing of homelands. Righteousness fulfilled is hard work, not easy to conceive and do solutions.

At the very least, let's reintroduce an idea: honesty, decency, and forthrightness and an expanding public awareness is more important than the dominance of money in politics and life. The middle class will never rise without that fundamental idea that all world religions profess: love is the gateway to heaven whether actual, spiritual, or imagined; and without clean, fresh Water, the elixir of life, and efficient Energy, the elixir of society, it's just going to get nasty. And if Congress can't pass a law without a loophole, it's time for Jesse (Ventura)... All in all, energy costs need to be reduced by half in mpge and fresh water must satisfy our environmental, health, and agricultural needs. Face the facts. They are more than opinions.

But we can strive for reconciliation the twentieth century had glory, trouble with excess, the need to acknowledge the state we're in, and the need to change right now. We must let reconciliation win the day and quickly prepare to accommodate nine billion people. Yes, populations must level out, but it won't until health and clean W&E and agriculture are actively prepared for. Given those cultures that have excess population growth, it should be clear that first we need a W&E culture and a path to health, and broad education with a path for economic uplifting coming from within. Only with greater prosperity will the culture of peace and understanding lead to leveling the population. Nations with leveling populations have a whole other set of issues with diminishing work forces and increasing productivity and extended life spans. So preparing for 2.5 billion vehicles and nine billion people is our reality, and success or failure in such that will be the only true legacy of the 21st Century. And it won't happen without a clear, aspiring Water & Energy transition *starting right now.*

To my skeptical brethren, I agree that the free market and individual choice is the ideal market for change, with all the implied check and balance associated with self-risk assessment. The problem is this is a market where the dominant suppliers are controlled by Kings and Military Juntas, coupled with multinational conglomerates and is 67% owned by "states", i.e. pseudo socialism. Not free enterprise. Further, discovery, led by world mining/engineering, is clearly shifting the percentage of reserves away from the Middle East and more around the Pacific Rim and the Americas. Further, the kinds of investments needed, including research to date, is something only the USA and capital intense participants can accomplish, and the dependence for agriculture is largely dominated by the US, the EU, The Middle East, and China in Africa and the around the world. Then the rise in population around the Pacific Rim and in Africa will be best supported by a rise in USA energy productivity, with the goal of reducing the image equivalent of the cost of energy by ½. So, the optimal plan, absent some breakthrough, is a **WE** project, as described. And it should be proceeded with a warlike fervor, a war for peace by leading the world in a fresh Water & clean Energy initiative. If needed to get buy-in, float **WE** bonds, and campaign for an all-in commitment. The point is funding is a matter of choice, a matter of will, of understanding the benefits.

Inclusion

What seems to be lost is the global village is an *inclusion* event. The USA is forecasted to grow to 450,000,000 people, because of needed immigration. All countries that have been culturally exclusive, Japan and several Euros are culturally isolationists, and are *all* suffering, resource-wise economically. Meanwhile, the world abounds with population growth. The USA, whose culture is inclusion, always bends to growth because they know people are a natural resource. Even the traditional Republicans know this. Iraq's troubles are that Iraq leadership (Shiite) failed to include Sunnis in its newfound government (mini-WWI) helped by the USA dismantling the Iraq army immediately after the fall of Sadam.

Now let's see Saudi Arabia is Sunni and Iran is Shiite. Iran must be trying to recreate Persia, and for completeness throw in Syria, Iran, Iraq, ultimately threatening Saudi Arabia's oil fields? (Pure speculation) Remember, Muslims (1.6 billion of them) are 85 % Sunni. **Egypt dismantled its revolution because the elected government tried to dismantle inclusion**. Yes, the Egyptian Army is smarter than the people. Or should I say, more experienced. Then there is Israel. Don't be mad at Israel, just because 15,000,000 Jews, world-wide, are seemingly more productive (except oil) than 1.6 billion Muslims. Don't respond with war, respond with education. USA conservatives won't reconcile the fact of anti-immigration politics...good for great "primary election wins" and equally bad for national election results (except for 2016?). Yes, we're a nation of immigrants and population increases are mostly through immigration and the populations they spawn. Yes, fix the energy problem and its high cost and pollution. Fix the fresh water problem, more capacity. Use our science to help implement efficient, clean Water & Energy strategies in high volume. It's important, no it's necessary. Water and Energy is an inclusion event that we can initiate, but the world will and is participating in, the underlying resource, low cost, highly efficient energy.

A strategy that we should: lead with and the world shares results and benefits from actions. Most emerging nations are our customers. If you can't see inaction's results on oil prices, you are living in denial. Choice, it's not a new idea, but is continually suppressed by the status quo. As the user of 25% of world energy, we have earned the need to lead. Embrace the global village. We had a lot to do with creating it. Americans understand global commerce, but many people don't. We seem to understand that national and regional cultures come along for the ride and financial benefits are expected. So, we fight over it instead of change. Meanwhile energy demand accelerates and freshwater declines. Rising population with limited resources?

It's a no brainer. Our thinking has to change...

There is no doubt that battery density and Sun-Gas and Syn-Gas rapid evolution, should be part of a "WE project" scope, a concentrated plan that includes Fresh Water "creation" whether that is driven by desalination, synthetic h2.0, creation, or both. This is the war to be fought and probably includes unbinding of the monopolization of the situation we have created. Return to the leadership we've earned and deserve. Sunshine to Petrol... it's here, for us and the world.

The Easy solution is to provide tax incentives to give our car owners choice at the pump. Gasoline, electric, natural gas, or hydrogen.

Without choice, there is no change. Think of it, an open market. All the alternative energy players and the O&G providers have an equal chance to succeed A closed distribution system put us where we are today, so open it to competition. It's a lot more economical than war.

Whatever the cost, it's the 21st Century and obviously it's time for a change, in our neighborhoods, our towns, cities, counties, states, nations and the world. If you don't think it's time to change, look at the world. We're retracting because it seems out of control, yet the world still expands. Do it or lose it. Don't look at optimal look at practical and synergistic. Can we have gasoline, electric, NG, and hydrogen at the pump. Of course!

Quell the Noise

You will hear lots of noise like let's go straight to batteries and hydrogen is too expensive and more. You'll even hear that shale oil capacity has been over-estimated by 98%. Another term for this noise is BS but we will shake out the near-term issues in the first year. The actual hybrid mix of battery, NG, and hydrogen will allow a phase in strategy based on results e.g. a three x battery density target, a decision on what and how to upgrade fueling stations, the establishment of sun-gas production network, and more.

Therefore, we are check pointing every critical path and why we are engaging the broad science and engineering community for this war reclaiming Water & Energy (WE). This is a war to win the century. We expect that Japan, Germany, S Korea, Russia, India and others will contribute because they will agree an action plan. If a strong result unfolds in batteries, for example or a rapid conversion plan for fresh water, we'll adjust. The purpose of this book is to tell you that we know the "moon landing" is possible and the initiative will adjust, invent, and assure that we will keep the American people and the world community aware of our progress. The point is the time to take a stand is now and we will restore your faith in humanity and reassurance, the confidence that science, engineering, and governments are reclaiming the 21st century because it must happen.

Fact: two grids exist...An Electric and a Natural gas grid. And conversion of Natural gas to Hydrogen exists and is scalable. Tesla has shown us that an electric recharging network is possible, even a solar based, self-contained system. We must do it, now!

The driving forces of the 21st century are:

Energy choice, free of artificial trade conglomerates to regulate supply and demand.

World trade, as opposed to shrinking into stove piped nationalism with symbolic "walls" of fear.

Ample fresh water, robust food sources, and pollution elimination are a fact of supporting an over 9-billion-person planet. This is a new paradigm caused by massive interdependency of our shrunken world. We should lead, not retract once more. No? Ask Reagan historians about strength with character.

The "trifecta dilemma"

All of this means nothing during international strife, particularly around North Korea, Syria/Russia, and Middle East Sunni/Shiite infighting. All of this is pressured by population growth and water shortage. This is a house of cards with the stacked deck of monopolization and its hold on the status quo.

1 North Korea

The painful and obvious is with a 90 % trade relationship, the path to peace must be through China. What's China's most pressing problem? Continued 5–7.5% GDP growth in an environment where **Pollution** is killing their people. North Korea is just a pain in their ass. The solution is POSITIVE incentives, not trade inhibitors. The USA, probably including at least India, should recognize that we could be perfect, and pollution is still killing the world. Therefore, China and perhaps India and the USA should have trilateral effort, including shared technology, in solving this problem which is obviously changing our "fuel mix". China would have its own agenda of quelling North Korea. We just must support S. Korea and other surrounding nations. North Korea will never attack the US, but they need to know how strong we are? Why do we report their missile range? Choice is the key word. If India wants to be all electric, for example, fine. If N. Dakota wants NG/hydrogen, fine.

2018 Interruptus Trump

In 2018, we are faced with the prospect of denuclearization of Korea. Note that N. Korean change coincided about a week after China and N Korea met in China.

If any kind of deal is possible, second-guessing Trump tactics is over, and probably post 2018 midterms, but the issue of China trade tariffs may be in the balance. If any tactic resulted in a major step toward Korean peace, who could blame President Trump for anything. Of course, Iran policy folds into that umbrella. If N Korea denuclearization is successful, Trump could ask the American people to trust him, after all.... his dream for 2020?

2 Syria/Russia

I combine these two because Russia has placed high stakes in Syria and Syrian refugees have caused the immigration problem that is haunting the EU. The "NATO" presence and always insufficient support lingering just prolongs all the problems. Of course, a full-on Military solution is worse than IRAQ because Syria's 350,000 standing army exceeds the operation of about 100,000 rebels (in many forms, including ISIS), and is backed by the Russian Air Force.

Meanwhile Russia is threatened by Cyprus and all the emerging clean energy initiatives discussed in this book. They seem to lack the willpower and wealth, of say Saudi Arabia (SA), to change their economic future, which SA announced they're doing. They have the small economic profile of OIL & Gas and weapons that must be redirected more broadly. The only solution is an EU / USA/ Russia reconciliation that lets us all evolve and eventually Russia can be trusted as part of NATO (obviously not immediately). Of course, they must change their KGB mentality which thinks disrupting other countries through cyber-attacks and more will let them win, which it never will. Of course, the USA needs instruction/ change also. When we accuse them of a KBG mentality, they retort the USA CIA, FBI, and secret service, you've got to be kidding. I think we're both right, or maybe both wrong.

Where is Gorbachevian and Reagan cooperation when we need them?

3 The Middle East

The directions of the Sunni or Shiite mess must change. EU and USA Israel position is unequivocal. While the Palestinian/ Israel 2 state solution is needed, it's not the real problem. Saudi Arabia, quite frankly, sees the handwriting on the wall, and they have the resources to change. The open question is "do dictatorships have to fall?" or can evolution persist.

The Middle Eastern regimes must understand that the energy paradigm has changed, and rapidly, so change and compete or stick your head in the sand and lose.

The Middle East must **"self-reconcile"** its issues between Shiite and Sunni Muslims, autocratic or democratic rule, Sharia law versus separation of powers, women's and all human rights, freedom and equality of religions, secular government with separation of church and state, religious punishment, and more. The reconciliation of those issues can't be resolved with world courts, the U.N., or on the battlefield. That can only be done in the Middle East, meaning that an ongoing strategy of energy markets and fresh water is a primary objective of the world in the 21st century. But we, the Russians, or the EU can't and won't resolve that, and the market of suppliers is no longer in the Middle East. I didn't create this reality, concentration of wealth and power did.

Forget the history of byzantine empires, Persia, etc. That's 19th and 20th century "stuff" (and maybe 1000 years before). The 21st Century is preparing for an 8.5-9.5 billion population and can only survive with widely available fresh water, clean air, and low cost, clean energy. Currently we seem to be preparing for war for no good reason, except some people think its 1965 and see wars of tanks, airplanes, and lots of dead bodies still possible, or desirable. It's not. Haven't 55+ years (1965-2017) of failed wars proven that to you?

CHAPTER XV

Conclusion

What we are part of today is the convergence of four factors: Europe, Trade, Asian emergence in the Pacific Century, and the world dancing with nationalism and isolationism, i.e., pre-world War II.

1. Europe is devastated because its EU have been rocked by millions (Syria-5mm in total including M.E. refugees) that, some of whom had slipped through the previously untested web of immigration, that is controlled by an international policy (EU) of previously marginally tested controls. At the same time, the northern European allies of Scotland, Denmark, Norway (not an EU member), and Germany are working with Canada, and individually companies in the USA but without exactly getting the support of President Trump, who is trying to "solve" the Middle East and to a degree, with Russia, by embracing Oil & Gas, the Saudis, and more.

2. At the same time The USA green movement has been stymied by the President who sees oil & gas and reduced regulation as a key to stimulating the USA economy. This, at the same time as EU is trying to unravel its immigration

and terrorism dilemma, as are we. Yes, we can absorb much more drilling, but we can't lose the markets we've spent over 100 years, and too many wars, developing. There's a fine line fair trade and isolation, and to go too far will be devastating.

3. This, however, is in the face of the 21st century, that is the Pacific Century. Cries from the nationalism **Trump**eters seem to ignore the fact that the USA's S&P 500 gets 40 % of its profit, overseas, and GM is selling more cars in China then the USA. (Now Ford is stepping up) and Apple is selling more iPhones in China than in the USA and most of Iowa's corn exports are sold to Mexico. Since the 1994 NAFTA agreement, (and soon affirmed update). Soon to be reconstituted, Mexican trade has grown tenfold, but we have $ 50 MM trade deficit. How many jobs are associated with that trade? Reality is we are a key proponent of the world market and are solidly in place. If we back down world leadership, we will lead the charge downhill to be a solid follower, which is opposite of where we should be. India and China, soon three (3) billion strong need cooperation and synergy with the USA and the EU. Meanwhile, the USA has a heroin problem brought to us by Mexican drug cartels, and Afghanistan, which produces 80% of the world's opium. The USA turns to "nationalism", as does Europe, who are also trying to control their borders. Yet the USA is less than five (5) percent of the world population, which means the international market (the other 95+ percent), with an emerging middle class, is an opportunity for American product and services. You don't have to be much of a capitalist to see that opportunity.

4. Meanwhile, ASIA is striving to address its growth with India and China approaching three (3) billion people and their emerging middle class, industry, agriculture, and people demand more Water and Energy. Meanwhile, China struggles with **Pollution** and its coal dominated energy position, but massive diversification is underway. The USA is under educated about China energy actions. World population is expected to grow by a billion is 10-12 years, mostly in western Asia, the Middle East, and Africa. Asia is expected to grow its automobile base leading to a billion more worldwide vehicles, which already accounts for some of GM's success. Meanwhile India has announced it will not sell gasoline powered cars anymore, in about 13 years. Their strategy... all electric. I should state that Warren Buffet has already invested in electric cars in China, whose leader is called "the Thomas Edison "of electric Cars. Asia is on the move and needs massive products, technology, and services in an "open" market, if you're a player in that market. That's us. The world won't change unless the energy Czar (the USA) moves forward.

5. At the same time, Iran and Pakistan's people are driving about seven (7) + million cars powered by Natural Gas, and Saudi Arabia plans to diversify its economy beyond Oil & Gas significantly, and Norway, whose wealth comes from the North Sea, will stop using Internal Combustion

Engine (ICE) (Gasoline based) cars in less than 10 years.

India announces it will shift to electric cars in ten+ years.

Persistence and Discipline

Understand our competitive position. As a culture, the USA excels at persistence–the freedom to pursue an idea, legally and morally, until it succeeds or fails. Asia, on a grand scale, excels in discipline. Hard work and creative pursuit often, despite constraints, but always to a safe conclusion. The USA needs more discipline, especially in a world stymied by monopolies, cartels, and paid off politicians. We can't even imagine what it would be like to support 3–4 times the people in the USA. It takes discipline.

To overcome this, we need to leverage our history of persistence but shift up our need <u>for financial, political, personal, and creative discipline; hard work and goal-oriented pursuit. The goal? Plentiful Water and Energy (WE) in a "global village" growing to 8-9.5 billion. People and suppressed by a Monopolistic Energy can (ME) ruling class. WE versus ME, that's a choice we must and will make.</u>

<u>To understand our approach, recognize that our culture of Freedom, with persistence, anyone can "make it". It's the freedom of choice and fair laws that made the USA great.</u>

Given all this, the USA should diversify its fuel at the pump and elsewhere, by providing aggressive tax credits for gasoline, electric, natural gas, and hydrogen additions to nationwide fuel depots and elsewhere. Don't fear fossil fuels, let the marketplace decide. Don't worry, the market will move the right way, once market dominance is opened, instead of suppressed. The resulting dramatic lowering of costs (real competition and absolute victory of clean supply over demand) will allow us to use a marginal tax to pay for desalination, in an energy market targeted at one dollar (1.00) per gallon of fuel. After all what is more American and pro capitalism as giving the citizens choice? Don't let the politicians bow to the conglomerates saying that the free market is dominant, when the freeway is dominated by lobby money. Allow competition and the market will drive us to clean Water and Energy solution(s). Current environment is a 20+ trillion-dollar debt with a status quo driven stagnation, mostly caused by War in Oil rich nations, from the supply side and the demand side, and must be thoughtfully addressed.

Do we need government sponsored incentives (tax credits) Yes! It's the 21st century, and we are up to our necks in challenges. We've done it to support businesses and entrepreneurship forever. Now, one for the people.

This direction should include working with the EU, India, China, Australia, Canada, and more to drive **pollution** to be a 20th century problem the 21st century world solved. Additionally, our aggressive understanding is what is best for America is to participate in the partnership to survive a 9+ billion-person planet and at least a 100+ trillion-dollar world GDP. We can be a dominant supplier of goods and services to the Pacific Rim and the world through. Fair trade, innovation, and hard work, as the USA moves from 330 million people to 450 million people through natural growth and immigration.

We withdrew from the Iranian Nuclear agreement and increased economic sanctions, and now tensions rise as we pressure Iran with oil sanctions, even though all international monitoring show Iran followed the nuclear pact that all Europe supports.

This is the light on the hill we need to brighten, **or be subordinated to a second-tier nation, who shrank when the world needed our forward leadership,** not regressive nationalism. Yes, fair trade, yes, controlled immigration, yes, improved Middle East progress to address the problems of terrorism, but yes, a full contributing partner in addressing the world need for eliminating pollution, producing water and agriculture, livestock, and fish farms across the globe. China and India understand how to support their growing need, caused by economic growth and a world with 9.5 billion people. They have the discipline to succeed. This focus spells jobs and a path for the American people through discipline and persistence, not reactionary retraction from a world which we helped create.

Yes, the Pacific Rim nations need to steer themselves and provide their own path, but the USA has the people, expertise, technology, and solutions to assist. Look at the breakup of AT&T in 1982 and the dissolution of Western Electric as AT&T's equipment provider, in stages up through 1996. Look what happens when the market was broken wide open. Likewise, our filling stations need to be assisted in opening fuel distribution, the secret behind massive diversification and growth. We are at a crossroads. Do we want to step back or move forward? Globalization is occurring and USA is crucial to our own growth and preventing Global Warring by embracing change that will happen with or without us. The solutions are in our hands, not in the hands of those who demand the status quo. A billion more people in about 10–12 years. Fair trade, yes, regressive isolationist policies, no, understanding our opportunities and risks in the world market, the other 95% of the world. That's the marketplace for the 21st century, more than ever, a global village.

We only need a moderate improvement of our international market share. There is enough for everyone. It requires immense discipline on our part, but we have the persistence to succeed.

Energy, abundant fresh water, clean air, and expanded healthy food. The rest is economic gravy...an open society that lets technology and innovation thrive, within a market of free enterprise–USA's specialties.

The combined will of Congress and the Executive is to hold back on changing the status quo while the whole world moves forward. We reduce healthcare, while we perpetuate Oil & Gas, increase our Military, and much more. We can't afford health care, don't maintain our infrastructure, withdraw services, and only pay for special services for congressional districts. Our main objectives are to satisfy our economic benefactors and lobbyists, so we can raise money for reelections. When President Obama tried to overcome distractors with healthcare: insurance companies, pharma, and more were spending one (1) million dollars per day to lobby against improving healthcare. Now we solve the problem by taking coverage away from 25 million people. So, we perpetuate the past by cutting services from the most vulnerable in society. The poor, lower class senior citizens, the indigent. If you follow this plan, you're asking the millennium generation to sacrifice their grandparents to save money. This would be fine, according to our elected officials, as we prepare for war and ignore the fact that the world is moving forward without us. In a recent survey of the top ten GDP nations, we ranked tenth in healthcare and life longevity expectations. The problem is that international society will stop buying our products and the "shining light on the hill" will extinguish. What's wrong? When you see India and China, together, approaching three (3) billion people, and the top quartile of their people (contributors, education, DNA, etc.

totaling 750 million people) more than twice our entire population, they will aggressively promote their people, their economy, their education, and more. You can see the consequences of our inaction, decline at best, and probably war, which we have been failing at for over sixty-five (65) years. What we are protecting, is our great history in the twentieth century. Or are we retracting, in the 21st century, to our own demise? We created an automation system that brings knowledge to the world, and they're using it. Remember, in 1960, we created the Peace Corps, trying to bring Africa, and others to a better standard of living. We used to believe that a rising tide lifts all boats. It reflected our Judeo or Christian beliefs. **Wake up America,** our founding principles dominated our culture and morals, and we need to continuously rediscover them. Our children and grandchildren need our mature, experienced, history. It's known as "change", what we've been doing so since 1776. Our brains, persistence, momentum, freedom to choose a positive direction, our moral fiber and our experience. We either use it or lose it. It's not a gift from our ancestors, it's an opportunity we must renew, refresh, and re-earn over and over. A nine-billion-person planet doesn't go to the strongest army, it goes to leadership that understands that, we're more than ever, a global village in a tiny spec of the universe.

This truth should be self-evident. The world population will grow. We are successful in the world marketplace, especially in China. This is a time to promote the positive aspects of the USA, from the Marshall plan, Mc Arthur's Japan, and Nixon's China. Since JFK, we saw the world as a positive marketplace. Now is the time to embrace our successes and change from our failures, not by cowering back, but by moving forward. The goal is to grow in health and security, and educated women will decrease family size, so that population will stabilize... get it? But we can't make that happen. *Only they can. Saudi Arabia just allowed their women to drive.*

Think of it this way...If India and China are right and add a billion cars to the world and we're not an active participant in the "clean" movement, what's going to happen when we're offered cleaner, more efficient cars at a much cheaper cost? The answer is good-by to the US auto industry. What if they step up to the next generation's silicon chip? Remember 85% of Intel's revenue comes from overseas, with today's population. Wake Up America! This moment is right for American momentum. While we struggle with the inconvenient truth and can't reconcile truth to power, India and China need to solve their pollution problems now. They enable a growing middle class, now. India, China, Indonesia, Japan. Germany, S Korea, Canada and more are moving forward...So, Wake Up America!

The world needs our multi-cultures and should be embraced through fair and free trade.

We need to move from a multiethnic monopoly-controlled energy cartel to a Water & Energy (**WE**) free society (in multi definitions) embracing clean and green goals, or die trying, which we won't.

Honesty and decency are our way of life and our foremost ideals. As a society we participate and complement each other.

If we don't like what we see, we seek to change it. But, if the world sees us as a hindrance, it will change us or ignore us. We must draw guidance from our growing standard as a free society, we need to embrace the world, or it will discard us. The global village is in motion and the best way to address it is fundamentally to participate **in fair trade**, open **Water** and

Energy (**WE**), and embrace the world as an **honest** participant and leader. In a growing marketplace that has 9+ billion brothers and sisters.

The fuel answer is clean diversity which can mix Gas, Hydrogen, and electric, in a hybrid FCEV and EV choice that can cost effectively diversify and react to new solutions that are not dominated in any geographic sector or outdated solution in a global economy. This must dominate our fair trade and politics, not monopolistic history-from ME to WE, *It's clear. The world needs to respond to a shrinking globe, enhanced education, and to change the mix of resource use, changing supply, and emergence of evidence that a nine-billion-person planet needs different, and is already on the move.*

With nations. Are we world leaders who want to rest on our laurels? Or are we engagers, who demand fair trade, but recognize that the 21st Century is the Pacific Century, and we're here to engage: Population. Water, Energy, Food, Pollution, and Economic rebound? Wake Up America! Step back and see that the world is changing because it must, and solutions are at hand. Our modus operandi needs to widen, not react in isolationist protectionism.

Restore our sense of purpose through liberty and world participation and peace with leadership driven by prudent action and cautious, but expanding, world markets. We will compete and succeed in world markets, with a strong manufacturing base in the USA. We will continue our leadership position in automation and motor vehicles.

Markets will be open and free of monopolistic, inhibiting forces.

We renew our positive attitude and our partnership with governments and world markets and the people we serve. We exist in a robust atmosphere of competitors who have a common understanding that pollution, fresh water, and clean energy is a global challenge, and we share our dedication to the fact that our atmosphere, oceans, and rivers have common, borderless, geographies.

Wake up, America

To all the existing auto manufacturers (Tesla, Ford, GM, Crysler, & all foreign manufacturers), with a capacity of 50 mpg. People do not realize that American internal combustion engines were based on German engineering.

With the current proliferation of electric vehicles, there should be a decrease in oil consumption (lubricating of gas engines) which can now be converted to gas to run the gas engines. Most people don't know that Germany created fuel artificially, representing 40% of the supply in 1940. Since 2015, a South African company (SASOL) is creating gasoline directly from natural gas and is trying to establish it in Louisiana but is being stymied by acquiring money.

Final end

1. Germany was the original petroleum engine (Benz).
2. Germany also created the Jet plane.
3. What's missing is new fuel capability.

This is the point of which the electric car as a change to the electric engine. Remember, the current car (Tesla requires no oil). If it's I.e., 50 mi/gal. Those who claim this is not true recognized that all current automobiles offer electric engine. Perhaps, the standard for the Tesla engine could be uniformed across the world just like it was Germany created the current gasoline engine.

Most people think that the technology is too expensive, this is because it will be opened as soon as they see that the world has really changed. As a comparison, this is an example, the television, the telephone have dramatically changed. The prices will be reduced. Guarantees, this means that the potential to 50 mi/gal. plus remember that these electric technology will be a better system than the petroleum system. For example, the Tesla system is a better way to provide a more efficient and cheaper to produce. I.e., No oil, 50mi/gal. and then it will be better. Guaranteed.

The right way

Capital GM, Tesla was to combine the efforts of the batteries of the Tesla engine to produce a worldwide common standard, similar to the Benz who created the standard in 1900s. However, this can be the worldwide solution, which was originated by Benz in the 1900s (far more complex than a standard system).

Germany

You may know that you have been dancing around the issue of Germany. How will you have the ability to enclose the Soviet Union, Saudi Arabia, (i.e., close the relationship between the oil and fuel.) Only the Germans have the ability to combine fuel components because we have learned how to make the beginning of the formula of fuel. Charlie Pedersen will allow the presentation to the world.

Fresh Water

You will know that the Atlantic Ocean is over filling, Florida, Manhattan, New York, to the Atlantic Ocean will be flooded. So, we must convert the excess water into fresh water. This converted water can be cured for USA and Europe. The middle of the country needs additional fresh water. All the reserve water can be converted from the Atlantic Ocean So the immediate result of fresh water can be available in New York and Florida. As a point, we are reducing the amount of excess water from Atlantic Ocean and deliver it to the middle of the country.

The Ogallala aquifer, spanning eight Midwestern states, is responsible for 30 percent of the water in the United States used for agriculture: it provides drinking water for two million people and is projected to risk being dry by 2021-2030. (Opinions vary) Ninety percent of the worlds fresh water is used for agriculture.

Desalination of the Atlantic Ocean system will enable the Mid-Atlantic states to replenish its fresh water supply. By having huge water tubes (pipes) that are unbreakable glass products, which can become a model that can be introduced throughout the water starved world.

This model can be workable in Australia, China, Africa, and Europe! The need of regions that suffer from a lack of sufficient potable water will no longer have such a problem.

Let me remind you that the only country that produces fresh water from the sea is Saudi Arabia! Remember, the Atlantic has an overabundance of water. So let's wake up America!

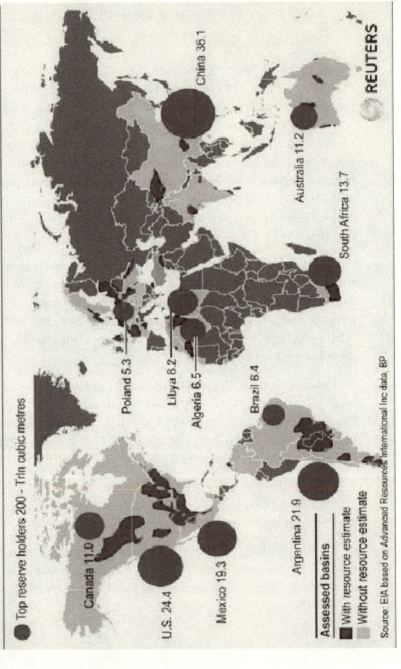

ABOUT THE AUTHOR

After a career in Technology management, including Aerospace and Finance, Charlie has engaged in literary efforts to change the World. Wake up America is his fourth book, and engaged him because of the directionless path the world and the USA, in particular, is on. If the USA and the World continues the current path it has no other path than war and depression. Charlie has four sons of diverse ancestry.

UnionBanCal Corporation and its principal subsidiary, Union Bank of California, today announced that Charles L. Pedersen, Executive Vice President, Systems Technology and Item Processing Group (STIP), will retire at the end of 2004, capping a 30-year career with the bank.

Pedersen, a member of the Union Bank of California's (Mitsubishi, previously Bank of Tokyo). executive management committee since 1994, is responsible for the bank's information technology and item processing operations that include central and distributed computing systems, systems development, data processing, telecommunications, security and contingency planning, information technology planning and engineering, and PC and LAN management. He oversees a staff of 1200 with round-the-clock operations located at Monterey Park, San Diego, San Francisco and Oakland, California, as well as Portland and Seattle operations centers.

Pedersen, 61, joined the bank in 1974 and has had management responsibility for virtually all aspects of the data processing, cash management and central operations before being appointed operations and automation group head in February 1991.

During his career he achieved a number of firsts, including deploying the bank's high performance item processing systems, and spearheading the formation of the Star System ATM network. The American Banker Association recognized his achievements in 1984 and awarded him a commendation for his efforts in creating the Star System which would later be sold for $2 billion.

Pedersen also was a pioneer and a leading advocate of automation within the financial services industry. During his tenure as Union Bank, he implemented and refined consumer electronic funds transfer, corporate cash management, domestic and international banking systems, branch automation, call center, check processing, imaging and online banking/web network underpinning the bank's leadership in the payments business and in core deposits growth.

"Charlie Pedersen has added immeasurably to the growth of productivity of our institution," said Norimichi Kanari, Union Bank President and Chief Executive Officer. "His leadership, management skills, and far-reaching insight into technology have created great value for our stockholders, our employees, and our customers," Kanari noted. "Our reputation for superior customer service rests on the foundations that Charlie built over three decades. We wish him all the best in retirement."

Kanari also announced that the Executive Vice President Linda Betzer, who heads the bank's Operations and Customer Service Group, will serve as acting group head of the Systems Technology and Item Processing Group, beginning January 1,

2005, until a national search is completed for Pedersen's successor.

"It's been a terrific journey. I'm so proud that I'm leaving an organization, colleagues, and a financial institution that is strong and has such a bright future," Pedersen said. "Most importantly during my tenure, I am proud to have been associated with a management team and line staff that has supported the bank through its growth–from $600 million to $47 billion in assets. We served a banking system that started in Southern California and his since grown to a worldwide distribution system."

Charlie Pedersen's Reach has been pervasive, not only in IT and operations, but in many other arenas. Over the last decade, he discovered many talented employees through the production of original songs, musicals, and plays associated with his annual CUBEE (Creating UBOC Efficiency and Effectiveness) show. The annual event, honoring STIP employees who operate out of cubicles and workstations, has been seen by thousands of bank employees and their families. "The success of Union Bank of California is built around an 'esprit de corps' that exists throughout the company. We not only work diligently, but we have had lots of reasons to laugh and smile along the way. The UBOC family is truly a competitive edge," he noted.

A native of long island New York, Pedersen is a graduate of Long Island University (CW Post). Prior to joining Union Bank, Pedersen managed the item processing systems of Chemical Bank in New York. He started his IT career working on the Apollo project for Grumman Aerospace in Bethpage, New York programming the abort guidance system. He is the original chairman member of the board of Star Systems Inc. Advisory Group, The Clearinghouse Payments Steering Committee, and

Primary Payments (PPS). In October 2004, he received WestPay's A.R. Zipf (invented MICR) award for Payment Systems innovations.

CPSIA information can be obtained
at www.ICGtesting.com
Printed in the USA
BVHW042204180723
667476BV00001B/1